basic
Korean

Learn to Speak Korean in 19 Easy Lessons

Soohee Kim, Emily Curtis & Haewon Cho

T0160539

TUTTLE Publishing

Tokyo| Rutland, Vermont |Singapore

"Books to Span the East and West"

Tuttle Publishing was founded in 1832 in the small New England town of Rutland, Vermont [USA]. Our core values remain as strong today as they were then—to publish best-in-class books which bring people together one page at a time. In 1948, we established a publishing outpost in Japan—and Tuttle is now a leader in publishing English-language books about the arts, languages and cultures of Asia. The world has become a much smaller place today and Asia's economic and cultural influence has grown. Yet the need for meaningful dialogue and information about this diverse region has never been greater. Over the past seven decades, Tuttle has published thousands of books on subjects ranging from martial arts and paper crafts to language learning and literature—and our talented authors, illustrators, designers and photographers have won many prestigious awards. We welcome you to explore the wealth of information available on Asia at **www.tuttlepublishing.com**.

Published by Tuttle Publishing, an imprint of Periplus Editions (HK) Ltd

www.tuttlepublishing.com

ISBN 978-0-8048-5244-9

First Tuttle edition, 2019
27 26 25 24 23   8 7 6 5 4
2303VP
Printed in Malaysia

Distributed by:

North America, Latin America & Europe
Tuttle Publishing
364 Innovation Drive
North Clarendon, VT 05759-9436 U.S.A.
Tel: 1 (802) 773 8930
Fax: 1 (802) 773 6993
info@tuttlepublishing.com
www.tuttlepublishing.com

Japan
Tuttle Publishing
Yaekari Building, 3F
5-4-12 Osaki, Shinagawa-ku
Tokyo 141-0032, Japan
Tel: (81) 3 5437-0171
Fax: (81) 3 5437-0755
sales@tuttle.co.jp; www.tuttle.co.jp

Asia Pacific
Berkeley Books Pte. Ltd.
3 Kallang Sector #04-01
Singapore 349278
Tel: (65) 6741 2178
Fax: (65) 6741 2179
inquiries@periplus.com.sg
www.tuttlepublishing.com

Contents

Introduction

This book is a light-weight guide on how to "pick up" the Korean language quickly and easily, and start using it right away in stores, on the street, and with friends or co-workers. In the process of learning everyday conversational Korean, you will obtain the pieces that make Korean work—how Korean verbs conjugate, the style of speech you need to use for each occasion—so you can start generating the language on your own once you have finished studying the book. This book covers a wide range of useful and practical topics that can be instantly adopted in everyday life: from the basics of Hangul, the Korean alphabet, and talking about yourself and your surroundings (e.g., introducing oneself, talking about housing and the neighborhood, getting around a building, etc.) to specific situational exchanges (e.g., shopping, getting a haircut at the salon, ordering food at a restaurant, visiting a hospital, etc.). For your practice, each chapter contains two model dialogues with cartoons, vocabulary, and expressions, along with thematic vocabulary lists, grammar notes, and culture notes. Likewise, you will have ample opportunity to practice new expressions and grammatical structures through pattern practices and exercises. We have laid the grammar out progressively, which, in some places, may seemingly be redundant, for the purposes of expansion and reinforcement.

In our previous book *Korean Grammar: The Complete Guide to Speaking Korean Naturally*, we adopted the Yale romanization system and received mixed feedback from users. Yale romanization is second to none in its systematicity in representing the Korean alphabet. Regardless, some readers found it difficult to follow, while others found it helpful. The following are explanations on the romanization and notations we used in this book.

Romanization

In this book, *Basic Korean*, we have adopted the revised romanization (RR) of the Korean government, which focuses on the pronunciation. We have varied it somewhat by transcribing the result of pronunciation rules that are potentially hard for learners to predict. That is, there is going to be no systematic one-to-one, Korean letter-to-romanized letter correspondence. For example, 한국 'Korea' is romanized **han.guk**, whereas for 한국말 'Korean language' **han.gungmal** is used to show the actual pronunciation of the words. (The latter shows a nasalization rule which we "spell out" in our romanization.) Another example is the varied romanization of 거 **geo**, which we sometimes romanize as **kkeo** based on its actual pronunciation: 내 거 **nae kkeo** 'mine,' 갈 거예요 **gal kkeoyeyo** 'I'll be going.' The RR itself incorporates a set of across-the-board phonological rules, romanizing 국 as **guk** 'soup,' trying to represent the phonetic difference between the initial and the final ㄱ ('g' or 'k' sound in English) in the word. We also adhere to the RR in romanizing proper nouns (e.g. 'Kim, Minjun' romanized as **GimMjinjun**). Similarly, you will see that we have spelled out the tensing of consonants in cases that are more difficult to predict (e.g. 신분증 **sinbunjjeung** 'ID card,' 문자 **munjja** 'text(ing),' 안고 **an.kko** 'hug-and,' or 갈게 **galkke** 'I'll go.') You will notice, however, "obstruent" tensing is not romanized (e.g. 옷장 **otjang**, not **otjjang**) because it is more intuitive. Likewise, palatalization or lip-rounding is not represented in romanization as it can be readily picked up. Thus, 식사 is romanized as **siksa** not **shiksa** (but 'ten' is invariably romanized as **ship**). Finally, we use a period to better represent the syllable divisions. Thus, 노래방에서 is romanized **noraebang.eseo**, which otherwise might mistakenly be read as **noraeban.geseo**.

As we mentioned earlier, we have chosen to represent words variously even when they contain the same parts (e.g. 한국 **han.guk** 'Korea,' 한국말 **han.gungmal** 'Korean language'). This is to clearly indicate the pronunciation. Because the Korean alphabet is remarkably easy to learn, we figure that if you do not have time to learn the alphabet, you are going to rely on the romanized text in this book, so the representation that is closest to actual pronunciation will help you the most. As with any spelling practice, approximating pronunciation makes it trickier to discern the relatedness of root words, but to help those who have no time to learn the Korean alphabet, it is a small cost to pay. Despite our good intentions and efforts, and thorough editing by the publisher, you may find inconsistencies or irregularities that are confusing. We strongly recommend that, in the course of your Korean study, you learn the alphabet and eventually use the 한글 **hangul** in this book.

Notations in vocabulary lists
In our introduction of new vocabulary for each lesson, we first present nouns (capitalized if they are proper nouns in English), then adverbs, markers, and lastly, adjectives and verbs that conjugate. Horizontally, we give the Korean word on the left-most column, which precedes romanization, which then is followed by the English translation. This order is not absolutely adhered to in other charts and tables. In the dialogues, for example, English then romanization show up first, and the Korean translation comes last.

The verbs and adjectives are presented first in the exact forms that appear in the dialogues. We then provide in parentheses their dictionary (or citation) forms with a hyphen '-' to indicate that they are root forms. For phrasal or compound verbs, dictionary forms for all involved verbs are listed. Also, the speech style in which the verb is conjugated in the dialogue is noted after its English translation:

만나서 반가워요 (만나-, 반갑-) **mannaseo ban.gawoyo (manna-, bangap-)**
Happy to meet you. (informal, polite)

Romanization "inconsistencies" can also be found in the vocabulary section. We have tried to be more faithful to the spelling in showing the dictionary forms and to the pronunciation once the form is "conjugated" and used in sentences. This is to help you find the dictionary forms with ease in case you are on your way to learning the Korean alphabet and need assistance. Some examples as they appear in the book are as follows:

살다 **salda** 'to live'   살아요 **sarayo** '(someone) lives'
괜찮다 **gwaenchanhda** 'to be OK'   괜찮아요 **gwaenchanayo** '(It's) OK, fine'
맛없다 **mas.eopsda** 'to be bland'   맛없어요 **madeopseoyo**
                                      '(It's) not delicious, unpalatable'

In the same vein, if the suffix is never pronounced as written but is pronounced only one way, we base the romanization on that pronunciation (e.g. -습니다 **-seumnida** (not ~~-seupnita~~)). If the suffix is pronounced differently depending on its surroundings, the base form is introduced (e.g. -겠 **-gess** [not ~~-get~~]), -겠어요 **-gesseoyo**, and -겠네 **-genne** [not ~~-gessne~~]).

To help learners practice, we are providing audio recordings of all the dialogues and vocabulary lists. For each lesson, the dialogue precedes its vocabulary list in the same sound file. The second dialogue and its vocabulary for Lesson 2, for example, is named as follows:

Lesson2_Dialog2__Voc.mp3

There is no dialogue for Lesson 1, but two files are provided for listening practice (Lesson1_Practice2-1.mp3 and Lesson1_Practice2-2.mp3).

We wish all users the best of luck in learning Korean and hope to have made it relatively EASY!

LESSON 1

The Alphabet

The Korean alphabet, called **Hangul**, is notoriously easy to learn. There are 21 vowel letters and 19 consonant letters, and each letter corresponds to a single sound, in principle. Korean letters are written left-to-right, top-to-bottom, but they are not written in a line of single letters, as English is. Instead, two to four letters are gathered into a graphical block that spells a single syllable.

Vowels

A vowel is a sound that you make with your mouth mostly open and unblocked. In English, the five vowel letters represent a number of different sounds while Korean vowel letters have a single pronunciation.

Six core vowels

The 10 basic vowels are built on the following six core vowels:

아 the **a** sound in the word "father"
어 a sound similar to **au** in the word "caught" or "awe"
오 the **o** sound in the word "tote" (made without rounding your lips at the end)
우 the **oo** sound in the word "moo" said with both lips sticking really far out
으 a sound similar to **oo** in the word "good" if you say it while smiling
    (Position your mouth to say "ee" but say "u" instead without changing the shape of your mouth.)
이 the **ee** sound in the word "see"

Korean vowels are written with a placeholder ○ before them when there is no consonant. Here, ○ is not pronounced.

If the vowel letter has a long vertical line, it is written to the right of the consonant or the placeholder ○ (as in 아, 어, 이). If the vowel has a long horizontal line, it is placed *under* the consonant or placeholder (as in 오, 우, 으).

Ten basic vowels

A short sidestroke is added to four of the basic vowels to add the **y** sound.

아 → 야 **ya**
어 → 여 **yeo**
오 → 요 **yoh**
우 → 유 **yoo (yu)**

The ten basic vowels are: 아, 야, 어, 여, 오, 요, 우, 유, 으, and 이.

EXERCISE 1

1. ㄴ is a consonant letter that sounds like *n*. Can you figure out the pronunciation of the following syllables?

    a. 노   b. 니   c. 뉴   d. 나   e. 너

2. Can you combine ㄴ with the correct vowel letter to write the following syllables in Hangul?

    a. **noo**   b. **nee**   c. **no**   d. **na**   e. **nya**

Long vs. Short vowels

There used to be a difference between long and short vowel sounds in Korean, but speakers do not make this difference any longer even if they say they know some words with long vowels. You can ask if they know which **mal** 말 should be long, *word* or *horse*?

Complex vowels

Complex vowels are called such because they are made up of more than one basic vowel. Two "complex" vowels are pronounced as simple vowels, but are made from two of the simple vowels.

애 (아 + ㅣ)   a vowel sound like "**bat**" or "**bet**"
에 (어 + ㅣ)   a vowel sound like "**bet**" or "**bait**"

In Seoul, Koreans would pronounce these two vowels as a vowel sound close to "bet." A short horizontal stroke is added to these vowels to add the **y** sound, and they are also pronounced the same, since there is no pronunciation difference between 애 and 에.

얘 **yeh**; **yeah**
예 **yeh**; **yay**

The last set of complex vowels are combinations of the **w** sound and a basic vowel. 오 and 우 are used to indicate the **w** sound in a very strict matching of what are known as "bright vowels" 오 with 아, as opposed to "dark vowels" 우 with 어:

오 combines with 아 to get 와 **wah**   It is not possible to combine 우 with 아.
오 combines with 애 to get 왜 **weh**   It is not possible to combine 우 with 애.
우 combines with 어 to get 워 **wuh**   It is not possible to combine 오 with 어.
우 combines with 에 to get 웨 **weh**   It is not possible to combine 오 with 에.

Both 오 and 우 can combine with 이:
오 + 이 makes 외 which is pronounced **weh** (not "wee" as you might expect)
우 + 이 makes 위 **wee**

So, you have three complex vowels that are pronounced as **weh**. The spelling just needs to be memorized:
왜, 웨, and 외

Lastly, ㅡ + ㅣ makes 의 which is pronounced with the emphasis on the first part, ㅡ, when it comes at the beginning of a word, otherwise on ㅣ.
ㅡ + ㅣ makes 의 **u-y** or **ee**

The eleven complex vowels are 애, 얘, 에, 예, 와, 왜, 외, 워, 웨, 위, and 의.

PRACTICE 1
1. Pronounce the following vowels out loud. What is the pronunciation of each of the complex vowels?
   a. 야 b. 여 c. 요 d. 유 e. 와
   f. 워 g. 왜 h. 웨 i. 외 j. 위 k. 의

2. Pronounce the following vowels out loud. Which three vowels are pronounced the same way?
   야, 여, 요, 유, 와, 워, 위, 의, 왜, 웨, 외

3. Can you write the **y** and **w** counterparts to each vowel in the chart? Be careful about choosing 오 or 우 for the **w** sound. The boxes in gray are impossible syllables, and there are two options under ㅣ. Remember: 어 or 워 are wrong!

	아	어	오	우	으	이	애	에
y+								
w+								

Consonants
A consonant is a sound you make by constricting some part of the mouth and obstructing the airflow.

Basic consonants
In the mid 15th century, when King Sejong the Great of the Joseon Dynasty created the Korean alphabet, he came up with the five basic consonant shapes, ㄱ, ㄴ, ㅁ, ㅅ, and ㅇ, based on the shape of articulatory organs like the tongue, teeth, roof of the mouth, and the lips.

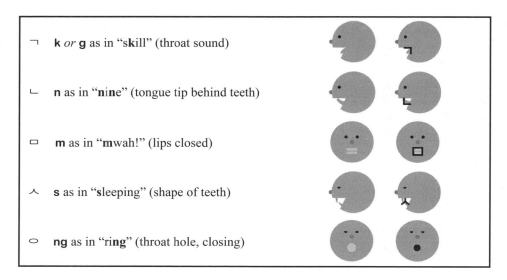

ㄱ	k *or* g as in "skill" (throat sound)
ㄴ	n as in "nine" (tongue tip behind teeth)
ㅁ	m as in "mwah!" (lips closed)
ㅅ	s as in "sleeping" (shape of teeth)
ㅇ	ng as in "ring" (throat hole, closing)

ㄱ represents the "k" sound being made with the back part of the tongue touching the top part of the throat. ㄴ represents the "n" sound being made with the tip of the tongue touching the front part of the mouth. ㅁ represents the lips seen from the front when pronouncing "m." ㅅ represents the teeth, which is where the air whistles through for "s," and ㅇ is a picture of the throat "hole" (seen from the front/inside the mouth) – and that is where the closure is for "ng" as in *ring*. (When ㅇ comes at the beginning of a syllable, it is not pronounced, and when it comes at the end of a syllable, it has this "ng" sound.)

Then, onto the basic consonant shapes, King Sejong added extra strokes to create more consonant letters.

ㄱ k/g	→ ㅋ kh as in cruise		("throat" sounds)
ㄴ n	→ ㄷ t/d as in still	→ ㅌ th as in attack	("tongue tip" sounds)
		→ ㄹ l or r as in ladder	
ㅁ m	→ ㅂ p/b as in spill	→ ㅍ ph as in please	("lip" sounds)
ㅅ soft s	→ ㅈ j/ch as in lunch or lunge	→ ㅊ chh as in chips	("teeth" sounds)
ㅇ ng	→ ㅎ h as in hat		("throat" sounds)

It is important to know that ㄱ, ㄷ, ㅂ, ㅅ, and ㅈ are called plain or **lax** consonants to distinguish them from ㅋ, ㅌ, ㅍ, and ㅊ, which are **aspirated** consonants, and from the doubled-letter **tense** consonants we'll talk about next. ㄱ, ㄷ, ㅂ, and ㅈ do not have a loud burst of air after them like English "k," "t," "p," and "ch" do. They sound like "g," "d," "b," and "j" (or "dg") much of the time, especially when they are in the middle of a word, although they sound similar to English "k," "t," "p," "ch" when they come at the beginning of a word. ㅋ, ㅌ, ㅍ, and ㅊ do have a loud and long burst of air after them (called "aspiration"), even more so than most English "k," "t," "p" and "ch" sounds.

ㅅ is a very soft-sounding "s"; try saying it as if there were an "h" sound before it (and after it). Your tongue is very briefly near the upper teeth before coming down.

ㄴ, ㅁ, ㅇ, and ㄹ are called **sonorant** or **resonant** sounds (because the sounds resonate, as in singing). They do not participate in the tense/lax distinction.

At the beginning or in the middle of a word, ㄹ is an "r" sound that is similar to that of Spanish or Japanese, or like the sound in the middle of "ki**tt**y" or "bu**dd**y" when said really fast. Don't curl your tongue or purse your lips as you would for English r. At the end of a word or syllable, it is a bit more like l. To correctly pronounce ㄹ as in 알 **al**, stick your tongue out, between your teeth or against your upper lip. Do not swallow the back of your tongue as if to say "all" or "doll" in English. Or, say "**l**emon" very slowly. Use that l for final ㄹ as in 알 **al**.

Double consonants

Yet another set of consonant letters was created based on the plain consonants, and they are written as doublets of ㄱ, ㄷ, ㅂ, ㅅ or ㅈ, a little squished together:

ㄲ   ㄸ   ㅃ   ㅆ   ㅉ

These are called **tense** consonants, and they have an extra build-up of air at the throat before they are released, and they have no aspiration. It may help to think of the way Homer Simpson said "ddoh!" This would be like 또 **tto**.

So there is a three-way distinction in non-sonorant consonant sounds in Korean: Plain vs. Aspirated vs. Tense. (There is no Aspirated ㅅ.)

PLAIN (LAX)	ASPIRATED	TENSE	EXAMPLES
ㄱ	ㅋ	ㄲ	기 **gi** "flag," 키 **ki** "height," 끼 **kki** "artistic talent"
ㄷ	ㅌ	ㄸ	달 **dal** "moon," 탈 **tal** "mask," 딸 **ttal** "daughter"
ㅂ	ㅍ	ㅃ	불 **bul** "fire," 풀 **pul** "grass," 뿔 **ppul** "horn"
ㅅ		ㅆ	사다 **sada** "to buy," 싸다 **ssada** "be cheap"
ㅈ	ㅊ	ㅉ	자다 **jada** "to sleep," 차다 **chada** "to kick," 짜다 **jjada** "be salty"

Plain consonants come with a low pitch on the following vowel, whereas aspirated and tense consonants have a higher pitch on the following vowel when you release all that air or energy.

PRACTICE 2

1. Listen carefully to the audio recording of the following words read by a native speaker. Mimic what you hear as closely as possible.
   a. 고기 meat
   b. 자주 frequently
   c. 비빔밥 mixed rice and veggie dish
   d. 도도하다 arrogant
2. Listen carefully to the audio recording of the following words. Listen for the differences. Can you figure out which word is being said?

   a. 기 "flag"   키 "height"   끼 "artistic talent"
   b. 달 "moon"   탈 "mask"   딸 "daughter"
   c. 불 "fire"   풀 "grass"   뿔 "horn"
   d. 사요 "buys"   싸요 "cheap"
   e. 자요 "sleeps"   차요 "kicks"   짜요 "salty"

COMBINING CONSONANTS AND VOWELS

The Korean letters are arranged into blocks that represent syllables.

Syllables with no final consonant

The simplest syllable in Korean is just a vowel (like ㅏ or ㅗ), but it is written with a silent 이응 (ㅇ), as you know.

Next, add a consonant to a vowel. Remember that vowels with long vertical strokes are written to the right of the preceding consonant (e.g., 아, 어, 이), and those with long horizontal strokes are written under it (e.g., 오, 우, 으). The same principle works when the first consonant is anything other than 이응 (ㅇ). Schematics and example words are given in the chart below. Tense consonants like ㅃ and ㅉ are treated as single consonants.

CV	다 da "all," 애 ae "kid," 걔 gyae "that kid," 저 jeo "I (humble)" 게 ge "crab," 네 ne "yes," 비 bi "rain," 짜 jja "salty," "to wring"
C V	소 so "cow," 오 o "five," 표 phyo "ticket," 구 gu "nine" 부부 bubu "married couple," 주소 juso "address," 뽀뽀 ppoppo "kiss"

Complex vowels are written with the first (horizontal) vowel under the consonant and the second (vertical) vowel to the right of everything else, as shown in the schematic below.

	과 gwa "lesson," 왜 wae "why," 최 choe "Choi (a last name)" 쥐 jui "mouse," 뒤 dwi "back," 의 ui "s," 꿔 kkwo "borrows," "dreams"

Any consonant, single or double, can come at the beginning of the syllable, but some are more rarely used than others. ㄹ, for example, is used as a word-initial consonant mainly in borrowed words (e.g., 라면 **ramyeon** "ramen," 라디오 **radio** "radio," 로데오 **rodeo** "rodeo") and is more commonly found in the middle of words (e.g., 머리 **meori** "head," 허리 **heori** "waist/lower back," 다리 **dari** "bridge," "leg," 꼬리 **kkori** "tail," 소리 **sori** "sound," 자리 **jari** "seat," 하루 **haru** "a day," 도로 **doro** "paved road").

One pronunciation note is in order: 시 **si** is pronounced like the English "she" not "see," (your lips should not be round or stuck out; instead, smile the whole time).

Syllables with a final consonant

Syllables may also end with a consonant in Korean. All consonant letters, except for the three doublets ㄸ, ㅃ, ㅉ, can come as the last consonant, known as 받침 **batchim**. (ㅇ is treated as a consonant letter.) The final consonants are always placed at the bottom of the syllable block regardless of whether the vowel is written to the right or under the initial consonant. There are syllables with two 받침 **batchim** consonants, but only single consonants come after complex vowels. All possible two-consonant 받침 **batchim** are shown schematically and with examples in the chart below. Try reading the examples.

CV C	CV CC	집 **jip** "house," 턱 **teok** "chin," 절 **jeol** "temple," 남 **nam** "others," 백 **baek** "hundred" 값 **gaps** "price," 얽히다 **eolkhida** "to get entangled," 짧다 **jjalpda** "short," 앉다 **anjda** "to sit"
C V C	C V CC	육 **yuk** "six," 눈 **nun** "eye," 숲 **sup** "forest" 끝 **kkeut** "end," 공 **gong** "ball," 옷 **ot** "clothes" 긁다 **geulkda** "to scratch," 곪다 **golmda** "to fester"
CV V C		꽉 **kkwak** "tight," 괌 **gwam** "Guam," 왕 **wang** "king" 된장 **doenjang** "soybean paste," 훨씬 **hwolssin** "far (more)"

Here are some syllables that exemplify all the possible final consonants (받침 **batchim**). Can you read them all?

각 꺾 만 곧 발 몸 밥 옷 갔 횡 찾 쫓 억 곁 앞 낳

샀 앉 끊 읽 젊 밟 곶 훑 읊 끓 없

Some of these are rarely used as final consonants (e.g., ㅋ, ㅌ, ㄲ, ㄽ, ㄾ, ㄿ), and others are quite common (e.g., ㄱ, ㅂ, ㅅ, ㅆ, ㄴ, ㄹ, ㅁ, ㅇ).

PRACTICE 3

Many words in the Korean lexicon have originated from foreign languages, just as the words, "spaghetti," "raccoon," "coffee," "moccasin," "chic," and "pajamas" were borrowed into English (and are now pronounced as English words). When words are borrowed into Korean, they are written according to certain conventions.

Read aloud the following Korean **loanwords** said by a native speaker and try to guess the matching English ancestor-word. Check your work by finding the match from the righthand column.

SET 1: (READ, GUESS, MATCH)		SET 2: (READ, GUESS, MATCH)	
a. 태스크	vanilla	a. 버스	pen
b. 스트라이크	chart	b. 재즈	pet
c. 맥도날드	coat or court	c. 퀴즈	bag or back
d. 아일랜드	game	d. 컵 (not 컾)	doughnut
e. 차트	task	e. 백	jazz
f. 코트	McDonald's	f. 펫 (not 펱 or 펜)	bus
g. 게임	desk	g. 팝 (not 팦)	quiz
h. 데스크	strike	h. 펜	cup
i. 바닐라	island	i. 도넛	pop
SET 3: (READ, GUESS, MATCH)		MORE EXAMPLES:	
a. 팀	ban or van	a. 호텔	hotel
b. 엘에이	pan or fan	b. 컷	cut (scenes)
c. 레인	lap, lab, rap or wrap	c. 커트	(hair) cut
d. 랩	Jen or Zen	d. 패드	pad
e. 팬	lane or rain	e. 픽	(guitar) pick
f. 밴	L.A.	f. 피크	peak
g. 젠	Ben	g. 핫도그	hotdog
h. 벤	car	h. 테이프	tape
i. 카	team or Tim	i. 칼	Carl

Names of the consonant letters

The name of the vowel letters in Korean is the sound the vowel represents. The name of each consonant letter follows the pattern of 이응 **ieung** (the name of the letter ㅇ). To make the name of ㄴ, replace the first and last ㅇ in 이응 **ieung** with ㄴ. You get 니은 **nieun**. Do the same for ㄹ, and you get its name, 리을 **lieul**. The same works for all but three names of letters: ㄱ is called 기역 **kiyeok**, ㄷ is called 디귿 **digeut**, and ㅅ is called 시옷 **siot**.

For the tense consonants, you use 쌍 **ssang**, which means "pair" or "twin," thus 쌍비읍 **ssangbieup** means "twin" 비읍 (ㅃ).

Here are the letters and their names:

ㄱ	ㄴ	ㄷ	ㄹ	ㅁ	ㅂ	ㅅ	ㅇ	ㅈ	ㅊ	ㅋ	ㅌ	ㅍ	ㅎ
g	n	d	r/l	m	b/p	s	ng	j	ch	k	t	p	h

ㄲ	ㄸ	ㅃ	ㅆ	ㅉ
kk	tt	pp	ss	jj

Names:

기역	니은	디귿	리을	미음	비읍	시옷
giyeok	nieun	digeut	rieul	mieum	bieup	siot

이응	지읒	치읓	키읔	티읕	피읖	히읗
ieung	jieut	chieut	kieuk	tieut	pieup	hieut

쌍기역	쌍디귿	쌍비읍	쌍시옷	쌍지읒
ssanggiyeok	ssangdigeut	ssangbieup	ssangsiot	ssangjieut

Some letters may look different depending on one's handwriting or computer fonts or even the other letters around it. For example, the first letter ㄱ has a more sideways-leaning downward stroke (like number 7) when it has a vowel to its right side (like 거 **geo**); it has a shorter downward stroke when the vowel is placed underneath (as in 구 **gu** or 고 **go**). The letters ㅈ, ㅊ, and ㅎ also have variant shapes:

  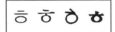

CULTURE NOTE Hangul

Koreans are very proud of their alphabet, and with good reason. It is one of only a very few writing systems that were intentionally created from scratch. King Sejong the Great, along with his cabinet of scholars, created **hangul** 한글 in the 15th century so that all his subjects could learn to read and write, not only the elite (who used Chinese characters at the time and were none too keen on ceding absolute control of information and knowledge to the commoners). If you're interested, you can find out more about it via a quick search online, in books or even through Korean films and shows. Many use the term **hangul** 한글 to refer to the language itself (as opposed to the writing system), but it is important to remember that the spoken language has existed for millennia, long before the writing system.

To ensure you're pronouncing each word correctly and like a native speaker, follow along with the audio recordings available from http://www.tuttlepublishing.com/basic-korean.

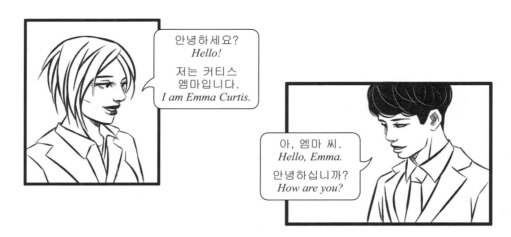

안녕하세요?
Hello!
저는 커티스 엠마입니다.
I am Emma Curtis.

아, 엠마 씨.
Hello, Emma.
안녕하십니까?
How are you?

처음 뵙겠습니다.
Nice to meet you.

제 이름은 김민준입니다.
My name is Kim Minjoon.
만나서 반갑습니다.
Nice to meet you!
여기 제 명함입니다.
Here is my business card.

네, 말씀 많이 들었습니다.
Yes, I've heard a lot about you.
잘 부탁드립니다.
I'm in your care.

LESSON 2
Introducing Yourself

🔘 **DIALOGUE 1** Hello! Nice to meet you!

Emma Curtis, an American, is a designer at the branch office in Seoul, Korea. She meets Kim Minjoon, the project leader, for the first time at the company party.

Emma: Hello! I am Emma Curtis.
Annyeonghaseyo? Jeoneun Keotiseu Emmamnida.
안녕하세요? 저는 커티스 엠마입니다.
Nice to meet you.
Cheo.eum boekesseumnida.
처음 뵙겠습니다.

Minjoon: Hello, Emma. How are you?
A, Emma ssi. Annyeonghasimnikka?
아, 엠마 씨. 안녕하십니까?
My name is Kim Minjoon. Nice to meet you!
Je ireumeun GimMinjunimnida. Mannaseo bangapseumnida.
제 이름은 김민준입니다. 만나서 반갑습니다.
Here is my business card.
Yeogi je myeonghamimnida.
여기 제 명함입니다.

Emma: Yes, I've heard a lot about you. I'm in your care.
Ne, malsseum mani deureosseumnida. Jal butakdeurimnida.
네, 말씀 많이 들었습니다. 잘 부탁드립니다.

VOCABULARY AND EXPRESSIONS

저	jeo	I (humble form)
제	je	my (humble form)
씨	ssi	Mr./Ms. (used after first or full name in formal situations)
네	ne	yes (humble form; also written and pronounced as **ye** 예)
이름	ireum	name
성함	seongham	name (respectful)
명함	myeongham	business card
말씀	malsseum	words, stories (honorific)
여기	yeogi	here
처음	cheo.eum	first time

많이	**mani**	a lot, much, many
잘	**jal**	well, often
-은	**eun**	topic marker after a noun that ends with a consonant
-는	**neun**	topic marker after a noun that ends with a vowel
-입니다	**imnida**	be (am, is, are): formal verb of identity
안녕하세요?	**annyeonghaseyo?**	Hello!/How are you? (informal, polite)
안녕하십니까?	**annyeonghasimnikka?**	Hello!/How are you? (formal, polite)
처음 뵙겠습니다.	**cheo.eum boekesseumnida.**	Nice to meet you. (formal, polite)
만나서 반갑습니다.	**mannaseo bangapseumnida.**	Nice to meet you/Pleased to meet you. (formal, polite)
말씀 많이 들었습니다.	**malsseum mani deureosseumnida.**	I have heard a lot about you. (formal, polite)
잘 부탁드립니다.	**jal butakdeurimnida.**	I'm in your care/Please take care of me. (formal, polite)

VOCABULARY PRACTICE 1
How would you say the following in Korean?
1. Yes!   2. Nice to meet you.   3. Hello!

VOCABULARY PRACTICE 2
Complete the words or expressions by filling in missing syllables.
1. 많_____ (a lot) **manh...**
2. _____음 ... (first time **eum**)
3. 잘 부_____드립니다. (I'm in your care.) **Jal bu...deurimnida.**
4. _____나서 반갑습니다 (Nice to meet you.) **... naseo bangapseumnida.**

Supplementary Vocabulary
Terms of address

학생	**haksaeng**	student, kid (from preschool to college)
언니	**eonni**	older sister (said by females)
누나	**nuna**	older sister (said by males)
오빠	**oppa**	older brother (said by females)
형	**hyung**	older brother (said by males)
남동생	**namdongsaeng**	younger brother
여동생	**yeodongsaeng**	younger sister
아가씨	**agassi**	miss, young lady
아저씨	**ajeossi**	sir, mister
아줌마	**ajumma**	ma'am (to a woman over 40)
아주머니	**ajummeoni**	ma'am (to a woman over 40; more polite)

할머니	halmeoni	grandma, ma'am (to an older woman)
할아버지	halabeoji	grandpa, sir (to an older man)
선생님	sunsaengnim	teacher, doctor
사장님	sajangnim	company chief
과장님	gwajangnim	section chief
부장님	bujangnim	department chief
대리님	daerinim	assistant manager

GRAMMAR NOTE **Basic sentence structure**

The word order is flexible in Korean as long as the verb comes last in the sentence order. The **subject** is often omitted in spoken Korean if it's clear from context. A marker is attached to a noun to indicate its role in the sentence, such as **topic** or **object**.

Romeo likes Juliet.

Romioneun	**Jullieseul**	**joahamnida.**
Romeo-topic marker	Juliet-object marker	like
Jullieseul	**Romioneun**	**joahamnida.**
Juliet-object marker	Romeo-topic marker	like

GRAMMAR NOTE **Topic marker –은/는 -eun/neun**

The marker **-eun/neun** -은/는 roughly translates to "speaking of" or "as for" in English, and marks the noun as the topic of the sentence. The topic marker can be used with the object to indicate a contrast. Use **-eun** -은 after nouns that end in a consonant, like **ireum** 이름 "name," and **-neun** -는 after nouns ending in a vowel, like **jeo** 저 "I (humble)."

| **je ireumeun** 제 이름은 | **jeoneun** 저는 |
| my name-topic | I (humble)-topic |

GRAMMAR NOTE **"A is B" with the formal verbal ending**

Imnida 입니다 is a verb of identity like the English "to be," used to equate items, e.g., "My name is Emma Curtis" but cannot be used with statements like "I am tired." It does not need to be conjugated differently for different subjects ("I," "you," "we," etc.), and it is written without a space between it and the preceding word.

Je ireumeun	**Keotiseu Emmaimnida.**
제 이름은	커티스 엠마입니다.
My (humble) name-topic marker	Emma Curtis-is
	= My name is Emma Curtis.

Jeoneun	**Gim.Minjunimnida.**
저는	김민준입니다.
I (humble)-topic marker	Kim Minjoon-am = I am Kim Minjoon.

PATTERN PRACTICE 1

Practice introducing yourself to someone else. You can follow the examples.

1. I am Kim Minjoon.
   Jeoneun Gim.Minjunimnida.
   저는 김민준입니다.

2. I am Emma Curtis.
   Jeoneun Keotiseu Emmaimnida.
   저는 커티스 엠마입니다.

3. My name is Kim Minjoon.
   Je ireumeun Gim.Minjunimnida.
   제 이름은 김민준입니다.

4. My name is Emma Curtis.
   Je ireumeun Keotiseu Emmaimnida.
   제 이름은 커티스 엠마입니다.

GRAMMAR NOTE Questions in the formal style

By simply replacing **da** 다 with **kka** 까 in **imnida** 입니다, you can make a formal question. Keep in mind that the subject is frequently omitted in Korean. Let's first construct a sentence like "This is Mr. Kim Minjoon's business card."

GimMinjun ssi   **myeonghamimnida.**
김민준 씨   명함입니다.
Kim Minjoon Mr.   business card-is-statement suffix
= This is Mr. Kim Minjoon's business card.

To make the statement into a question, we drop the **-da** -다 ending and replace it with the question marker **-kka** -까.

GimMinjun ssi   **myeonghamimnikka?**
김민준 씨   명함입니까?
Kim Minjoon Mr.   business card-is-question suffix
= Is this Mr. Kim Minjoon's business card?

GRAMMAR NOTE How to express possession

To express possession, put the item's owner before the item itself: "Kim Minjoon" (**GimMinjun** 김민준) precedes the "business card" (**myeongham** 명함) to show that he owns the card.

PATTERN PRACTICE 2

Practice asking questions in Korean, using the formal ending. You can follow the examples.

1. (Are you/is this) Mr. Kim Minjoon?
   Gim.Minjun ssiimnikka? 김민준 씨입니까?

2. (Are you/is this) Ms. Emma?
   Emma ssiimnikka? 엠마 씨입니까?

3. (Is this) Mr. Kim Minjoon's business card?
   Gim.Minjun ssi myeonghamimnikka? 김민준 씨 명함입니까?
4. (Is that) Ms. Emma's business card?
   Emma ssi myeonghamimnikka? 엠마 씨 명함입니까?

CULTURE NOTE **Formal vs. informal registers**

If you hear someone saying in **-mnida** -ㅂ니다 or **-mnikka** -ㅂ니까, the person speaking is being _formal_ (common in work situations or if you are talking to someone in a higher position than you are). If you hear **-yo** -요 at the end, they are being less formal, but still _polite_. In the dialogue, Emma begins with the greeting **Annyonghaseyo?** 안녕하세요? and Minjoon responds with **Annyeonghasimnikka?** 안녕하십니까?. Older men tend to use the formal style when first meeting someone, although Korean does not have a strict male or female speech. Once they get to know each other well, people will usually start using the _informal polite_ ending **-yo** -요.

CULTURE NOTE **Korean names**

One's family name (or surname) comes before their given name, i.e., Kim (surname) Minjoon (given name). The five most common Korean family names (45 per cent of the population) are Kim, Lee/Yi, Park, Choi, and Cheong/Jung. When introducing yourself or others, remember to start with the surname first followed by the given name, i.e., **Keotiseu Emmaimnida** 커티스 엠마입니다 for "(I am/This is) Emma Curtis."

CULTURE NOTE **Addressing Korean people**

Koreans usually use titles like "Section chief" or "Manager," or kinship terms like "older brother/sister" or "Auntie" to address each other. Otherwise, you can also use the person's first name plus **ssi**, if they are an adult about the same age or younger, i.e., **Minjoon-ssi** 민준 씨. **Ssi** 씨 can be roughly translated as Mr., Mrs., Miss or Ms. in English, but it is not as formal or polite. Do not use this with your own name, or to address your boss(es) or seniors.

CULTURE NOTE **Exchanging business cards**

It is very common to exchange business cards in Korea in formal situations. Exchanging cards is a common way to introduce oneself. Once you know others' status, age, and station in life, you can then use the appropriate forms of address, formality level and honorifics.

When receiving a business card, take a moment to read the card and carefully put it away in your wallet or a business card holder. Do not simply jam it in your back pocket.

EXERCISE 1

What would you say in the following situations?
1. Say hello to the manager Ms. Kim in the office.
2. Say hello to your older friend you've met on the street.
3. Tell your new co-worker, whom you're meeting for the first time, that you are pleased to meet him/her.
4. Tell your new co-worker your name (Sarah).
5. Give your business card to your client.

EXERCISE 2

You have just met someone for the first time. Introduce yourself and say "Nice to meet you." Follow the example.

Minjoon: Hello, My name is Kim Minjoon. Nice to meet you! I'm in your care.
Annyeonghasimnikka? Je ireumeun Gim.Minjunimnida.
Mannaseo ban.gapseumnida. Jal butakdeurimnida.
안녕하십니까? 제 이름은 김민준입니다. 만나서 반갑습니다. 잘 부탁드립니다.

1. Kristine Kim (**Gim Kristin**)
   김 크리스틴
2. Michelle Wang (**Wang Mishel**)
   왕 미셸
3. Jamie Parker (**Pakeo Jeimi**)
   파커 제이미
4. Jonathan Brown (**Buraun Jonadan**)
   브라운 조나단

DIALOGUE 2 Where are you from?

Lee Eunbi works with Emma as a graphic designer and she meets Aiden Tyler, who is an employee in the marketing department, at the company party.

Eunbi: Hello! My name is Lee Eunbi. What is your name?
Annyeonghaseyo? Jeoneun I.Eunbirago haeyo. Ireumi mwoyeyo?
안녕하세요? 저는 이은비라고 해요. 이름이 뭐예요?

Aiden: I am Aiden Tyler. Pleasure (meeting you).
Je ireumeun Tailleo Eideunieyo. Ban.gawoyo.
제 이름은 타일러 에이든이에요. 반가워요.

Eunbi: Good to meet you. Which country are you from, Aiden? Are you an American?
Ban.gawoyo. Eideun ssineun eoneu nara saramieyo? Miguk saramieyo?
반가워요. 에이든 씨는 어느 나라 사람이에요? 미국 사람이에요?

Aiden: No, I'm not an American. I'm a Canadian. Where did you come from, Eunbi?
          Aniyo. Miguk sarami anieyo. Kaenada saramieyo. Eunbi ssineun eodieseo wasseoyo?
          아니요. 미국 사람이 아니에요. 캐나다 사람이에요. 은비 씨는 어디에서 왔어요?
Eunbi: Hahaha. I am Korean. I "came from" my house this morning. Nice to meet you!
          Hahaha. Jeoneun Han.guk saramieyo. Oneul achime jibeseo wasseoyo. Mannaseo ban.gawoyo!
          하하하. 저는 한국 사람이에요. 오늘 아침에 집에서 왔어요. 만나서 반가워요!

VOCABULARY AND EXPRESSIONS

뭐	mwo	what
어느	eoneu	which
나라	nara	country
어디	eodi	where
사람	saram	person
미국	Miguk	U.S.
미국 사람	Miguk saram	American (person)
캐나다	Kaenada	Canada
한국	Han.guk	Korea
오늘	oneul	today
내일	naeil	tomorrow
아침	achim	morning
집	jip	house, home
-이	i	subject marker after a noun that ends in a consonant
-가	ga	subject marker after a noun that ends in a vowel
-에서	eseo	from
-이라고 해요	irago haeyo (i-, ha-)	be called—after consonant-ending nouns (informal, polite)
-라고 해요	rago haeyo ((i-), ha-)	be called—after vowel-ending nouns (informal, polite)
-이에요	ieyo (i-)	be—after consonant-ending nouns (informal, polite)
-예요	yeyo (i-)	be—after vowel-ending nouns (informal, polite)
아니요	aniyo	no (informal, polite)
아니에요 (아니-)	anieyo (ani-)	not be (informal, polite)

왔어요 (오-)	**wasseoyo (o-)**	came (informal, polite)
(만나서) 반가워요	**(mannaseo) ban.gawoyo**	Happy (to meet you). (informal, polite)
(만나-, 반갑-)	**(manna-, bangap-)**	

VOCABULARY PRACTICE 3

How would you say the following in Korean?

1. this morning　　　　2. an American　　　　3. a Canadian
4. What?!　　　　5. I came from home.　　　　6. Nice to meet you!

Supplementary Vocabulary

Nationalities

Here are some names of countries. If your country is not listed, you can look it up online (or on Google Translate).

미국	**Miguk**	United States
캐나다	**Kaenada**	Canada
멕시코	**Meksiko**	Mexico
영국	**Yeong.guk**	United Kingdom
프랑스	**Peurangseu**	France
스페인	**Seupein**	Spain
이탈리아, 이태리	**Itallia, Itaeri**	Italy
독일	**Dogil**	Germany
네덜란드	**Nedeollandeu**	Netherlands
덴마크	**Denmakeu**	Denmark
러시아	**Reosia**	Russia
중국	**Jung.guk**	China
월남, 베트남	**Wollam, Beteunam**	Vietnam
일본	**Ilbon**	Japan
싱가포르	**Singgaporeu**	Singapore
호주	**Hoju**	Australia
뉴질랜드	**Nyujillaendeu**	New Zealand

To talk about a person from a country, simply add **in** 인 or **saram** 사람 after the country. **Saram** 사람 is more appropriate in conversation and is less formal than **in** 인:

　　Kaenada saram 캐나다 사람　a Canadian (person),
　　Jung.gugin 중국인　a Chinese (person)

To refer to the language of a country, simply add **eo** 어 or **mal** 말 to the country name. Use **mal** 말 in conversation as it is less formal than **eo** 어. English and Spanish are exceptions (and cannot use **mal** 말).

Han.gungmal 한국말 Korean   **Han.gugeo** 한국어 Korean
Seupeineo 스페인어 Spanish   **Yeongeo** 영어 English

To talk about something from that country, you just need to use the country name before the item: **Han-gung munhwa** 한국 문화 Korean culture

PATTERN PRACTICE 3

Read the sentences to practice asking someone's nationality.

1. A: Where are you from, Emma? **Emma ssineun eoneu nara saramieyo?**
      엠마 씨는 어느 나라 사람이에요?
   B: I am an American (person). **Jeoneun miguk saramieyo.**
      저는 미국 사람이에요.
2. A: Where are you from, Minjoon? **Minjun ssineun eoneu nara saramieyo?**
      민준 씨는 어느 나라 사람이에요?
   B: I am a Korean (person). **Jeoneun Han.guk saramieyo.**
      저는 한국 사람이에요.
3. A: Where are you from, Jiang? **Jiang ssineun eoneu nara saramieyo?**
      지앙 씨는 어느 나라 사람이에요?
   B: I am a Chinese (person). **Jeoneun Junggugeseo wasseoyo.**
      저는 중국에서 왔어요.

GRAMMAR NOTE Formal and Polite conjugations of verb of identity 이 *i*

There are at least two ways to conjugate "to be" in Korean. One is the formal **imnida** 입니다, which you saw in the first dialogue of Lesson 2, and the other is the still polite but informal **ieyo** 이에요 (for nouns that end in a consonant) and **yeyo** 예요 (for nouns that end in a vowel).

Yeogi	**je**	**myeonghamimnida.**
여기	제	명함입니다.
Here	my (humble)	business card-is = This is my business card.

Je	**ireumeun**	**Syue Singyuyeyo.**
제	이름은	싱유예요.
my (humble)	name-top	Xue Xingyu-is = My name is Xue Xingyu.

Jeoneun	**Jung.guk**	**saramieyo.**
저는	중국	사람이에요.
I (humble)-topic	China	person-am = I am (a) Chinese (person).

PATTERN PRACTICE 4

Practice answering with your name politely, then formally. You can follow the examples.

1. A: What is your name? **Ireumi mwoyeyo?** 이름이 뭐예요?
   B: My name is Lee Jihye. **Lee.Jihyeyeyo.** 이지혜예요.
   B': My name is Lee Jihye. **Lee.Jihyeimnida.** 이지혜입니다.
2. A: What is your name? **Ireumi mwoyeyo?** 이름이 뭐예요?
   B: My name is Jung Taeyang. **Jeong.Taeyangieyo.** 정태양이에요.
   B': My name is Jung Taeyang. **Jeong.Taeyangimnida.** 정태양입니다.

GRAMMAR NOTE Yes/no questions

To ask and answer a yes/no question in the informal polite speech style, raise your intonation at the very last syllable. There is no need to change the form of **ieyo** 이에요 (or **yeyo** 예요).

Jung.guk	**saramieyo.**
중국	사람이에요.
China	person is = (Someone is/I am) a Chinese (person)/I am Chinese.

Jung.guk	**saramieyo?**
중국	사람이에요?
China	person is (Is someone/are you) Chinese?/Are you Chinese?

GRAMMAR NOTE Negative verb of identity 아니 *ani*

To negate an identity verb and make it "A is <u>not</u> B" in Korean, you have to use the negative verb **animnida** 아닙니다 (formal version) or **anieyo** 아니에요 (informal) "(it) is not." Use the subject marker **-i/ga** -이/가 after the noun you are negating and then a space before **anieyo** 아니에요 in its written form.

Jeoneun	**Han.guk**	**sarami**	**animnida.**
저는	한국	사람이	아닙니다.
I (humble)-topic	Korea	person-subject	be-not
= I am not (a) Korean (person).			

Jeo sarameun	**Emmaga**	**anieyo.**
저 사람은	엠마가	아니에요.
that person-topic	Emma-subject	be-not = That person is not Emma.

A: **Eideun ssineun   Yeong.guk saramieyo?**
   에이든 씨는   영국 사람이에요?
   Aiden-Mr.-topic   British   person is? = Are you British, Aiden?

B: **Aniyo. Jeoneun**   **Yeong.guk sarami**   **animnida/anieyo.**
아니요. 저는   영국   사람이   아닙니다/아니에요.
No   I (humble)-topic   U.K.   person-subj. be-not
= No, I am not British.

PATTERN PRACTICE 5

Answer someone's questions in the negative. Follow the example below:

Reporter: **Jiyoung ssiyeyo?** 지영 씨예요?
You: **Aniyo. Jeoneun Jiyoungi anieyo.** 아니요. 저는 지영이 아니에요.

1. Are you Jihye? **Jihye ssiyeyo?** 지혜 씨예요?
2. Are you a student? **Haksaeng.ieyo?** 학생이에요?
3. Are you Japanese? **Ilbon saramieyo?** 일본 사람이에요?
4. Are you Korean? **Han.guk saramieyo?** 한국 사람이에요?

GRAMMAR NOTE The subject marker –이/가 -i/ga

The subject marker, **-i/ga** -이/가 marks a noun as the subject of the sentence. **-i** -이 is used after nouns with consonants as their last letter, like **ireum-i**, 이름-이 and **-ga** -가 is used (when written) with nouns and names that have vowels as their last letter, like **Emili-ga** 에밀리-가. We have so far only used -i -이 and -ga -가 to make negative sentences and in the question **Ireumi mwoyeyo** 이름이 뭐예요? "What is your name?"

Nouns marked with the subject marker typically start a new topic, give information that is new or is the focus of the conversation related to the person the conversation is about.

Jega	**geugeo**	**kkaesseoyo.**
제가	그거	깼어요.
I-subject	that	broke = It is I who broke it.

Jeimseuga	**NyuYogeseo**	**wasseoyo.**
제임스가	뉴욕에서	왔어요.
James-subject	New York-from	have come

= James has come (back or just arrived) from New York.

PATTERN PRACTICE 6

Practice stating the person's nationality.
1. A: Who is from the U.S.? (Ms. Emma) **Nuga Miguk saramieyo? (Emma ssi)**
누가 미국 사람이에요? (엠마 씨)
B: Ms. Emma is (American). **Emma ssiga Miguk saramieyo.**
엠마 씨가 미국 사람이에요.

B: The teacher is (Korean). **Seonsaengnimi Han.guk saramiyo.**
선생님이 한국 사람이에요.

2. A: Who is Chinese? (my friend) **Nuga Jung.guk saramieyo? (je chin.gu)**
누가 중국 사람이에요? (제 친구)

B: My friend is (Chinese). **Je chin.guga Jung.guk saramieyo.**
제 친구가 중국 사람이에요.

GRAMMAR NOTE Revisiting the topic marker -은/는 *-eun/neun*

The subject of an English sentence can either be said with the subject marker or a topic marker in Korean. Nouns marked with a topic marker speak of what is already known (either from the context or because it has been mentioned previously) or in comparison to something else (which may not be explicitly mentioned).

Jeoneun oneul an gayo.
저는   오늘 안 가요.
I-topic   today not go
= I am not going today (I don't know about everyone else).

Jeimseuneun   NyuJeojieseo   wasseoyo.
제임스는   뉴저지에서   왔어요.
James-topic   New Jersey-from   have come
= James (the person who we just introduced) is from New Jersey.

GRAMMAR NOTE The perfective aspect—"Something has already been done"

When you hear words with the suffix **-sseoyo** -ㅆ어요, the speaker is talking about something that he/she assumes has already taken place (as in, "Did you eat there yesterday?" or "Have you eaten?"). Thus, **wassseoyo** 왔어요 means "came" or "have come" in the question "Where are you from?" (*Lit.*, "Where have you come from?")

Jeoneun Miguk   NyuJeojieseo   wasseoyo.
저는   미국   뉴저지에서   왔어요.
I-topic America   New Jersey-from   have come
= I am/have come from New Jersey, in the US.

Jingeun   Jung.guk   Syanghaieseo   wasseoyo.
저는   중국   샹하이에서   왔어요.
Jing-topic China   Shanghai-from   has come
= Jing is/has come from Shanghai, China.

PATTERN PRACTICE 7

Practice saying the expression "Someone is/someone came from…"

1. I am/came from Thailand. **Jeoneun Taegugeseo wasseoyo.**
   저는 태국에서 왔어요.
2. Ngyuen is/came from Vietnam. **Ngyueneun Beteunameseo wasseoyo.**
   뉴엔은 베트남에서 왔어요.
3. Jessie is/came from Hawaii. **Jessineun Hawaieseo wasseoyo.**
   제시는 하와이에서 왔어요.

CULTURE NOTE **Greetings among peers**

Eunbi and Aiden use the informal polite ending **-yo** -요 in this dialogue because they are of a similar status (similar age and at a similar station in life), but not on familiar terms yet.

CULTURE NOTE 잘 부탁드립니다 *Jal butakdeurimnida* — "Please treat me kindly."

The phrase **Jal butakdeurimnida** 잘 부탁드립니다, or **Jal butakaeyo** 잘 부탁해요 in the informal polite form, is said by a newcomer to ask for kindness and patience or just to be polite when he/she meets someone. It is very common in Korean, although its English rendition may sound overly formal. **Jal** 잘 means "well" or "often," and **butakdeurimnida** 부탁드립니다 or **butakaeyo** 부탁해요 "make a request," thus it means that the speaker is making a request to be taken care of "well."

CULTURE NOTE **Asking someone's name**

There are two things to note about asking names. First, when asking someone's name in the informal style, be sure to use the subject marker with **ireum** 이름 (name): **Ireum imwoyeyo?** 이름이 뭐예요?

Secondly, refrain from asking someone older or of higher status their name as it's considered to be rude, and address them with a title instead. There is a special way to ask a person's name with proper honorific and formal forms (but still avoid this with much older persons), e.g., "Pardon me, but what is your name?" **Sillyejiman seonghami eotteoke doesimnikka?** 실례지만 성함이 어떻게 되십니까?

CULTURE NOTE **Bowing**

When Koreans meet for the first time, they bow by lowering their head slightly. They may close their eyes or their gaze might drop somewhat along with their head, as it is considered to be quite rude to keep eye contact as you bow.

In very formal situations, for example, to express deep appreciation or greet the company's CEO or to welcome a customer at a department store, people may lower their upper body as much as 90 degrees. If you want to try this, keep your hands at your sides or folded on your belly and tuck in your behind.

EXERCISE 3

Your new colleague is asking some questions about people in your office. Answer his/her questions. Follow the example.

Your colleague: **Jenipeo ssineun Migugeseo wasseoyo?**
제니퍼 씨는 미국에서 왔어요?

You: **Ne. Migugeseo wasseoyo.**   OR   **Aniyo. Yeonggugeseo wasseoyo.**
네. 미국에서 왔어요.   OR   아니요. 영국에서 왔어요.

Jennifer Kim (**Gim.Jenipeo**) (김 제니퍼)	American
Jason Zhang (**Jang Jeiseun**) (장 제이슨)	Chinese
Peter Brown (**Beuraun Piteo**) (브라운 피터)	English
Park Minho (**Bak.Minho**) (박민호)	Korean
Nakamura Aiko (**Nakamura Aiko**) (나카무라 아이코)	Canadian

1. **Jang Jeiseun ssineun Jung.guk saramieyo?**
   장 제이슨 씨는 중국 사람이에요?
2. **Beuraun Piteo ssineun eoneu nara saramieyo?**
   브라운 피터 씨는 어느 나라 사람이에요?
3. **Bak.Minho ssineun eodieseo wasseoyo?**
   박민호 씨는 어디에서 왔어요?
4. **Nakamula Aiko ssineun Ilbon saramieyo?**
   나카무라 아이코 씨는 일본 사람이에요?

EXERCISE 4

You overheard Jennifer saying the following in Korean. What do you think the other person asked? Answer in Korean.

1. **Ne, Jenipeoyeyo.** 네, 제니퍼예요.
2. **Yeong.guk saramieyo.** 영국 사람이에요.
3. **Aniyo. Jeoneun haksaeng.i anieyo. Jang Maikeul ssiga haksaeng.ieyo.**
   아니요. 저는 학생이 아니에요. 장 마이클 씨가 학생이에요.
4. **Maikeul ssineun Beteunameseo wasseoyo.**
   마이클 씨는 베트남에서 왔어요.

LESSON 3
Getting to Know Your Friends

🔘 **DIALOGUE 1** **What's your phone number?**

Eunbi and Emma want to exchange telephone numbers so they can hang out together after work.

Emma: Ms. Eunbi, what is your (house) telephone number?
Eunbi ssi, jip jeonhwabeonhoga mwoyeyo?
은비 씨, 집 전화번호가 뭐예요?

Eunbi: I only have a cell phone. My cell number is 016-123-7890.
Hyudaeponman isseoyo. Je hyudaepon beonhoneun gong.il.lyuk il.li.same chil.pal.gu.gong.ieyo.
휴대폰만 있어요. 제 휴대폰 번호는 016-123-7890이에요.
What is your number, Ms. Emma?
Emma ssi jeonhwa beonhoneun mwoyeyo?
엠마 씨 전화 번호는 뭐예요?

Emma: It is 017-987-4321.
Gong.il.chil gu.pal.chire sa.sam.i.irieyo.
017-987-4321이에요.

Eunbi: Do you have a Kakao Talk I.D. as well?
Katok aidido isseoyo?
카톡 아이디도 있어요?

Emma: Yes. It's Emma123.
Ne. Emma il.i.samieyo.
네. 엠마123이에요.

Eunbi: Yay! We are now Kakao Talk friends.
Yaho! Urineun ije katok chin.guyeyo.
야호! 우리는 이제 카톡 친구예요.

Emma: Is that so? Let's text often.
Geuraeyo? Uri jaju munjahaeyo!
그래요? 우리 자주 문자해요!

VOCABULARY AND EXPRESSIONS

전화	jeonhwa	phone
번호	beonho	number
휴대폰	hyudaepon	cell phone
우리	uri	we, us

카톡	**Katok**	Kakao Talk (Korean messaging application)
아이디, 신분증	**aidi, sinbunjjeung**	I.D.
친구	**chin.gu**	friend
야호	**Yaho!**	Yay! Hooray!
이제	**ije**	now, unlike before
−도	**do**	also, as well, too (noun marker)
−만	**man**	only (noun marker)
그래요 (그렇−)	**geuraeyo (geureoh-)**	OK, it is so, let's do
문자해요 (문자하−)	**munjahaeyo (munjaha-)**	let's text, text (me)

VOCABULARY PRACTICE 1

Give the Korean terms for the words described below.
1. Now we are friends.
2. Let's talk on the phone often!
3. I only have my I.D.
4. Do you have a cell phone, too?

Supplementary Vocabulary

Popular social media and search engines in Korea

SNS	**Eseu.eneseu**	Social media
카카오 톡	**Kakao tok**	Kakao Talk (instant messaging application)
라인	**Lain**	Line (instant messaging application)
페이스북, 페북	**Peiseubuk, Pebuk**	Facebook
트위터	**Teuwiteo**	Twitter
인스타그램	**Inseutageuraem**	Instagram
카카오 스토리	**Kakao seutoli**	Kakao Story (social media)
네이버 밴드	**Neibeo baendeu**	Naver Band (mobile community application)
네이버	**Neibeo**	Naver (search portal)
다음	**Da.eum**	Daum (search portal)

Sino-Korean numbers

공/영	gong/yeong	0	구	gu	9
일	il	1	십	ship	10
이	i	2	십일	shibil	11
삼	sam	3	십오	shibo	15
사	sa	4	칠십	chilship	70
오	o	5	구십구	gushipgu	99
육	(r)yuk	6	백	baek	100
칠	chil	7	천	cheon	1,000
팔	pal	8	만	man	10,000

Months of the year

The names of the months in Korean are made up of the Sino-Korean number representing the month plus the affix **wol** 월, which means "month." The 6th month "June," and the 10th month, "October," drop the final consonant in the number word.

일월	Irwol	January	팔월	Parwol	August
이월	Iwol	February	구월	Guwol	September
삼월	Samwol	March	시월	Shiwol	October
사월	Sawol	April	십일월	Shibirwol	November
오월	Owol	May	십이월	Shibiwol	December
유월	Yuwol	June	몇 월	Myeot dweoi?	what month?
칠월	Chirwol	July			

Days of the month

The days of the month use Sino-Korean numbers plus the "day" suffix, **il** 일.

일일	iril	the 1st (day) of the month	이십삼일	ishipsamil	the 23rd
이일	iil	the 2nd	삼십일일	samshibiril	the 31st
십오일	shiboil	the 15th	며칠이에요?	Myeochirieyo?	What's the date?

PATTERN PRACTICE 1

Practice exchanging telephone numbers in Korean. You can follow the examples.

1. A: What is your telephone number? **Jeonghwabeonhoga mwoyeyo?**
    전화번호가 뭐예요?

    B: (My telephone number is) 050-9564-9823.
    (Je jeonhwabeonhoneun) gong.o.gong gu.o.ryuk.sa.e guparisamieyo.
    (제 전화번호는) 공오공의 구오육사의 구팔이삼이에요.

2. A: What is Mr. Aiden's telephone number?
    Eideun ssi jeonhwabeonhoga mwoyeyo?
    에이든 씨 전화 번호가 뭐예요?

    B: (Mr. Aiden's phone number is) 019-702-8804. **(Eideun ssi jeonhwabeonhoneun) gong.il.gu.e chilgong.i.e palpalgongsayeyo.**
    (에이든 씨 전화번호는) 공일구의 칠공이의 팔팔공사예요.

PATTERN PRACTICE 2

Practice asking and answering the following.

1. A: What's the date today? **Oneuri myeochirieyo?** 오늘이 며칠이에요?

    B: It's December 16th. **Shibiwol shimnygirieyo.** 12월 16일이에요.

2. A: When is your birthday? **Saeng.iri myeochirieyo?**
       생일이 며칠이에요?
    B: It's March 24th. **Samwol ishipsairieyo.** 3월 24일이에요.
3. A: What month is it now? **Jigeum myeodworieyo?** 지금 몇 월이에요?
    B: It is May. **Oworieyo.** 오월이에요.

GRAMMAR NOTE *WH* Questions in Korean

To make questions that involve "wh" question words (*who*, *what*, *where*, *when*, *why*, and *how*), replace the unknown information in the sentence with the question word. When using the formal question ending, **-kka** -까, use the question intonation similar to English (high then low at the very end). With the polite ending **-yo** -요, lower the last syllable and raise it back a little (make a dip in the intonation).

    A: What time is the meeting? **Miting.i myeot siimnikka?**
       미팅이 몇 시입니까?
    B: It's (at) 10:00 a.m. **Ojeon yeol siyeyo.** 오전 열 시예요.

    A: Where do you live? **Eodi sarayo?** 어디 살아요?
    B: I live in Itaewon. **Itaewone sarayo.** 이태원에 살아요.

GRAMMAR NOTE Markers to show "also," "too" and "only"

"Also" and "too" in English can be expressed with the marker **-do** -도 in Korean. It is attached to the noun that is "added." Likewise, the concept "only" is captured with the marker **-man** -만 in Korean. These markers replace, instead of being added to, the topic or the subject marker.

    I also live in Hyoja Dong!
    Jeodo Hyojadong.e sarayo! 저도 효자동에 살아요.

    I, too, like tennis.
    Jeodo teniseureul joahaeyo. 저도 테니스를 좋아해요.

    I only have a cell phone.
    Hyudaeponman isseoyo. 휴대폰만 있어요.

PATTERN PRACTICE 3
Practice saying the following, using -도 **-do** and -만 **-man**.
1. I am Korean. Ms. Eunbi is Korean, too.
    Jeoneun Han.guk saramieyo. Eunbi ssido Han.guk saramieyo.
    저는 한국 사람이에요. 은비 씨도 한국 사람이에요.

2. I have a cell phone. Ms. Eunbi also has a cell phone.
   Jeoneun haendeuponi isseoyo. Eunbi ssido haendeuponi isseoyo.
   저는 핸드폰이 있어요. 은비 씨도 핸드폰이 있어요.
3. I do not have a home phone. I only have a cell phone.
   Jip jeonhwaga eopseoyo. Hyudaeponman isseoyo.
   집 전화가 없어요. 휴대폰만 있어요.
4. I do not have a Kakao Talk ID. I only have an email ID.
   Kakao tok aidiga eopseoyo. Imeil aidiman isseoyo.
   카카오톡 아이디가 없어요. 이메일만 있어요.

GRAMMAR NOTE Changing topics and contrasting statements with -은/는 –eun/neun

The topic marker **-eun/neun** -은/는 can also be used to switch topics in the same way you would use "what about," "on the other hand" or "however" in English.

Oh, and what about today's meeting?
Cham, oneul miting.eunyo? 참, 오늘 미팅은요?

By the way, where is the restroom?/And.., the restroom?
Geureonde hwajangsireun eodie isseoyo?
그런데 화장실은 어디에 있어요?

And what is your phone number, Eunbi?
Eunbi ssi jeonhwabeonhoneun myeoyeyo?
은비 씨 전화번호는 뭐예요?

The topic marker **-eun/neun** -은/는 also sets up a contrast or provides an undertone "on the other hand" or "however" without explicitly contrasting.

I do have a cell phone (however). vs. I have a cell phone.
Hyudaeponeun isseoyo. vs. **Hyudaeponi isseoyo.**
휴대폰은 있어요.   휴대폰이 있어요.

GRAMMAR NOTE Personal pronouns

The following two tables are a simplified version of Korean personal pronouns.

	BASE FORM	POSSESSIVE	PLURAL
1st person, humble	저 **jeo** I, me	제 **je** my	저희(들) **jeohui(dul)** we, us; our
3rd person, honorific	그 분 **geu bun** he/she, him/her; his/her		그 분들 **geu bundul** they, them; their
3rd person, inanimate	그거/그것 **geugeo/geugeot** it, it; its		그것들 **geugeotdeul** they, them; their

When you speak to strangers who seem older than you or if it is difficult to guess their age, use the humble pronoun **jeo** 저 to refer to yourself. It is always safer to be polite and humble.

Use **geu bun** 그 분 "he"/"she" when you are talking about someone who should be honored and fully respected, like a teacher or boss. For an item, use **geugeo** 그거 "it." (The final consonant ㅅ, pronounced as **t**, is added for written Korean (**geugeot** 그것).) Now look at the following pronoun table.

	BASE FORM	POSSESSIVE	PLURAL
1st person, familiar	나 **na** I, me	내 **nae** my	우리(들) **uri(deul)** we, us; our
2nd person minor, directed	너 **neo** you	네 [니] **ne** your	너희(들) **neohui(deul)** you, you; your
3rd person minor, directed	걔 **gyae** he/she, him/her; his/her		걔들 **gyaedeul** they, them; their
	쟤 **jyae** he/she, him/her; his/her (over there)		쟤들 **jyaedeul** they, them; their (over there)
3rd person adult, equal	그 사람 **geu saram** he/she, him/her; his/her		그 사람들 **geu saramdeul** they, them; their
	저 사람 **jeo saram** he/she, him/her; his/her (over there)		저 사람들 **jeo saramdeul** they, them; their (over there)

Use minor-directed pronouns when speaking to and about children, sometimes up to college age, or your childhood friends. With this group (and your close friends), you can use the familiar "I," **na** 나, but not with people older than you (even those three or four years older), as they may consider you to be uncultured and insolent. It's always best to start out with the humble form if you know you are younger.

For the second person "you," that is not minor-directed, use the person's job title (e.g., section chief) or family relationship term (e.g., older brother). The minor-directed **neo** 너 can be used up till one graduates high school or college, or only for younger family members and close friends. Personal pronouns can be omitted if it is clear who is being talked about.

When talking about a third person "he" or "she," use **gyae** 걔 or **jyae** 쟤 if it's a child you are referring to, and use **geu saram** 그 사람 "the person close to you/the person we are talking about" or **jeo saram** 저 사람 "that person over there" if it is a person of equal status as you.

Some pronouns have special forms when the subject marker is attached: **jega** 제가 and **nega** 네가. To differentiate the first person form **naega** 내가 from the second person minor-directed form **nega** 네가, you *pronounce* (but not write) the latter as [**niga** 니가].

GRAMMAR NOTE Numbers (Sino-Korean)

There are two kinds of numbers in Korean. One is the set above, "Sino-Korean" numbers, borrowed from Chinese and used for identifying things, e.g., pointing to a specific floor in a building, a page in a book, the amount on the dollar bill, months, or one's address and phone number. It's also used in Maths. For numerals more than 10, use "ten-one" for "eleven," and "two-ten" for "twenty," and so on.

There is a restroom on the second floor.
I cheung.e hwajangsiri isseumnida. 이 층에 화장실이 있습니다.

Eleven plus twenty is thirty-one.
Shibil deohagi ishibireun samshibil. 십일 더하기 이십일은 삼십일.

CULTURE NOTE **Catching nuances**
Some Korean words might have a similar English translation, but nuances can vary significantly. **Ije** 이제 and **jigeum** 지금 are both translated as "now," but **ije** 이제 conveys a strong sense of a change of situation, which is different from before.

Emma is not home now.
Emmaneun jigeum jibe eopseoyo. 엠마는 지금 집에 없어요.

Emma is not home now (She is not home any longer).
Emmaneun ije jibe eopseoyo. 엠마는 이제 집에 없어요.

EXERCISE 1
Tell your co-workers the names of the people at the company party, responding appropriately to the pronouns they use (honorific or not). Follow the example.
A: **Geu saram ireumi mwoyeyo?** (Emma Curtis)
  그 사람 이름이 뭐예요? (커티스 엠마)
B: **Geu sarameun Keotiseu Emmayeyo.**
  그 사람은 커티스 엠마예요.
A: **Jeo bun seonghami mwoyeyo?** (Jiyoung Park)
  저 분 성함이 뭐예요? (박지영)
B: **Jeo buneun Bak.Jiyeong ssiyeyo.**
  저 분은 박지영씨예요.

1. **Piteoseun Sara** Sarah Peterson (그분 **Geubun**)
2. **Jang Keuriseu** Chris Zhang (그 사람 **Geu saram**)
3. **Dakeda Hiro** Takeda Hiro (그 친구 **Geu chin.gu**)
4. **Adel** Adele (그 사람 **Geu saram**)
5. **I Hai** Lee Hi (그 사람 **Geu saram**)

EXERCISE 2

Ask and answer the following questions about Sara <u>in Korean</u> based on the information you see on Sara's business card.

Business card (front)

피터슨 사라
디자이너

베스트 마케팅
서울시 강남구 논현동 123-4
전화번호: 02-123-4567
휴대폰: 010-9876-5432
이메일. Sara_loveall@email.co.kr

Business card (back)

Sara Peterson
Designer

BEST MARKETING
123-4, Nonhyeon-dong, Gangnam-gu, Seoul, Korea
Tel: 02-123-4567
Mobile: 010-9876-5432
Email: Sara_loveall@email.co.kr

1. Is Sara a marketing manager (마케팅 매니저 **maketing maenijeo**)?
2. What is Sara's cell phone number?
3. Does she have an email?
4. What is Sara's email address?

EXERCISE 3

Ask and answer the following questions about telephone numbers based on the given information.

Minjoon	민준	050-9564-9823	**Aiden**	에이든	019-902-8805
Emma	엠마	02-895-3364	**Eunbi**	은비	070-435-2301

A: **Minjun ssi jeonhwabeonhoga mwoyeyo?** 민준 씨 전화번호가 뭐예요?
B: **Gong.o.gong gu.o.yuk.sae gu.pal.i.samieyo.** 050-9564-9823이에요.

1. What is Mr. Minjoon's telephone number?
2. What is Ms. Emma's telephone number?
3. What is Ms. Eunbi's telephone number?
4. What is Mr. Aiden's telephone number?

EXERCISE 4

Answer your friend who wants to know the following days. Follow the example.

Friend: **Oneuri myeochirieyo?** What's the date today? 오늘이 며칠이에요?
You: **Yuwol ishibirieyo.** It's June 20th. 유월 이십일이에요.

1. What date is Valentine's Day? **Ballentain Deiga myeochirieyo?**
   발렌타인 데이가 며칠이에요?
2. What date is Halloween? **Hallowini myeochirieyo?** 할로윈이 며칠이에요?
3. What date is *Ebeo.i Nal* (Parents' Day, May 8th)? **Eobeo.i nari myeochirieyo?**
   어버이날이 며칠이에요?
4. What date is Chuseok (Korean Thanksgiving, August 15th by the lunar
   calendar 음력 **eumnyeok**)? **Chuseogi myeochirieyo?** 추석이 며칠이에요?

EXERCISE 5

Translate the following statements using -도 **-do**, -만 **-man**, and -은/는 **-eun/
neun** (topic marker).

1. I am an American. Ms. Emma is also an American. How about Mr. Aiden? (add
   the politeness marker -요 **-yo**)
2. Ms. Sara is not an American. Only Jason is an American.
3. I only have a home phone. As for the cell phone, I do not have it.
4. I have an email. I also have a Kakao Talk ID. How about you, Tina?

DIALOGUE 2 **Where do you live?**

Aiden is assisting Minjoon on a project as part of his internship training, and the
two are chatting while on a break.

Minjoon: Where do you live, Aiden?
Eideun ssineun eodie sarayo?
에이든 씨는 어디에 살아요?

Aiden: I live in Hyoja Dong. How about you, Minjoon Seonbaenim?
Jeoneun Hyojadong.e sarayo. Minjun seonbaenimeunyo?
저는 효자동에 살아요. 민준 선배님은요?

Minjoon: Oh, I live in Hyoja Dong, too!
A, nado Hyojadong.e sarayo!
아, 나도 효자동에 살아요!

Aiden: Wow, really?
Wa, jeongmarieyo?
와, 정말이에요?

Minjoon: I am glad (to learn that). By the way, what will you be doing this
weekend?

Ban.gawoyo! Cham, ibeon jumare mwo haeyo?
반가워요! 참, 이번 주말에 뭐 해요?

Aiden: I like exercising, so I (will) play tennis this weekend.
Jeoneun undong.eul joahaeyo. Geuraeseo ibeon jumare teniseureul chyeoyo.
저는 운동을 좋아해요. 그래서 이번 주말에 테니스를 쳐요.

Minjoon: I like tennis, too. Let's play together!
Jeodo teniseureul joahaeyo. Uri gachi chyeoyo!
저도 테니스를 좋아해요. 우리 같이 쳐요!

Aiden: Then, let's play together this Saturday! And, let's have a meal together.
Geureom ibeon ju toyoire gachi chyeoyo! Geurigo gachi bap meogeoyo.
그럼 이번 주 토요일에 같이 쳐요! 그리고 같이 밥 먹어요.

VOCABULARY AND EXPRESSIONS

정말	jeongmal	truth, really
모레	more	the day after tomorrow
주말	jumal	weekend
운동	undong	exercise
테니스	teniseu	tennis
이번 주	ibeon ju	this week
토요일	Toyoil	Saturday
밥	bap	meal, cooked rice
아!	A!	Oh!
와!	Wa!	Wow!
참!	Cham!	Oh, by the way
그래서	geuraeseo	so
그럼 (= 그러면)	geureom (= geureomyeon)	(if so) then
그리고	geurigo	and
같이	gachi	together
혼자	honja	alone, by oneself
-에	e	at, on, in; to
-을	eul	object marker after a noun that ends in a consonant
-를	reul	object marker after a noun that ends in a vowel
살아요 (살-)	sarayo (sal-)	live
좋아해요 (좋아하-)	joahaeyo (joh.aha-)	like
운동해요 (운동하-)	undonghaeyo (undongha-)	exercise
쳐요 (치-)	chyeoyo (chi-)	play, hit
만나요 (만나-)	mannayo (manna-)	meet
먹어요 (먹-)	meogeoyo (meok-)	eat

VOCABULARY PRACTICE 2

Connect the words that are associated with each other.

1. early breakfast   a. **sarayo** 살아요
2. my best friend   b. **undonghaeyo** 운동해요
3. in Seoul   c. **meogeoyo** 먹어요
4. the piano   d. **joahaeyo** 좋아해요
5. at the gym   e. **chyeoyo** 쳐요

VOCABULARY PRACTICE 3

Which of the three Korean connectors, 그리고 **geurigo**, 그래서 **geuareseo**, 그럼 **geureom**, would you use in the following sentences?

1. 저는 운동을 좋아해요. _____ 테니스를 쳐요.
   Jeoneun undong.eul joahaeyo. _____ **teniseureul chyeoyo.**
   I like sports. _____ I play tennis.
2. 나는 효자동에 살아요. _____ 민준 씨도 효자동에 살아요.
   Jeoneun Hyojadong.e sarayo. Minjun ssido Hyojadong.e sarayo.
   I live in Hyoja Dong. _____ Minjoon lives in Hyoja Dong, too.
3. A: 테니스 좋아해요? Do you like tennis? **Teniseu joahaeyo?**
   B: 네. 좋아해요. Yes, I like it. **Ne. Joahaeyo?**
   A: _____ 같이 쳐요! Let's play tennis together! **Gachi chyeoyo!**

VOCABULARY PRACTICE 4

How would you say the following in Korean?

1. Is (it) true?   2. I live by myself.   3. Today is Saturday.

Supplementary Vocabulary

Days of the week

월요일	Woryoil	Monday	금요일	Geumyoil	Friday
화요일	Hwayoil	Tuesday	토요일	Toyoil	Saturday
수요일	Suyoil	Wednesday	일요일	Iryoil	Sunday
목요일	Mogyoil	Thursday			

The suffix **yoil** 요일 is paired with the Sino-Korean root word for each day: **wol** 월 "moon," **hwa** 화 "fire," **su** 수 "water," **mok** 목 "tree," **geum** 금 "gold," **to** 토 "soil," and **il** 일 "sun." The time marker **-e** -에 is frequently used with these words.

See (meet) you on Monday! **Woryoire mannayo!** 월요일에 만나요!
See you on Saturday. **Toyoire bwayo.** 토요일에 봐요!

PATTERN PRACTICE 4

Practice the following conversations about days of the week.

A: What day is it today?
   Oneuri museun yoirieyo? 오늘이 무슨 요일이에요?
B: It's Friday. **Geumyoirieyo.** 금요일이에요.
A: What day is it tomorrow?
   Nae.iri museun yoirieyo? 내일이 무슨 요일이에요?
B: It's Saturday. **Toyoirieyo.** 토요일이에요.

Supplementary Vocabulary
Frequently used verbs

가요 **gayo**	go	와요 **wayo**	come
일어나요 **ireonayo**	get up	깨요 **kkaeyo**	wake up
물 마셔요 **mul masyeoyo**	drink water	전화해요 **jeonhwahaeyo**	talk on the phone
앉아요 **anjayo**	sit	기다려요 **gidaryeoyo**	wait
세수해요 **sesuhaeyo**	wash face	찾아요 **chajayo**	look for/find
이 닦아요 **i dakkayo**	brush teeth	쇼핑 가요 **syoping gayo**	go shopping
운동해요 **undonghaeyo**	exercise	쇼핑해요 **syopinghaeyo**	shop
화장실에 가요 **hwajangsire gayo**	go to the restroom	버스에서 내려요 **beoseueseo naelyeoyo**	get off a bus
숙제해요 **sukjehaeyo**	do homework	사요 **sayo**	buy
씻어요 **ssiseoyo**	wash	돈 내요 **don naeyo**	pay
나가요 **nagayo**	go out	문자해요 **munjahaeyo**	text
버스 타요 **beoseu tayo**	get on a bus	영화 봐요 **yeonghwa bwayo**	watch a movie
노래해요 **noraehaeyo**	sing	누워요 **nuwoyo** 집에	lie down
일해요 **ilhaeyo**	work	목욕해요 **mogyokaeyo**	take a bath
공부해요 **gongbuhaeyo**	study	책 읽어요 **chaek ilgeoyo**	read a book
설거지해요 **seolgeojihaeyo**	do the dishes	음악 들어요 **eumak deueoyo**	listen to music
미팅해요 **mitinghaeyo**	have a meeting	집에 들어가요/와요 **jibe deureogayo/wayo**	go/come back home
인사해요 **insahaeyo**	greet	자요 **jayo**	sleep

GRAMMAR NOTE The time and place point marker -에 -e

The marker **-e** -에 comes after a time or a location expression to indicate a POINT in time or place, i.e., **Toyoire wasseyo** 토요일에 왔어요 "I came on Saturday" or **Jeoneun Hyojadong.e sarayo** 저는 효자동에 살아요. "I live in Hyoja Dong."
     When stating dates, the year precedes the month and the month precedes the day, e.g., on 2017 July 17. The time marker will be placed at the end of the whole time expression, e.g., **2017 nyeon 7 wol 17 ire** 2017 년 7 월 17 일에.

-E -에 also marks where the destination is with the verbs "go" **ga** 가 and "come" **wa** 와. It can be left out after place adverbs, e.g., "where" **eodi** 어디, "here" **yeogi** 여기, and "over there" **jeogi** 저기. The markers **-do** -도, **-man** -만, and **-eun/neun** -은/는 can be added after **-e** -에, e.g., **jeogiedo** 저기에도 "over there too," **jeogieman** 저기에만 "over there only," **jeogieneun** 저기에는 "speaking of over there."

I'll go tomorrow morning at nine o'clock.
Naeil achim ahop sie galkkeyo. 내일 아침 아홉 시에 갈게요.
I'm going to a friend's house. **Chin.gu jibe gayo.** 친구 집에 가요.
I have come to Korea. **Han.guge wasseoyo.** 한국에 왔어요.
Where is it? **Eodi isseoyo?** 어디 있어요?
It's over there, too. **Jeogido isseoyo.** 저기도 있어요.
It's only here. **Yeogiman isseoyo.** 여기만 있어요.

PATTERN PRACTICE 5

Follow the example and ask and answer the question below.
A: Where do you live? **(Hyoja Dong)** 어디에 살아요?
B: I live in Hyoja Dong. **Hyoja Dong.e sarayo.** 효자동에 살아요.

1. I live in an apartment 아파트에 살아요.
2. I live in Seoul. 서울에 살아요.
3. (your answer)

GRAMMAR NOTE **The object marker -을/를 _-eul/reul_**

-Eul/reul -을/를 is the object marker in Korean. It is attached to a noun that is the grammatical _direct object_ of the verb, such as "I will eat <u>an apple</u>." In spoken Korean, this marker is often dropped unless you are emphasizing _exactly_ what. Otherwise, you may hear just a hint of the marker as ㅣㄹ. The full forms are used in writing, however. Use **-reul** -를 after vowel-ending nouns and **-eul** -을 after nouns that end in a consonant.

I, too, like tennis.
Jeodo teniseureul joahaeyo. 저도 테니스를 좋아해요.

I am looking for a one-room (apartment).
Wonrumeul chatgoisseoyo. 원룸을 찾고 있어요.

Who did you meet yesterday?
Eoje nugul mannasseoyo? 어제 누굴 만났어요?

I'll call. (OK?) **Jega jeonhwa halkkeyo.** 제가 전화 할게요.

PATTERN PRACTICE 6

Practice talking about activities using the object particle -을/를 **-eul/reul**.

1. A: What do you do on weekends? **Jumare mwo haeyo?** 주말에 뭐 해요?
   B: I exercise. **Undong.eul haeyo.** 운동을 해요.
2. A: What do you do on Saturdays? **Toyoire mwo haeyo?** 토요일에 뭐 해요?
   B: I play tennis. **Teniseureul chyeoyo.** 테니스를 쳐요.
3. A: What are you eating? **Mwo meogeoyo?** 뭐 먹어요?
   B: I am eating *bulgogi*. **Bulgogireul meogeoyo.** 불고기를 먹어요.

GRAMMAR NOTE Informal-style conjugation
(For consonant-ending verbs)

The most common speech style is the informal style, which typically has the
suffixes **a(yo)** 아(요) or **eo(yo)** 어(요). **-Yo** -요 is added to make the *polite*
informal style. The informal style is extremely useful because it uses the same
ending for statements, questions, suggestions, and even commands. Its meaning
can also cover what's going on now (the present tense), what's usually the case
(generalization), and what's going to happen soon (immediate future). (For the past
tense, add **-ss.eoyo** -ㅆ어요 after conjugating in the informal style):

I'm going to the bowling alley now.
Jigeum bollingjang.e gayo. 지금 볼링장에 가요.

I go to the bowling alley every day.
Maeil bollingjang.e gayo. 매일 볼링장에 가요.

I'm going to the bowling alley tomorrow.
Naeil bollingjang.e gayo. 내일 볼링장에 가요.

When conjugating verbs, start by finding the root in the *dictionary form* with **-da**
-다 at the end. (For example, in **gada** 가다 ("to go" in the dictionary form), **ga** 가
is the root.) If the root ends in a consonant, conjugation is simple.

Add **a** ㅏ to the verb root if its last vowel is **a** ㅏ or **o** ㅗ, and **eo** ㅓ for all other
root-final vowels, then add **-yo** -요 (as needed) to be polite. Thus, **salda** 살다
"to live" (last vowel in the root being **a** ㅏ) becomes **sara** 살아 and then **sarayo**
살아요 for the informal polite form. Likewise, **mandeulda** 만들다 "to eat" (the
last vowel in the verb root being **eo** ㅓ) becomes **mandeureo** 만들어 and then
mandeureoyo 만들어요. (The letter ㄹ in Korean is represented as **l** or **r** in
romanization because of changes in its pronunciation. You will also see a similar
correlation between ㄱ and **k/g** below.)

DICTIONARY FORM	CONJUGATION	DICTIONARY FORM	CONJUGATION
살다 **salda** to live	살아요 **sarayo**	녹다 **nokda** to melt	녹아요 **nogayo**
있다 **issda** to be present	있어요 **isseoyo**	만들다 **mandeulda** to eat	만들어요 **mandeureoyo**
없다 **eopsda** to be absent	없어요 **eopseoyo**	묶다 **mukkda** to tie	묶어요 **mukkeoyo**

GRAMMAR NOTE Informal-style conjugation (for ㅣ *i*–ending verbs)

Verb roots that end in a vowel undergo some additional changes. Verbs whose root <u>ends</u> in the vowel **i** ㅣ will use the **eo** ㅓ suffix, but they are written and pronounced as **yeo** (**i** + **eo** = **yeo**) ㅕ (ㅣ + ㅓ = ㅕ), e.g., **chida** 치다 "to hit, play" becomes **chyeo** 쳐요 and then **chyeoyo** 쳐요.

DICTIONARY FORM	CONJUGATION	DICTIONARY FORM	CONJUGATION
치다 **chida** to hit, play	쳐요 **chyeoyo**	마시다 **masida** to drink	마셔요 **masyeoyo**
이기다 **igida** to win	이겨요 **igyeoyo**	지다 **jida** to lose	져요 **jyeoyo**
다치다 **dachida** to get hurt	다쳐요 **dachyeoyo**	시다 **sida** to be sour	셔요 **syeoyo**

I drink apple juice.
Jeoneun sagwajuseureul masyeoyo. 저는 사과주스를 마셔요.

We won! **Uriga igyeosseoyo!** 우리가 이겼어요!

GRAMMAR NOTE Four frequently used vowel-ending verbs

There are four common vowel-ending verbs with irregular conjugation—two of them end in the vowel **i** ㅣ, **ida** 이다 "to be" and **anida** 아니다 "to be not" as well as **doeda** 되다 "to become" and **hada** 하다 "to do." When connecting to nouns that end in consonants, **ida** 이다 becomes **ieyo** 이에요, and for nouns that end in vowels, **yeyo** 예요. **Anida** 아니다 becomes **anieyo** 아니에요. **Doeda** 되다, which has a number of idiomatic usages, conjugates as **dwaeyo** 돼요, and **hada** 하다, which combines with other words to make compound verbs, conjugates as **haeyo** 해요, e.g., **undonghada** 운동하다 "to exercise" becomes **undonghaeyo** 운동해요 in the informal polite form.

I am a student. **Jeoneun haksaeng.ieyo.** 저는 학생이에요.
It's now time. **Ije sigani dwaesseoyo.** 이제 시간이 됐어요.
I like exercising. **Jeoneun undong.eul joahaeyo.** 저는 운동을 좋아해요.

CULTURE NOTE **Establishing social relations**

People determine others' relative status and social distance by the relationships they have cultivated—in school, the workplace, family and other organizations one might belong to. Don't be surprised if they ask you your age, when you graduated high school, if you are married, etc. This is done so that they can use the correct mode of address, with formality, politeness and honorifics, if necessary. One thing to note is that the elderly are always treated with respect and honor, whether they are acquaintances or not.

EXERCISE 6

Answer the question based on the given information. Follow the example.

A: Where do you live, Minjoon?
   Minjun ssineun eodie sarayo? 민준 씨는 어디에 살아요?
B: I live in Hyoja Dong. **Hyojadong.e sarayo.** 효자동에 살아요.

NAME OF PERSON	WHERE THE PERSON STAYS	NAME OF PERSON	WHERE THE PERSON STAYS
Minjoon	Hyoja Dong	Sieun	Idae ap
Emma	Shinchon	Eunbi	Hongdae ap
Xinyi	Jamsil	Aiden	Hyoja Dong

1. Sieun   2. Xinyi   3. Emma   4. Aiden   5. Eunbi

EXERCISE 7

Tell your friends what Korean food you like. Don't forget to use the object marker. Follow the example.

A: **Mwo joahaeyo?** (*bulgogi*) 뭐 좋아해요? (불고기)
B: *Bulgogoreul* joahaeyo. 불고기를 좋아해요.

1. *galbi* 갈비
2. *tteobokki* 떡볶이
3. *haemulpajeon* 해물파전
4. *sundubujjigae* 순두부찌개
5. *japchae* 잡채

EXERCISE 8

What does each person do on a certain day of the week? Answer the questions based on the given information. Follow the example.

A: What does Minjoon do on Monday? **Minjun ssineun woryoire mwo haeyo?**
민준은 월요일에 뭐 해요?

B: **Teniseureul chyeoyo.** 테니스를 쳐요.

Monday	Minjoon plays tennis.
Tuesday	Eunbi meets Emma.
Wednesday	Jinhui sees a movie.
Friday	Emma listens to music.
Sunday	Toni exercises.

1. What does Eunbi do on Tuesday?
2. What does Jinhui do on Wednesday?
3. What does Emma do on Friday?
4. What does Toni do on Sunday?

LESSON 4
Accepting Invitations

🔘 **DIALOGUE 1** **Are you free this Friday night?**

Eunbi wants to invite Emma to her party.

Eunbi:　Emma, are you usually free on the weekends?
　　　　Emma ssi, jumare botong sigani isseoyo?
　　　　엠마 씨, 주말에 보통 시간이 있어요?

Emma:　Which day (*Lit.*, when) on the weekend?
　　　　Jumal eonjeyo?
　　　　주말 언제요?

Eunbi:　Next Friday evening[1]?
　　　　Da.eum ju Gumyoil jeonyeok?
　　　　다음 주 금요일 저녁?

Emma:　Yes, it's an OK time.
　　　　Ne, sigan gwaenchanayo.
　　　　네, 시간 괜찮아요.

Eunbi:　I'm having a party at my place. Please come, Emma!
　　　　Uri jibeseo patireul haeyo. Emma ssido oseyo!
　　　　우리 집에서 파티를 해요. 엠마 씨도 오세요!

Emma:　Really? What time is the party?
　　　　Jeongmalyo? Myeot sie haeyo?
　　　　정말요? 몇 시에 해요?

Eunbi:　Please come around six-thirty. It'll be a World Cup party.
　　　　Jeonyeok yeoseot si banjjeume oseyo. WoldeuKeop patiyeyo.
　　　　저녁 6 시 반쯤에 오세요. 월드컵 파티예요.

Emma:　We are watching TV together? I like that. Who else is coming?
　　　　Gachi tellebijeon bwayo? Joayo. Tto nuga wayo?
　　　　같이 텔레비전 봐요? 좋아요. 또 누가 와요?

Eunbi:　I have invited Aiden, too.
　　　　Eideun ssido chodaehaesseoyo.
　　　　에이든 씨도 초대했어요.

Emma:　How about Mr. Kim?
　　　　Gim timjangnimeunyo?
　　　　김 팀장님은요?

1　To Koreans, the "weekend" starts on Friday evening.

Eunbi: He can't. I'll prepare the food.
Mot oseyo. Jega eumsigeul junbihalkkeyo.
못 오세요. 제가 음식을 준비할게요.

Emma: Six-thirty is good. Then, I will bring some dessert.
Yeoseot si ban joayo. Geureom dijeoteureul gajyeo galkkeyo.
6 시 반 좋아요. 그럼 디저트를 가져 갈게요.

Eunbi: Sounds good!
Joayo!
좋아요!

VOCABULARY AND EXPRESSIONS

주말	jumal	weekend
시간	sigan	(duration of) time
언제	eonje	when; sometime
다음 주	da.eum jju	next week
저녁	jeonyeok	evening (dinner time)
우리 집	uri jip	my house (*Lit.*, "our house")
몇	myeot	how many
시	si	hour (on the clock; time of day)
몇 시	myeot si?	What time?
월드컵	WoldeuKeop	World Cup
팀장(님)	timjang(nim)	team captain, head of the team
파티	pati	party
누가/누구	nuga/nugu	who (as the subject)/non-subject
음식	eumsik	food
디저트	dijeoteu	dessert
보통	botong	usually, in general
또	tto	(what/who) else; and; again
안	an	not, will not
못	mot	can't
-쯤	jjeum	about, approximately
-에서	eseo	at (point of activity), from
있어요 (있-)	isseoyo (iss-)	there is, one has (informal)
괜찮아요 (괜찮-)	gwaenchanayo (gwaenchanh-)	good, fine; fair, not bad, OK, no big deal
해요 (하-)	haeyo (ha-)	does
오세요! (오-)	oseyo! (o-)	Please come! (honorific, polite)
초대했어요 (초대하-)	chodaehaesseoyo (chodaeha-)	has invited
좋아요 (좋.)	joayo (joh-)	good
봐요 (보-)	bwayo (bo-)	sees, watches
준비할게요 (준비하-)	junbihalkkeyo (junbiha-)	will prepare
가져 갈게요 (가지-, 가-)	gajyeo galkkeyo (gaji-, ga-)	will bring/take (offer, promise)

Supplementary Vocabulary
Native numbers

1	하나; 한 (before a noun)	hana; han	2	둘; 두 (before a noun)	dul; du
3	셋; 세 (before a noun)	set; se	4	넷; 네 (before a noun)	net; ne
5	다섯	daseot	6	여섯	yeoseot
7	일곱	ilgop	8	여덟	yeodeol
9	아홉	ahop	10	열	yeol
11	열하나; 열한 (before a noun)	yeolhana; yeolhan	12	열둘; 열두 (before a noun)	yeoldul; yeoldu
13	열여덟	yeolyeodeol	14	열아홉	yeolahop

VOCABULARY PRACTICE 1
Conjugate the following verbs for the informal style. Check the conjugation against the word list given in the chart above and memorize their meaning.
1. **issda** 있다
2. **johda** 좋다
3. **hada** 하다
4. **gwaenchanda** 괜찮다

GRAMMAR NOTE The native number system

The native number system is used for *counting*. Numbers one through four have a modifying form that is used when they come before a noun. To count numbers beyond ten, simply tack on the number (one through nine) after the word for ten, e.g., "All together (it is) 13 people." **Modu yeolse myeong.ieyo.** 모두 열세 명이에요.

GRAMMAR NOTE Making a negative sentence with 안 *an* and 못 *mot*

Add the adverb **an** 안 "not" in front of the verb. **An** 안 may come across as someone *purposely* refusing to do something, so if the circumstances are out of one's control, use **mot** 못 "can't." Compare "Minjoon is not coming." **Minjun ssineun an wayo.** 민준 씨는 안 와요. with "Minjoon can't come to the party." **Minjun ssineun patie mod wayo.** 민준 씨는 파티에 못 와요.

PATTERN PRACTICE 1
Practice reading out the following negative sentences.
1. I do not exercise. **Jeoneun undong.eul an haeyo.** 저는 운동을 안 해요.
2. Mr. Minjoon does not like parties. **Minjun ssineun patireul an joahaeyo.** 민준 씨는 파티를 안 좋아해요.
3. Emma can't play tennis. **Emmaneun teniseureul mot chyeoyo.** 엠마는 테니스를 못 쳐요.
4. Aiden can't come. **Eideuneun mot wayo.** 에이든은 못 와요.

GRAMMAR NOTE -에서 *-eseo* + activity verb "Where something is happening"

-Eseo -에서 marks the source or origin with the verbs **gayo** 가요 "goes" and **wayo** 와요 "comes." **Junggugeseo wasseoyo** 중국에서 왔어요 "I came <u>from</u> China." With activity (not direction) verbs, **-eseo** -에서 also marks the location where an activity is taking place, rather than where something is located (in which case **-e** -에 is used), e.g., "You are <u>at</u> some place + you <u>do</u> something <u>there</u>."

I play tennis at the park.
Gongwoneseo teniseu chyeoyo. 공원에서 테니스 쳐요.

I work at the office. **Samusireseo ilhaeyo.** 사무실에서 일해요.

We sing at the *noraebang*.
Noraebang.eseo noraehaeyo. 노래방에서 노래해요.

PATTERN PRACTICE 2
Practice reading out the following conversations.
1. A: Where are you meeting your friend? **Eodieseo chin.gureul mannayo?** 어디에서 친구를 만나요?
   B: I am meeting (them) at the party. **Patieseo mannayo.** 파티에서 만나요.
2. A: Where do you exercise? **Eodieseo undong.haeyo?** 어디에서 운동해요?
   B: I exercise in the park. **Gongwoneseo undong.haeyo.** 공원에서 운동해요.
3. A: Where do you work? **Eodieseo ilhaeyo?** 어디에서 일해요?
   B: I work at Samsung. **Samseong.eseo ilhaeyo.** 삼성에서 일해요.
4. A: Where do you shop? **Eodieseo shyoping.haeyo?** 어디에서 쇼핑해요?
   B: I shop at the Hongdae district. **Hongdae.apeseo shyoping.haeyo.** 홍대 앞에서 쇼핑해요.

GRAMMAR NOTE Telling the time
Use Sino-Korean numbers for the hour (시 **si**) and native Korean numbers for the minutes (분 **bun**).

9:00 AM	**ojeon ahop si** 오전 아홉 시
2:45 PM	**ohu du si sashibo bun** 오후 두 시 사십오 분
3:15 in the afternoon	**ohu se si shibo bun** 오후 세 시 삼십오 분
7:30 in the evening	**jeonyeok ilgop si ban, ilgop si samship bun** 저녁 일곱 시 반, 일곱 시 삼십 분
1:00 in the morning	**saebyeok han si** 새벽 한 시
Let's meet at two o'clock.	**Du sie mannayo.** 두 시에 만나요.

PATTERN PRACTICE 3

Practice asking for and telling the time.

1. A: What time is it now? **Jigeum myeot siyeyo?** 지금 몇 시예요?
   B: It's 11:20 at night. **Bam yeolhan si iship bunieyo.**
   밤 열한 시 이십 분이에요.
2. A: What time is it now? **Jigeum myeot siyeyo?** 지금 몇 시예요?
   B: It's 2:30 in the afternoon. **Ohu du si banieyo.** 오후 두 시 반이에요.
3. A: What time is the meeting? **Miting.i myeot siyeyo?** 미팅이 몇 시예요?
   B: It's at 10.00 in the morning. **Achim yeol siyeyo.** 아침 열시예요.
4. A: What time is the party? **Patiga myeot siyeyo?** 파티가 몇 시예요?
   B: It's at 7.00 in the evening. **Jeonyeok ilgop siyeyo.** 저녁 일곱 시예요.

GRAMMAR NOTE Using honorifics -(으)세요 –*(eu)seyo* to make a polite command

In the dialogue, Eunbi uses an honorific ending and says **oseyo** 오세요, made up of the verb root **o** 오, the honorific suffix **-(eu)se** -(으)세 (in this conjugation) and the polite ending **-yo** -요 to ask Emma to come to her party, e.g., "Come around 6 in the evening, please." **Jeonyeok yeoseot si banjjeume oseyo** 저녁 여섯 시 반쯤에 오세요. The 으 **eu** vowel in honorific **euse** 으세 is used after verbs that end in consonants (e.g. **anj** 앉 "sit," **ilk** 읽 "read"), so it is <u>not</u> used to conjugate **oseyo** 오세요.

Honorifics are mainly used when you're talking **about** someone of a higher social status, like a boss, grandmother or customer. Even if you're directly asking them to do something, you are still talking "about" their action (eg., Can you close the door? Will you sit here?).

While you could use the polite informal form **wayo** 와요 as a *somewhat* polite command, it's always safer to use the honorific suffix **oseyo** 오세요 to soften the request, even if you and the listener are of similar status. Another common verb in this form is **juseyo** 주세요 "please give (me)" replacing its polite informal form **jwoyo** 줘요.

Useful Tip: The verb preceding the honorific suffix **-(eu)se** -(으)세 loses its final consonant if it is l ㄹ, e.g., **nolda** 놀다" to hang out, play" → **noseyo** 노세요.

PATTERN PRACTICE 4

Practice these phrases using the polite command ending.

1. Please sit on the chair. **Uijae anjeuseyo.** 의자에 앉으세요.
2. Please watch from here. **Yeogieseo boseyo.** 여기에서 보세요.
3. Please read a book. **Chaegeul ilgeuseyo.** 책을 읽으세요.
4. Please come at two o'clock. **Du sie oseyo.** 두 시에 오세요.

EXERCISE 1

Answer the following questions based on the information provided.

A: **Miting.i myeot siyeyo?** 미팅이 몇 시예요?

B: **Achim ahop si shibo bunieyo.** 아침 아홉 시 십오 분이에요.

lunch time **jeomsim sigan** 점심시간	12:30 PM	now **jigeum** 지금	8:55 at night
party **pati** 파티	7:00 in the evening	class **sueop** 수업	10.30 AM

1. What time is lunch?
3. What time is it now?

2. What time is the party?
4. What time is the class?

EXERCISE 2

Answer the questions based on the information given below. Use the negative **an/mot** 안/못 as needed.

Sara	does not exercise	Jian	doesn't like parties
Jeonghun	can't eat *kimchi*	Mori	can't play tennis

1. **Sara ssineun undong.eul haeyo?** 사라 씨는 운동을 해요?
2. **Jeonghun ssineun gimchireul jal meogeoyo?**
   정훈 씨는 김치를 잘 먹어요?
3. **Jian ssineun patireul joahaeyo?** 지안 씨는 파티를 좋아해요?
4. **Mori ssineun teniseureul jal chyeoyo?** 모리 씨는 테니스를 잘 쳐요?

EXERCISE 3

Ask and answer the "where" questions based on the given information.

A: **Emmaneun eodieseo undonghaeyo?** 엠마는 어디에서 운동해요?

B: **Gongwoneseo undonghaeyo.** 공원에서 운동해요.

Emma 엠마	exercise at the park (공원 **gong.won**)	Minjoon 민준	watch a movie at home (집 **jip**)
Aiden 은비	listen to music in his room (방 **bang**)	Suji 수지	write a report in the office (보고서 **bogoseo**, 사무실 **samusil**)
Eunbi 에이든	meet a friend at a café (카페 **kape**)		

1. Where does Eunbi meet a friend?
3. Where does Minjoon watch a movie?

2. Where does Aiden listen to music?
4. Where does Suji write a report?

EXERCISE 4

It's Emma's first day at the internship. Practice what Emma's boss would say to her in Korean using polite command forms.

1. Please come by 8:30 AM.
2. Please use this desk. (to use: **sseuda** 쓰다; this desk: **i chaeksang** 이 책상)
3. Please sit here.
4. Please give me your phone number.

DIALOGUE 2 How much is it?

On his way to Eunbi's party, Aiden stops by a store to get some fruit.

Shopkeeper: Welcome!/Come on in!
Eoseo oseyo!
어서 오세요!

Aiden: Do you have beer?
Maekju isseoyo?
맥주 있어요?

Shopkeeper: Yes, it's over there.
Ne, jeojjoge isseumnida.
네, 저쪽에 있습니다.

Aiden: Do you have apples?
Sagwado isseoyo?
사과도 있어요?

Shopkeeper: Sorry, we don't have apples. We do have mandarin oranges.
Joesonghamnida. Sagwaneun eopseumnida. Gyureun inneundeyo.
죄송합니다. 사과는 없습니다. 귤은 있는데요.

Aiden: Is that so? How much are the mandarin oranges?
A, geuraeyo? Gyureun eolmayeyo?
아, 그래요? 귤은 얼마예요?

Shopkeeper: They are 3,000 won per package. One package has 10 of them.
Gyureun han paeg.e samcheon wonieyo. Han paege yeol gae deureo isseoyo.
귤은 한 팩에 3,000 원이에요. 한 팩에 10 개 들어 있어요.

Aiden: Hmmm… then, how about these chips?
Heum…geureom i gwajaneun eolmayeyo?
흠… 그럼 이 과자는 얼마예요?

Shopkeeper: It's 2,000 won per bag.
Han bongjie icheon wonimnida.
한 봉지에 2,000 원입니다.

Aiden: Then, please give me six bottles of beer and two bags of chips.
                Geureom maekju yeoseot byeonghago gwaja du bongji juseyo.
                그럼 맥주 6병하고 과자 2 봉지 주세요.

Shopkeeper: Yes, I got it. 6,500 won for six bottles of beer, and 4,000 won for
                two bags of chips. All together, it's 10,500 won.
                **Ne, algesseumnida. Maekju yeoseot byeong.e yukcheon
                obaeg won, gwaja du bongji.e sacheon won, modu man.
                obaeg wonimnida.**
                네, 알겠습니다. 맥주 6병에 6,500원, 과자 2 봉지에 4,000원,
                모두 10,500원입니다.

VOCABULARY AND EXPRESSIONS

가게	gage	store
주인	juin	owner, master
맥주	maekju	beer
저쪽	jeojjok	that side over there
사과	sagwa	apple
귤	gyul	mandarin orange
팩	paek	pack, sealed package
삼천 원	samcheon won	3,000 won
열 개	yeol gae	10 items
얼마	eolma	how much (price only)
과자	gwaja	snack chips, crackers, cookies
봉지	bongji	bag (plastic, paper)
병	byeong	bottle
모두	modu	all together
-에	e	per
흠…	heum...	hmmm…
없습니다 (없-)	eopseumnida (eop-)	does not exist, does not have (formal)
있는데요 (있-)	inneundeyo (iss-)	exists, there is (what do you think..?)
들어 있어요 (들-, 있-)	deureo isseoyo (deul-, iss-)	is in, has in it (informal, polite)
어서 오세요! (오-)	eoseo oseyo! (o-)	Welcome/Come on in! (honorific, polite)
죄송합니다 (하-)	joesonghamnida (joesongha-)	I am sorry (formal)
얼마예요? (이-)	eolmayeyo? (eolmai-)	how much is it/are they? (informal, polite)
주세요 (주-)	juseyo (ju-)	please give me (informal, honorific, polite)
알겠습니다 (알-)	algesseumnida (al-)	I understand; got it (formal)

VOCABULARY PRACTICE 2
What would you say in the following situations?
1. A guest rang your doorbell, and you just opened the door.
2. You need to ask the price of an item you want to buy.
3. You just stepped on someone's foot.
4. You want to tell your boss that you understand and acknowledge his/her instructions on a new project.
5. You want to say the restroom is occupied. (**hwajangsil** 화장실 restroom, **nuga** 누가 someone)

VOCABULARY PRACTICE 3
Fill in the blanks to come up with as many words as possible.
1. _____ **gogi** 고기   2. _____ **ju** 주   3. _____ **gi** 기

Supplementary Vocabulary
Fruits, vegetables and other food

과일	gwail	fruit	배	bae	Asian pear
포도	podo	grape	딸기	ttalgi	strawberry
참외	chamoe	Korean melon	수박	subak	watermelon
감	gam	persimmon	복숭아	bogsung.a	peach
채소	chaeso	vegetable	무	mu	radish
배추	baechu	napa cabbage	양배추	yangbaechu	cabbage
호박	hobak	zucchini, pumpkin	오이	o.i	cucumber
파	pa	scallion, green onion	양파	yangpa	onion
감자	gamja	potato	고구마	goguma	sweet potato
마늘	maneul	garlic	생강	saenggang	ginger
고기	gogi	meat	생선	saengseon	fish
닭고기	dakgogi	chicken	돼지고기	dwaejigogi	pork
소고기	sogogi	beef	새우	sae.u	shrimp
오징어	ojing.eo	squid	조개	jogae	clam
음료수	eumnyosu	beverage	콜라	kolla	cola
사이다	saida	Sprite	커피	keopi	coffee
차	cha	tea	주스	juseu	juice
술	sul	alcohol	소주	soju	soju
막걸리	maggeolli	unrefined rice wine	양주	yangju	hard liquor
아이스크림	aiseukeurim	ice cream	케이크	keikeu	cake

GRAMMAR NOTE Big (Sino-Korean) numbers

Big numbers are all expressed, using Sino-Korean numbers. Remember that there are separate names for 10,000 **man** 만 and 100,000,000 **ireok** 일억.

백 **baek**	100		천 **cheon**	1,000
만 **man**	10,000		십만 **shimman**	100,000
백만 **baengman**	1,000,000		천만 **cheonman**	10,000,000
일억 **ireok**	100,000,000		십억 **shibeok**	1,000,000,000

All together it is 10,500 won.
Modu man.obaek wonimnida. 모두 만 오백원입니다.

I hear that the monthly rent is 800,000 won.
Han dal wol sega palsimman woniraeyo. 한 달 월세가 팔십만원이래요.

GRAMMAR NOTE Counters

When you count things in Korean, you use native Korean numbers **han** 한, **du** 두, **se** 세… etc, along with counters, e.g., "a piece of paper" or "a bottle of beer." First you say what you are counting, then the number, followed by the counter. (See the examples below.) The most widely used counter is **gae** 개 for small inanimate objects. If there is no "official" counter for the thing you are counting, you can use a word for the container (**byeong** 병 "bottle," **keop** 컵 "cup," **sangja** 상자 "box" etc.). If a marker is used, it can appear on the noun being counted or on the counter itself.

one apple	three students	two pencils	one dog
sagwa han gae	**haksaeng se myeong**	**yeonpil du jaru**	**gae han mari**
상자 한 개	학생 세 명	연필 두 자루	개 한 마리

Give me an express ticket for 6:00, please.
Gosogeuro yeoseot si pyo han jang juseyo.
고속으로 여섯 시 표 한 장 주세요.

There is one six o'clock bus.
Yeoseot si beoseuga han dae isseumnida.
여섯 시 버스가 한 대 있습니다.

You drank all three bottles by yourself?
Se byeong.eul honja da masyeosseo? 세 병을 혼자 다 마셨어요?

How many shall I give you?
Myeot gae deurilkkayo? 몇 개 드릴까요?

Commonly used counters

COUNTERS			EXAMPLES		
개	gae	item	사과 한 개	sagwa han gae	one apple
사람/명	saram/ myeong	person	동생 한 명	dongsaeng han myeong	one younger brother
분	bun	person (honorific)	선생님 한 분	seonsaengnim han bun	one teacher
마리	mari	animal	고양이 한 마리	goyang.i han mari	one cat
권	gwon	book	책 한 권	chaek han gwon	one book
장	jang	paper, thin object	티셔츠 한 장, 종이 한 장	tisyeocheu han jang, jong.i han jang	one t-shirt, one piece of paper
병	byeong	bottle	맥주 한 병	maekju han byeong	one bottle of beer
잔	jan	glass, cup	우유 한 잔	uyu han jan	one glass of milk
곡	gok	song	노래 한 곡	norae han gok	one song
대	dae	electronics, car	텔레비전 한 대	tellebijeon han dae	one TV
자루	jaru	pencil, pen	연필 한 자루	yeonpil han jaru	one pencil
상자	sangja	box	배 한 상자	bae han sangja	one box of pears
송이	song.i	flower	장미 한 송이	jangmi han song.i	one rose stem
켤레	kyeolle	socks, shoes	구두 한 켤레	gudu han kyeolle	one pair of dress shoes

PATTERN PRACTICE 4

Practice these phrases using the polite command ending and counters.
1. Please give me ten apples. **Sagwa yeol gae juseyo.** 사과 열 개 주세요.
2. Please give me two bottles of lemon-lime. **Sa.ida du byeong juseyo.** 사이다 두 병 주세요.
3. Please give me three bags of chips. **Gwaja se bongji juseyo.** 과자 세 봉지 주세요.
4. Please give me four packages of mandarin oranges. **Gyul ne paek juseyo.** 귤 네 팩 주세요.

GRAMMAR NOTE "To have" and "to exist"

The verb **isseoyo** 있어요 (or its formal form **isseumnida** 있습니다) means "exists" (or "there is") but is also used to express someone "having" something. Its negative counterpart, for "don't have" or "there isn't any," is **eopseoyo** 없어요 (informal polite) or **eopseumnida** 없습니다 (formal). The roots of these verbs are **iss** 있 and **eops** 없.

Do you have beer? **Maekju isseoyo?** 맥주 있어요?

There is no (cooked) rice./We have no (cooked) rice.
Babi eopseoyo. 밥이 없어요.

There are no apples./We have no apples.
Sagwaga eopseumnida. 사과가 없습니다.

PATTERN PRACTICE 5

Practice the following conversations in Korean.
1. A: Do you have tea? **Cha(ga) isseoyo?** 차(가) 있어요?
   B: Yes, we do. **Ne, isseoyo.** 네, 있어요.
   A: Do you also have chips? **Gwajado isseoyo?** 과자도 있어요?
   B: No, we don't. **Aniyo. Eopseoyo.** 아니요. 없어요.
2. A: Do you have mandarin oranges? **Gyur(i) isseoyo?** 귤(이) 있어요?
   B: Yes, we do. **Ne, isseumnida.** 네, 있습니다.
   A: Do you also have apples? **Sagwado isseoyo?** 사과도 있어요?
   B: No, we don't. **Aniyo. Eopseumnida.** 아니요. 없습니다.

GRAMMAR NOTE The -에 *–e* marker, "per"

The marker **-e** -에 is also used to mean "per," e.g., "How much per (one) bottle of
beer?" **Maekju han byeong.e eolmayeyo?** 맥주 한 병에 얼마예요?

PATTERN PRACTICE 6

Practice the following conversations in Korean.
1. A: How much is cola? **Kolaga eolmayeyo?** 콜라가 얼마예요?
   B: It's 3,000 won per bottle. **Han byeong.e samcheon wonieyo.**
   한 병에 3,000 원이에요.
2. A: How much are chips? **Gwajaga eolmayeyo?** 과자가 얼마예요?
   B: They're 1,500 won per bag. **Han bongji.e cheon obaeck wonieyo.**
   한 봉지에 1,500 원이에요.
3. A: How much are mandarin oranges? **Gyuri eolmayeyo?** 귤이 얼마예요?
   B: They're 10,000 won per pack. **Han paege man wonieyo.**
   한 팩에 10,000 원이에요.
4. A: How much are apples? **Sagwaga eolmayeyo?** 사과가 얼마예요?
   B: They're three for 2,000 won. **Se gae.e i cheon wonieyo.**
   세 개에 2,000 원이에요.

GRAMMAR NOTE Informal-style conjugation (ㅗ *o-* and ㅜ *u-* verbs)

To conjugate verbs whose last vowel is **o** ㅗ in the informal speech style, you add a vowel suffix **a** ㅏ to the verb root then add **-yo** -요 to be polite. To conjugate verbs whose last vowel is **u** ㅜ, add a vowel suffix **eo** ㅓ to the root then add **-yo** -요 to be polite. The vowels normally get contracted.

DICTIONARY FORM	CONJUGATION	DICTIONARY FORM	CONJUGATION
보다 **boda** to see, look	봐요 **bwayo** (←보아요 **boayo**)	주다 **juda** to give	줘요 **jwoyo** (←주어요 **ju.eoyo**)
쏘다 **ssoda** to shoot	쏴요 **sswayo** (←쏘아요 **sso.ayo**)	나누다 **nanuda**	나눠요 **nanwoyo** (←나누어요 **nanu.eoyo**)
오다 **oda** to come	와요 **wayo** (←오아요 **oayo**)	춤추다 **chumchuda**	춤춰요 **chumchwoyo** (←춤추어요 **chumchu.eoyo**)
돌보다 **dolboda** to look after	돌봐요 **dolbwayo** (←돌보아요 **dolboayo**)	꿈꾸다 **kkumkkuda**	꿈꿔요 **kkumkkwoyo** (←꿈꾸어요 **kkumkku.eoyo**)

GRAMMAR NOTE Making other verbs and adjectives with 해요 *haeyo*

Haeyo 해요 is a verb form that has been conjugated irregularly for the informal style. Its root is **ha** 하 so it would look like **hamnida/hamnikka** 합니다/합니까 in the formal style. If you see **haseyo** 하세요, it is **ha** 하 conjugated for the *honorific* polite form (to talk *about* someone honorable and to someone you need to be polite to). If you see **hasimnida/hasimnikka** 하십니다/하십니까, that is the honorific formal form (which is used to talk about someone honorable and to someone you are being formal with). As an independent verb, **hada** 하다 means "to do," but it attaches to many Sino-Korean and other words borrowed from foreign languages to make new verbs.

I am playing a computer game now.
Jigeum keompyuteo geimhaeyo. 지금 컴퓨터 게임해요.

Grandmother is taking a walk.
Halmeoni sanchaekaseyo. 할머니 산책하세요.

Is your grandfather jogging?
Harabeoji joging hasimnikka? 할아버지 조깅하십니까?

There is usually no space before the conjugated **hae** 해 (or **ha** 하) verb in the written language except when it is separated with adverbs or when the object marker is used.

(Someone) isn't doing homework. **Sukje an haeyo.** 숙제 안 해요.
(Someone) plays basketball well. **Nonggu jal haeyo.** 농구 잘 해요.
(Someone) is bragging/showing off. **Jarang.eul haeyo.** 자랑을 해요.

Haeyo 해요 also works as a suffix to make *adjectives*, that is, to express "(something is) in that state."

How are you? (*Lit.*, "Are you in good peace and comfort?")
Annyeonghaseyo? 안녕하세요?
(I am/It is) comfortable/convenient. **Pyeonhaeyo.** 편해요.

CULTURE NOTE **Sharing a meal**

It is very common for a newcomer to be invited to a meal or other food-centered outing. Eating is indeed central to Korean socializing and hospitality, a beloved pastime, and an important part of life and well-being. Koreans are proud of their food and the variety it comes in, and meals are generally "family style," where it is expected that everyone shares the food. Restaurants often specialize in one dish or kind of food, such as grilled meats, and traditionally, a restaurant is judged by the variety and quality of the **banchan** 반찬 ("side dishes" of *kimchi*, pickled foods and other usually salty treats made to accompany rice). A lot of Korean food is spicy, but not all. There are also many vegetarian options.

CULTURE NOTE **Accepting or rejecting an invitation**

Unless you are talking with close friends or family, avoid being too straightforward in turning down others' invitations. Here are some useful phrases for declining an invitation:

I have some work to do/I have to take care of something.
Iri inneundeyo. 일이 있는데요.

I have a prior engagement.
Yagsogi inneundeyo. 약속이 있는데요.

I am a little busy…. **Jom bappeundeyo.** 좀 바쁜데요.

The person inviting will usually insist and repeat the invitation—whether for a gathering, eating or tasting something—twice or thrice out of courtesy.

CULTURE NOTE **Possession and familial relations**

Refer to your family members and family belongings using the plural possessor, "our" and not "my," for example, **uri jip** 우리 집 "our house," **uri eomma** 우리 엄마 "our mom," **uri oppa** 우리 오빠 "our older brother." To refer to your younger sibling use either **nae dongsaeng** 내 동생 or **uri dongsaeng** 우리 동생 "my/our younger sibling."

EXERCISE 5

You are doing some grocery shopping. Use 있어요 **isseoyo?** to ask if the store has the items, and request them using **juseyo** 주세요.

A: **Sagwa.ga isseoyo?** 사과가 있어요?
B: **Ne. Isseoyo.** 네, 있어요.
A: **Sagwa ne gae juseyo.** 사과 네 개 주세요.

Your shopping lists:
1. 4 apples, 6 peaches, 10 mandarin oranges
2. 6 bottles of beer, 2 bags of chips
3. 2 ice creams, 1 cake, 4 cups of coffee
4. 3 fishes, 1 radish, 2 onions

EXERCISE 6

Answer the questions based on the given information using the -에 **-e** marker.

chips **gwaja** 과자	₩ 3,000 per bag
mandarin oranges **gyul** 귤	₩ 900 per three
coffee **keopi** 커피	₩ 1,800 per one cup
orange juice **orenji juseu** 오렌지 주스	₩ 2,500 per bottle

1. **Gwajaga eolmayeyo?** 과자가 얼마예요?
2. **Gyuri eolmayeyo?** 귤이 얼마예요?
3. **Keopiga eolmayeyo?** 커피가 얼마예요?
4. **Orenji juseuga eolmayeyo?** 오렌지 주스가 얼마예요?

엠마 씨, 좋은 아침!
Ms. Emma, good morning!

다음 주 월요일 아침에 미팅이 있을 거예요.
We're going to have a meeting next Monday morning.

네, 알겠습니다.
I see.

미팅이 몇 시예요?
What time is the meeting?

오전 10시입니다.
At ten o'clock.

삼층 회의실로 오세요.
Please go to the meeting room on the third floor.

네, 갈게요.
Yes, I will be there.

무슨 미팅이에요?
What (kind of) meeting is it?

예산에 대한 미팅이에요.
It's a meeting about the budget.

그럼, 월요일에 봐요.
Then, see you Monday.

네, 알겠습니다.
Got it.

월요일에 뵙겠습니다!
I will see you on Monday!

LESSON 5

Getting Around in a Building

DIALOGUE 1 What time is the meeting?

Minjoon: Ms. Emma, good morning! We're going to have a meeting next
            Monday morning.
            **Emma ssi, Jo.eun achim! Da.eumju Woryoir achime miting.i
            isseul kkeoyeyo.**
            엠마 씨, 좋은 아침! 다음 주 월요일 아침에 미팅이 있을 거예요.
Emma: I see. What time is the meeting?
            Ne, algesseumnida. Miting.i myeot siyeyo?
            네, 알겠습니다. 미팅이 몇 시예요?
Minjoon: At ten o'clock. Please go to the meeting room on the third floor.
            Ojeon yeol si.imnida. Samcheung hoe.uisillo oseyo.
            오전 10시입니다. 삼층 회의실로 오세요.
Emma: Yes, I will be there. What (kind of) meeting is it?
            Ne, galkkeyo. Museun miting.ieyo?
            네, 갈게요. 무슨 미팅이에요?
Minjoon: It's a meeting about the budget. Then, see you Monday.
            Yesane daehan miting.ieyo. Geureom, Woryoire bwayo.
            예산에 대한 미팅이에요. 그럼, 월요일에 봐요.
Emma: Got it. I will see you on Monday!
            Ne, algesseumnida. Woryoire boekesseumnida!
            네, 알겠습니다. 월요일에 뵙겠습니다!

VOCABULARY AND EXPRESSIONS

월요일	**Woryoil**	Monday
미팅 (= 회의)	**miting (= hoe.ui)**	meeting
오전	**ojeon**	morning, A.M
층	**cheung**	-th floor (in a building)
회의실	**hoe.uisil**	meeting room
예산	**yesan**	budget
무슨	**museun**	what kind of/what for
-로	**lo**	to, towards, by way of (after a noun that ends in a vowel or l)
-으로	**euro**	to, towards, by way of (after a noun that ends in a consonant)
-에 대한	**e daehan**	about, on (used before a noun)
있을 거예요 (있-, 이-)	**isseul kkeoyeyo (iss-, i-)**	there will be (formal)

알겠습니다 (알-)   **algesseumnida (al-)**   knows (formal, humble)
뵙겠습니다 (뵙-)   **boepgesseumnida (boep-)**   will see (formal, humble)
봅시다 (보-)   **bopsida (bo-)**   let's see each other (formal)

VOCABULARY PRACTICE 1
Give the Korean terms for the words described below.
1. an estimate of income and expenditure of an organization for a set period of time: _____
2. an office room where meetings are held: _____
3. third floor: _____

GRAMMAR NOTE Semi-formal "Let's!" -(으)ㅂ시다 -(eu)psida
While the same ending **-eoyo** -어요 in the informal polite speech style can be used for statements, commands, and invitations ("let's" sentences), adults usually favor **-(eu)seyo** -(으)세요 for polite commands (as mentioned in Lesson 4) and **-(u)psida** -(으)ㅂ시다 for "let's" suggestions. The verb loses its final consonant if it ends in l ㄹ so some words may have the same pronunciation but different meanings.

> Let's sit here. **Yeogi anjeupsida.** 여기 앉읍시다.
> Let's go together. **Gachi gapsida.** 같이 갑시다.
> Let's live here. **Yeogi sapsida** 여기 삽시다. (from **salda** 살다 "to live")
> Let's buy (it) here. **Yeogieseo sapsida.** 여기에서 삽시다. (from **sada** 사다 "to buy")

PATTERN PRACTICE 1
Practice saying the following.
1. Let's meet (see) at the meeting room. **Hoe.uisireseo bopsida.**
   회의실에서 봅시다.
2. Let's meet tomorrow. **Nae.il mannapsida.** 내일 만납시다.
3. Let's eat. **Babeul meogeupsida.** 밥을 먹읍시다.
4. Let's watch a movie. **Yeonghwareul bopsida.** 영화를 봅시다.

GRAMMAR NOTE The Future Tense in Korean -(으)ㄹ 거예요 -(eu)l kkeoyeyo
The simplest way to express the "future tense" in Korean would be to add **-eul kkeoyeyo** -을 거예요 to verb roots that end in consonants and **-l kkeoyeyo** -ㄹ 거예요 to verb roots that end in vowels or l ㄹ. The formal version of this is **-(eu) l kkeomnida** -(으)ㄹ 겁니다.

> I am going to eat dinner at home.
> **Jibeseo jeonyeogeul meogeul kkeoyeyo.** 집에서 저녁을 먹을 거예요.

We are going to the *noraebang* tonight.
Oneul ppame noraebang.e gal kkeoyeyo.
오늘 밤에 노래방에 갈 거예요.

We're going to have a meeting next Monday morning.
Da.eum jju Woryoire miting.eul hal kkeomnida.
다음 주 월요일에 미팅을 할 겁니다.

PATTERN PRACTICE 2

Practice the following conversations.

1. A: What are you going to do tomorrow? **Naeil mwo hal kkeoyeyo?**
      내일 뭐 할 거예요?
   B: I am going to watch a movie. **Yeonghwareul bol kkeoyeyo.**
      영화를 볼 거예요.

2. A: When are we going to have a meeting?
      Eonje miting.i isseul kkeomnikka? 언제 미팅이 있을 겁니까?
   B: We're going to have a meeting next Monday morning.
      Da.eum ju Woryoir achime isseul kkeomnida.
      다음 주 월요일 아침에 있을 겁니다.

3. A: What are you going to eat for lunch? **Jeomsime mwo meogeul kkeoyeyo?**
      점심에 뭐 먹을 거예요?
   B: I'm going to eat *sundubu.* **Sundubu meogeul kkeoyeyo.**
      순두부 먹을 거예요.

GRAMMAR NOTE Making a promise or offer -(으)ㄹ게요 *-(eu)lk–keyo* and -겠습니다 *-gesseumnida* "I will"

If you want to express a promise or offer to do something, you can use the "future tenses" **-gesseumnida** -겠습니다 and **-(eu)lkkeyo** -(으)ㄹ게요 which include a sense of "if that works for you" or "if you agree." For very formal situations, **-gesseumnida** -겠습니다 is used; for less formal situations, **-eulkkeyo** -을게요 (after consonant-ending verb roots) and **-lkkeyo** -을게요 (after vowel-ending or ㅣㄹ-ending verb roots) are used. Although these endings often imply a need for a response, they should never be used as a question.

	INFORMAL	FORMAL
I'll come again tomorrow.	**Naeil dasi olkkeyo.**	**Naeil dasi ogesseumnida.**
	내일 다시 올게요.	내일 다시 오겠습니다.
I'll stay here.	**Yeogi isseulkkeyo.**	**Yeogi itgessumnida.**
	여기 있을게요.	여기 있겠습니다.

PATTERN PRACTICE 3
Practice offering to do things.
1. I will be here (if that's okay). **Yeogie isseulkkeyo./Yeogie itgesseumnida.**
   여기에 있을게요./ 여기 있겠습니다.
2. I will watch from here (if that works for you).
   Yeogieseo bolkkeyo./Yeogieseo bogesseumnida.
   여기에서 볼게요./ 여기에서 보겠습니다.
3. I will read tomorrow (if that's okay). **Naeil ilgeulkkeyo./Naeil ilkesseumnida.**
   내일 읽을게요./내일 읽겠습니다.
4. I will come tomorrow (if that works). **Naeil olkkeyo./Naeil ogesseumnida.**
   내일 올게요./내일 오겠습니다.

GRAMMAR NOTE "To be" verbs

In English, the verb "to be" is used to express identification (e.g., A *is* B) as well as existence and location (e.g., "There *is* a problem" and "The magazine *is* on the table"). Korean uses two different verbs. For identification or equation, **ieyo** 이에요 / **yeyo** 예요 (informal) / **imnida** 입니다 (formal) is used. The verb of location and existence is **isseoyo** 있어요 (informal) / **isseumnida** 있습니다 (formal).

	INFORMAL	FORMAL
My name is Kim Minjoon.	**Je ireumeun GimMinjunieyo.** 제 이름은 김민준이에요.	**Je ireumeun GimMinjunimnida.** 제 이름은 김민준입니다.
What time is the meeting?	**Miting.i myeot siyeyo?** 미팅이 몇 시예요?	**Miting.i myeot siimnikka?** 미팅이 몇 시입니까?
Is there a meeting tomorrow?	**Naeil achime miting.i isseoyo?** 내일 아침에 미팅이 있어요?	**Naeil achime miting.i isseumnikka?** 내일 아침에 미팅이 있습니까?
Is Emma (located) in/at the office?	**Emmaga samusire isseoyo?** 엠마가 사무실에 있어요?	**Emmaga samusire isseumnikka?** 엠마가 사무실에 있습니까?

EXERCISE 1

Practice responding to your friend Tina's suggestions using -(으)ㅂ시다 **-(eu)-psida**.

Tina: **Naeil gachi jeomsim meogeoyo**. 내일 같이 점심 먹어요.
You: **Joayo, gachi jeomsim meogeupsida**. 좋아요. 같이 점심 먹읍시다.

1. **Yeoldu si bane hoesa lobi.eseo mannayo.**
   열두 시 반에 회사 로비에서 만나요.
2. **Hoesa yeop Jung.guk sikdang.e gachi gayo.**
   회사 옆 중국 식당에 같이 가요.
3. **Jeonyeoge gachi yeonghwa bwayo.** 저녁에 같이 영화 봐요.
4. **Bame Han.gang Gongwoneseo gachi sanchaekaeyo.**
   밤에 한강 공원에서 같이 산책해요. (**Han.gang Gongwon** Han River Park)

EXERCISE 2

What are these people going to do this weekend? Answer in Korean.

Emma 엠마	Go hiking
Aiden 에이든	Meet friends at a party
Minjoon 민준	Take a walk with his dog
Eunbi 은비	Drink coffee with her friends

1. **Emmaneun jumare mwo hal kkeoyeyo?** 엠마는 주말에 뭐 할 거예요?
2. **Minjuneun jumare mwo hal kkeoyeyo?** 민준은 주말에 뭐 할 거예요
3. **Eideuneun jumare mwo hal kkeoyeyo?** 에이든은 주말에 뭐 할 거예요?
4. **Eunbineun jumare mwo hal kkeoyeyo?** 은비는 주말에 뭐 할 거예요?

EXERCISE 3

Practice the following conversations. Use -(으)ㄹ게요 **-(eu)lkkeyo** and (으)세요 **(eu)seyo**.

1. You: I will sit here (if that works).
   Friend: Yes, please sit.
2. You: I will come at 10 AM tomorrow (if that's okay).
   Friend: Yes, please come at 10 AM tomorrow.
3. You: I will go now (if that's okay).
   Friend: Yes, please go now.
4. You: I will call you tomorrow.
   Friend: Yes, please call tomorrow.

EXERCISE 4

Which "to be" verb would you use to say the following? Use either the formal or informal ending.

1. **Je ireumeun Emma** _____. 제 이름은 엠마 _____.
2. **Naeil miting.i** _____. 내일 미팅이 _____.
3. **Emmaga samusire**_____? 엠마가 사무실에 _____.
4. **Miting.i myeot si**_____? 미팅이 몇 시 _____.

⊙ DIALOGUE 2 Where is the cafeteria?

Aiden is out running errands, and he doesn't know his way around very well. He is looking for the cafeteria in the building he is visiting and is asking the receptionist (**annaewon** 안내원) for help.

Aiden:	Excuse me. Where is the cafeteria in this building?
	Sillyehamnida. Yeogi gunae sikdang.i eodie isseoyo?
	실례합니다. 여기 구내 식당이 어디에 있어요?
Receptionist:	It's on Basement 1. Take the elevator down.
	Jiha il cheung.e isseumnida. Ellibeiteoreul tago naeryeogasipsio.
	지하 1층에 있습니다. 엘리베이터를 타고 내려가십시오.
Aiden:	Thank you. By the way, is there no restroom on this floor?
	Gamsahamnida. Geureonde i cheung.e hwajangsireun eopseoyo?
	감사합니다. 그런데, 이 층에 화장실은 없어요?
Receptionist:	There is one next to the elevator.
	Ellibeiteo yeope isseumnida.
	엘리베이터 옆에 있습니다.
Aiden:	Let me ask just one more question.
	Hanaman deo yeojjwobolkkeyo.
	하나만 더 여쭤볼게요.
Receptionist:	Yes, please ask.
	Ne, mureoboseyo.
	네, 물어보세요.
Aiden:	Where is the ATM?
	Hyeon.geuminchulgineun eodie isseoyo?
	현금인출기는 어디에 있어요?
Receptionist:	There isn't one in the building, but there is one in front of the store to the right of this building.
	Bilding aneneun eopjiman geonmul oreunjjok gage ape isseumnida.
	빌딩 안에는 없지만 건물 오른 쪽 가게 앞에 있습니다.

Aiden: Thank you!
              Gamsahamnida!
              감사합니다!

VOCABULARY AND EXPRESSIONS

안내원	**annaewon**	(information booth) receptionist; guide
여기	**yeogi**	here (where I am)
그런데 (= 근데)	**geureonde (= geunde)**	by the way; however
이	**i**	this (needs a noun after)
구내	**gunae**	in the building, facilities affiliated with X
식당	**sikdang**	restaurant, cafeteria
지하	**jiha**	basement
일	**il**	one
엘리베이터	**ellibeiteo**	elevator
화장실	**hwajangsil**	restroom
옆	**yeop**	next to, beside
빌딩 (= 건물)	**bilding (= geonmul)**	building
현금 인출기	**hyeon.geuminchulgi**	ATM
안	**an**	inside
오른쪽	**oreunjjok**	right side
앞	**ap**	(in) front (of)
더	**deo**	more
-고	**go**	and (used with verb roots)
-지만	**jiman**	but (used with verb roots)
실례합니다 (실례하-)	**sillyehamnida (sillyeha-)**	excuse me (formal)
감사합니다 (감사하-)	**gamsahamnida (gamsaha-)**	thank you (formal)
여쭤볼게요 (여쭤보-)	**yeojjwobolkkeyo (yeojjwobo-)**	let me ask (someone honored, older)
물어보세요 (물어보-)	**mureoboseyo (mureobo-)**	go ahead and ask (informal, honorific)
타고 (타-)	**tago (ta-)**	rides and
내려가십시오 (내려가-)	**naeryeogasipsio (naeryeoga-)**	please go down(stairs) (formal)

VOCABULARY PRACTICE 2

How would you say the following in Korean?
1. right side   2. front   3. next to   4. inside

Supplementary Vocabulary
Location words

Korean location words (e.g. "the front", "the side", etc.) are used with the point marker **-e** –에 to say "at the front" or "on the side." The reference point noun, e.g. "next to *THE HOUSE*," comes *BEFORE* the location word.

LOCATION WORDS		EXAMPLES	
옆 **yeop**	side	제니퍼 옆에 **Jenipeo yeope**	next to/beside Jennifer
앞 **ap**	front	제니퍼 앞에 **Jenipeo ape**	in front of Jennifer
뒤 **dwi**	back	학교 뒤에 **hakkyo dwi.e**	behind the school
LOCATION WORDS		EXAMPLES	
위 **wi**	above	책 위에 **chaek wi.e**	above the book
아래 **arae**	below	시계 아래에 **sigye arae.e**	under the clock/watch
밑 **mit**	under/bottom	바다 밑에 **bada mite**	under the sea
밖 **bak**	side	학교 밖에 **hakkyo bakke**	outside the school
안 **an**	inside	학교 안에 **hakkyo ane**	inside/in the school
속 **sok**	(deep) inside	마음 속에 **ma.eum soge**	deep inside your mind
왼쪽 **oenjjok**	left side	책상 왼쪽에 **chaeksang oenjjoge**	to the left of the desk (desk's left side)
오른쪽 **oreun jjok**	right side	사과 오른쪽에 **sagwa oreunjjoge**	to the right of the apple (apple's right side)

PATTERN PRACTICE 4
Practice the following conversations about location.
1. A: Where is the restroom? **Hwajangsiri eodi(e) isseumnikka**
   화장실이 어디(에) 있어요?
   B: It is next to the elevator. **Ellibeiteo yeope isseumnida.**
   엘리베이터 옆에 있어요.
   A: Where is the elevator? **Ellibeiteoga eodi(e) isseumnikka?**
   엘리베이터가 어디(에) 있어요?
   B: It is in front of the meeting room. **Hoe.uisil ape isseumnida.**
   회의실 앞에 있어요.
2. A: Where is the meeting room? **Hoe.uisiri eodi(e) isseumnikka?**
   회의실이 어디(에) 있어요?
   B: It is on the third floor. **Sam cheung.e isseumnida.**
   3층에 있어요.

PATTERN PRACTICE 5
Practice the following brief exchanges in Korean.
1. A: Where is the wallet? **Jigabi eodie isseoyo?**
   지갑이 어디에 있어요?
   B: On (top of) the desk. **Chaeksang wieyo.** 책상 위에요.

2. A: Where is Charles? **Chalseu ssiga eodie isseoyo?**
찰스 씨가 어디에 있어요?
   B: He is next to Maya. **Maya ssi yeope isseoyo.** 마야 씨 옆에 있어요.
3. A: Where is the orange juice? **Orenji juseuga eodie isseoyo?**
오렌지 주스가 어디에 있어요?
   B: In the fridge. **Naengjanggo aneyo.** 냉장고 안에요.
4. A: Where is the ATM? **Hyeon.geuminchulgiga .i eodie isseoyo?**
현금 인출기가 어디에 있어요?
   B: It is on the first floor. **Il cheung.e isseumnida.** 일층에 있습니다.

GRAMMAR NOTE Deictic expressions "here/there/over there," "this/that/that over there"

Korean has a three-way distinction among place/distance words, where English has only two-way distinction, "here" and "there." In Korean, **yeogi** 여기 means "here" (close to the speaker), **geogi** 거기 means "there (over there, nearby)," and **jeogi** 저기 means "over there (further away)." To express the equivalent of "this (thing)" and "that (thing)" in English, Korean uses three words **igeo** 이거, **geugeo** 그거, and **jeogeo** 저거 (with a final ㅅ—pronounced **t**—in more formal Korean).

이 **i** this...	그 **geu** that...	저 **jeo** that... way over there
이 사람 **i saram** this person	그 사람 **geu saram** that person	저 사람 **jeo saram** that person over there
이거 **igeo**/이것 **igeot** this (thing)	그거 **geugeo**/그것 **geugeot** that (thing)	저거 **jeogeo**/저것 **jeogeot** that (thing) over there

Geu saram 그 사람 and **geugeo** 그거 also work as pronouns ("him/her" and "it"). The idiomatic phrases "**yeogi jeogi** 여기 저기" and "**igeot jeogeot** 이것 저것" are also useful:

I found it after asking <u>around</u> (*Lit.*, "here and there").
Yeogi jeogi susomunhaeseo chajasseoyo.
여기 저기 수소문해서 찾았어요.

Don't touch <u>anything</u>. (*Lit.*, "this and that")
Igeot jeogeot manjiji maseyo. 이것 저것 만지지 마세요.

PATTERN PRACTICE 6
Practice asking the following expressions out loud in Korean.
1. Is it raining over there now? **Geogineun jigeum biga wayo?**
거기는 지금 비가 와요?
2. Where is it? **Geugeo eodie isseoyo?** 그거 어디에 있어요?
3. Let's go over there. **Jeogiro gapsida.** 저기로 갑시다.

GRAMMAR NOTE -고 *-go* "and" and -지만 *-jiman* "but"

The suffix **-go** -고 "and" is attached to verb roots to connect two actions. The suffix **-jiman** -지만 is attached to verb roots to connect two actions with the meaning "but."

Please take the elevator and go down.
Ellibeiteoreul <u>tago</u> naeryeogasipsio. 엘리베이터를 타<u>고</u> 내려가십시오.

There isn't one in the building, but there is one outside.
Geonmul aneneun eopjiman geonmul bakke hana isseumnida.
건물 안에는 없<u>지만</u> 건물 밖에 하나 있습니다.

PATTERN PRACTICE 7

Practice the following phrases using -고 **-go** and -지만 **-jiman**.
1. Restrooms are on the first floor, and the meeting room is on the second floor.
   Hwajangsireun il cheung.e itgo hoe.uisireun i cheung.e isseumnida.
   화장실은 일 층에 있고 회의실은 이 층에 있습니다.
2. Please take the elevator and go down. **Ellibeiteoreul tago naeryeo gasipsio.**
   엘리베이터를 타고 내려 가십시오.
3. There are restrooms on the first floor, but there aren't any on the second floor.
   Hwajangsireun il cheung.eneun itjiman i cheung.eneun eopseumnida.
   화장실은 일 층에는 있지만 이 층에는 없습니다.
4. We don't have a meeting today, but we have one tomorrow.
   Oneureun hoe.uiga eopjiman naeil hoe.uiga isseoyo.
   오늘은 회의가 없지만 내일 회의가 있어요.

GRAMMAR NOTE Formal honorific command -(으)십시오
                        -(eu)sipsio

-(Eu)sipsio -(으)십시오 is the *formal honorific command* form, used mostly by people in the service industry or company employees. The vowel **eu** 으 is inserted after verb roots that end in consonants.

As with the semi-formal suggestion suffix **-(eu)psida** -(으)ㅂ시다, the verb loses its final consonant if it ends in **l** ㄹ for the **-(eu)sipsio** -(으)십시오 conjugation, resulting in words with the same pronunciation but different meanings.

Welcome! **Eoseo osipsio.** 어서 오십시오.

Please sit/have a seat over here.
Ijjogeuro anjeusipsio. 이쪽으로 앉으십시오.

Please hang it here. (**dalda** "hang") **Yeogie dasipsio.** 여기에 다십시오.

PATTERN PRACTICE 8

Practice these phrases using polite honorific commands.
1. Please take the elevator. **Ellibeiteoreul tasipsio.** 엘리베이터를 타십시오.
2. Please come this way. **Ijjogeuro osipsio.** 이쪽으로 오십시오.
3. Please have a seat over this way. **Yeogie anjeusipsio.** 여기에 앉으십시오.
4. Please wait for a minute. **Jamkkanman gidarisipsio.** 잠깐만 기다리십시오.

GRAMMAR NOTE Informal style conjugation
(ㅏ *a*, ㅐ *ae*, ㅓ *eo*, ㅔ *e*–verbs)

In conjugating verbs in the formal style, if the verb root ends in a ㅏ, ae ㅐ, eo ㅓ, or e ㅔ, then you do not need to do anything further to the verb but add other suffixes.

DICTIONARY FORM	[VERB] + and -고 *-go*	FUTURE -(으)ㄹ게요/-(으)ㄹ 거예요 *-(eu)lkkeyo/-(eu)l kkeoyeyo*	PRESENT, PAST -어/아요, -었/았어요 *-eo/ayo, -eoss/asseoyo*
타다 **tada** to ride, burn	타고 **tago**	탈게요/탈 거예요 **talkkeyo/tal kkeoyeyo** will ride, burn	타요, 탔어요 **tayo, tasseoyo** ride, rode
보내다 **bonaeda** to send	보내고 **bonaego**	보낼게요/보낼 거예요 **bonaelkkeyo/bonael kkeoyeyo** will send	보내요, 보냈어요 **bonaeyo, bonaesseoyo** send, sent
서다 **seoda** to stand, stop	서고 **seogo**	설게요/설 거예요 **seolkkeyo/seol kkeoyeyo** will stand, stop	서요, 섰어요 **seoyo, seosseoyo** stand, stood
세다 **seda** to count	세고 **sego**	셀게요/셀 거예요 **selkkeyo/sel kkeoyeyo** will count	세요, 셌어요 **seyo, sesseoyo** count, counted

GRAMMAR NOTE Informal style conjugation ㅗ *o*, ㅜ *u*, ㅣ i–verbs

There are three different "types" of suffixes in Korean according to the different verb conjugations. The first column in the table below shows a consonant type, where the suffix begins with a consonant **g** ㄱ (of -go -고). The second column shows the **-eu** -으 type and the third the **-eo** -어 type.

For verb roots that end in **o** ㅗ, **u** ㅜ, or **i** ㅣ, there is contraction of the root vowels before **-eo** -어 type suffixes. Compare the conjugations in the chart below.

DICTIONARY FORM	[VERB] + and -고 *-go*	FUTURE -(으)ㄹ게요/-(으)ㄹ 거예요 *-(eu)lkkeyo/-(eu)l kkeoyeyo*	PRESENT, PAST -어/아요, -었/았어요 *-eo/ayo, -eoss/asseoyo*
돌보다 **dolboda** to take care of	돌보고 **dolbogo**	돌볼게요/돌볼 거예요 **dolbolkkeyo/dolbol kkeoyeyo** will take care of	돌봐요/돌봤어요 **dolbwayo/dolbwasseoyo** take care of, took care of

DICTIONARY FORM	[VERB] + and -고 -go	FUTURE -(으)ㄹ게요/-(으)ㄹ 거예요 -(eu)lkkeyo/-(eu)l kkeoyeyo	PRESENT, PAST -어/아요, -었/았어요 -eo/ayo, -eoss/asseoyo
바꾸다 bakkuda to (ex)change	바꾸고 bakkugo	바꿀게요/바꿀 거예요 bakkulkkeyo/bakkul kkeoyeyo will exchange	바꿔요/바꿨어요 bakkweoyo/bakkwosseoyo exchange, exchanged
던지다 deonjida to throw	던지고 deonjigo	던질게요/던질 거예요 deonjilkkeyo/deonjil kkeoyeyo will throw	던져요/던졌어요 deonjyeoyo/ deonjyeosseoyo throw, threw

CULTURE NOTE **Basic pleasantries and responses**

Respond to commands or reminders by your superiors with the phrase, **Ne, algesseumnida** 네, 알겠습니다 (*Lit.,* "yes, I will know that," or the formal form of saying "OK, I got it.").

Another basic pleasantry is to mention in closing <u>when</u> you will meet again. In the formal style, you'll use a time expression, such as **nae.il** 내일 "tomorrow" plus **boepgesseumnida** 뵙겠습니다 (*Lit.,* "(I) will be seen") to mean "see you tomorrow." Here are some other time expressions:

어제 **eoje** yesterday	오늘 **oneul** today	모레 **more** day after tomorrow
아침 **achim** (early) morning	오전 **ojeon** before noon	점심 **jeomsim** lunchtime
오후 **ohu** afternoon	저녁 **jeonyeok** evening/dinner time	밤 **bam** nighttime
지난 주 **jinan ju** last week	이번 주 **ibeon ju** this week	다음 주 **da.eumju** next week
지난 달 **jinan dal** last month	이번 달 **ibeon dal** this month	다음 달 **da.eum dal** next month
작년 **jangnyeon** last year	올해 **olhae** this year	내년 **naeyeon** next year
곧 **got** soon	다시 **dasi** again	다음에 **da.eume** next time

CULTURE NOTE **Polite expressions**

There are different ways to say common phrases such as "thank you" in Korean, with different degrees of formality or affection.

"Thank you": The most formal way to say this is **gamsahamnida** 감사합니다. **Gomapseumnida** 고맙습니다 is a more personal way to say "I appreciate it" while still being formal. The most informal (but still polite) is **gomawoyo** 고마워요.

"Excuse me" and **apologizing: Jeosonghamnida** 죄송합니다 is a very formal way of apologizing for grave mistakes that you may have personally committed. **Sillyehamnida** 실례합니다 works for getting someone's attention politely and is the most commonly used. **Mianhamnida** 미안합니다 is a lighter way of apologizing, perhaps to someone who is younger or as old as you, but still in the formal speech style. **Mianhaeyo** 미안해요 is the informal (polite) counterpart for apologizing among friends.

CULTURE NOTE **Using negatives to be polite**

In the second dialogue, Aiden asks "is there <u>no</u> bathroom on this floor?" Some Korean speakers use negative questions to be more polite.

EXERCISE 5

Practice the following conversations using the given information.

restroom	next to the elevator	elevator	in front of the meeting room
meeting room	5th floor	Minjoon's office	behind the meeting room

1. **Hwajangsiri eodie isseoyo?** 화장실이 어디에 있어요?
2. **Ellibeiteoga eodie isseoyo?** 엘리베이터가 어디에 있어요?
3. **Hoe.uisiri eodie isseoyo?** 회의실이 어디에 있어요?
4. **Minjun ssi samusiri eodie isseoyo?** 민준 씨 사무실이 어디에 있어요?

EXERCISE 6

Imagine you are working at the information desk. Give information about the building using -고 **-go** and -지만 **-jiman**.
1. The elevator is on the first floor, and the restrooms are next to the elevator.
2. Please take the elevator to go up.
3. There are restrooms on the second floor, but there aren't any on the third floor.
4. There isn't an ATM in the building, but there is one in front of the store.

EXERCISE 7

Imagine you are working at the information desk. Give directions to visitors using -(으)십시오 **-(eu)sipsio**.
1. Welcome. (*Lit.,* "Please come quickly.")
2. Please come this way.
3. Please sit here.
4. Please take the elevator to go down.

LESSON 6

Talking About Housing and Neighborhood

DIALOGUE 1 How is living in your apartment?

Minjoon and Emma are chatting in front of the coffee vending machine at work.

Minjoon: Hi, Emma. How is life in Korea?
Annyeonghaseyo, Emma ssi. Han.guk saenghwari eottaeyo?
안녕하세요, 엠마 씨. 한국 생활이 어때요?

Emma: Hello, Mr. Kim. It's great.
Annyeonghaseyo, timjangnim. Aju joayo.
안녕하세요, 팀장님. 아주 좋아요.

Minjoon: Where are you living now?
Jigeum eodi salgo isseoyo?
지금 어디 살고 있어요?

Emma: (In) an apartment.
Apateuyo.
아파트요.

Minjoon: How is your apartment (for living)?
Apateuga salgiga eottaeyo?
아파트가 살기가 어때요?

Emma: It's very modern and convenient. There is a refrigerator and a washing machine.
Aju hyeondaesigigo salgi pyeonhaeyo. Naeng.janggohago setakgido isseoyo.
아주 현대식이고 살기 편해요. 냉장고하고 세탁기도 있어요.

Minjoon: Oh, that's good. Is there a separate bedroom, too?
Jaldwaenneyo. Chimsildo ttaro isseoyo?
잘됐네요. 침실도 따로 있어요?

Emma: Yes, there is a separate bedroom and a bathroom.
Ne, chimsirirang yoksildo ttaro isseoyo.
네, 침실이랑 욕실도 따로 있어요.

Minjoon: Oh, then it is pretty big! Is the rent expensive?
Geureom kkwae keugunyo! Wolsega bissayo?
그럼 꽤 크군요! 월세가 비싸요?

Emma: Even the monthly rent is cheap.
Wolsedo aju sssayo.
월세도 아주 싸요.

Minjoon: Good for you!
           Jaldwaenneyo!
           잘됐네요!

VOCABULARY AND EXPRESSIONS

생활	**saenghwal**	X life, life as a…, life in … (usually after a descriptive noun)
아파트	**apateu**	apartment
냉장고	**naen.janggo**	refrigerator
세탁기	**setakgi**	washing machine
침실	**chimsil**	bedroom
욕실	**yoksil**	bathroom (for showering)
지금	**jigeum**	(right) now, this moment, these days
아주	**aju**	very
따로	**ttaro**	separately
꽤	**kkwae**	quite
-기	**gi**	temporary noun-making suffix (usually for idiomatic expressions; used with verb roots)
-하고	**hago (= irang)**	and (noun connector)
-이랑	**irang (= hago)**	and (noun connector; used after nouns ending in consonants), more colloquial than 하고
-랑	**rang**	and (noun connector; used after nouns ending in vowels), more colloquial than 하고
-을	**eul**	marker of the direct object of the sentence (used after nouns ending in consonants)
-를	**reul**	marker of the direct object of the sentence (used after nouns ending in vowels)
살고 있어요 (살-, 있-)	**salgo isseoyo (sal-, iss-)**	is living
어때요 (어떻-)	**eeottaeyo (eotteoh-)**	How is…?
살기 (살-)	**salgi (sal-)**	living, to live
현대식이고 (현대식이-)	**hyeondaesigigo (hyeondaesigi-)**	modern and
편해요 (편하-)	**pyeonhaeyo (pyeonha-)**	convenient, comfortable
크군요 (크-)	**keugunyo (keu-)**	big, I see
잘됐네요 (잘되-)	**jaldwaenneyo (jaldoe-)**	oh, good for you! (*Lit.,* "well done/turned out well")

VOCABULARY PRACTICE 1

Give the Korean terms for the words described below.
1. It keeps your food cool so it won't spoil easily: _____
2. You can take a shower in this room: _____
3. It makes washing clothes easy: _____
4. This room usually has a bed in it: _____

GRAMMAR NOTE Loanwords from English

Korean has many words adopted from English: **apateu** 아파트 "apartment," **keopi** 커피 "coffee," **tisyeocheu** 티셔츠 "t-shirt," **keonpeom** 컨펌 "confirm(ation)," and so on. But there are occasional differences in usage, i.e., **wonrum** 원룸 ("one room"), means a studio, not a one-bedroom apartment with a separate living room and kitchen.

Supplementary Vocabulary
Household appliances and furniture

가구 **gagu** furniture	카페트 **kapeteu** carpet/rug 전등 **jeondeung** ceiling light 의자 **uija** chair 서랍장 **seorapjang** dresser 책상 **chaeksang** desk 액자 **aekja** (picture) frame	램프 **laempeu** lamp 스위치 **seuwichi** light switch 콘센트 **konsenteu** outlet 소파 **sopa** sofa 식탁/상 **siktak/sang** (tall/low) table 　(for eating)
가전제품 **gajeonjepum** electrical 　(household) 　appliances	믹서기 **mikseogi** blender 선풍기 **seonpunggi** fan 보온밥통/전기밥솥 **bo.on** 　**baptong/jeon.gi bapsot** rice 　warmer/(electric) rice cooker 김치 냉장고 **gimchi naengjanggo** 　kimchi refrigerator	전자레인지 **jeonjareinji** microwave 오븐 **obeun** oven 냉장고 **naengjanggo** refrigerator 냉동고/냉동실 **naengdonggo/** 　**naengdongsil** (independent/ 　compartment) freezer 가스레인지 **gaseureinji** stovetop 토스트기 **toseuteugi** toaster 텔레비전 **tellebijeon** TV 세탁기 **setakgi** washing machine
도구/연장 **dogu/** 　**yeonjang** tools	빗자루 **bitjaru** broom 식기세제/주방세제 **sikgiseje/** 　**jubangseje** dish soap 풀 **pul** glue 망치 **mangchi** hammer 대걸레 **daegeolle** mop (주방용) 수세미 **(jubangyong)** 　**susemi** kitchen scourer (주방용) 스폰지 **(jubangyong)** 　**seuponji** kitchen sponge 못 **mot** nail 바늘 **baneul** needle	걸레 **geolle** rag 노끈 **nokkeun** rope 가위 **gawi** scissors (스카치) 테이프 **(seukachi) teipeu** 　Scotch tape 끈 **kkeun** string 실 **sil** thread 티슈 **tisyu** tissue (두루마리) 휴지 **(durumari) hyuji** 　toilet paper 수건 **sugeon** towel

GRAMMAR NOTE Frequently used adjectives

DICTIONARY FORM	-어요/아요	DICTIONARY FORM	-어요/아요
크다 big **keuda**	커요 is big **keoyo**	작다 small **jakda**	작아요 is small **jagayo**
넓다 spacious, wide **neolpda**	넓어요 is spacious **neolbeoyo**	좁다 **jopda** not spacious, narrow	좁아요 **jobayo** is not spacious
싸다 cheap **ssada**	싸요 is cheap **ssayo**	비싸다 expensive **bissada**	비싸요 is expensive **bissayo**
좋다 good **johda**	좋아요 is good **joayo**	나쁘다 bad **nappeuda**	나빠요 is bad **nappayo**
예쁘다 pretty **yeppeuda**	예뻐요 is pretty **yeppeoyo**	편리하다 convenient **pyeonlihada**	편리해요 **pyeollihaeyo** is convenient
편하다 comfortable **pyeonhada**	편해요 **pyeonhaeyo** is comfortable	불편하다 **bulpyeonhada** inconvenient, uncomfortable	불편해요 **bulpyeonhaeyo** is inconvenient
피곤하다 tired **pigonhada**	피곤해요 is tired **pigonhaeyo**	아프다 sick **apeuda**	아파요 is sick **apayo**
바쁘다 busy **bappeuda**	바빠요 is busy **bappayo**	괜찮다 okay, fine **gwaenchanhda**	괜찮아요 is okay **gwaenchanayo**
힘들다 tiring, hard **himdeulda**	힘들어요is tiring **himdeureoyo**	어떻다 how **eotteohda** (ㅎ h-irregular)	어때요 how is **eottaeyo**
맛있다 delicious **masissda**	맛있어요 **masisseoyo** is delicious	맛없다 not delicious **mas.eopsda**	맛없어요 **madeopseoyo** is not delicious
재미있다 fun **jaemiissda**	재미있어요 is fun **jaemiisseoyo**	재미없다 not fun **jaemi.eopsda**	재미없어요 **jaemi.eopseoyo** is not fun
깨끗하다 clean **kkaekkeus.hada**	깨끗해요 is clean **kkaekkeutaeyo**	더럽다 dirty **deoreopda** (ㅂ p-irregular)	더러워요 is dirty **deoreowoyo**
조용하다 quiet **joyonghada**	조용해요 is quiet **joyonghaeyo**	시끄럽다 noisy **sikkeureopda** (ㅂ p-irregular)	시끄러워요 is noisy **sikkeureowoyo**
쉽다 **swipda** easy (ㅂ p-irregular)	쉬워요 is easy **swiwoyo**	어렵다 difficult **eo.ryeopda** (ㅂ p-irregular)	어려워요 is difficult **eo.ryeowoyo**
가깝다 close **gakkapda** (ㅂ p-irregular)	가까워요 is close **gakkawoyo**	멀다 far **meolda**	멀어요 is far **meoreoyo**

Korean adjectives conjugate just like verbs, and they come at the very end of a sentence. You do not need to use the "be" verb with adjectives in Korean.

(My) house is close from here.
Jibi yeogieseo gakkawoyo. 집이 여기에서 가까워요.

I am tired today.
Oneul pigonhaeyo. 오늘 피곤해요.

GRAMMAR NOTE **-도 *-do* as an emphasis marker "even"**
The suffix **-do** -도 normally adds yet another item to the list just introduced. When it is used singly, it adds emphasis with the meaning "even," e.g., "Even the monthly rent is cheap." **Wolsedo aju sssayo.** 월세도 아주 싸요.

GRAMMAR NOTE **Connecting nouns with -하고 *-hago* and -(이)랑 *-(i)rang***
The suffix **-hago** -하고 connects two nouns by attaching to the first noun. **-Irang** -이랑 does the same job but is a little more colloquial. The vowel I 이 drops after a noun that ends in a vowel.

Neorang na 너랑 나 vs. **neohago na** 너하고 나 "you and I"
Namchinhago na 남친이랑 나 vs. **namchinirang na** 남친하고 나 "(my) boyfriend and I"

PATTERN PRACTICE 1
Practice these phrases using the two different ways of connecting nouns in Korean.
1. mandarin oranges and apples **gyulhago sagwa** 귤하고 사과
2. mandarin oranges and apples **gyurirang sagwa** 귤이랑 사과
3. Eunbi and Minjoon **Eunbihago Minjun** 은비하고 민준
4. Eunbi and Minjoon **Eunbirang Minjun** 은비랑 민준

GRAMMAR NOTE **Expressing an ongoing action with -고 있어요 *-go isseoyo***
Use **-go isseoyo** -고 있어요 to talk about something that is ongoing (progressive) at the moment. Normally, verbs conjugated with **-eoyo/ayo** -어요/아요 can express an activity over a span of time ("I am dancing"), a repeated or habitual action ("I dance"), or even an immediate future plan ("I'm going to dance later"). **-Go isseoyo** -고 있어요 limits the interpretation to an activity that is going on <u>now</u>. The suffix **-go** -고 attaches to the verb root. Compare the following sets of sentences.

Where are you living now?	Where do you live?
Jigeum eodi salgo isseoyo?	**Jigeum eodi sarayo?**
지금 어디 살고 있어요?	요즘 어디 살아요?
What are you reading now?	What are you reading these days?
Jigeum mwo ilkgo isseoyo?	**Yojeum mwo ilgeoyo?**
지금 뭐 읽고 있어요?	요즘 뭐 읽어요?
Who are you meeting with now?	Who are you seeing these days?
Jigeum nugu mannago isseoyo?	**Yojeum nugu mannayo?**
지금 누구 만나고 있어요?	요즘 누구 만나요?

PATTERN PRACTICE 2
Practice these phrases using "be …ing" ," -고 있어요 **-go isseoyo** in Korean.
1. I am working now. **Jigeum ireul hago isseoyo.** 지금 일을 하고 있어요.
2. I am watching a movie now. **Jigeum yeonghwareul bogo isseoyo.** 지금 영화를 보고 있어요.
3. I am taking a rest now. **Jigeum swigo isseoyo.** 지금 쉬고 있어요.
4. I am living in Hyoja Dong. **Hyojadong.e salgo isseoyo.** 효자동에 살고 있어요.

GRAMMAR NOTE "For doing...," "to do..." suffix -기(가) *-gi(ga)*

The suffix **-gi** -기 makes verbs into (temporary) nouns, to be used in idiomatic expressions such as "it is easy to/convenient/good to …" The subject marker **-i/ga** -이/가 that comes after the suffix **-gi** -기 is optional. You can also use the point marker **-e** -에 before the adjectives such as **joayo** 좋아요 "good."

It's easy to find that house.
Geu jibeun chatgi(ga) swiwoyo. 그 집은 찾기(가) 쉬워요.

Living in Korea is good.
Han.gugeun salgi(ga) joayo. 한국은 살기(가) 좋아요.

It's comfortable/convenient to live in this apartment. (*Lit.,* "As for this apartment, living is convenient/comfortable.")
I apateuneun salgi.e pyeonhaeyo. 이 아파트는 살기에 편해요.

PATTERN PRACTICE 3
Practice these phrases using "it is (good) to… , -기 **-gi** (adjective)" in Korean.
1. It's good to live in Korea (Korea is good to live in). **Han.gugeun salgi joayo.** 한국은 살기 좋아요.
2. It's difficult to find this apartment. **I apateuneun chatgi himdeureoyo.** 이 아파트는 찾기힘들어요.

3. It's easy to study math. **Suhageun gongbuhagi swiwoyo.**
   수학은 공부하기 쉬워요.
4. It's easy to ride this bicycle. **I jajeon.geoneun tagi pyeonhaeyo.**
   이 자전거는 타기 편해요.

EXERCISE 1

Your friends came over to your house to have snacks and hang out. Everyone brought something with them. Say what each person has, using -(이)랑 **-(i)rang** and -하고 **-hago**.

1. Eunbi has three apples and one pear. (pear: **bae** 배)
2. Minjoon has two bottles of beer and five bottles of juice.
3. Aiden has *kimbap* and *ramyeon* noodles. (김밥; 라면)
   (**gimbap** 김밥 seaweed rice rolls; **ramyeon** 라면 ramen noodles)
4. Emma has four bags of chips and five mandarin oranges.

EXERCISE 2

After having snacks, all your friends are making themselves comfortable. Answer the following questions in Korean using -고 있어요 **-go isseoyo** based on the given information.

Emma	is exercising
Aiden	is watching a movie
Eunbi	is sleeping
Minjoon	is drinking coffee

1. **Emmaneun jigeum mwo hago isseoyo?** 엠마는 지금 뭐 하고 있어요?
2. **Eunbineun jigeum mwo hago isseoyo?** 은비는 지금 뭐 하고 있어요?
3. **Eideuneun jigeum mwo hago isseoyo?** 에이든은 지금 뭐 하고 있어요?
4. **Minjuneun jigeum mwo hago isseoyo?** 민준은 지금 뭐 하고 있어요?

EXERCISE 3

Answer your friend's questions in Korean using -기 **-gi** + ("it is (adjective) to …"), based on the given information.

1. **I apateu salgi eottaeyo?** (good to live [in]: **salda** 살다)
2. **I chaek ilkgi eottaeyo?** (easy to read: **ilkta** 읽다)
3. **I naengjanggo eottaeyo?** (convenient to use: **sayonghada** 사용하다)
4. **I jajeon.geo eottaeyo?** (comfortable to ride: **tada** 타다)

DIALOGUE 2 What is the room like?

Eunbi:	Aiden, how is the room you are living in now?
	Eideun ssi, jigeum salgo inneun bang.i eottaeyo?
	에이든 씨, 지금 살고 있는 방이 어때요?
Aiden:	It's alright. But I'm looking for another place.
	Gwaenchanayo. Geureonde dareun dereul chatgo isseoyo.
	괜찮아요. 그런데 다른 데를 찾고 있어요.
Eunbi:	Why?
	Waeyo?
	왜요?
Aiden:	The rent is too expensive so I'm looking for a cheaper place. I prefer a studio, but…
	Bang.sega neomu bissaseo deo ssan dereul chatgo isseoyo. Wonrumi jo.eunde…
	방세가 너무 비싸서 더 싼 데를 찾고 있어요. 원룸이 좋은데…
Eunbi:	My older sister is moving out of her studio.
	Uri eonniga wonrumeseo isareul naganeunde.
	우리 언니가 원룸에서 이사를 나가는데.
Aiden:	Oh? What is the room like?
	Geuraeyo? Bang.i eotteondeyo?
	그래요? 방이 어떤데요?
Eunbi:	It's a nice place. It has a private bathroom and (there are) heated floors. And it's nearby.
	Kkwae gwaenchanayo. Gaein hwajangsildo itgo, ondol maruyeyo. Yeogieseo aju gakkawoyo.
	꽤 괜찮아요. 개인 화장실도 있고, 온돌 마루예요. 여기에서 아주 가까워요.
Aiden:	Sounds great, then!
	Geureom gwaenchaneundeyo!
	그럼 괜찮은데요!
Eunbi:	There are many restaurants and convenience stores nearby, too. There's no air conditioning in the unit, though.
	Geuncheo.e sikdang.irang pyeonuijeomdo manayo. Geunde apateu.e e.eokeoni eopseoyo.
	근처에 식당이랑 편의점도 많아요. 근데 아파트에 에어컨이 없어요.
Aiden:	That's not a problem.
	Gwaenchanayo.
	괜찮아요.
Eunbi:	Shall we go see it tomorrow?
	Naeil gachigaseo bolkkayo?
	내일 같이 가서 볼까요?

Aiden: Sure. Thank you.
              Geuraeyo. Gomawoyo.
              그래요. 고마워요.

VOCABULARY AND EXPRESSIONS

방	**bang**	room
방세	**bang.sse**	rent (money)
언니	**eonni**	older sister (of a female)
원룸	**wonnum**	one-room, studio
데	**de**	place, location (used only when modified)
왜	**wae**	why
이사	**isa**	moving
개인	**gaein**	individual, private
온돌	**ondol**	heated stone floor (traditionally wood-floored)
마루	**maru**	living room, space between rooms
근처	**geuncheo**	vicinity, nearby
식당	**sikdang**	restaurant
편의점	**pyeonuijeom**	convenience store
에어컨	**e.eokeon**	air conditioner, air conditioning
내일	**nae.il**	tomorrow
너무	**neomu**	too, overly
근데 (= 그런데)	**geunde (= geureonde)**	but, however
좋은데	**jo.eunde (joh-)**	good, but
비싸서 (비싸-)	**bissaseo (bissa-)**	expensive so,
다른 (다르-)	**dareun (dareu-)**	(an)other, different
싼 (싸-)	**ssan (ssa-)**	cheap (used before a noun)
찾고 있어요 (찾-, 있-)	**chatgo isseoyo (chaj-, iss-)**	is looking for
나가는데 (나가-)	**naganeunde (naga-)**	going/moving out so/but/and…
그래요? (그렇-)	**geuraeyo? (geureoh-)**	Is that right? Is that so?
어떤데요? (어떻-)	**eotteondeyo? (eotteoh-)**	How is it (can you tell me)?
가까워요 (가깝-)	**gakkawoyo (gakkap-)**	close, nearby
괜찮은데요 (괜찮-)	**gwaenchaneundeyo (gwaenchanh-)**	fair, not bad, OK, no big deal
많아요 (많-)	**manayo (manh-)**	a lot, plenty
가서 (가-)	**gaseo (ga-)**	go and…
볼까요? (보-)	**bolkkayo? (bo-)**	Shall we look?
그래요 (그렇-)	**geuraeyo (geureoh-)**	it is so; yes, please
고마워요 (고맙-)	**gomawoyo (gomap-)**	thank you

VOCABULARY PRACTICE 2

Give the Korean terms for the words described below.
1. It keeps your room cool in the summer: _____
2. A place to eat outside the home: _____
3. Not far away but _____
4. When you change where you live: _____

Supplementary Vocabulary

Family terms

어머니	eomeoni	mother (formal)	아버지	abeoji	father (formal)
엄마	eomma	mom, mother (informal)	아빠	appa	dad, father (informal)
할머니	halmeoni	one's grandmother	할아버지	harabeoji	one's grandfather
할머님	halmeonim	grandmother (honorific)	할아버님	harabeonim	grandfather (honorific)
오빠	oppa	older brother of a female	형	hyeong	older brother of a male
언니	eonni	older sister of a female	누나	nuna	older sister of a male
동생	dongsaeng	younger sibling	사촌	sachon	cousin
외삼촌	oesamchon	maternal uncle	친삼촌	chinsamchon	paternal uncle
이모	imo	maternal aunt	고모	gomo	paternal aunt
이모부	imobu	maternal aunt's husband	고모부	gomobu	paternal aunt's husband

When speaking of family members and possessions, use the "plural" possessives: **uri eomma** 우리 엄마 "my/our mom," **uri eonni** 우리 언니 "my/our sister," **uri jip** 우리 집 "my/our house," **uri cha** 우리 차 "our car" or to speak humbly to elders, **jeohui abeoji** 저희 아버지 "my/our father."

GRAMMAR NOTE Turn-taking/hedging/hesitation suffix -(으)ㄴ데/는데 -(eu)nde/neunde

Added at the end of a verb (or a sentence) **-(eu)nde/neunde** -(으)ㄴ데/는데 gives the impression that the speaker hasn't quite ended the conversation—that she is still thinking or giving the opportunity for the listener to consider the situation and then chime in. It is sort of like adding a long "Well …" in English, or a dangling "but…" or "so… ." This suffix is used mostly in conversation.

The speakers in the dialogue above can use the informal polite ending **-eoyo** -어요, but this ending is used for giving information and in conversation may come across as very factual or even too curt and rude. Compare the two responses to the same question.

Eunbi: Shall we go see it tomorrow? **Naeil gachi gaseo bolkkayo?**
내일 같이 가서 볼까요?

Aiden: I am a little busy tomorrow… (implied: perhaps some other time)
Naeireun jom bappeundeyo. 내일은 좀 바쁜데요.
  OR   I am busy tomorrow. (implied: that's final) **Naeireun bappayo.**
내일은 바빠요.

The **-(eu)nde/neunde** -(으)ㄴ데/는데 suffix is also used to emotionally connect with the interlocutor, that is, to let the speaker know that the listener is fully engaged in the conversation at hand (and ready to continue with the topic).

Eunbi: I just got this bag. **I gabang saero sasseoyo.**
이 가방 새로 샀어요.
Aiden: It looks cool! **Meosinneundeyo!** 멋있는데요!

The same suffix can also connect two short sentences to mean "well, however," not to contrast two different situations but to give some background before introducing another situation.

There are many restaurants and convenience stores nearby, too, but no air conditioning in the unit… **Geuncheo.e sikdang.irang pyeonuijeomdo maneunde apateu.e e.eokeoni eopseoyo.**
근처에 식당이랑 편의점도 많은데 아파트에 에어컨이 없어요.

They were open yesterday, but are closed today.
Eojeoneun yeoreonneunde oneureun dadasseoyo.
어제는 열었는데 오늘은 닫았어요.

Use **-eunde** -은데 with adjectives ending in a consonant, and **-nde** -ㄴ데 with adjectives that end in a vowel. For verbs, use **-neunde** -는데 for the present tense and **-nneunde** -ㅆ는데 for the past tense.

PATTERN PRACTICE 4
Practice the following conversations using the hedging suffix, -(으)ㄴ/는데 **-(eu)n/neunde**.
1. A: Here is my room. **Yeogiga naebang.ieyo.** 여기가 내 방이에요.
   B: It is pretty spacious! **Kkwae neolbeundeyo!** 꽤 넓은데요!
2. A: It's 10,000 won per bottle of beer. **Maekjuga han byeong.e man wonieyo.**
맥주가 한 병에 만 원이에요.
   B: Wow, it's really expensive! **Wa, jeongmal bissandeyo!**
와, 정말 비싼데요!

3. A: How's life in Korea? **Han.guk saenghwari eottaeyo?**
    한국 생활이 어때요?
    B: It is fun, but busy. **Jaemiinneunde bappayo.** 재미있는데 바빠요.
4. A: How's your apartment? **Apateuga ettaeyo?** 아파트가 어때요?
    B: It is very clean, but expensive. **Aju kkaekkeutande bissayo.**
    아주 깨끗한데 비싸요.

GRAMMAR NOTE -어서 *-eoseo* "so, therefore"

The connector **-eoseo** −어서 provides a logical reason or explanation for what
follows, equivalent to "so," "therefore" or "thus" in English.

It's on sale so it's (only) 50,000 won.
Jigeum seilhaeseo oman wonieyo. 지금 세일해서 오만 원이에요.

It's cheap so I'm going to buy it.
Ssaseo sal kkeoyeyo. 싸서 살 거예요.

It's close to work so I moved there.
Jikjang.eseo gakkawoseo geogiro isa gasseoyo.
직장에서 가까워서 거기로 이사 갔어요.

Thank you for coming. (*Lit.,* "you have come so I feel thankful")
Wajwoseo gomawo. 와줘서 고마워요.

PATTERN PRACTICE 5
Practice the following conversations using the logical consequence connector
-어서 **-eoseo**.
1. A: Why are you moving out? **Wae isagayo?** 왜 이사가요?
    B: The rent is expensive, so I am moving out. **Bangsega bissaseo isagayo.**
    방세가 비싸서 이사가요.
2. A: Why did you buy so much water? **Wae mureul ireoke mani sasseoyo?**
    왜 물을 이렇게 많이 샀어요?
    B: It was on sale, so I bought it/them. **Seilhaeseo sasseoyo.**
    세일해서 샀어요.
3. A: Why do you go to that convenience store? **Wae geu pyeonuijeome gayo?**
    왜 그 편의점에 가요?
    B: It is nearby, so I go (there). **Gakkawoseo gayo.** 가까워서 가요.

GRAMMAR NOTE The suffix -(으)ㄹ까요 *-(eu)lkkayo* "Shall we?"

The basic sense of the verb ending **-(eu)lkkayo** -(으)ㄹ까요 is *wondering*. It can
mean "I wonder…" or "Do you think…?," but when using it in a conversation
with someone else, it is often interpreted as "Should I?" or "Shall we?" and is
always a question.

Shall I come at 3 tomorrow? **Naeil se sie olkkayo?** 내일 세 시에 올까요?

Shall we go together? **Uri gachi galkkayo?** 우리 같이 갈까요?

Do you think it will rain again tomorrow?
Naeildo biga olkkayo? 내일도 비가 올까요?

Should I eat this, I wonder? **Igeo meogeulkkayo?** 이거 먹을까요?

PATTERN PRACTICE 6
Practice the following conversations using -(으)ㄹ까요 **-(eu)lkkayo** "shall we?"
1. A: Shall we meet at two? **Du sie mannalkkayo?** 두시에 만날까요?
   B: Yes, let's do it. **Ne, geuraeyo.** 네, 그래요.
2. A: Shall we watch a movie? **Yeonghwareul bolkkayo?** 영화를 볼까요?
   B: Yes, that sounds good. **Ne, joayo.** 네, 좋아요.
3. A: Shall we eat *bibimbap*? **Bibimbabeul meogeulkkayo?**
   비빔밥을 먹을까요?
   B: Well, how about *bulgogi*? **Geulsseyo. Bulgogiga eottaeyo?**
   글쎄요. 불고기가 어때요?

GRAMMAR NOTE ㅂ *p* and ㅎ *h*–irregulars

There are irregular verbs and adjectives in Korean, and they conjugate irregularly only with vowel-type suffixes, that is, those beginnig with **-eo/a** -어/아 or **-eu** -으 type.

    P ㅂ- irregular verbs and adjectives are those whose roots end in a **p** ㅂ that changes to **u** ㅜ (or sometimes ㅗ **o**) before vowel suffixes. The **u** ㅜ vowel contracts with the **-eo/a** -어/아 ending. Not all **p** ㅂ- final verbs are irregular.

DICTIONARY FORM	VERB *GO* (DO) AND -고 *-go*	PRESENT *EOYO/AYO* (DOES/IS) -어/아요 *-eo/ayo*	FUTURE *(EU)L KKEOYEYO* (WILL) -(으) 거예요 *-(eu)l kkeoyeyo*
돕다 **dopda** to help	돕고 **dopko**	도와요 (←도오+아요) **dowayo**	도울 거예요 (NOT 도오을 거예요) **doul kkeoyeyo**
가깝다 **gakkapda** be close	가깝고 **gakkapgo**	가까워요 (←가까우+어요) **gakkawoyo**	가까울 거예요 (NOT 가까우을 거예요) **gakkaul kkeoyeyo**
고맙다 **gomapda** be appreciative	고맙고 **gomapgo**	고마워요 (←고마우+어요) **gomawoyo**	고마울 거예요 (NOT 고마우을 거예요) **gomaul kkeoyeyo**

DICTIONARY FORM	VERB GO (DO) AND -고 -go	PRESENT EOYO/AYO (DOES/IS) -어/아요 -eo/ayo	FUTURE (EU)L KKEOYEYO (WILL) -(으) 거예요 -(eu)l kkeoyeyo
반갑다 ban.gapda be happy/pleased	반갑고 **ban.gapgo**	반가워요 (←반가우+어요) **ban.gawoyo**	반가울 거예요 (NOT 반가우을 거예요) **ban.gaul kkeoyeyo**

There are also **h** ㅎ-irregular adjectives. The final consonant **h** ㅎ disappears before **eu** 으-type suffixes and the vowel also changes to **ae** ㅐ before **eo/a** 어/아-type suffixes.

DICTIONARY FORM	VERB GO (IS) AND -고 -go	PRESENT EOYO/AYO (IS) -어/아요 -eo/ayo	(EU)LKKAYO I WONDER -(으)ㄹ까요 -(eu)lkkayo
어떻다 **eotteohda** how to be	어떻고 **eotteoko**	어때요 **eottaeyo**	어떨까요? **eotteolkkayo?**
그렇다 **geureohda** be so, be like that	그렇고 **geureoko**	그래요 **geuraeyo**	그럴까요? **geureolkkayo?**
빨갛다 **ppalgahda** be red	빨갛고 **ppalgako**	빨개요 **ppalgaeyo**	빨갈까요? **ppalgalkkayo?**

CULTURE NOTE **Where to live**

Unless they move to a larger city for schooling, Koreans usually live with their parents until they get married and begin a household of their own. In large cities, students are often able to attend a college in their hometown and commute to school, as public transportation is convenient. Some, however, will live in the dormitory or rent a tiny **wonnum** 원룸 (studio) or a single room, which comes with a bathroom and a kitchen. Other options include **dandokjutaek** 단독주택 (single houses), **apateu** 아파트 (similar to condos in the U.S.), **jusangbokap** 주상복합 (buildings with offices and retail spaces on lower floors and residences on upper floors), usually with a refrigerator and a washer/dryer in the unit, and **opiseutel** 오피스텔 (office + residence). Home, in Korea, is mainly a place to sleep, study, and be with one's family.

CULTURE NOTE **Physical space**

As is the case in a lot of cities around the world, including Seoul, physical space can be somewhat restrictive. People sit and stand quite close to each other, even with strangers, on the subway and in busy public spaces. It is common for people not to hold the door for others and to bump into people, especially on public transportation during rush hour. People may not always apologize, since the concept of "social circles" (politeness and honorifics in the language) also works in the physical culture.

EXERCISE 4

Minjoon and Emma are chatting. Answer Minjoon's questions, based on the given information using −(은)데/는데 -(eu)nde/neunde.

1. **Han.guk saenghwari eottaeyo?** 한국 생활이 어때요? (It is busy, but good)
2. **Apateuga eottaeyo?** 아파트가 어때요? (It is okay, but far.)
3. **Sikdang.i eottaeyo?** 식당이 어때요? (It is delicious, but expensive.)
4. **Iri eottaeyo?** 일이 어때요? (It is a little difficult, but fun.)

EXERCISE 5

At an M-mart, you ran into a Korean friend. Answer his questions using -어서 -eoseo.

1. Friend: **Wae eoje patie an wasseoyo?**
   왜 어제 파티에 안 왔어요?
   You: I (just) moved into a new studio, so I couldn't go.
2. Friend: **Wae isahaesseoyo?** 왜 이사했어요?
   You: The rent was expensive, so I moved out.
3. Friend: **Wae maekjureul sayo?** 왜 맥주를 사요?
   You: I have a party today, so I am buying beer.
4. Friend: **Mworeul chatgo isseoyo?** 뭐를 찾고 있어요?
   You: There is no refrigerator in the apartment, so I am looking for one.

EXERCISE 6

What would the following people suggest? Create questions based on the given information using −(으)ㄹ까요 -(eu)lkkayo?

Name	wants to
Aiden	watch a movie
Emma	go skiing (seuki tada) (스키 타다)
Minjoon	take a walk (sanchaekada) (산책하다)
Eunbi	cook together (yorihada) (요리하다)

1. **Aiden** 에이든 would suggest:
2. **Emma** 엠마 would suggest:
3. **Minjoon** 민준 would suggest:
4. **Eunbi** 은비 would suggest:

LESSON 7
Going Shopping

DIALOGUE 1 **What is the price?**

Emma is looking to buy a rice cooker for her apartment.

Sales Clerk: Come on in! What can I do for you? (*Lit.,* "What are you looking for?")
Eoseo oseyo. Mwo chajeuseyo?
어서 오세요. 뭐 찾으세요?

Emma: I'm looking for a rice cooker. (*Lit.,* "I have come, trying to see some rice cookers.")
Jeon.gi bapsot jom boryeogo wasseoyo.
전기 밥솥 좀 보려고 왔어요.

Sales Clerk: (A cooker that will make rice) for how many people?
Myeodinnyong chajeuseyo?
몇인용 찾으세요?

Emma: Do you have one for three people?
Sam innyong isseoyo?
3인용 있어요?

Sales Clerk: Of course. Please come this way and check things out.
Ne, geureomnyo. Ijjogeuro osyeoseo boseyo.
네, 그럼요. 이쪽으로 오셔서 보세요.
How about this one? It's a new item that came out this month.
I jepumi eotteoseyo? Ibeon dare naon sinjepumieyo.
이 제품이 어떠세요? 이번 달에 나온 신제품이에요.

Emma: Yes. It looks good. What is the price? I'm looking for one on the cheaper end.
Ne, joa boineyo. Gagyeogi eolmayeyo? Jom ssan geollo chatgo isseoyo.
네, 좋아 보이네요. 가격이 얼마예요? 좀 싼 걸로 찾고 있어요.

Sales Clerk: It's on sale now at 50,000 won. It can pressure-cook as well.
Jigeum seilhaeseo o.man wonieyo. Amnyeokdo dwaeyo.
지금 세일해서 5만 원이에요. 압력도 돼요.

Emma: Not bad! Please give me one of those.
Gwaenchanneyo. Geugeuro juseyo.
괜찮네요. 그거로 주세요.

VOCABULARY AND EXPRESSIONS

직원	jigwon	(sales) clerk
전기	jeon.gi	electric
밥솥	bapsot	rice cooker
몇인용	myeodinnyong	for use for how many people
삼인용	saminnyong	(designed for) three people
제품	jepum	product, sales item
이번 달	ibeon ttal	this month
신제품	sinjepum	new product
가격	gagyeok	price
오만 원	o.man won	50,000 won
압력	amnyeok	pressure
그거	geugeo	that one, that thing
좀 (= 조금)	jom (= jogeum)	a little (conversational softener used when making a request)
그럼요	geureomnyo	of course, certainly, sure (polite)
걸로 (= 것으로)	geollo (= geoseuro)	with/by that choice
-네요	-neyo	Gee…hmm! (suffix used with verb roots to express emotion)
찾으세요? (찾-)	chajeuseyo (chaj-)	look for, looking for (honorific, polite)
보려고요 (보-)	boryeogoyo (bo-)	trying to look at, intending to see
오셔서 (오-)	osyeoseo (o-)	come and… (honorific)
보세요 (보-)	boseyo (bo-)	please take a look (honorific)
어떠세요 (어떻-)	eoteoseyo (eotteoh-)	how is/how do you like…?
나온 (나오-)	naon (nao-)	(something that) came out
좋아 보이네요 (좋-, 보이-)	joa boineyo (joh-, boi-)	looks/seems good (polite)
싼 (싸-)	ssan (ssa-)	cheap
세일해서 (세일하-)	seilhaeseo (seilha-)	it's on sale so…
괜찮네요 (괜찮-)	gwaenchanneyo (gwaenchanh-)	fair, not bad, OK, no big deal
돼요 (되-)	dwaeyo (doe-)	possible

VOCABULARY PRACTICE 1

Give the Korean terms for the words described below.

1. You have to plug it in: _____
2. Something new to consider buying: _____
3. How much it costs: _____
4. Of course! _____

Supplementary Vocabulary

Color words

There are five native Korean color adjectives which are **h**-irregular. They take on different endings when used as nouns, when modifying nouns and when used at the end of a sentence. Other color terms are inherently nouns.

DICTIONARY FORM	NOUN	NOUN-MODIFYING FORM	PREDICATE FORM
빨갛다 **ppalgahda** to be red	빨간색 **ppalgansaek** the color red	빨간 가방 red bag **ppalgan gabang**	가방이 빨개요. **Gabang.i ppalgaeyo.** The bag is red.
노랗다 **norahda** to be yellow	노란색 **noransaek** the color yellow	노란 손수건 **noran sonsugeon** yellow handkerchief	손수건이 노래요. **Sonsugeoni noraeyo.** The handkerchief is yellow.
파랗다 **parahda** to be blue	파란색 **paransaek** the color blue	파란 셔츠 **paran syeocheu** blue shirt	셔츠가 파래요. **Sheocheuga paraeyo.** The shirt is blue.
까맣다 **kkamahda** to be black	까만색 **kkamansaek** the color black	까만 바지 **kkaman baji** black pants	바지가 까매요. **Bajiga kkamaeyo.** The pants are black.
하얗다 **hayahda** to be white	하얀색 **hayansaek** the color white	하얀 장갑 **hayan janggap** white gloves	장갑이 하얘요. **Janggabi hayaeyo.** The gloves are white.
회색 **hoesaek** the color gray	회색 **hoesaek** the color gray	회색 운동화 **hoesaek undonghwa** gray sneakers	운동화가 회색이에요. **Undonghwaga hoesaegieyo.** The sneakers are gray.
핑크색 **pinkeusaek** the color pink	핑크색 **pinkeusaek** the color pink	핑크색 구두 **pinkeusaek gudu** pink dress shoes	구두가 핑크색이에요. **Guduga pinkeusaegieyo.** The dress shoes are pink.
초록색 **choroksaek** the color green	초록색 **choroksaek** the color green	초록색 코트 **choroksaek koteu** green coat	코트가 초록색이에요. **Koteuga choroksaegieyo.** The coat is green.
오렌지색 **orenjisaek** the color orange	오렌지색 **orenjisaek** the color orange	오렌지색 펜 **orenjisaek pen** orange pen	펜이 오렌지색이에요. **Peni orenjisaegieyo.** The pen is orange.
보라색 **borasaek** the color purple	보라색 **borasaek** the color purple	보라색 공책 **borasaek gongchaek** purple notebook	공책이 보라색이에요. **Gongchaegi borasaegieyo.** The notebook is purple.

GRAMMAR NOTE Intention suffix -(으)려고 *-(eu)ryeogo*

You can use **-(eu)ryeogo** -(으)려고 when you want to express an intention, i.e., "trying to," "(in order) to," "intending to," or "thinking of" in English. Use the vowel **eu** 으 after verb roots that end in a consonant. In answering a question about why you are doing something, you can simply use up to **-(eu)ryeogo** -(으)려고 (and add **-yo** -요 for politeness) and leave the rest out.

I've come to find my friend.
Chin.gureul chajeuryeogo wasseoyo. 친구를 찾으려고 왔어요.

I made Korean friends in order to/so I could learn Korean.
Han.gungmareul bae.uryeogo Han.guk chin.gureul sagwi.eosseoyo.
한국말을 배우려고 한국 친구를 사귀었어요.

A: Why are you going there? **Geogie wae ga?** 거기 왜 가?
B: In order to get my lost wallet (back)/Trying to find my lost wallet.
Ireobeorin jigabeul chajeuryeogo. 잃어버린 지갑을 찾으려고.

PATTERN PRACTICE 1

Practice expressing your intentions using -(으)려고 **-(eu)ryeogo**.
1. A: What can I do for you? (*Lit.,* "What are you looking for?")
   Mwo chajeuseyo? 뭐 찾으세요?
   B: I'm looking for a rice cooker. **Jeon.gi bapsot jom boryeogo (wasseo)yo.**
   전기 밥솥 좀 보려고(왔어)요.
2. A: What are you doing? **Mwo haseyo?** 뭐 하세요?
   B: I am about to eat dinner. **Jeomsim meoreuryeogo (hae)yo.**
   점심 먹으려고(해)요.
3. A: What are you going to do tonight? **Oneul bame mwo haseyo?**
   오늘 밤에 뭐 하세요?
   B: I intend to watch a movie. **Yeonghwaleul bolyeogo (hae)yo.**
   영화를보려고(해)요.
4. A: When are you moving? **Eonje isahaseyo?** 언제 이사하세요?
   B: I plan to move next month. **Daeum dare isahaharyeogo (hae)yo.**
   다음 달에 이사하려고(해)요.

GRAMMAR NOTE Using -어 보여요/어 보이네요 *-eo boyeoyo/eo boineyo* to say "it looks..."

You can use **boyeoyo** 보여요 after another verb in **-eo/a** -어/아 form to express how something looks, e.g., "It *looks* good." **-Neyo** 네요 at the end helps to connect with the person you are interacting with. That is, it is a suffix to comment on others' and never yourself.

It looks good. **Joah boyeoyo.** 좋아 보여요.
It doesn't look bad, eh? **Gwaenchana boineyo.** 괜찮아 보이네요.
Gee, it looks comfortable! **Pyeonhae boineyo.** 편해 보이네요.

PATTERN PRACTICE 2

Practice these phrases using -어 보여요 **-eo boyeoyo**.
1. The room looks spacious. **Bang.i neolbeo boyeoyo.** 방이 넓어 보여요.
2. The apple looks delicious. **Sagwaga masisseo boyeoyo.**
   사과가 맛있어 보여요.
3. The rice cooker looks okay. **Jeon.gi bapsochi gwaenchana boyeoyo.**
   전기 밥솥이 괜찮아 보여요.
4. The book looks difficult. **Chaegi eoryeowo boyeoyo.** 책이 어려워 보여요.

GRAMMAR NOTE Sequential connector -어/아서 *-eo/aseo* "and there/then"

Attached to simple movement verbs like "go, come, sit, stand," and "lie down," the verbal connector **-eo/aseo** -어/아서 signals that the first action has taken place, and it was done to prepare for the next action to take place then and there.

Go (and) see it. **Gaseo bwayo.** 가서 봐요.

Sit and wait here. **Yeogi anjaseo gidariseyo.** 여기 앉아서 기다리세요.

Please come out and go right.
Nawaseo oreunjjogeuro gaseyo. 나와서 오른쪽으로 가세요.

Cut it and eat it. **Jallaseo deuseyo.** 잘라서 드세요.

PATTERN PRACTICE 3

Practice the following phrases.
1. Please come and sit down. **Yeogi waseo anjeuseyo.** 여기 와서 앉으세요.
2. Please go outside and go left. **Bakkeuro nagaseo oenjjogeuro gaseyo.**
   밖으로 나가서 왼쪽으로 가세요.
3. A: Shall we meet and watch a movie?
   Gachi mannaseo yeonghwa bolkkayo? 같이 만나서 갈까요?
   B: Yes, that sounds good. **Ne, joayo.** 네, 좋아요.

EXERCISE 1

What do you intend to do, or what are you thinking of doing? Answer the following questions using −(으)려고 **-(eu)ryeogo** based on the given information.

1. Sales Clerk: **Eoseo oseyo. Mwo chajeuseyo?**
   어서 오세요. 뭐 찾으세요?
   You: I am here to buy a rice cooker.
2. Real Estate Agent: **Eoseo oseyo. Etteoke osyeosseoyo?**
   어서 오세요. 어떻게 오셨어요?
   You: I am looking for a studio.
3. Roommate: **Jigeum mwo hago isseo?** 지금 뭐 하고 있어?
   You: I am about to eat lunch.
4. Friend: **Oneul bame mwo hal kkeoyeyo?**
   오늘 밤에 뭐 할 거예요?
   You: I plan to go shopping.

EXERCISE 2

Your Korean friend is asking how things look. Give her your opinion using −어 보여요 **-eo boyeoyo** based on the given information.

1. How does that rice cooker look to you? (looks expensive)
   Jeo jeon.gi bapsochi eottae boyeoyo? 전기 밥솥이 어때 보여요?
2. How does the room look to you? (looks nice)
   Bang.i eottae boyeoyo? 방이 어때 보여요?
3. How does that movie look to you? (looks like fun)
   Jeo younghwa eottae boyeo? 저 영화 어때 보여요?
4. How does this restaurant look to you? (looks okay)
   I sikdang eottae boyeoyo? 이 식당이 어때 보여요?

EXERCISE 3

Use −어서 **-eoseo** to invite your Korean co-worker to do things with you.

1. Please come here and eat with me.
2. Please sit here and watch TV with me.
3. Let's go out and have dinner together.

DIALOGUE 2 I'll pay with a credit card.

Aiden is looking for a dresser for his apartment.

Aiden: Excuse me…Do you have dressers?
   Jeo.. seorapjang isseoyo?
   저.. 서랍장있어요?

Salesman:	Yes, which color are you looking for?
	Ne, eotteon saeg chajeuseyo?
	네, 어떤 색 찾으세요?
Aiden:	A white one, please.
	Hayan saegiyo.
	하얀 색이요.
Salesman:	How about this one? It's a DIY one.
	Igeo eotteoseyo? Joripsigieyo.
	이거 어떠세요? 조립식이에요.
Aiden:	Oh, that's too big. Do you have something a bit smaller?
	A, Neomu keuneyo. Jom deo jageun geo isseoyo?
	아, 너무 크네요. 좀 더 작은 거 있어요?
Salesman:	Too big? How about this?
	Neomu keoyo? Igeon eotteoseyo?
	너무 커요? 이건 어떠세요?
Aiden:	It's just right. How much is it?
	Ttak jonneyo. Eolmayeyo?
	딱 좋네요. 얼마예요?
Salesman:	The total is 70,000 won. I'll ring it up. (*Lit.,* check it out).
	Modu chilman wonimnida. Gyeoljje dowadeurigesseumnida.
	모두 70,000만 원입니다. 결제 도와드리겠습니다.
Aiden:	I'll pay with a credit card.
	Sinyongkadeuro naelkkeyo.
	신용카드로 낼게요.
Salesman:	Is this a one-time payment or a monthly installment?
	Ilsibullo hasigesseoyo? Animyeon halburo hasigesseoyo?
	일시불로 하시겠어요? 아니면 할부로 하시겠어요?
Aiden:	It'll be a one-time payment.
	Ilsibullo halkkeyo.
	일시불로 할게요.
Salesman:	Got it. Just a moment, please. Please sign here. Do you need a receipt?
	Ne, algesseumnida. Jamsiman gidaryeo juseyo. Yeogi seomyeong butakdeurigesseumnida. Yeongsujeung piryohaseyo?
	네, 알겠습니다. 잠시만 기다려 주세요. 여기 서명 부탁드리겠습니다. 영수증 필요하세요?
Aiden:	(signing) Yes, please.
	Ne, juseyo.
	네, 주세요.
Salesman:	70,000 won has been charged to your BC card. Thank you!
	Bissi kadeuro chilman won gyeoljjehae deuryeosseumnida. Gamsahamnida.
	비씨 카드로 7만 원 결제해 드렸습니다. 감사합니다.

Aiden: OK. Thank you. Bye now.
            Ne, sugohaseyo. Annyeonghi gyeseyo.
            네, 수고하세요. 안녕히 계세요.

VOCABULARY AND EXPRESSIONS

조립식	**joripsik**	self-assembly, do-it-yourself
서랍장	**seorapjang**	dresser
색	**saek**	color
결제	**gyeoljje**	(credit card) processing
신용카드	**sinyongkadeu**	credit card
일시불	**ilsibul**	one-time payment/pay all at once
할부	**halbu**	monthly installment
서명	**seomyeong**	signature
영수증	**yeongsujeung**	receipt
잠시만 (= 잠깐만)	**jamsiman (= jamkkanman)**	for a minute, for a second
-으로	**euro**	choice marker after a noun ending in a consonant
-로	**lo**	choice marker after a noun ending in a vowel or ㄹ
어떤 (어떻-)	**eotteon (eotteoh-)**	what sort/kind of (modifier)
하얀 (하얗-)	**hayan (hayah-)**	white (used before a noun)
큰 (크-)	**keun (keu-)**	big
작은 (작-)	**jageun (jak-)**	small
주세요 (주-)	**juseyo (ju-)**	Please give (honorific, polite)
크네요 (크-)	**keuneyo (keu-)**	big, eh?
커요 (크-)	**keoyo (keu-)**	(it) is big
드릴까요 (드리-)	**deurilkkayo (deuri-)**	shall I give (humble, polite)
도와드리겠습니다 (돕-, 도와드리-)	**dowa.deurigesseumnida (dop-, deuri-)**	I will help you (humble, formal)
하시겠어요 (하-)	**hasigesseoyo (ha-)**	would you (honorific, polite)
낼게요 (내-)	**naelkkeyo (nae-)**	I will pay (informal)
알겠습니다 (알-)	**algesseumnida (al-)**	got it (humble, formal)
기다려주세요 (기다리-, 주-)	**gidaryeojuseyo (gidari-, ju-)**	wait, please (honorific, polite)
부탁드리겠습니다 (부탁드리-)	**butak.deurigeseumnida (deuri-)**	please, may I ask that you (humble, formal)
필요하세요? (필요하-)	**piryohaseyo? (piryoha-)**	do you need (honorific, polite)
결제해드렸습니다 (결제하-, 드리-)	**gyeoljjehae deuryeosseumnida. (gyeoljeha-, deuri.)**	I have processed (it) for you (humble, formal)
수고하세요 (수고하-)	**sugohaseyo (sugoha-)**	thank you (to a service provider)
안녕히 계세요 (안녕히 계시-)	**annyeonghi gyeseyo (gyesi-)**	goodbye (to the one staying)

VOCABULARY PRACTICE 2

Give the Korean terms for the words described below.
1. Instead of paying with cash or check: _____
2. Write this at the bottom of your checks or credit card receipts: _____
3. Where you keep your clothes: _____
4. I understand/Got it.: _____

GRAMMAR NOTE The choice marker -(으)로 –*(eu)ro* "by, as, with"

-(Eu)ro -(으)로 is a versatile marker that usually expresses a choice to accomplish something, e.g., when Aiden says **sinyongkadeuro** 신용카드로 "with a card" or **ilsibullo** 일시불로 "one-time payment," he is expressing his *choice* of payment methods. In Lesson 5, we used **Samcheung hoe.uisillo oseyo** 삼층 회의실로 오세요 "Please come to the meeting room on the third floor," showing the choice of rooms. Use the vowel **eu** after consonants except **l**.

for the first time	(toward) this way	with/using water	with/in Korean
cheo.eumeuro	**ijjogeuro**	**mullo**	**Han.gugeoro**
처음으로	이쪽으로	물로	한국어로

PATTERN PRACTICE 4

Practice these phrases with the choice marker -(으)로 **-(eu)ro**.
1. Please come this way. **Ijjogeuro oseyo.** 이쪽으로 오세요.
2. Please go to the meeting room. **Hoe.uisillo gasipsio.** 회의실로 가십시오.
3. It'll be a one-time payment. **Ilsibullo halkkeyo.** 일시불로 할게요.
4. I paid with a credit card. **Sinyongkadeuro gyeoljehaesseoyo.**
   신용카드로 결제했어요.

GRAMMAR NOTE Humble politeness suffix -겠 *-gess*

-Gess -겠 is a suffix that comes after a verb root and before other suffixes to express various ideas. One of these is to show the humbleness and politeness of the person speaking or asking a question. **-Gess** -겠 also replaces **-(eu)l kkeoyeyo** -(으)ㄹ 거예요 for polite and formal future tense (when asking others about their plans).

Could you sign here, please? **Yeogi seomyeong putak.deurigesseumnida.**
여기 서명 부탁드리겠습니다.

I will go tomorrow (humble statement). **Naeil gagesseumnida.**
내일 가겠습니다.

Would you like to pay for it all at once? (humble). **Ilsibullo hasigesseoyo?**
일시불로 하시겠어요?

PATTERN PRACTICE 5

Practice the following conversations with the humble politeness suffix −겠 **-gess**.

1. A: Would you like to pay for it all at once? **Ilsibullo hasigesseoyo?**
   일시불로 하시겠어요?

   B: Yes, I would like to pay for it all. **Ne, ilsibullo halkkeyo.**
   네, 일시불로 할게요.

2. A: When would you like to come? **Eonje osigesseoyo?**
   언제 오시겠어요?

   B: I would like to come tomorrow. **Naeil gagesseumnida.**
   내일 가겠습니다.

3. A: Could you sign here, please? **Yeogi seomyeong butak. deurigessumnida.**
   여기 서명부탁드리겠습니다.

   B: Yes, I see. (Yes, I will.) **Ne, algesseumnida.** 네, 알겠습니다.

GRAMMAR NOTE The honorific suffix -(으)시 *–(eu)si*

-(Eu)seyo -(으)세요 is the honorific suffix **-(eu)si** -(으)시 conjugated in the informal polite-style speech ending **-(eo)yo** -(어)요. This honorific suffix is often used in commands, but it can also be used when talking *about* the doer of an action who is someone of high social status or honor, such as when talking to a sibling or child *about* what your boss or grandparents do, e.g., **Halmeonido oseyo?** 할머니도 오세요? "Is Grandmother also coming?" Never use this honorific suffix to talk about yourself.

Waiter: How many of you? **Myeot buniseyo?** 몇 분이세요?
You: (There are) three of us. **Se myeong.ieyo.** 세 명이에요.

-(Eu)si -(으)시 can be used with any speech style and with various kinds of suffixes, following the verb root. With the formal **-mnida** -ㅂ니다/**mnikka** ㅂ니까 suffix, it becomes **-(eu)simnida** -(으)십니다/**(eu)simnikka** (으)십니까. With the past tense, you get **-(eu)syeoss** -(으)셨, and with the future tense **-(eu)sil** -(으)실.

Who are you?   Who are you, if I may ask?
Nuguyeyo? 누구예요?   **Nuguseyo?** 누구세요?

Where are you?   Might I ask where you are?
Eodiyeyo? 어디예요?   **Eodiseyo?** 어디세요?

Sit down, please.   Please have a seat.
Anjayo. 앉아요.   **Anjeuseyo.** 앉으세요.

The verb loses its final consonant if it ends in **l** ㄹ for **-(eu)se** -(으)세 conjugations.

Are you going to buy this?	Would you be planning to buy this?
Igeuro sal kkeoyeyo?	**Igeoseuro sasigesseumnikka?**
이거로 살 거예요?	이것으로 사시겠습니까?
Are you going to live there?	Would you be planning to live there?
Geogi sal kkeoyeyo?	**Geogi sasail kkeoyeyo/kkeomnikka?**
거기 살 거예요?	거기 사실 거예요/겁니까?
Where did he/she go?	Where did he/she (the honorable person) go?
Eodi gasseoyo?	**Eodi gasyeosseoyo** (informal)/
어디 갔어요?	**gasyeosseumnikka** (formal)**?**
	어디 가셨어요/가셨습니까?

PATTERN PRACTICE 6
Practice the following conversations. Pay attention to the honorific suffix -(으)시 **-(eu)si**.
1. A: Who is it? **Nuguseyo?/Nugusimnikka?** 누구세요?/ 누구십니까?
   B: It's me. **Jeoyeyo.** 엠마예요.
2. A: Where are you going? **Eodi gaseyo?/gasimnikka?**
   어디 가세요?/가십니까?
   B: I am going to the office. **Samusire gayo.** 사무실에 가요.
3. A: What are you doing? **Jigeum mwo haseyo?/hasimnikka?**
   지금 뭐 하세요?/ 하십니까?
   B: I am about to eat lunch. **Jeomsim meogeuryeogo(hae)yo.**
   점심 먹으려고(해)요.

GRAMMAR NOTE **Informal style conjugation -으 -eu-verbs**
To conjugate verbs ending in **eu** ㅡ for **eu** ㅡ-type and consonant-type suffixes, just add the suffix. For the **-eo** ㅓ-type suffixes, drop the vowel **eu** ㅡ, then follow the core conjugation rule based on the previous vowel. If the second from the last vowel in the verb root is **a** ㅏ or **o** ㅗ, then the suffix vowel to use is **a** ㅏ; for all others, use **eo** ㅓ. If there is no "previous" vowel, simply use the default vowel **eo** ㅓ.

DICTIONARY FORM	[VERB] + AND -고 -go	FUTURE -(으) 거예요 - (eu)l kkeoyeyo	PAST -었/았어요 -eoss/asseoyo
크다 keuda big, grow	크고 keugo	클 거예요 keul kkeoyeyo	컸어요 keosseoyo
모으다 moeuda collect	모으고 moeugo	모을 거예요 moeul kkeoyeyo	모았어요 moasseoyo
담그다 damgeuda dunk, sink	담그고 damgeugo	담글 거예요 damgeul kkeoyeyo	담갔어요 damgasseoyo

GRAMMAR NOTE **Endings and connectors**

By now you have learned a number of endings that attach to verbs for different meanings and speech styles. "Connector endings" link two sentences together into one long sentence, and "mood endings" show the speaker's attitude or mood mental state (such as surprise, realization, wondering, etc.) or her social relationship to the listener (e.g., polite and formal vs. informal endings).

Shall we/I go there and sleep (and then come back)?
Gaseo jago olkka? 가서 자고 올까?

I have come to Korea to learn Korean.
Han.gungmareul bae.uryeogo Han.guge wasseoyo.
한국말을 배우려고 한국에 왔어요.

If it rains, don't go out.
Biga omyeon nagaji maseyo. 비가 오면 나가지 마세요.

CULTURE NOTE **Where to shop in Korea**

A range of shopping options can be found in Korea, from hole-in-the-wall mom-and-pop grocery stores, to daily amenity stores to **pyeonuijeom** 편의점 (chain convenience stores). Many apartment complexes have food courts, grocery and other useful stores on the ground floor (**jusang bokap bilding** 주상 복합 빌딩) or in a separate building (**sang.ga** 상가). Various products like clothing, shoes and household items are also available at large supermarkets (e.g., E-Mart and HomePlus), many of which offer free delivery service with a minimum purchase. Alternatively, you can shop online at G Market, Auction, Lotte Mart and E Mart.

Public market places, and cheap, trendy clothing stores are also located near major college districts in Seoul. Then there are underground/basement stores (**jihasang.ga** 지하상가), around subway and intercity bus stations, with shops selling clothes, shoes, cosmetics, and gift items, often with snack bars and restaurants at especially reasonable prices.

EXERCISE 4

How would you say the following in Korean using the choice marker -(으)로 **-(eu)ro**?

1. Please go this way.
2. Please do a one-time payment.
3. I will go down by elevator (if it's okay).
4. I will pay by credit card (if it's okay).

EXERCISE 5

What did the sales clerk say in Korean for you to answer as follows? Use the humble politeness suffix -겠 **-gess** .

1. Sales Clerk: How would you like to pay?
   You: **Keuredit kadeuro naelkkeyo.** 크레딧 카드로 낼게요.
2. Sales Clerk: Would you like to pay it all?
   You: **Ne, ilsibullo halkkeyo.** 네, 일시불로 할게요.
3. Sales Clerk: Would you please sign here?
   You: **Ne, geureolkkeyo.** 네, 그럴게요.

EXERCISE 6

Describe what these people do using the honorific suffix -(으)시 **-(eu)si**.

1. Grandmother exercises.
2. Father goes to church (교회 **gyohoe**) on Sundays.
3. Mother is reading a book.
4. Grandfather is playing tennis now.

엠마 씨, 안녕하세요?
Hi Emma!

오랜만이에요!
Long time no see!

안녕하세요, 팀장님.
Hello, Mr. Kim.

오늘 회사 끝나고 동료들이랑 노래방에 가기로 했어요.
Some co-workers and I are going to a noraebang tonight after work.

같이 안 가실래요?
Don't you want to come with us?

글쎄요.
Oh, I don't know.

노래 잘 못 하는데요.
I'm not a good singer.

못 불러도 돼요!
You don't have to sing well!

같이 갑시다!
Come with (us)!

네. 갈게요.
Okay, I'll go.

LESSON 8

Inviting Friends to a *Noraebang*

🔘 **DIALOGUE 1** **Don't you want to come with us?**

Minjoon and Emma haven't seen each other for a while. Minjoon invites Emma to a *noraebang* outing with other colleagues.

Minjoon: Hi Emma! Long time no see!
            Emma ssi, annyeonghaseyo? Oraenmanieyo!
            엠마 씨, 안녕하세요? 오랜만이에요!
Emma: Hello, Mr. Kim. Is your baby growing well (how's your baby)?
            Annyeonghaseyo, timjang.nim, agineun jal keoyo?
            안녕하세요, 팀장님, 아기는 잘 커요?
Minjoon: Oh, he's growing well! By the way, some co-workers and I are going to a *noraebang* tonight after work. Don't you want to come with us?
            Aju jal keugo isseoyo. Geureonde oneul hoesa kkeunnago dongnyodeurirang noraebang.e gagiro haesseoyo. Gachi an gasillaeyo?
            아주 잘 크고 있어요. 그런데 오늘 회사 끝나고 동료들이랑 노래방에 가기로 했어요. 같이 안 가실래요?
Emma: Oh, I don't know. I'm not a good singer.
            Geulsseyo. Norae jal mot haneundeyo.
            글쎄요. 노래 잘 못 하는데요.
Minjoon: You don't have to sing well! Come with (us)! We are going to meet at the company's main entrance at 6 PM.
            Mot bulleodo dwaeyo! Gachi gapsida! Hoesa jeongmun apeseo yeoseot sie mannagiro haesseoyo.
            못 불러도 돼요! 같이 갑시다! 회사 정문 앞에서 6 시에 만나기로 했어요.
Emma: Okay, I'll go.
            Ne. Galkkeyo.
            네. 갈게요.

VOCABULARY AND EXPRESSIONS

아기	agi	baby
오늘	oneul	today
회사	hoesa	company
동료들	dongnyodeul	colleagues, co-workers
노래방	noraebang	karaoke room, singing room

노래	norae	song, singing
잘	jal	well
같이	gachi	together
안	an	not
못	mot	can't
글쎄요	geulsseyo	not sure, I don't know
정문	jeongmun	main gate, main entry
-이랑	irang	together with; and (used after a noun that ends in a consonant)
-랑	rang	together with; and (used after a noun that ends in a vowel)
-에	e	to
오랜만이에요 (오랜만이-)	oraenmanieyo (oraenmani-)	It's been a long time!
커요 (크-)	keoyo (keu-)	grows
크고 있어요 (크-, 있-)	keugo isseoyo (keu-, iss-)	is growing
끝나고 (끝나-)	kkeunnago (kkeutna-)	after (it) ends
가기로 했어요 (가-, 하-)	gagiro haesseoyo (ga-, ha-)	decided to go
가실래요 (가-)	gasillaeyo (ga-)	want to go, feel like going
불러도 (부르-)	bulleodo (bureu-)	even if you sing/call out
돼요 (되-)	dwaeyo (doe-)	it's OK, it works
갑시다 (가-)	gapsida (ga-)	let's go (semi-formal)
만나기로 했어요 (만나-, 하-)	mannagiro haesseoyo (manna-, ha-)	decided to meet, are going to meet
알았어요 (알-)	arasseoyo (al-)	knew it, got it
갈게요 (가-)	galkkeyo (ga-)	will go (promise, offer)

VOCABULARY PRACTICE 1

Give the Korean terms for the words described below.

1. a place to sing songs with friends: _____
2 the people you work with: _____
3. the day before tomorrow: _____
4. Long time, no see!: _____

GRAMMAR NOTE -기로 했어요 *-Giro haesseoyo* "have made an arrangement to/have decided to"

-Giro haesseoyo -기로 했어요 attaches to the verb root and adds the meaning "(I) have decided to (thus, am going to)." You can also use it to talk about an arrangement that has been made by someone else.

Some co-workers and I have arranged to go to a *noraebang* tonight after work.
Oneul hoesa kkeunnago dongnyodeuriang noraebang.e gagiro haesseoyo.
오늘 회사 끝나고 동료들이랑 노래방에 가기로 했어요.

I have decided to quit smoking as of today.
Oneulbuteo dambaereul kkeunkiro haesseoyo.
오늘부터 담배를 끊기로 했어요.

PATTERN PRACTICE 1

Practice expressing your resolution using −기로 했어요 **-giro haesseoyo** in the following conversations.

1. A: What are you doing tonight after work?
      Oneul hoesa kkeunnago mwo haseyo? 오늘 회사 끝나고 뭐 하세요?
   B: I've decided to go to the *noraebang*.
      Noraebang.e gagiro haesseoyo. 노래방에 가기로 했어요.
2. A: What are you doing today after class?
      Oneul sueop kkeunnago mwo haseyo? 오늘 수업 끝나고 뭐 하세요?
   B: I've decided to study with my friend.
      Chin.gurang gongbuhagiro haesseoyo. 친구랑 공부하기로 했어요.
3. A: When did you decide to quit smoking?
      Eonjebuteo dambaereul kkeunkiro haesseoyo?
      언제부터 담배를 끊기로 했어요?
   B: I've decided to quit smoking starting tomorrow.
      Naeilbuteo kkeunkiro haesseoyo. 내일부터 끊기로 했어요.
4. A: When are you going to move? **Eonje isahagiro haesseoyo?**
      언제 이사하기로 했어요?
   B: I've decided to move next month. **Da.eum dare isahagiro haesseoyo.**
      다음 달에 이사하기로 했어요.

GRAMMAR NOTE Immediate plan/desire suffix -(으)ㄹ래요 -(eu)llaeyo "I feel like"

-(Eu)llaeyo -(으)ㄹ래요, which can only be used between "I" and "you," captures a light-hearted intention or immediate desire, the Korean equivalent of "I wanna…" or "I'm gonna…" or "Do you feel like (doing something)?" The honorific version is **-(eu)sillaeyo?** -(으)실래요?, and there is no formal form because of the informality of the meaning.

Would you like to come with? **Gachi gasillaeyo?** 같이 가실래요?
I don't wanna eat. **Nan an meogeullaeyo.** 난 안 먹을래요.

PATTERN PRACTICE 2

Practice expressing your immediate plan/desire using -(으)ㄹ래요 -(eu)llaeyo in the following conversations.

1. A: What do you wanna do/what shall we do? **Mwo hallaeyo?** 뭐 할래요?
   B: I wanna go to the *noraebang*! **Noraebang gallaeyo!** 노래방 갈래요.

2. A: Do you want to buy this rice cooker?
       I jeon.gi bapsot sallaeyo? 이 전기 밥솥 살래요?
    B: Yes, I wanna buy it! **Ne, sallaeyo!** 네, 살래요!
3. A: Shall we drink coffee? **Keopi masilkkayo?** 커피 마실까요?
    B: No, I don't wanna drink any.
       Aniyo. An masillaeyo. 아니요. 안 마실래요.
4. A: Shall we watch a comedy movie?
       Komedi yeonghwa bolkkayo? 코메디 영화볼까요?
    B: No, I wanna watch an action movie.
       Aniyo. Aeksyeon yeonghwa bollaeyo. 아니요. 액션 영화볼래요.

GRAMMAR NOTE "Even though (something) happens" -어도
                  -eodo

-Eodo dwaeyo -어도 돼요 (variations include **-ado dwaeyo** -아도 돼요 or
just **-do dwaeyo** -도 돼요) is a composite ending that has two parts **-eodo**
-어도 "although" or "even though" and **dwaeyo** 돼요 "becomes," "works" or
"is OK." Together they mean "Even if this happens, it's okay." **Dwaeyo** 돼요 is
just a filler word for "OK," so you can use other words such as **gwaenchanayo**
괜찮아요 and **joayo** 좋아요.

Can I sit here? (Is it okay if I sit here?)
Yeogi anjado dwaeyo? 여기 앉아도 돼요?

You may read that book. **Geu chaek ilgeodo joayo.** 그 책 읽어도 좋아요.

You don't have to sing well. (It's OK to not sing well.)
Norae motbulleodo gwaenchanayo. 노래 못불러도 괜찮아요.

PATTERN PRACTICE 3
Practice asking for permission to do using -어도 돼요 **-eodo dwaeyo** in the
following conversations.
1. A: May I sit here? **Yeogi anjado dwaeyo?** 여기 앉아도 돼요?
    B: Yes, please sit. **Ne, anjeuseyo.** 네, 앉으세요.
2. A: May I read this book? **I chaek ilgeodo gwaenchanayo?**
       이 책 읽어도 괜찮아요?
    B: Yes, please read. **Ne, ilgeuseyo.** 네, 읽으세요.
3. A: I don't have money now. **Jigeum doni eopseoyo.** 지금 돈이 없어요.
    B: You may pay by credit card. **Sinyongkadeuro naedo dwaeyo.**
       신용카드로 내도 돼요.
4. A: I cannot sing. **Jeoneun norae mot bulleoyo.** 저는 노래 못 불러요.
    B: You don't need to sing well. (It is okay not to be good at singing.)
       Norae mot bulleodo gwaenchanayo. 노래 못 불러도 괜찮아요.

GRAMMAR NOTE **Irregular verbs**

There are several kinds of verbs that have alternative root shapes such as **chupgo** 춥고 "cold and" and **chuwoyo** 추워요 "is cold." As you saw in Lesson 6, the **chupda** 춥다 kind is called "p-irregular." The root ends in a **p** that turns into an **u** (showing up as **wo** 워 or **wa** 와) in the alternative root form (before the **eo** 어 and **eu** 으-type vowel suffixes). You already know **geureohda** 그렇다 to be a **h** ㅎ-irregular verb as well.

There are also **t** ㄷ irregular verbs (the final **t** ㄷ is replaced by **r** ㄹ), **s** ㅅ-irregular verbs (the final **s** ㅅ alternates with nothing, or, "the ghost of **s** ㅅ,") and the **reu** 르 irregular verbs (**reu** 르 alternates with **ll** ㄹㄹ). Consonant-initial suffixes like **-go** -고, **-gi** -기, and **-giro** -기로 do not affect these verbs and adjectives. Simply add the suffix to the verb root.

When the suffix starts with a vowel like **-eoyo** -어요 or **-eodo dwaeyo** -어도 돼요 (i.e., the **eo** 어-type) and **-(eu)seyo** -(으)세요 or **-(eu)ryeogo** -(으)려고 (i.e., the **eu** 으-type), the alternative root is used.

DICTIONARY FORM	-고 *-go* (DO) AND	PRESENT -어요/아요 *eoyo/ayo* (DOES/IS)	FUTURE -(으)ㄹ 거예요 *(eu)l geyeyo* (WILL)
걷다 **geotda** to walk	걷고 **geotgo** walk and	걸어요 **georeoyo** walk/walking	걸을 거예요 **georeul kkeoyeyo** will walk
묻다 **mutda** to ask	묻고 **mutgo** ask and	물어요 **mureoyo** ask/asking	물을 거예요 **mureul kkeoyeyo** will ask
낫다 **nasda** to get/be better	낫고 **nasgo** get better and	나아요 **na.ayo** get/getting better	나을 거예요 **na.eul kkeoyeyo** will get better
젓다 **jeosda** to stir	젓고 **jeosgo** stir and	저어요 **jeoeoyo** stirring	저을 거예요 **jeo.eul kkeoyeyo** will stir

Reu 르- irregular verbs are a little different; you use their alternative forms only before the **eo** 어 suffixes in standard Korean. For fast-spoken colloquial Korean, however, native speakers frequently use the alternative form before the **eu** 으 suffixes as well.

DICTIONARY FORM	-고 *-go* (DO/IS) AND	PRESENT -어요 *eoyo* (DOES/IS)	FUTURE -(으)ㄹ 거예요 *(eu)l geyeyo* (WILL)
목마르다 **mokmareuda** thirsty	목마르고 **mokmareugo** thirsty and	목말라요 **mokmallayo** is thirsty	목마를 거예요 **mokmareul kkeoyeyo** will be thirsty
배부르다 **baebureuda** full	배부르고 **baebureugo** full and	배불러요 **baebulleoyo** is full	배부를 거예요 **baebureul kkeoyeyo** will be full

CULTURE NOTE Body language and 글쎄요 *geulsseyo*

When saying **geulsseyo** 글쎄요 "I am not sure. I don't know…," to act more like a native Korean, inhale between the teeth and tilt your head to one side. Koreans will be amused that you have picked up the language properly!

EXERCISE 1

Minjoon has decided to do the following in the new year. Use -기로 했어요 **-giro haesseoyo** to describe Minjoon's resolutions.
1. Minjoon has decided to exercise every day.
2. Minjoon has decided to quit smoking.
3. Minjoon has decided not to watch TV.
4. Minjoon has decided to study English harder. (harder: 더 열심히 **deo yeolsimhi**)

EXERCISE 2

Role play with your friend. Ask and answer the questions in Korean based on the given information.
1. Shall we watch this movie?   (No, I don't wanna watch it.)
2. Shall we go to the *noraebang*?   (Yes, I wanna go.)
3. Do you want to eat *bibimbap*?   (No, I don't wanna eat.)
4. Do you want to go shopping?   (Yes, I wanna go shopping.)

EXERCISE 3

Your new colleague asks a lot of questions regarding what is allowed in the office. Practice the following conversations in Korean, using -어도 되다 **-eodo doeda**.
1. May I use this computer?   (Yes, you may.)
2. May I drink this coffee?   (Yes, you may.)
3. May I do this work tomorrow?   (Yes, you may.)
4. May I pay by credit card at the cafeteria?   (No, you may not.)

DIALOGUE 2 I'm sorry, I have another appointment.

Eunbi invites Aiden to the after-work *noraebang* outing, but he has a previous engagement.

Eunbi: Hi, Aiden. We're all going to a *noraebang* tonight. Wanna come with?
Eideun ssi, oneul jeonbu noraebang.e ganeunde, gachi an gallaeyo?
에이든 씨, 오늘 전부 노래방에 가는데, 같이 안 갈래요?

Aiden: Oh. I'm sorry, I have another appointment, so I don't think I can go today.
A. Mianhandeyo, dareun yaksogi isseoseo oneul mot gagesseoyo.
아. 미안한데요, 다른 약속이 있어서 오늘 못 가겠어요.

Eunbi: Oh, really? What time is your appointment? Can you meet us there after it ends? Let's go!
A, jeongmallyo? Yaksogi myeot siyeyo? Yaksok kkeunnago mot wayo? Gapsida!
아, 정말요? 약속이 몇 시예요? 약속 끝나고 못 와요? 갑시다!

Aiden: We're meeting for drinks, so it'll be late.
Sul yaksogiraseo neujeojil kkeoyeyo.
술 약속이라서 늦어질 거예요.

Eunbi: Then you can come with us at 6 PM and then go to your appointment. Emma will come, too.
Geureomyeon yeoseot sie urihago meonjeo nolgo geu da.eume yaksoge gaseyo. Emma ssido ol kkeoyeyo.
그러면 6 시에 우리하고 먼저 놀고 그 다음에 약속에 가세요. 엠마 씨도 올 거예요.

Aiden: Haha. It sounds like fun. But I really can't join you (*Lit.,* play together) this time. I'll come along next time.
Haha. Jaemiitgenneyo. Geunde ibeonen jeongmal gachi mon norayo. Da.eume gachi galkkeyo.
하하. 재미있겠네요. 근데 이번엔 정말 같이 못 놀아요. 다음에 같이 갈게요.

Eunbi: OK. We'll make sure you'll join us next time!
Joayo. Geureom da.eumen kkok gachi gapsida!
좋아요. 그럼 다음엔 꼭 같이 갑시다!

VOCABULARY AND EXPRESSIONS

약속	yaksok	promise, appointment
술	sul	alcohol, booze, liquor
우리	uri	we, us
전부	jeonbu	altogether, everyone, everything

먼저	meonjeo	first, before others
다음	da.eum	next (time, one)
다	da	every(one, thing), all
이번엔 (= 이번에는)	ibeonen (= ibeonenun)	this time (around)
다음엔 (= 다음에는)	da.eumen (= da.eumeneun)	next time (around)
-하고	hago	together with, and
		(connects two nouns)
와요 (오-)	wayo (o-)	come
이라서 (= 이어서) (이-)	iraseo (= ieoseo) (i-)	(it is the case) so
늦어질 거예요 (늦어지-, 이-)	neujeojil kkeoyeyo (neujeoji-, i-)	will be late, will get late
놀고 (놀-)	nolgo (nol-)	play and (then)
알지요? (알-)	aljiyo (al-)	(I) know, right?
재미있겠네요 (재미있-)	jaemiitgenneyo (jaemiiss-)	sounds (like) fun

VOCABULARY PRACTICE 2

Give the Korean terms for the words described below.
1. after this: _____
2. wine, beer, other spirits: _____
3. none, some, or _____
4. a commitment to do something: _____

GRAMMAR NOTE Noun-modifying suffix for adjectives -(으)ㄴ
-(eu)n

As you might have noticed, predicate adjectives (at the end of the sentence) conjugate just like verbs do in Korean:

(It's) convenient/comfortable. **Pyeonhaeyo.** 편해요.
I need more time.
Sigani deo pirohaeyo. 시간이 더 필요해요. (*Lit.*, More time is needed.)

When adjectives come before the noun they modify, however, use the suffix **-eun** -은 after adjective roots that end in a consonant or **-n** ㄴ after those that end in a vowel. Remember that **piryoha** 필요하 "need" is an adjective in Korean, and there will be some irregularities in conjugation for some adjectives because the suffix begins with the vowel **eu** 으:

(pyeonha-)	pyeonhan uija	a comfortable chair
편하-	편한 의자	
(piryoha-)	piryohan don	the necessary money
필요하-	필요한 돈	(the amount needed)
(gwaenchanh-)	gwaenchaneun sosik	decent news
괜찮-	괜찮은 소식	

(bangap-) 반갑-	ban.gawun saram 반가운 사람	someone you are happy to see
(keu-) 크-	keun il 큰 일	a big deal, a huge matter
(dareu-) 다르-	dareun yaksok 다른 약속	a different appointment

PATTERN PRACTICE 4

Practice these phrases using the noun-modifying suffix for adjectives, -(으)ㄴ -(eu)n.
1. The dresser is cheap. **Otjang.i ssayo.** 옷장이 싸요.
   Do you have a cheap dresser? **Ssan otjang isseoyo?** 싼 옷장이 있어요?
2. The room is okay. **Bang.i gwaenchanayo.** 방이 괜찮아요.
   Do you have a good/"okay" room? **Gwaenchanun bang isseoyo?**
   괜찮은 방 있어요?
3. The apartment is big. **Apateuga keoyo.** 아파트가 커요.
   I need a big apartment. **Keun apateuga piryohaeyo.** 큰 아파트가 필요해요.
4. The movie is fun. **Yeonghwaga jaemiisseoyo.** 영화가 재미있어요.
   Do you want to go see a fun movie?
   Jaemiinneun yeonghwa boreo gallaeyo? 재미있는 영화 보러 갈래요?

GRAMMAR NOTE Expressing change of state: -어지 *–eoji*

-Eoji -어지 attaches to an adjective to show change of state, "become" or "get" such-and-such. It also gives the sense of comparison "more than expected." You will mostly hear this used in completed events (**-eojyeosseoyo** -어졌어요) or events that have not yet occurred (**-eojil kkeoyeyo** -어질 거예요).

The weather has gotten colder.
Nalssiga deo chuwojyeosseoyo. 날씨가 더 추워졌어요.

I've got some business (to take care of) so I'll be late again today.
Iri isseoseo onuldo neujeojil kkeoyeyo.
일이 있어서 오늘도 늦어질 거예요.

PATTERN PRACTICE 5

Practice the following conversations. Pay attention to -어지 **-eoji**, which is used to express a change.
1. A: How's the weather? **Nalssiga eottaeyo?** 날씨가 어때요?
   B: The weather has gotten colder. **Deo chuwojyeosseoyo.** 더 추워졌어요.
2. A: How's your room? **Bang.i eottaeyo?** 방이 어때요?
   B: It has gotten cleaner. **Deo kkaekkeutaejyeosseoyo.** 더 깨끗해졌어요.

3. A: What do you think the weather will be tomorrow?
       Naeireun nalssiga eotteolkkayo? 내일은 날씨가 어떨까요?
    B: It will become better. **Joajil kkeoyeyo.** 좋아질 거예요.

GRAMMAR NOTE Using -(으)ㄹ 거예요 *-(eu)l kkeoyeyo* "going to" or "I'm sure"

-(Eu)l kkeoyeyo -(으)ㄹ 거예요 is used to state your own plans (first person "I") or ask about those of the person you are talking to (second person "you"). When used with a third person ("it", "she," or "he"), it expresses your conjectures about what they are going to do only when you are quite certain. **-(Eu)l kkeoyeyo** -(으)ㄹ 거예요 is a simple objective conjecture about the future, and a space precedes **kkeoyeyo** 거예요.

Other "future" endings come with an added nuance: **-(eu)lkkeyo** -(으)ㄹ게요 conveys the sense "if you are OK with my proposal," and **-gess** 겠 conveys the sense of "based on my personal judgment, I think it will be the case."

Emma will be coming, too (I'm sure).
Emma ssido ol kkeoyeyo. 엠마 씨도 올 거예요.

It looks like it's going to rain. **Biga ogesseoyo.** 비가 오겠어요.

PATTERN PRACTICE 6
Practice expressing a strong prediction or future plan using -(으)ㄹ 거예요 **-(eu)l kkeoyeyo**.
1. A: Is Emma coming? **Emma ssido wayo?** 엠마씨도 와요?
    B: Yes, she will be coming. **Ne, ol kkeoyeyo.** 네, 올 거예요.
2. A: Are you coming to the *noraebang*? **Noraebang.e ol kkeoyeyo?**
       노래방에 올 거예요?
    B: Yes, but I will probably be late. **Ne, geureonde ama neujeul kkeoyeyo.**
       네, 그런데 아마 늦을 거예요.
3. A: When do you think Emma will be moving out?
       Emma ssiga eonje isahal kkeoyeyo? 엠마씨가 언제 이사할 거예요?
    B: Maybe next month or so. **Ama da.eum daljjeum isahal kkeoyeyo.**
       아마 다음 달쯤 이사할 거예요.

GRAMMAR NOTE Coming and going

Koreans use the word **gayo** 가요 "go," whenever they move away from where they are (or where they will be). In situations when English speakers may say "come," Koreans say "go."

A: Are you coming to my house today?
   Oneul uri jibe ol kkeoyeyo? 오늘 우리 집에 올 거예요?

B: No, I'll come tomorrow. (*Lit.,* I'll <u>go</u> tomorrow.)
Ani. Naeil galkkeyo. 아니. 내일 갈게요.

Useful Tip: Pronunciation of 못 *mot*

Mot 못 may be pronounced differently, depending on how fast you're speaking and the words that follow.

Mot wayo? 못 와요? Can't you come?	[**Modwayo?**] 모돠요?
Mot gayo. 못 가요. I can't go.	[**Mokkayo.**] 목까요
Mot norayo? 못 놀아요? Can't you play?	[**Monnorayo?**] 몬노라요
Mot haeyo. 못 해요. I can't.	[**Motaeyo.**] 모태요

CULTURE NOTE **Major cultural events**

설날 **seolnal**, Lunar New Year's Day, and 추석 **chuseok,** the Fall Moon Harvest, are the two main traditional holidays when Koreans visit their parents and relatives. Other national holidays such as Memorial Day, Independence Day, and National Foundation Day offer Korean families breaks from school and work. Buddha's Birthday is a colorful and festive holiday for many Korean Buddhists, and Christmas brings Christians to churches. For non-believers, however, Christmas is a time when young people organize parties with their friends. You may be invited to a Christmas party or an end-of-the-year party, but other days are either tight-knit family gatherings or just days off to rest at home. The festival dates below follow the Gregorian calendar, unless specified otherwise.

New Year's Day	January 1st
Lunar New Year's Day	the first day of the first month of the lunar calendar— usually end of January to early February
Independence Movement Day	March 1st
Buddha's Birthday	the eighth day of the fourth month on the lunar calendar—usually sometime in the first three weeks of May
Children's Day	May 5th
Memorial Day	June 6th
Independence Day	August 15th
Fall Moon Harvest Day	the 15th day of the eighth month on the lunar calendar, usually in September to early October
National Foundation Day	October 3rd
Korean Alphabet Day	October 9th
Christmas	December 25th

Two milestone birthdays are the first and 60th. The first birthday is called **dol** 돌. (Korean-Americans may use the older spelling **dols** 돐.) The one-year old is dressed in a traditional outfit called the **dolbok** 돌복 and seated at a table with various objects. The object the toddler first grabs is said to predict his/her future, i.e., a brush or pen symbolizes scholarship, money for wealth, noodles or cotton thread for longevity. This tradition is called **doljabi** 돌잡이.

The 60th birthday is called **hwan.gap** 환갑. Huge celebrations are organized, involving many guests, foods, and traditional activities. **Hwan.gap** 환갑 celebrates the completion of a full cycle of the zodiac; that is, when one reaches the same alignment of heaven and earth signs as the birth year. (There are ten heaven signs and twelve earth signs.)

Weddings and funerals also serve as occasions for inviting people outside the family to celebrate. Guests give gift money in a <u>white</u> envelope (**chug.uigeum** 축의금 for wedding or birthday celebrations, and **jo.uigeum** 조의금 for funerals) and the hosts offer food to guests. At weddings and birthdays, the hosts often give guests small gifts such as rice cakes, candles, umbrellas, and towels.

CULTURE NOTE | **Other traditional customs to take note of**

When in Korea, remove your shoes when entering a house. When in the presence of someone older than you, refrain from putting your feet on the furniture, smoking, chewing gum and drinking "in front of" them—the younger person should turn his head to the side to drink. Always sit up straight in school (and in front of your elders), and give and receive things from elders using <u>both hands</u>. A simple nod will suffice when seeing someone you know, and a bow when you meet someone older or of higher status.

CULTURE NOTE | *Noraebang* – **Korean karaoke**

Korean *noraebang* 노래방 (karaoke clubs) offer individual rooms for each party and may come in different sizes to accommodate the number of people in the party. The room (charged according to the length of your stay) will usually contain a microphone or two and a system to choose your songs—usually with a wide variety of English pop and folk songs as well as modern hits. Most also sell drinks and snacks.

EXERCISE 4
Brag about what you have in Korean. Use the appropriate adjective forms.
1. I have a big car. (car 차 **cha**)
2. I have a decent rice cooker.
3. I have delicious *kimchi*.
4. I have a good friend.

EXERCISE 5

How would you respond in Korean to the following questions about changes? Use the information given in parentheses.

1. **Oneul nalssiga eottaeyo?** 오늘 날씨가 어때요 (gotten warmer)
2. **I sikdang bibimbap eottaeyo?** 이 식당 비빔밥 어때요?
   (gotten more delicious)
3. **Sae apateunga eottaeyo?** 새 아파트가 어때요? (gotten farther from work)

EXERCISE 6

Your friends and colleagues are seeking your infinite wisdom. Answer their questions.

1. **Wonrum apateuga salgi gwaenchaneulkkayo?**
   원룸 아파트가 살기 괜찮을까요? (It will be okay.)
2. **Jogeum gidarimyeon jeon.gi bapsochi ssajilkkayo?**
   이 전기 밥솥이 싸질까요? (It will become cheaper.)
3. **Naeil nalssiga chuulkkayo?** 내일 날씨가 추울까요?
   (It will not be cold tomorrow.)
4. **Eideun ssiga oneul yaksoge neujeulkkayo?**
   에이든 씨가 오늘 약속에 늦을까요?
   (He will not be late today.)

LESSON 9
Around Town

 **DIALOGUE 1** **Take me to Kyobo Book Center, please.**

Emma is heading out to meet Aiden in town and is taking a taxi.

Taxi Driver:	Welcome! Where should I take you?
	Eoseo oseyo. Eodiro mosilkkayo?
	어서 오세요. 어디로 모실까요?
Emma:	Can you take me to Kyobo Book Center, Gwanghwamun branch store, please? How long do you think it will take?
	Gyobomun.go Gwanghwamunjeomeuro ga juseyo. Eolmana geollilkkayo?
	교보문고 광화문점으로 가 주세요. 얼마나 걸릴까요?
Taxi Driver:	Since it's rush hour, there is going to be some traffic now. It looks like it's going to take about 30 minutes.
	Jigeum toegeun siganinikka giri jom makil kkeoyeyo. Ama samsip bunjjeum geollil geo gasseumnida.
	지금 퇴근 시간이니까 길이 좀 막힐 거예요. 아마 30 분쯤 걸릴 거 같습니다.
Emma:	OK.
	Algesseumnida.
	알겠습니다.
Taxi Driver:	Ma'am, we are almost there. Where do you want me to stop?
	Sonnim, geo.ui da wasseumnida. Eodie naeryeo deuryeoyo?
	손님, 거의 다 왔습니다. 어디에 내려 드려요?
Emma:	Over there in front of the main gate, please.
	Jeogi jeongmun ape naeryeo juseyo.
	저기 정문 앞에 내려 주세요.
Taxi Driver:	OK. 15,000 won, please.
	Ne. Man.ocheon wonimnida.
	네. 15,000 원입니다.
Emma:	OK. Do you take credit cards?
	Ne, sinyongkadeu badeuseyo?
	네, 신용카드 받으세요?
Taxi Driver:	Of course. We take cash, T-cards, and credit cards. All of them. Here.
	Mullonijyo. Hyeongeum, ti kadeu, sinyongkadeu da basseumnida. Yeogiyo.
	물론이죠. 현금, 티 카드, 신용카드 다 받습니다. 여기요.

Emma: OK. Thank you for your service.
             Ne, gamsahamnida. Sugohasyeosseoyo.
             네, 감사합니다. 수고하셨어요.
Taxi Driver: OK. Thank you. Goodbye!
             Ne. Gamsahamnida. Annyeonghi gaseyo!
             네. 감사합니다. 안녕히 가세요!

VOCABULARY AND EXPRESSIONS

택시 기사	**taeksi gisa**	taxi driver
교보문고	**Kyobomun.go**	Kyobo Book Center
광화문점	**Gwanghwamunjeom**	Gwanghwamun branch store
퇴근 시간	**toegeun sigan**	when people get off work
길	**gil**	road, street, way
삼십 분	**samsip bun**	thirty minutes
손님	**sonnim**	guest, customer, client
정문	**jeongmun**	main gate, main entry
현금	**hyeon.geum**	cash
티 카드	**ti kadeu**	T(ransit)-card
어느	**eoneu**	which
얼마나	**eolmana**	how (long, much)
아마	**ama**	perhaps, probably
거의	**geo.i**	nearly
저기	**jeogi**	over there
모실까요 (모시-)	**mosilkkayo (mosi-)**	where to take (you) (humble)
막힐 거예요 (막히-, 이-)	**makil kkeoyeyo (makhi-, i-)**	it will be blocked up, congested
걸릴 거 같습니다 (걸리-, 같-)	**geollil geo gasseumnida (geolli-, gat-)**	it looks like it will take (time)
내려 드려요 (내리-, 드리-)	**naeryeo deuryeoyo (naeri-, deuri-)**	drop you off, let you out (humble)
내려 주세요 (내리-, 주-)	**naeryeo juseyo (naeri-, ju-)**	drop me off, let me out (honorific)
받으세요 (받-)	**badeuseyo (bat-)**	receive, take, get (honorific)
물론이죠 (물론이-)	**mullonijyo (mulloni-)**	it goes without saying; of course!

VOCABULARY PRACTICE 1

Give the Korean terms for the words described below.

1. a more positive way to say "not quite": _____
2. bills and coins: _____
3. the person you invited or the person buying in your store: _____
4. half an hour: _____

GRAMMAR NOTE Making a polite request -어 주세요 *-eo juseyo* "please do it for me"

Juda 주다 means "to give" and **juseyo** 주세요 is the polite command form (using the honorific suffix) to mean "please give (me)." It is used after a verb conjugated with **-eo** -어 (or **-a** -아), to make a request gentler and more polite, i.e., "please (do) for me."

Please give me some water. **Mul jom juseyo.** 물 좀 주세요.

Ladies and gentlemen, please take a seat now.
Yeoreobun, ije anja juseyo. 여러분, 이제 앉아 주세요.

Let me out in front of Kyobo Book Center, please.
Gyobomun.goro ape naeryeo juseyo. 교보문고 앞에 내려 주세요.

To ask very humbly whether *you* could do the <u>other</u> person a favor, you can use the helping verb **deuryeoyo** 드려요 (the humble version of **jwoyo** 줘요) in place of **juseyo** 주세요.

How can I help you? (*Lit.*, what shall I give you?)
Mwo deurilkkayo? 뭐 드릴까요?

Where do you want me to drop you off?
Eodie naeryeo deuryeoyo? 어디에 내려 드려요?

PATTERN PRACTICE 1

Practice the following conversations using -어 주세요 **-eo juseyo**.

1. A: What would you like to have? **Mwo deurilkkayo?** 뭐 드릴까요?
   B: Please give me water. **Mul jom juseyo.** 물 좀 주세요.
2. A: Where should I take you? **Eodiro mosilkkayo?**
   어디로 모실까요?
   B: Please go to Gwanghwamun. **Gwanghwamuneuro ga juseyo.**
   광화문으로 가 주세요.

3. A: Where should I put this bag? **I gabang eodie noeulkkayo?**
   이 가방 어디에 놓을까요?
   B: Please put it next to the desk. **Chaeksang yeope noa juseyo.**
   책상 옆에 놓아 주세요.
4. A: When should I call you? **Eonje jeonhwa halkkayo?** 언제 전화할까요?
   B: Please call me this evening. **Oneul jeonyeoge jeonhwahae juseyo.**
   오늘 저녁에 전화해 주세요.

GRAMMAR NOTE Subjective justification -(으)니까 -(eu)nikka "since"

The connecting suffix **-(eu)nikka** -(으)니까 "since" is used on a personal judgment that is the basis for anything where a little reasoning might be needed. The **-(eu)nikka** -(으)니까 clause is always said first in Korean.

Since it's rush hour, there will be some traffic.
Jigeum toegeun siganinikka jom makil kkeoyeyo.
지금 퇴근 시간이니까 좀 막힐 거예요.

Take that route, since this way is blocked.
I giri makyeosseunikka jeo killo gaseyo.
이 길이 막혔으니까 저 길로 가세요.

The difference between the suffix **-eoseo** -어서 "so" and **-(eu)nikka** -(으)니까 is that the former provides a logical and objective explanation (that is, a *reason*) for what follows while **-(eu)nikka** -(으)니까 offers reasoning, which may be subjective and even a little defensive. **-Eoseo** -어서 is not used before commands or suggestions.

I decided to buy since it was cheap (otherwise I might not have.)
Gagyeogi ssanikka sagiro haesseoyo.
가격이 싸니까 사기로 했어요.

The price was low so I chose (and bought) that product (neutral statement/ report). **Gagyeogi ssaseo geu jepumeuro sasseoyo.**
가격이 싸서 그 제품으로 샀어요.

PATTERN PRACTICE 2
Practice the following conversations using the personal judgment suffix -(으) 니까 **-(eu)nikka**.
1. A: Shall we take a taxi? **Taeksi talkkayo?** 택시 탈까요?
   B: It's rush hour, so let's take the subway. **Toegeun siganinikka jihacheol tayo.**
   퇴근 시간이니까 지하철 타요.

2. A: Should I buy this rice cooker? **I jeon.gi bapsot salkkayo?**
        이 전기 밥솥 살까요?
    B: It's expensive, so buy a different one.
        Bissanikka dareun bapsot saseyo. 비싸니까 다른 밥솥 사세요.
3. A: Shall we drink coffee? **Keopi masilkkayo?** 커피 마실까요?
    B: It's late, so I don't want to drink any. **Baminikka an masillaeyo.**
        밤이니까 안 마실래요.
4. A: Shall we go to a Chinese restaurant for lunch?
        Jeomsime Jung.guk sikdang galkkayo? 점심에 중국 식당 갈까요?
    B: I went yesterday, so I want to go to a Korean restaurant today.
        Eoje gasseunikka oneureun Han.guk sikdang.e gallaeyo.
        어제 갔으니까 오늘은 한국 식당에 갈래요.

GRAMMAR NOTE Using -(으)ㄹ 거 같아요 -(eu)l kkeo gatayo "it seems like"

If you want to avoid sounding too certain or assertive in expressing your opinion, use the suffix **-(eu)l** -(으)ㄹ combined with **kkeo gatayo** 거 같아요 to say "it seems like." The ending is both a guess about the unknown (either present or future situations) and a softer, more indirect way of stating a personal judgment. **Gatayo** 같아요 is pronounced as **gataeyo** 같애요 or **gateoyo** 같어요 in casual speech by many speakers.

It looks like it's going to rain. **Biga ol geo gatayo.** 비가 올 거 같아요.

It's probably going to take about 30 minutes.
Samsip bunjjeum geollil geo gasseumnida. 삼십 분쯤 걸릴 거 같습니다.

(I am not certain, but) I think it's cold out.
Bakkeun jigeum chu-ul geo gatayo. 밖은 지금 추울 거 같아요.

(I am not sure but) it's probably expensive.
Bissal geo gatayo. 비쌀 거 같아요.

PATTERN PRACTICE 3
Practice making a non-committal statement with -(으)ㄹ 거 같아요 **-(eu)l kkeo gatayo**.
1. A: How long will it take? **Eolmana geollilkkayo?** 얼마나 걸릴까요?
    B: It looks like it's going to take about 30 minutes.
        Samsip bunjjeum geollil kkeo gatayo. 삼십 분쯤 걸릴 거 같아요.
2. A: How's the weather? **Nalssiga eottaeyo?** 날씨가 어때요?
    B: It looks like it's going to rain. **Biga ol kkeo gatayo.** 비가 올 거 같아요.

3. A: Do you want to take a break? **Jom swillaeyo?** 좀 쉴래요?
    B: I have so much to do, so I don't think I can.
       Iri manaseo mot swil kkeo gatayo. 일이 많아서 못 쉴 거 같아요.
4. A: Do you want to go to the *noraebang* with me?
       Gachi noraebang.e gallaeyo? 같이 노래방에 갈래요?
    B: I have work, so I don't think I can.
       Iri isseoseo oneureun mot gal kkeo gatayo.
       일이 있어서 오늘은 못 갈 거 같아요.

GRAMMAR NOTE 얼마나 *Eolmana* "how much"

Eolmana 얼마나 "how (much)" is often used with adjectives, to ask about the extent or degree. If the adjective is not there, it means "how long (does it take)" or "how much (do you want)."

How cold is it outside? **Bakki eolmana chuwoyo?** 밖이 얼마나 추워요?

How fast is the subway?
Jihacheori eolmana ppallayo? 지하철이 얼마나 빨라요?

How long does it take? **Eolmana geollyeoyo?** 얼마나 걸려요?

How much do you want? (*Lit.* How much should I give you?)
Eolmana deuryeoyo? 얼마나 드려요?

GRAMMAR NOTE Combining verbs

The most common way to put Korean verbs together for added meaning or function is to conjugate the first verb in the informal style (to end in **-eo/a** -어/아) and then add on the second verb. There is a space between the two verbs in written Korean (but no pause in speaking). The space is often ignored when the verbs are short.

Please let me out in front of the main gate.
Jeongmun ape naeryeo juseyo. 정문 앞에 내려 주세요.

Please come this way. **Ijjogeuro wajuseyo.** 이쪽으로 와주세요.
It looks odd. **Isanghae boyeoyo.** 이상해 보여요.

CULTURE NOTE Situational expressions

There are a number of polite expressions in Korean that are used in particular situations. The function of these phrases is understandable, but there's often no good equivalent in English.

Emma says to the taxi driver: **sugohasyeosseoyo** 수고하셨어요 "you worked hard." This expression is used to thank someone in a service position. Never use this for teachers, as they are not providing a "service."

When parting ways, the person leaving says **annyeonghi gyeseyo** 안녕히 계세요 "goodbye" to the person staying (*lit.*, "stay well") and the person staying says **annyeonghi gaseyo** 안녕히 가세요 "goodbye" to the person leaving (*Lit.*, "go well.") The informal sayings are **jal isseo** 잘 있어 and **jal ga** 잘 가. If a family member is leaving the house, you will hear people say **annyeonghi danyeo.oseyo** 안녕히 다녀오세요 (honorific) or **jal gatda wa** 잘 갔다 와 (to those who are younger or of equal status) "go and come back well."

Before a meal, the person serving (especially in a restaurant), might say **masitge deuseyo** (*Lit.*, "Please, eat deliciously") or, "Enjoy your meal." If you are about to eat something someone else made for you, you should say **jal meokgesseumnida** (*Lit.*, "I will eat well").

EXERCISE 1
Emma is calling a taxi service to go to the Gangnam Station from Kyobo Book Center. Practice the following in Korean based on the given information.
1. Please come to Kyobo Book Center.
2. Please take me to Gangnam Station. (강남역 **Gangnam yeok**)
3. Please let me off in front of the main gate.

EXERCISE 2
You have a new friend who just got into town. Suggest what she should do, giving your justification. Practice the following conversations in Korean based on the given information.
1. Taxis are expensive here, so please take (the) subway.
2. (The) coffee here is good, so buy coffee here.
3. A rice cooker is convenient (useful), so buy one.
4. One-room studios are cheap and clean, so find one.

EXERCISE 3
Politely make an excuse using -(으)ㄹ 거 같아요 **-(eu)l geo gatayo**.
1. **Bakke nagalkkayo?** 밖에 나갈까요? (It looks cold outside.)
2. **Naeil mannalkkayo?** 내일 만날까요? (I think I will be busy tomorrow.)
3. **I keompyuteoreul sallaeyo?** 이 컴퓨터를 살래요?
   (I think it will be too expensive)
4. **Ohue teniseureul chillaeyo?** 오후에 테니스를 칠래요?
   (It looks like it's going to rain.) (to rain: 비가 오다 **biga oda**)

🔘 DIALOGUE 2 Take the subway toward City Hall.

Aiden is heading out to meet Emma in town and is getting directions from Minjoon.

Aiden: I'm meeting Emma at the Kyobo Bookstore, Gwanghwamun branch. How do I go to Gwanghwamun from here?
Oneul Emma ssihago Gyobomungo Gwanghwamunjeomeseo mannagiro haesseoyo. Yeogieseo Gwanghwamunkkaji eotteoke gaya dwaeyo?
오늘 엠마 씨하고 교보문고 광화문점에서 만나기로 했어요.
여기에서 광화문까지 어떻게 가야 돼요?

Minjoon: The subway is faster so try that. But you have to (make a) transfer.
Jihacheori ppareunikka taboseyo. Geureonde garataya dwaeyo.
지하철이 빠르니까 타보세요. 그런데 갈아타야 돼요.

Aiden: It's OK. Please tell me (how).
Gwaenchanayo. Gareuchyeo juseyo.
괜찮아요. 가르쳐 주세요.

Minjoon: First, take Line 2 at the Shinchon Station. You gotta take the train that takes you toward City Hall. You shouldn't take the one going towards the Hongdae Entrance.
Useon Sinchonyeogeseo jihacheol i hoseoneul taseyo. Sicheong jjogeuro ganeun jihacheoreul taya dwaeyo. Hongdaeipgu jjogeuro gamyeon an dwaeyo.
우선 신촌역에서 지하철 2 호선을 타세요. 시청 쪽으로 가는 지하철을 타야 돼요. 홍대입구 쪽으로 가면 안 돼요.

Aiden: I see. And then?
A, geureokunyo. Geurigoyo?
아, 그렇군요. 그리고요?

Minjoon: Get off the subway at the Chungjeong station after three stops.
Yeogeul se gae jinaseo chungjeongno yeogeseo naeriseyo.
역을 3 개 지나서 충정로 역에서 내리세요.
Then transfer to Line 5 and pass two stops, and then get off at the Kwanghwamun station.
Geurigo o hoseoneuro garataseo (hwanseunghaeseo) yeok du gaereul jinaseyo. Geurigo Gwanghwamun yeogeseo naeriseyo.
그리고 5 호선으로 갈아타서 (환승해서) 역 2 개를 지나세요.
그리고 광화문 역에서 내리세요.
When you get out of the station, it's directly connected to the Kyobo building.
Yeogeseo nagamyeon Gyobomun.goro jikjeop yeon.gyeoldoe.eo isseoyo.
역에서 나가면 교보문고로 직접 연결되어 있어요.

Aiden:	I see. Thank you! But it sounds complicated (*Lit.,* difficult)!
	A, gamsahamnida! Geureonde neomu eo.ryeowoyo!
	아, 감사합니다! 그런데 너무 어려워요!
Minjoon:	Use the Naver map app then. You just need to type in the departure and the arrival under the "Find Route" window.
	Geumreom Neibeo jido aebeul iyonghae boseyo. "Gilchatgi"eseo chulbaljihago dochakjireul neo.eumyeon dwaeyo.
	그럼 네이버 지도 앱을 이용해 보세요. "길찾기"에서 출발지하고 도착지를 넣으면 돼요.
Aiden:	That would be really convenient! I'll use this app then.
	Jeongmal pyeonhagenneyo! Geureom i aebeul iyonghae bolkkeyo.
	정말 편하겠네요! 그럼 이 앱을 이용해 볼게요.

VOCABULARY AND EXPRESSIONS

충정로	**Chungjeongno**	Chungjeong Road, Chungjeong Street
네이버	**Neibeo**	Naver (a Korean search engine)
기억*	**gieok**	memory; *to remember
이용*	**iyong**	use; *to use
시청	**Sicheong**	City Hall
지하철	**jihacheol**	subway
쪽	**jjok**	side
신촌	**Shinchon**	Shinchon
홍대입구	**Hongdae.ipgu**	Hongik University Entrance
역	**yeok**	(train) station
지도	**jido**	map
앱	**aep**	phone/computer application
길찾기	**gilchatgi**	get directions, finding one's way around
출발지	**chulbalji**	departing point
도착지	**dochakji**	arriving point
어떻게	**eotteoke**	how
직접	**jikjeop**	directly
X-호선	**X.hoseon**	Line # X
-까지	**kkaji**	up to (and including), up until (a point), by
-부터	**buteo**	starting with (a point), starting from, since
빨라요 (빠르-)	**ppallayo (ppareu-)**	fast
갈아타야 (갈-, 타-)	**garataya (gal-, ta-)**	have to transfer
가르쳐 (가르치-)	**gareuchyeo (gareuchi-)**	teach, inform
지나서 (지나-)	**jinaseo (jina-)**	having passed
내리세요 (내리-)	**naeriseyo (naeri-)**	please get off (e.g., the subway)
그렇군요 (그렇-)	**geureokunyo (geureoh-)**	oh, I see.

연결되어 (연결되-)	**yeon.gyeoldoe.eo (yeon. gyeoldoe-)**	connected
어려워요 (어렵-)	**eo.ryeowoyo (eo.ryeop-)**	difficult
넣으면 (넣-)	**neo.eumyeon (neoh-)**	if put in

*See Grammar Notes

Supplementary Vocabulary
Useful Applications

Map	Naver Maps (http://map.naver.com/), Kakao Maps (cell phone app)
Dictionary	Naver Dictionary (http://dic.naver.com), Daum Dictionary (http://alldic.daum.net)
Taxi service	Kakao Taxi
Texting	Kakao Talk, Line

VOCABULARY PRACTICE 2

Give the Korean terms for the words described below.
1. without stopping or turning: _____
2. not easy: _____
3. underground railway: _____
4. opposite of forgetting: _____

GRAMMAR NOTE -어 봐요 *–Eo bwayo,* -어 보세요 *–eo boseyo*
"Please try (it) out"

-Eo bwayo 봐요 and its honorific variant **-eo boseyo** 보세요 suggest that the listener "try something out":

Try (eating) this. It's delicious.
Igeo meogeo bwayo. Masisseoyo. 이거 먹어 봐요. 맛있어요.

The subway is faster so try (riding) it. But you'll have to transfer.
Jihacheori ppareunikka taboseyo. Geureonde garataya dwaeyo.
지하철이 빠르니까 타보세요. 그런데 갈아타야 돼요.

Try (using) the Naver map application next time.
Da.eum ppeoneneun Neibeo jido aebeul iyonghae boseyo.
다음 번에는 네이버 지도 앱을 이용해 보세요.

PATTERN PRACTICE 4

Invite someone to try something out using -어 봐요 **-eo bwayo** or -어 보세요 **-eo boseyo**.

1. A: How can I get to Gwanghwamun?
     Gwanghwamune eotteoke gaya dwaeyo?
     광화문에 어떻게 가야 돼요?
   B: The subway is fast. Try the subway.
     Jihacheori ppallayo. Jihacheoreul ta boseyo.
     지하철이 빨라요. 지하철을 타 보세요.

2. A: How do I get to Namsan from here?
     Yeogeiseo Namsankkaji eotteoke gayo?
     여기서 남산까지 어떻게 가요?
   B: Well... try the map application. **Geulsseyo... jido aebeul iyonghae boseyo.**
     글쎄요. 지도 앱을 이용해 보세요.

3. A: Where do they sell rice cookers? (Where can I buy a rice cooker?)
     Jeon.gi bapsocheul eodieseo parayo?
     전기 밥솥을 어디에서 팔아요?
   B: Try E-Mart. **I mateu.e ga boseyo.** 이마트에 가 보세요.

4. A: Please lend me some dress shoes. **Gudu jom billyeo juseyo.**
     구두 좀 빌려 주세요.
   B: Try (on) this pair of dress shoes. **I gudureul sineo boseyo.**
     이 구두를 신어 보세요.

GRAMMAR NOTE "Need to, have to" -어야 돼요 *-eoya dwaeyo*

The suffix **-eoya** -어야, combined with the helping verb **dwaeyo** 돼요 (all together **-eoya dwaeyo** -어야 돼요), expresses that something needs to be done. The English translation can mean "should," "need to," "have to" or "ought to." In formal Korean, **haeyo** 해요 is used instead of **dwayo** 돼요.

You need to transfer there.
Geogiseo garataya dwaeyo. 거기서 갈아타야 돼요.

How should I get there ("go")? **Otteoke gaya dwaeyo?** 어떻게 가야 돼요?

You ought to take the subway that goes toward City Hall.
Sicheong jjogeuro ganeun jihacheoreul taya dwaeyo.
시청 쪽으로 가는 지하철을 타야 돼요.

PATTERN PRACTICE 5

Practice expressing obligation and necessity using −어야 돼요 **-eoya dwaeyo**.

1. I have to go to work today. **Oneul hoesa.e gaya dwaeyo.**
   오늘 회사에 가야 돼요.
2. I have to move next month. **Dadeum dare isahaeya dwaeyo.**
   다음 달에 이사해야 돼요.
3. You are late, so you should take a taxi.
   Neujeosseunikka taeksireul taya dwaeyo. 늦었으니까 택시를 타야 돼요.
4. I should use a credit card because I do not have cash.
   Hyeongeumi eopseoseo sinyongkadeureul sseoya haeyo.
   현금이 없어서 신용카드를 써야 해요.

GRAMMAR NOTE Conditional suffix -(으)면 *-(eu)myeon* "if" or "when"

-(Eu)myeon -(으)면 is a suffix that expresses a condition similar to the English "if" and "when," the latter for future actions.

Ask me *if* you don't know. **Moreumyeon mureoboseyo.** 모르면 물어보세요.

Call me *when* you get home.
Jipe gamyeon jeonhwahaseyo. 집에 가면 전화하세요.

When you get off at the Gwanghwamun Station, it's connected.
Gwanghwamunyeoge naerimyeon yeongyeoldwae isseoyo.
광화문역에 내리면 연결돼 있어요.

With **dwaeyo** 돼요 "something works," you can express such ideas as "if you just do…then it works," "all you have to do is...," and, in the negative **an dwaeyo** 안 돼요, "it won't work if you do."

You just need to type in the places of departure and the arrival under the "Find road" window.
"Giljatgi"eseo chulbaljihago dochakjireul neoeumyeon dwaeyo.
"길찾기"에서 출발지하고 도착지를 넣으면 돼요.

You shouldn't go toward the Hapjeong or the Hongdaeipku direction.
Hapjeong.ina hongdaeipku jjogeuro gamyeon an dwaeyo.
합구정이나 홍대입구 쪽으로 가면 안 돼요.

PATTERN PRACTICE 6

Practice the following phrases using the conditional suffix −(으)면 **-(eu)myeon**.

1. Please ask me if you don't know. **Moreumyeon mureo boseyo.**
모르면 물어보세요

2. Please take a taxi if you are tired. **Pigonhamyeon taeksi taseyo.**
피곤하면 택시 타세요.

3. Please call me when you get home. **Jibe gamyeon jeonhwahaseyo.**
집에 가면 전화하세요.

4. Please pay by credit card if you don't have money.
Doni eopseumyeon kadeuro naeseyo. 돈이 없으면 카드로 내세요.

GRAMMAR NOTE Sino-Korean nouns as verbs

We have mentioned that there are a number of verbs and adjectives that use the "dummy" verb **hada/haeyo** 하다/해요 such as **gongbuhaeyo** 공부해요 "to study" and **pigonhaeyo** 피곤해요 "to be tired." In many cases, the verb or adjective is based on a Sino-Korean *noun* and that noun can be used with or without **hada/haeyo** 하다/해요 (or another verb such as **nada/nayo** 나다/나요 "to come out"). In the vocabulary list in this Lesson (and throughout the rest of this book), Sino-Korean nouns that are listed with an asterisk indicate that a dummy verb (usually **hada/haeyo** 하다/해요) can be added to make them into a verb (or adjective).

The spa voucher is free.
Seupa iyonggwoneun muryoimnida. 스파 이용권은 무료입니다.

Enjoy making use of the new facilities.
Sae siseoreul mani iyonghae juseyo. 새 시설을 많이 이용해 주세요.

(Someone) has a good memory. **Gieongnyeoki joayo.** 기억력이 좋아요.

Now I remember! **Gi.eongnayo!** 기억나요!

GRAMMAR NOTE Counters and marker positions

There are three ways to say the sentence "get off the subway at the Chungjeong station after three stops" without changing its meaning.

Yeok se gaereul jinaseo Chungjeongno yeogeseo naeriseyo.
역 세 개를 지나서 충정로 역에서 내리세요.
Yeok se gae jinaseo Chungjeongno yeogeseo naeriseyo.
역을 세 개 지나서 충정로 역에서 내리세요.
Yeogeul se gaereul jinaseo Chungjeongno yeogeseo naeriseyo.
역을 세 개를 지나서 충정로 역에서 내리세요.

CULTURE NOTE | Use of Sino-Korean words in public spaces

Official notices and announcements in public spaces are usually made using Sino-Korean vocabulary. The first of the two directions below, with more native Korean vocabulary, is likely said by a passerby to a foreigner and the second, with more Sino-Korean "big words," by a student to a native speaker to sound educated and polite.

After you transfer to Line 5 and pass two stops, get off at Gwanghwamun station.

1. **O hoseoneuro garatasyeoseo yeok du gaereul jinan da.eum Gwanghwamun yeogeseo naeriseyo.**
5호선으로 갈아타셔서 역 두 개를 지난 다음 광화문 역에서 내리세요.
2. **O hoseoneuro hwanseunghasyeoseo yeok du gaereul janan da.eum Gwanghwamun yeogeseo hachahaseyo.**
5 호선으로 환승하셔서 역 두 개를 지난 다음 광화문 역에서 하차하세요.

EXERCISE 4

Suggest that your friend try something in your town using −어 보세요 **-eo boseyo**.
1. Try eating Korean food at this restaurant.
2. Try walking at Hangang Park.
3. Try going to Kyobo bookstore.
4. Try making Korean friends.

EXERCISE 5

Your friend wants to do something together, but you cannot. Explain why you cannot join him using −어야 돼요 **-eoya dwaeyo** and based on the given information.
1. Friend: **Oneul yeonghwa bolkkayo?** 친구: 오늘 영화 볼까요?
You: Sorry. I have to go to my mother's house.
2. Friend: **Naeil teniseu chilkkayo?** 친구: 내일 테니스 칠까요?
You: Sorry. I have to work tomorrow.
3. Friend: **Jigeum keopi masilkkayo?** 친구: 지금 커피 마실까요?
You: Sorry. I have to meet my younger sibling.
4. Friend: **Gachi noraebang.e galkkayo?** 친구: 같이 노래방에 갈까요?
You: Sorry. I have to rest because I am sick.

EXERCISE 6

Reply to your friend using −(으)면 **-(eu)myeon**.

1. Friend: **Pigonhaeyo.** 친구: 피곤해요.
   You: If you are tired, take a taxi.
2. Friend: **Oneul iri manayo.** 친구: 오늘 일이 많아요.
   You: If you have a lot of work today, shall we meet tomorrow?
3. Friend: **Chuwoyo.** 친구: 추워요.
   You: If you are cold, come in. (to come inside 들어오다 **deureo.oda**)
4. Friend: **Jigeum jibe gaya dwaeyo.** 친구: 지금 집에 가야 돼요.
   You: If/when you get home, please call (me).

LESSON 10
Seeing a Doctor

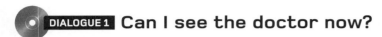 **DIALOGUE 1 Can I see the doctor now?**

Aiden caught the flu and is visiting a doctor's office.

Aiden: Hello. Can I see the doctor now? (*Lit.,* Can I get examined now?)
         Annyeonghaseyo. Jigeum jillyo badeul su isseoyo?
         안녕하세요. 지금 진료 받을 수 있어요?

Nurse: What brought you here? (*Lit.,* where hurts so you came?)
         Eodiga apaseo osyeosseumnikka?
         어디가 아파서 오셨습니까?

Aiden: Well, because of a cold, I continually have high fever and am cold.
         And my nose is clogged and I have a bad cough, so I can't sleep.
         **Ne. Gamgi ttaemuneyo. Gyesok yeori nago chuwoyo. Geurigo
         koga makigo gichimi simhaeseo jal suga eopseoyo.**
         네. 감기 때문에요. 계속 열이 나고 추워요. 그리고 코가 막히고
         기침이 심해서 잘 수가 없어요.

Nurse: Is this the first time you are visiting our hospital?
         Jeohui byeongwone cheo.eum osyeosseoyo?
         저희 병원에 처음 오셨어요?

Aiden: Yes.
         Ne.
         네.

Nurse: Do you have an ID or insurance card?
         Sinbunjjeung.ina uiryoboheomjeung isseusimnikka?
         신분증이나 의료보험증 있으십니까?

Aiden: Here it is. I'm Canadian.
         Yeogi isseumnida. Kaenadasaramieyo.
         여기 있습니다. 캐나다사람이에요.

Nurse: Please write your name here. Have a seat over there and wait until
         your name is called.
         **Yeogie seonghameul jeogeo juseyo. Geurigo jeogi anjeusyeoseo
         seonghameul bureul ttaekkaji gidaryeo jusipsio. Oneureun
         hwanjabundeuri manki ttaemune jogeum gidarisyeoya
         doemnida.**
         여기에 성함을 적어 주세요. 그리고 저기 앉으셔서 성함을 부를
         때까지 기다려 주십시오. 오늘은 환자분들이 많기 때문에 조금
         기다리셔야 됩니다.

VOCABULARY AND EXPRESSIONS

진료*	jillyo	medical exam and treatment, *to give a medical exam
간호사	ganhosa	nurse
감기	gamgi	a cold
열	yeol	fever
코	ko	nose
기침	gichim	cough
병원	byeongwon	hospital
신분증	sinbunjeung	identification card
의료보험증	uiryoboheomjeung	insurance card
때	ttae	(at the) time (of)
성함	seongham	name (formal, official, honorific)
환자분	hwanjabun	patient (honorific)
계속	gyesok	continually, constantly
저희	jeohui	we, our (humble)
처음	cheo.eum	first time
조금 (= 좀)	jogeum (= jom)	a little (conversational softener used when making a request)
-이나	ina	or (after consonant-ending nouns)
-나	na	or (after vowel-ending nouns)
때문에	ttaemune	because of (something)
받을 수 있어요 (받-, 있-)	badeul su isseoyo (bat-, iss-)	can receive, get
아파서 (아프-)	apaseo (apeu-)	sick/hurt so…
오셨습니까 (오-)	osyeosseumnikka (o-)	came (honorific-formal)
오셨어요 (오-)	osyeosseoyo (o-)	came (honorific-polite)
나고 (나-)	nago (na-)	come out and
추워요 (춥-)	chuwoyo (chup-)	feel cold
막히고 (막히-)	makigo (makhi-)	is blocked up/congested and
심해서 (심하-)	simhaeseo (simha-)	severe, so…
잘 수가 없어요 (자-, 없)	jal ssuga eopseoyo (ja-, eops-)	can't sleep
있으십니까? (있-)	isseusimnikka? (iss-)	do you have/is there? (honorific-polite)
앉으셔서 (앉-)	anjeusyeoseo (anj-)	having sat (honorific)
부를 때 (부르-)	bureul ttae (bureu-)	when (I) call
적어 주세요 (적-, 주-)	jeogeo juseyo (jeok-, ju-)	please write down (honorific-polite)
기다려 주십시오 (기다리-, 주-)	gidaryeo juseyo (gidari-, ju-)	please wait (honorific-formal)
기다리셔야 됩니다 (기다리-, 되-)	gidarisyeoya doemnida (gidari-, doe-)	you have to wait (honorific-formal)

VOCABULARY PRACTICE 1

Give the Korean terms for the words described below.

1. when a virus makes your nose stuffy or runny (and other symptoms):

   _____

2. the person who helps doctors take care of patients: _____
3. the place where people with injuries and illnesses are cared for: _____
4. When you need time to do something, ask the other (honored person) to wait:

   _____

GRAMMAR NOTE -(으)ㄹ 수 있어요 -*(eu)l ssu isseoyo* "can; is possible to..."

-(Eu)l ssu isseoyo -(으)ㄹ 수 있어요 literally means "there is a way to... ." The subject **-i/ga** -이/가 or the topic marker **-eun/neun** -은/는 may show up after the word **su** 수 "way" or "means" for emphasis. The negative "can't" is **-(eu)l ssu eopseoyo** -(으)ㄹ 수 없어요.

Can I see a doctor (get examined)?
Jigeum jillyo badeul ssu isseoyo? 지금 진료 받을 수 있어요?

I can't sleep because my nose is congested.
Gichimi simhaeseo jal ssuga eopseoyo. 코가 막혀서 잘 수가 없어요.

PATTERN PRACTICE 1

Practice the following conversations about possibility using -(으)ㄹ 수 있어요 **-(eu)l su isseoyo.**

1. A: May I talk to you for a minute now? **Jigeum jamkkan yaegihal su isseoyo?**
   지금 잠깐 얘기할 수 있어요?
   B: Sure. **Ne, gwaenchanayo.** 네, 괜찮아요.
2. A: Where does it hurt? **Eodiga apeuseyo?** 어디가 아프세요?
   B: I have a bad cough, so I can't sleep.
   Gichimi simhaeseo jal ssu eopseoyo. 기침이 심해서 잘 수 없어요.
3. A: Can you ride a bicycle? **Jajeon.geo tal ssu isseoyo?**
   자전거 탈 수 있어요?
   B: No, I can't. **Aniyo. Motaeyo.** 아니요. 못 타요.
4. A: Can you go home alone? **Honja jibe gal su isseoyo?**
   혼자 집에 갈 수 있어요?
   B: Yes, I can go (home on my own). **Ne, gal ssu isseoyo.** 네, 갈 수 있어요.

GRAMMAR NOTE A point in time with 때 *ttae* "the time when..."

A composite expression **-(eu)l ttae** -(으)ㄹ 때, with the noun **ttae** 때, "time" in it, is used to mean "times when (you do something)" in a general present tense (for repeated actions).

Turn off the light <u>when</u> you (go to) sleep.
Jal ttae bureul kkeuseyo. 잘 때 불을 끄세요.

Don't make noises when you eat.
Bap meogeul ttae, sori naeji ma. 밥 먹을 때 소리 내지 마.

For the "past tense" or a completed action, use **-eoss/asseul ttae** -었/았을 때.

When I went (got) home, there was nobody (there).
Jibe gasseul ttae amudo eopseosseoyo.
집에 갔을 때 아무도 없었어요.

I had many friends when I was young.
Eoryeosseul ttae chin.guga manasseoyo. 어렸을 때 친구가 많았어요.

Ttae 때 can also be used for future actions, but in this case it highlights the point when an action begins or while it is going on. More often you will use **-(eu) myeon** -(으)면 for future tense actions. Since it is more of a conditional ("if"), it is typically used for "if you happen to do that," or "once you have finished doing that."

Call me (at the point) when you (set out to) go home.
Jibe gal ttae jeonhwahae. 집에 갈 때 전화해.

If/when you go (/get) home, call me.
Jibe gamyeon jeonhwahae. 집에 가면 전화해.

Ttae 때 is often used with nouns as well:

점심 때	**jeomsim ttae**	at lunch time
저녁 때	**jeonyeok ttae**	at dinner time
방학 때	**banghak ttae**	at vacation time
그 때	**geu ttae**	at that time
크리스마스 때	**keuriseumaseu ttae**	at Christmas time

PATTERN PRACTICE 2

Practice the following phrases with 때 **ttae**, which shows the exact point in time.

1. When it's cold, I do not go out. **Chu.ul. ttae bakke an nagayo.**
   추울 때 밖에 안 나가요.
2. You should drink lots of water (any time) when you take medicine.
   Yak meogeul ttae mureul mani masyeoya dwaeyo.
   약 먹을 때 물을 많이 먹어야 돼요.
3. When I went/was going to Korea, I took a plane from LA.
   Han.guge gal ttae ellei.eseo bihaenggireul tasseoyo.
   한국에 갈 때 LA에서 비행기를 탔어요.
4. When I went/got to Korea, I went to a *noraebang.*
   Han.guge gasseul ttae noraebang.e gasseoyo.
   한국에 갔을 때 노래방에 갔어요.

GRAMMAR NOTE Giving a specific reason with -기 때문에 *-gi ttaemune* "because of (doing/being)..."

To name (or blame) a specific cause, use **ttaemune** 때문에 after a noun. Use **-gi ttaemune** -기 때문에 if the cause is an action (verb) or description (adjective), and **-eotgi/atgi** -었기/았기 for a completed action.

I won't be going to the party today because of work.
Il ttaemune oneul patie an gal kkeoyeyo.
일 때문에 오늘 파티에 안 갈 거예요.

I can't use chopsticks because my hand hurts.
Soni apeugi ttaemune jeotgarakjireul hal ssu eopseoyo.
손이 아프기 때문에 젓가락질을 할 수 없어요.

Because I was very cold, I closed the door.
Neomu chuwotgi ttaemune muneul dadasseoyo.
너무 추웠기 때문에 문을 닫았어요.

PATTERN PRACTICE 3

Practice the following phrases with -(기) 때문에 **-gi ttaemune**, which gives a specific reason.

1. I can't go to the party because of work. **Il ttaemune pati.e mot gayo.**
   일 때문에 못 가요.
2. Because it is cold today, I'm staying home.
   Oneul chupgi ttaemune jibe isseoyo. 오늘 춥기 때문에 집에 있어요.
3. Because I have a severe cough, I can't sleep.
   Gichimi simhagi ttaemune jameul jal suga eopseoyo.
   기침이 심하기 때문에 잠을 잘 수가 없어요.

4. I can't go to the party because I caught a cold.
    Gamgie geollyeotgi ttaemune pati.e mot gayo.
    감기에 걸렸기 때문에 파티에 못 가요.

GRAMMAR NOTE Identifying the subject and omitted information in a sentence

The Korean language leaves out who is doing what if that information is understandable—but non-native speakers will need to pay close attention to what has been said. Let us look at the following sentence:

"(He/she) won't come until (someone) calls (him/her)."
Jeonhwa <u>deuril</u> ttaekkaji an <u>osil</u> geoya. 전화 <u>드릴</u> 때까지 안 <u>오실</u> 거야.

Neither of the two actions, calling and coming, is said with a subject. However, from the humble verb **deuri** 드릴 "to give" and the honorific **-(eu)si** -(으)시, attached to the verb **o** 오 "to come," one can glean that the person making the phone call is honoring its recipient and the person coming is honored, thus the same person.

EXERCISE 1
Emma sprained her ankle while running, so she went to see a doctor. Practice the following dialogue with the doctor using −(으)ㄹ 수 있어요/없어요 **-(eu)l su isseoyo/eopseoyo**, based on the given information.
1. Emma: Can I walk today?
    Doctor: No, you cannot walk.
2. Emma: Can I go to work tomorrow? (go to work: 출근하다 **chulgeunhada**)
    Doctor: No, you cannot go.
3. Emma: Can I ride a bicycle this weekend? (ride a bicycle: 자전거 타다 **jajeon.geo tada**))
    Doctor: No, you cannot ride one.

EXERCISE 2
Tell your friend about what you usually do on each occasion using −(으)ㄹ 때 **-(eu)l ttae**.
1. When I exercise, I listen to music.
2. When I am tired, I drink coffee.
3. When it rains, I stay home.
4. When I am sick, I drink citron tea. (citron tea: 유자차 **yujacha**)

EXERCISE 3

Answer your friend's questions using −(기) 때문에 **-(gi) ttaemune**.

1. Friend: **Oneul wae teniseu an chyeoyo?** 오늘 왜 테니스 안 쳐요?
   You: Because it is very cold...
2. Friend: **Wae jameul mot jayo?** 왜 잠을 못 자요?
   You: Because I caught a cold...
3. Friend: **Wae chulgeun an haesseoyo?** 왜 출근 안 했어요?
   (go to work: 출근하다 **chulgeunhada**)
   You: Because I had a headache...
4. Friend: **Wae wonrumeuro isahaesseoyo?** 왜 원룸으로 이사했어요?
   You: Because the rent was cheap...

DIALOGUE 2 It looks like you have the flu.

After waiting a while, Aiden gets to see the doctor.

Nurse: Patient Aiden Tyler. Please come this way.
          Tailleo Eideun nim. Ijjogeuro oseyo.
          타일러 에이든 님. 이쪽으로 오세요.
Doctor: Hello. What brought you here? (*Lit.,* where is not well?)
          Annyeonghasimnikka? Eodiga an jo.eusimnikka?
          안녕하십니까? 어디가 안 좋으십니까?
Aiden: Hello. I have a fever and I feel very cold. And I have a bad cough.
          Annyeonghaseyo. Yeori nago aju chuwoyo. Geurigo gichimdo simhaeyo.
          안녕하세요. 열이 나고 아주 추워요. 그리고 기침도 심해요.
Doctor: I see. When did the fever start? And do you have a headache?
          Geureokunyo. Eonjebuteo yeori nasseumnikka? Meorido apeuseyo?
          그렇군요. 언제부터 열이 났습니까? 머리도 아프세요?
Aiden: I started being cold and having a fever yesterday. I don't have a headache, but my nose is congested so it's very uncomfortable.
          Eojebuteo chupgo yeori nasseoyo. Meorineun apeuji anayo. Geureochiman koga makyeoseo gwoengjanghi bulpyeonhaeyo.
          어제부터 춥고 열이 났어요. 머리는 아프지 않아요. 그렇지만 코가 막혀서 굉장히 불편해요.
Doctor: Oh, is that so? Do you have body aches, vomiting, or diarrhea? Are you able to eat?
          A, geureosseumnikka? Momdo apeugeona guto, seolsaga isseuseyo? Siksaneun jal haseyo?
          아, 그렇습니까? 몸도 아프거나 구토, 설사가 있으세요? 식사는 잘 하세요?

Aiden: I had body aches starting in the middle of the night. I can eat just fine. I don't have any other symptoms.
           Hanbamjjung.e momi apeugi sijakaesseoyo. Meongneun geon amu munje eopseoyo.
           한밤중에 몸이 아프기 시작했어요. 먹는 건 아무 문제 없어요. 다른 증상은 없습니다.

Doctor: It looks like you have the flu. I'll write a prescription for you. Get your prescription as you pay at the counter (*Lit.*, window).
           Gamgi momsarin geot ganneyo. Yageul cheobanghae deurilkkeyo. Sunapcheo.eseo cheobangjeon bada gaseyo.
           감기 몸살인 것 같네요. 약을 처방해 드릴게요.수납처에서 처방전 받아 가세요.

Aiden: Where is the pharmacy?
           Yakgugi eodi isseoyo?
           약국이 어디 있어요?

Doctor: You'll see a drugstore right after you leave the hospital. Take the prescription to get it filled.
           Byeongwon nagasimyeon baro yakgugi isseumnida. Cheobangjeoneul gajyeo gasyeoseo yageul badeuseyo.
           병원 나가시면 바로 약국이 있습니다. 처방전을 가져 가셔서 약을 받으세요.
           Take the medicine an hour after each meal for three days. Get lots of sleep at night, and take a rest. It's better if you don't go to work tomorrow.
           Yageun saheulgan siku han siganmada deuseyo. Jameul puk jumusigo swiseyo. Nae.ireun ireul an nagasineun ge joayo.
           약은 사흘간 식후 한 시간마다 드세요. 잠을 푹 주무시고 쉬세요. 내일은 일을 안 나가시는 게 좋아요.

Aiden: Yes, I understand.
           Ne, algesseumnida.
           네, 알겠습니다.

VOCABULARY AND EXPRESSIONS

의사	uisa	doctor
식사*	siksa	meal, *to have a meal
시작*	sijak	beginning, *to start
처방*	cheobang	prescribing, *to prescribe
일*	il	matter, job, business, *to work
머리	meori	head, hair
증상	jeungsang	symptom
몸	mom	body
구토	guto	vomiting

설사	**seolsa**	diarrhea
부터	**buteo**	since
한밤중	**hanbamjjung**	in the middle of the night
문제	**munje**	problem
약	**yak**	medicine, drug
밖	**bakk**	outside
수납처	**sunapcheo**	service window
처방전	**cheobangjeon**	prescription (note)
약국	**yakguk**	drug store, pharmacy
잠	**jam**	sleeping
식후	**siku**	after a meal
아무	**amu**	any (used with negatives and questions)
그럴지만 (= 하지만)	**geureochiman** (= hajiman)	but, however
바로	**baro**	directly, right away, straight
사흘	**saheul**	three days
푹	**puk**	deeply, sufficiently
-거나	**geona**	or (attached to verb roots)
-는 거	**-neun geo**	(the act of do)ing; what one does
-는 건	**-neun geon**	(the act of do)ing (topic marker)
-는 게	**-neun ge**	(the act of do)ing (subject marker)
-간 (= 동안)	**-gan (= dong.an)**	for (marker for duration)
-마다	**-mada**	every, each
굉장히	**goengjanghi**	awfully, greatly
먹는 건 (먹-)	**meongneun geon (meok-)**	(the act of) eating; what one eats
-지 않아요	**ji anayo (ji anh-)**	not (formal, used with verb roots)
불편해요 (불편하-)	**bulpyeonhaeyo (bulpyeonha-)**	inconvenient, uncomfortable
나가시면 (나가-)	**nagasimyeon (naga-)**	if you go out (honorific)
가져 가셔서 (가지-, 가-)	**gajyeo gasyeoseo (gaji-, ga-)**	take it with you and (honorific)
주무시고 (주무시-)	**jumusigo (jumusi-)**	sleep and (honorific)
쉬세요 (쉬-)	**swiseyo (swi-)**	please rest (honorific)
나가시는 게 (나가-)	**nagasineun ge (naga-)**	(the act of) going out (honorific)

VOCABULARY PRACTICE 2
Give the Korean terms for the words described below.
1. what you ingest to treat an illness: _____
2. _____ and end (opposites)
3. children need to play _____ (where?) 에서 **eseo**

Supplementary Vocabulary
Describing Your Symptoms

혓바늘이 돋았어요.	Hyeotbaneuri dodasseoyo.	I have a sore on my tongue.
입술이 부르텄어요.	Ipsuri bureuteosseoyo.	I have a cold sore on my lip.
목이 따가워요.	Mogi ttagawoyo.	My throat is burning/stinging.
목에 가래가 껴요.	Moge garaega kkyeoyo.	I have phlegm.
피곤해요.	Pigonhaeyo.	I am tired.
머리가 아파요.	Meoriga apayo.	My head hurts.
기침이 나요.	Gichimi nayo.	I have a cough.
재채기가 나요.	Jaechaegiga nayo.	I'm sneezing.
땀이 나요.	Ttami nayo.	I sweat.
오한이 나요.	Ohani nayo.	I get chills.
고열이 나요.	Goyeori nayo.	I have a high fever.
미열이 나요.	Miyeori nayo.	I have a slight fever.
몸살이 났어요.	Momsari nasseoyo.	I have body aches.
두드러기가 나요.	Dudeureogiga nayo.	I'm getting hives.
토해요.	Tohaeyo.	I'm vomiting.
설사가 나요.	Seolssaga nayo.	I am having diarrhea.
변비에 걸렸어요.	Byeonbie geollyeosseoyo.	I am constipated.

GRAMMAR NOTE Formal grammatical negation -지 않아요
-ji anayo "not"

-Ji anayo -지 않아요 is a longer and more formal version of "not." As a suffix, it attaches to the verb root to negate the verb or adjective, instead of coming before it like the negative adverb **an** 안.

My head does not hurt. **Meorineun apeuji anayo.** 머리는 아프지 않아요.
I am not cold. **Chupji anayo.** 춥지 않아요.

PATTERN PRACTICE 4
Practice the following conversations using the formal grammatical negation -지 않아요 **-ji anayo**.
1. A: Do you have a headache? **Meoriga apeuseyo?** 머리가 아프세요?
   B: My head doesn't hurt. **Aniyo. Meorineun apeuji anayo.**
   아니요. 머리는 아프지 않아요.

2. A: Is your cough severe? **Gichimi simhaseyo?** 기침이 심하세요?
   B: No. My cough is not severe. **Aniyo. Gichimeun simhaji anayo.**
      아니요. 기침은 심하지 않아요.
3. A: Are you cold? **Chu.useyo?** 추우세요?
   B: No, I am not cold. **Aniyo. Chupji anayo.** 아니요. 춥지 않아요.
4. A: Do you have a fever? **Yeori naseyo?** 열이 나세요?
   B: No, I don't have a fever. **Aniyo. Yeoreun naji anayo.**
      아니요. 열은 나지 않아요.

GRAMMAR NOTE "Begin to" -기 시작해요 *-gi sijakaeyo*

You learned in Lesson 6 that **gi** 기 makes a temporary noun from a verb. Thus, since **sijakaeyo** 시작해요 means "begin," **-gi sijakaeyo** -기 시작해요 means "start doing (something)."

Now then, please start the song.
Ije noraereul sijakaseyo. 이제 노래를 시작하세요.

My body began to hurt.
Momi apeugi sijakaesseoyo. 몸이 아프기 시작했어요.

Oh, it started snowing just in that short time.
A! Geusae nuni naerigi sijakaenneyo.
아! 그새 눈이 내리기 시작했네요.

PATTERN PRACTICE 5

Practice the following phrases with -기 시작해요/시작했어요 **-gi sijakaeyo/ sijakaesseoyo**.
1. I am beginning to cough. **Gichimi nagi sijakaeyo.** 기침이 나기 시작해요.
2. I am starting to have a fever. **Yeori nagi sijakaeyo.** 열이 나기 시작해요.
3. My head began to hurt. **Meoriga apeugi sijakaesseoyo.**
   머리가 아프기 시작했어요.
4. It started to rain. **Biga ogi sijakaesseoyo.** 비가 오기 시작했어요.

GRAMMAR NOTE The suffix -는 거 *-neun geo* "-ing"

The suffix **-neun geo** -는 거 attaches to the verb root to turn it into a concept (noun)—similar to the "ing" in English. **-Neun geo** -는 거 is grammatically similar to **-gi** -기, but its use is wider and more general. If you say **noraereul joahaeyo** 노래를 좋아해요 that means "I like songs," but if you say **noraehaneun geol joahaeyo** 노래하는 걸 좋아해요, it becomes "I like singing." The subject version is **-neun ge** -는 게, the topic version (as in "Singing is ...") is **-neun geon** -는 건, and **-neun geol** -는 걸 is the object-marked version.

I have no problem with eating.
Meongneun geon munje eopseoyo. 먹는 건 문제 없어요.

It's better if you don't go to work tomorrow. (Not going to work tomorrow is good.) **Naeireun ireul an nagasineun ge joayo.**
내일은 일을 안 나가시는 게 좋아요.

PATTERN PRACTICE 6
Practice the following phrases using the suffix -는 거 **-neun goe** "-ing."
1. I like reading (books).
   Jeoneun chaek ingneun geol joahaeyo. 저는 책 읽는 걸 좋아해요.
2. I do not like walking. **Jeoneun geonneun geol an joahaeyo.**
   저는 걷는 걸 안 좋아해요.
3. I have no problem with reading. **Ingneun geon munje eopseoyo.**
   읽는 건 문제 없어요.
4. It's better if you rest tomorrow. **Naeireun swisinun ge joayo.**
   내일은 쉬시는 게 좋아요.

GRAMMAR NOTE Expressing options with -(이)나 *-(i)na*, -거나 *-geona*, 아니면 *animyeon*

There are a few ways to express the English concept of "or" in Korean. You can use **-ina** -이나 (after nouns ending in a consonant) or **-na** -나 (after nouns ending in a vowel) to connect two <u>nouns</u>:

Would you like me to give you a reminder call or text message?
Jeonhwana munjja deurilkkayo? 전화나 문자 드릴까요?

If you are choosing one <u>action</u> out of two possible options, you do not need a connector, but instead just list each whole action, complete with verb endings. You can add **animyeon** 아니면 (*Lit.,* "if not"):

Will we be doing a perm or (if not,) doing a color treatment today?
Pamahasil kkeoyeyo? (animyeon) yeomsaekasil kkeoyeyo?
파마하실 거예요? (아니면) 염색하실 거예요?

If you are considering more than a couple of optional actions to take, use the connector suffix **-geona** -거나. In the following example, the speaker is not committed to either option.

I'll either come in the afternoon or stop by again tomorrow morning (or something). **Ohue ogeona naeil ojeone dasi deulleulkkeyo.**
오후에 오거나 내일 오전에 다시 들를게요.

CULTURE NOTE Insurance and identification

If you have a full-time work visa in Korea, your employer is required to provide you with at least three of the the four basic insurances: national pension insurance (retirement benefits) **gungmin yeon.geumboheom** 국민 연금보험; health insurance **geon.gangboheom** 건강보험; industrial accident insurance **sanjaeboheom** 산재보험; and the optional (un)employment insurance **goyongboheom** 고용보험.

Even if you are in Korea for purposes other than work, you can be "locally" insured for your area of residence (that is, not through your employer). If you have a clear, legal reason for your stay (e.g., marriage, studying), you can obtain your local insurance on the day of your arrival. If you are a long-term tourist, you may be locally insured three months *after* you arrive in Korea.

If you are staying in Korea for work purposes, you will likely need to get a certificate of alien registration (foreigners' ID card) **oegugin deungnokjeung** 외국인 등록증, which needs to be renewed every year (or every three years, depending on your visa). When you visit a hospital, you can present this ID or your passport. Your employer may ask you to submit a medical certificate if you work for a big, established company. However, you do not need to present your medical history to local doctors, unless you have pre-existing conditions that the doctor should be aware of.

"Going to the hospital" (**byeongwon** 병원) is the Korean equivalent to "seeing a doctor," wherever that doctor may practice. If you need to stay in a hospital, it is called **ibwonhaeyo** 입원해요 and getting released from the hospital to go home is called **toewonhaeyo** 퇴원해요. Don't be surprised when Koreans say they have a cold and need to go "to the hospital" **byeongwone gaya doeyo** 병원에 가야 돼요.

CULTURE NOTE Don't over-exert yourself! 무리하지 마세요!
Murihaji maseyo!

According to a survey conducted in 2015 (https://data.oecd.org/emp/hours-worked.htm), Korean people worked 2,113 hours per year, which is the second-longest among 35 OECD countries. Many Koreans believe that illness stems from overwork and other stressors such as poor diet, lack of sleep and emotional stress. Warnings to keep warm, sleep well and not overwork are common, and you'll likely hear recommendations to get more rest rather than to take medicine. For illnesses, the Korean approach is to address the root cause and not just the symptoms. Natural remedies like herbal teas, honey or radish, hot baths and "sweating it out" are also common—and probably good advice! That said, Koreans do seek their doctor's advice and treatment when they get colds and the flu.

EXERCISE 4

Tell your colleague that you are okay, using the formal negation −지 않아요 **-ji anayo**, based on the given information.

1. Colleague: **Gichimi simhaseyo?** 기침이 심하세요?
   You: No, my cough is not severe.
2. Colleague: **Meoriga apeuseyo?** 머리가 아프세요?
   You: No, my head does not hurt.
3. Colleague: **Yageul meogeosseoyo?** 약을 먹었어요?
   You: No, I did not take medicine.
4. Colleague: **Byeongwone gasseoyo?** 병원에 갔어요?
   You: No, I did not go to the hospital.

EXERCISE 5

You are sick. Tell your doctor when the symptoms started using −기 시작했어요 **-gi sijakaeasseoyo.**

1. My fever started yesterday.
2. I started to cough last night.
3. I've had a headache since this morning.

EXERCISE 6

Write a sentence using -는 걸 좋아해 **-neun geol joahae** to describe the following people's hobbies.

Emma	walking in the morning or evening	Eunbi	watching a scary movie or reading books
Minjoon	playing basketball or going to a *noraebang*	Aiden	eating Chinese food or sleeping

1. 엠마는
2. 은비는
3. 민준은
4. 에이든은

점심시간이네요!
It's lunch time!

오늘은 뭐 먹을까요?
What should we eat today?

오늘은 한식을 먹고 싶은데요.
I'd like a traditional Korean meal.

한국에 있는 동안 한국 음식을 많이 먹고 싶어요.
I'd like to eat a lot of Korean food while I am here.

그럼 지하에 한식당이 있는데 거기 갑시다.
Then, there is a Korean restaurant in the basement. Let's go there.

뭐 먹을래요?
What would you like to eat?

여기 뭐가 맛있어요?
What's good here?

여기 순두부가 맛있어요.
Sundubu *is yummy here.*

그럼 오늘은 순두부를 먹어 볼게요.
Then I'll try sundubu *today.*

LESSON 11
Dining Out and In

 **One seafood *sundubu*, please.**

Minjoon and Emma go out for lunch near the office.

Minjoon: It's lunch time! What should we eat today?
          Jeomsimsiganineyo! Oneureun mwo meogeulkkayo?
          점심시간이네요! 오늘은 뭐 먹을까요?

Emma: I'd like a traditional Korean meal. I'd like to eat a lot of Korean food
          while I am here.
          **Oneureun hansigeul meokgo sipeundeyo. Hanguge inneun
          dong.an Hangug eumsigeul mani meokgo sipeoyo.**
          오늘은 한식을 먹고 싶은데요. 한국에 있는 동안 한국 음식을
          많이 먹고 싶어요.

Minjoon: Then, there is a Korean restaurant in the basement. Let's go there.
          Geureom jiha.e hansikdang.i inneunde geogi gapsida.
          그럼 지하에 한식당이 있는데 거기 갑시다.

At the restaurant…

Minjoon: What would you like to eat?
          Mwo meogeullaeyo?
          뭐 먹을래요?

Emma: What's good here?
          Yeogi mwoga masisseoyo?
          여기 뭐가 맛있어요?

Minjoon: *Sundubu* is yummy here.
          Yeogi sundubuga masisseoyo.
          여기 순두부가 맛있어요.

Emma: Then I'll try *sundubu* today.
          Geureom oneureun sundubureul meogeo bolkkeyo.
          그럼 오늘은 순두부를 먹어 볼게요.

A waitress brings a pitcher of water and two cups.

Waitress: What would you like (to order)?
          Mwo deusigesseoyo?
          뭐 드시겠어요?

Minjoon: One seafood *sundubu*, please.
          Haemul sundubu hana juseyo.
          해물 순두부 하나 주세요.

Emma: For me, one beef *sundubu*, please.
           Jeoneun sogogi sundubu hanayo.
           저는 소고기 순두부 하나요.
Waitress: OK. Please wait a bit.
           Algesseumnida. Jamsiman gidaryeo juseyo.
           알겠습니다. 잠시만 기다려 주세요.
Emma: Where are the spoons and chopsticks?
           Sujeoneun eodie itjiyo?
           수저는 어디에 있지요?
Waitress: They are in the drawer on the side of the table.
           Teibeul yeope seorabeul yeosimyeon isseoyo.
           테이블 옆의 서랍을 여시면 있어요.
Emma: OK. Thank you!
           Ne, gamsahamnida!
           네, 감사합니다!

VOCABULARY AND EXPRESSIONS

점심	**jeomsim**	lunch, lunch time
한식	**hansik**	Korean food
한식당	**hansikdang**	restaurant that only serves Korean food
순두부 (찌개)	**sundubu (jjigae)**	soft tofu (stew)
해물	**haemul**	seafood
소고기	**sogogi**	beef
수저	**sujeo**	spoon(s) and chopsticks
숟가락	**sutgarak**	spoon(s)
젓가락	**jeotgarak**	chopsticks
테이블	**teibeul**	table
서랍	**seorap**	drawer
-지요	**-jiyo**	we both know/right?
먹고 싶은데요 (먹, 싶)	**meokgo sipeundeyo (meok-, sip-)**	I want to/would like to eat…
갑시다 (가-)	**gapsida (ga-)**	Let's go.
맛있어요 (있-)	**masisseoyo (iss-)**	delicious
드시겠어요 (드시-)	**deusigesseoyo (deusi-)**	would you like to eat (honorific)
여시면 (열-)	**yeosimyeon (yeol-)**	if you open (honorific)

VOCABULARY PRACTICE 1

Give the Korean terms for the words described below.

1. Utentils that Koreans (and other Asian cultures) traditionally eat with:
   _____

2. Sea creatures eaten as food: _____

3. A restaurant that serves Korean food only: _____
4. Tastes good!: _____

Supplementary Vocabulary
Korean food and related words

비빔냉면	**bibimnaeng-myeon**	spicy cold noodles	갈비	**galbi**	barbecued (beef) ribs
불고기	**bulgogi**	barbecued beef	국	**guk**	soup
순두부	**sundubu**	tofu stew (spicy)	반찬	**banchan**	side dishes
비빔밥	**bibimbap**	rice mixed with vegetables and hot sauce	나물	**namul**	seasoned steamed vegetables
잡채	**jabchae**	clear noodles with seasoned vegetables	양념치킨	**yangnyeom chikin**	seasoned fried chicken
밥	**bap**	cooked rice	간장	**ganjang**	soy sauce
물냉면	**mulnaeng-myeon**	cold noodles in soup	된장	**doenjang**	soy bean paste
(해물) 파전	**(haemul) pajeon**	(seafood) scallion pancake	고추장	**gochujang**	hot pepper paste
양념	**jjigae**	salty stew	설탕	**seoltang**	sugar
갈비탕	**galbitang**	beef rib soup	소금	**sogeum**	salt
갈비찜	**galbijjim**	braised (beef) rib	김	**gim**	roasted seaweed
생선 구이	**saengseon gui**	grilled fish	참기름	**chamgireum**	sesame oil
볶음밥	**bokkeum-bap**	fried rice	김치	**gimchi**	*kimchi*
오징어 볶음	**ojing.eo bokkeum**	stir fried squid	깍두기	**kkagdugi**	radish *kimchi*

GRAMMAR NOTE *"Would like to," "want to" -고 싶어요 -go sipeoyo*

While **-(eu)llaeyo** -(으)ㄹ래요 has the idea of "I want to so I'm going to do (it)," and can thus sound rather self-centered, **-go sipeoyo** -고 싶어요 can be used for wishes that may take a while to achieve or are not entirely under one's control. It is more neutral. The object of the person's desire (that is, of the desired action) is normally paired with the object marker, but it can also take the subject marker in emphatic or idiomatic uses.

I would like a traditional Korean meal (what do you think?).
Oneureun hansigeul meokgo sipeundeyo.
오늘은 한식을 먹고 싶은데요.

I want to see Mom./I miss Mom.
Eommaga bogo sipeoyo. 엄마가 보고 싶어요

If talking about a third party's wishes, you must use the extended version of this ending, **-go sipeohaeyo** -고 싶어해요, e.g., "My sister wants to rest." **Nunaga swigo sipeohaeyo** -고 싶어해요.

PATTERN PRACTICE 1
Practice the following conversations with -고 싶어요 **-go sipeoyo.**
1. A: What would you like to have for lunch?
      Jeomsim mwo meogeullaeyo? 점심 뭐 먹을래요?
   B: I would like a traditional Korean meal today.
      Oneureun hansigi meokko sipeoyo. 오늘은 한식이 먹고 싶어요.
2. A: What would you like to do during the break?
      Banghage mwo hago sipeoyo? 방학에 뭐 하고 싶어요?
   B: I want to travel. **Yeohaeng gago sipeoyo.** 여행가고 싶어요.
3. A: What are you going to do this weekend?
      Ibeon jumare mwo hal kkeyeyo? 이번 주말에 뭐 할 거예요?
   B: I am so tired, so I would like to rest.
      Neomu pigonhaeseo swigo sipeoyo. 너무 피곤해서 쉬고 싶어요.
4. A: I want to see my family... **Gajokdeuri bogo sipeoyo...**
      가족들이 보고 싶어요⋯ (family: 가족 **gajok**)
   B: Try making a video call. **Hwasangtonghwareul hae boseyo.**
      화상통화를 해 보세요. (video call: 화상통화 **hwasangtonghwa**)

GRAMMAR NOTE Using the -지요 *-jiyo* "You should know" suffix
You use the suffix **-jiyo** -지요 when you think the listener would definitely know the information or answer, e.g., today's date or where something is, and you are trying to confirm it. It is often shortened to **-jyo** -죠:

I am (of course) not going. **Jeoneun an gajiyo.** 저는 안 가지요.
Hmmm, what's the date today? **Oneul myeochirijyo?** 오늘 며칠이지요?

Where are the spoons and chopsticks?
Sujeoneun eodie itjiyo? 수저는 어디에 있지요?

What would be good to eat today?
Oneureun mwo meokjyo? 오늘은 뭐 먹죠?

PATTERN PRACTICE 2

Practice the following conversations with -지요 **-jiyo**.

1. A: It's cold today, isn't it? **Oneul nalssiga chupjiyo?** 오늘 날씨가 춥지요?
   B: Yes, it is. **Ne, geuraeyo.** 네, 그래요.
2. A: The food at this restaurant is good, right?
   I sikdang eumsik gwaenchanchiyo? 이 식당 음식 괜찮지요?
   B: Yes, it is good! **Ne, gwaenchanneyo!** 네, 괜찮네요!
3. A: What's good here? **Yeogi mwoga masitjiyo?** 여기 뭐가 맛있지요?
   B: *Bibimbap* is good here. **Yeogin bibimbabi masisseoyo.**
   여긴 비빔밥이 맛있어요.
4. A: Where are the spoons and chopsticks? **Sujeoneun eodi itjiyo?**
   수저는 어디 있지요?
   B: They are there if you open the drawer on the side of the table.
   Teibeul yeopuy seorap ane isseumnida.
   테이블 옆의 서랍 안에 있습니다.

GRAMMAR NOTE Adding -는 동안 *-neun dong.an* "while," "during"
to verbs

-Neun dong.an -는 동안 attaches to an active verb that is the backdrop for another
action.

Don't use your phone while having dinner.
Jeonyeok meongneun dong.an jeonhwa sayonghaji maseyo.
저녁 먹는 동안 전화 사용하지 마세요.

You just played games while you were home, right?
Jipe inneun dong.an geimman haetji?
집에 있는 동안 게임만 했지?

PATTERN PRACTICE 3

Practice the following sentences with -는 동안 **-neun dong.an**.

1. I slept for eight hours. **Yeodel sigan dong.an jasseoyo.**
   여덟 시간 동안 잤어요.
2. I would like to travel a lot while I am in Korea.
   Han.guge innun dong.an yeohaeng.eul mani hago sipeoyo.
   한국에 있는 동안 여행을 많이 하고 싶어요.
3. I read a book while taking the subway.
   Jihacheoreul taneun dong.an chaegeul ilksseumnida.
   지하철을 타는 동안 책을 읽습니다.
4. While Emma was working, Eunbi watched TV.
   Emmaga ilhaneun dong.an Eunbineun telebijeoneul bwasseoyo.
   엠마가 일하는 동안 은비는 텔레비전을 봤어요.

CULTURE NOTE **Typical Korean dishes**

Normally, a meal in a Korean home will include the basics such as **bap** 밥 "cooked rice" (as opposed to **ssal** 쌀 "uncooked rice"), **jjigae** 찌개 "salty stew/casserole," and **guk** 국 "clear, bland soup."

As for **banchan** 반찬 "side dishes" other than **kimchi** 김치, the spicy fermented cabbage mainstay of the table, there may be **namul** 나물 (seasoned steamed vegetables), **jjim** 찜 (seasoned steamed/simmered meat), **bokkeum** 볶음 (any sauteed dish with sauce) or **gu.i** 구이 (grilled meat or fish).

Gogi 고기 "meat" includes **sogogi** 소고기 "beef," **dwaejigogi** 돼지고기 "pork," and **talkgogi** 닭고기 "chicken meat" and others, but the concept does not include fish **saengsun** 생선, or seafood **haemul** 해물.

Two most common types of seaweed are **kim** 김 (dried laver, like the wrap on sushi, but seasoned with sesame oil and salt) and **miyeok** 미역 (kelp, sea mustard), which is thicker and used in soups. Seaweed is very nutritious and seaweed soup is a traditional birthday soup in Korea.

CULTURE NOTE **Cutlery**

Koreans use **sutgarak** 숟가락 "spoon" and **jeotgarak** 젓가락 "chopsticks" thin metal chopsticks. Spoons are traditionally for rice and soup or **jjigae** and chopsticks are for **banchan** 반찬. **Pokeu** 포크 "fork" and **kal/naipeu** 칼/나이프 "knife" are used at Western restaurants. You may be given scissors **gawi** 가위 at a restaurant to cut **kalbi** 갈비 (meat) or noodles. Napkins **naepkin** 냅킨 are usually provided in restaurants.

CULTURE NOTE **Korean table manners**

At a meal everyone waits for the most senior person to start eating. Leave your bowl on the table—rice bowls are usually made of ceramic and metal and they would be too hot to hold anyway. Use a spoon for rice and soup, and chopsticks for side dishes. It is okay to make a little slurping sound when drinking hot soup, but you should not blow your nose at the table. To show your gratitude for someone cooking or buying a meal for you, use these expressions: **jal meokgesseumnida** 잘 먹겠습니다 "I will eat well" before eating, and **jal meogeosseumnida** 잘 먹었습니다 "I ate well" or **aju masitge meogeosseumnida** 아주 맛있게 먹었습니다 "I ate really well" after you have finished.

EXERCISE 1

Answer Eunbi's questions in Korean using 고 싶다 **-go sipda**.
1. Eunbi: **Jeomsime mwo meogeullaeyo?** 점심에 뭐 먹을래요?
   You: I want to eat *sundubu*.
2. Eunbi: **Jumare mwo hal kkeoyeyo?** 주말에 뭐 할 거예요?
   You: I wish to sleep a lot.

3. Eunbi: **Emmaga jibe gamyeon mwo hago sipeohaeyo?**
   엄마 씨가 집에 가면 뭐 하고 싶어해요?
   You: She wants to rest.
4. Eunbi: **Eideuni ibeon hyuga-e mwo hago sipeohaeyo?**
   에이든이 이번 휴가에 뭐 하고 싶어해요?
   You: He wants to travel to China. (to travel to: 여행 가다 **yeohaeng gada**)

EXERCISE 2
Ask for your friend's agreement using −지요 **-jiyo**.
1. It's very hot today, isn't it?
2. *Sundubu* is really delicious, right?
3. The subway in Seoul is really convenient, isn't it?
4. *Noraebang* is really fun, don't you think?

EXERCISE 3
Emma and Eunbi are great friends. Translate the following statements about them using −는 동안 **-neun dong.an**.
1. While Emma and Eunbi were working together, they became closer.
   (close: 친하다 **chinhada**)
2. While Eunbi rests, Emma watches TV.
3. While Emma sings, Eunbi dances.
4. While Eunbi exercises, Emma goes grocery shopping.

DIALOGUE 2 Can you deliver now?

Eunbi is helping Aiden pack for his move. They get hungry and decide to get some food.

Aiden: I'm hungry! What shall we eat?
         Bae gopeuda! Mwo meogeulkkayo?
         배고프다! 뭐 먹을까요?
Eunbi: We eat Chinese food on moving day in Korea.
         Hangugeseoneun isahaneun nare Jung.gug eumsigeul meogeoyo.
         한국에서는 이사하는 날에 중국 음식을 먹어요.
Aiden: OK! I'll have *jjajangmyeon*.
         Joayo! Jung.gugeumsik meogeupsida. Nan jjajangmyeon meogeullaeyo.
         좋아요! 중국음식 먹읍시다. 난 짜장면 먹을래요.
Eunbi: I'll have *jjamppong*. I'll order in. Should we order *tangsuyuk*, too?
         Nan, jjamppong. Naega jumunhalkkeyo. Tangsuyukdo sikilkkayo?
         난, 짬뽕. 내가 주문할게요. 탕수육도 시킬까요?

Aiden: Yes, let's order a small one.
Jageun geollo hana sikipsida.
작은 걸로 하나 시킵시다.

Eunbi calls a Chinese restaurant.

Staff: Hello, this is Hong Kong Chinese Restaurant.
Ne, hongkongbanjeomipnida.
네, 홍콩반점입니다.

Eunbi: Hello. Can you deliver now?
Yeoboseyo. Jigeum baedaldoejyo?
여보세요. 지금 배달되죠?

Staff: Yes. Go ahead.
Ne, malsseumhaseyo.
네, 말씀하세요.

Eunbi: We are calling from the Shilla building, room 301. We would like one *jjajangmyeon*, one *jjamppong* and one small *tangsuyuk*, please.
Yeogi silla bilding sambaegil ho.indeyo. Jjajangmyeon hana, jjamppong hana, tangsuyuk jageun geo hana butakdeurilkkeyo.
여기 신라 빌딩 301호인데요. 짜장면 하나, 짬뽕 하나, 탕수육 작은 거 하나 부탁드릴게요.

Staff: OK, got it. One *jjajangmyeon*, one *jjamppong* and one small *tangsuyuk*, right?
Ne, ne. Jjajangmyeon hana, jjamppong hana, tangsuyuk jageun geo hanayo?
네, 네. 짜장면 하나, 짬뽕 하나, 탕수육 작은 거 하나요?

Eunbi: Yes. How much is it?
Ne, eolmayeyo?
네, 얼마예요?

Staff: (You ordered) one *jjajangmyeon*, one *jjamppong* and one small *tangsuyuk*. The total is 21,500 won. (Are you paying with) cash?
Jjajangmyeon hana, jjamppong hana, tangsuyuk sojja hana, hasyeotgoyo. Modu imancheonobaeg wonimnida. Hyeongeumisimnikka?
짜장면 하나, 짬뽕 하나, 탕수육 소자 하나, 하셨고요. 모두 21,500 원입니다. 현금이십니까?

Eunbi: No, we'll pay with a card.
Aniyo. Gyesaneun kadeuro halkkeyo.
아니요. 계산은 카드로 할게요.

Staff: OK.
Ne, algesseumnida.
네, 알겠습니다.

Eunbi: How long will it take? We are really hungry.
            Eolmana geollilkkayo? Jeohuiga jom baega gopaseoyo.
            얼마나 걸릴까요? 저희가 좀 배가 고파서요.
Staff: We'll deliver within 20 minutes. Don't worry.
            Isip bun ane gatda deurilkkeyo. Geokjeong maseyo.
            20 분 안에 갖다 드릴게요. 걱정 마세요.
Eunbi: OK. Then please hurry. Thank you.
            Geureom ppalli gatda juseyo. Gomapseumnida.
            그럼 빨리 갖다 주세요. 고맙습니다.
Staff: OK. Thank you.
            Ne, gamsahamnida.
            네, 감사합니다.

VOCABULARY AND EXPRESSIONS

이사*	**isa**	moving, *to move
주문*	**jumun**	ordering, *to order
배달*	**baedal**	delivering, *to deliver
계산*	**gyesan**	calculation, paying, *to calculate
걱정*	**geokjeong**	worrying, *to worry
배	**bae**	belly, stomach
날	**nal**	day
짜장면	**jjajangmyeon**	noodles with black bean sauce
짬뽕	**jjamppong**	spicy seafood noodle soup
탕수육	**tangsuyuk**	breaded, glazed sweet-and-sour pork
홍콩	**Hong Kong**	Hong Kong
반점	**banjeom**	suffix often used with Chinese restaurants
신라	**Silla**	Shilla (Kingdom)
호	**ho**	# used for numbering a series
소자	**sojja**	small one, small size
빨리	**ppalli**	quickly, hurriedly
여보세요	**Yeoboseyo**	hello (on the phone)
배고프다 (배고프-)	**baegopeuda (baegopeu-)**	hungry
이사하는 (날) (이사하-)	**isahaneun (nal) (isaha-)**	moving (day)
시킬까요? (시키-)	**sikilkkayo? (siki-)**	should I/we order?
작은 (걸로) (작-)	**jageun (geollo) (jak-)**	(by) the small one
갖다 드릴게요 (갖-, 드리-)	**gatda deurilkkeyo (gaj-, deuri-)**	I'll get/bring (it to you) (humble)
걱정 마세요 (말-)	**geokjeong maseyo (mal-)**	don't worry
갖다 주세요 (갖-, 주-)	**gatda juseyo (gaj-, ju-)**	please bring (X) (to me) (honorific)

VOCABULARY PRACTICE 2

Give the Korean terms for the words described below.

1. When you haven't eaten in a long time, you feel: _____
2. Where the food goes to be digested (in your body): _____
3. Paying the check in a restaurant: _____
4. When you are uneasy or anxious about something: _____

Supplementary Vocabulary

Taste and food-related words

배고파요	baegopayo	hungry
배불러요	baebulleoyo	full
목말라요	mongmallayo	thirsty
맛있어요	masisseoyo	delicious
맛없어요	madeopseoyo	not tasty
매워요	maewoyo	spicy
싱거워요	singgeowoyo	bland, not salty enough
셔요	syeoyo	sour
달아요	darayo	sweet
써요	sseoyo	bitter
고소해요	gosohaeyo	savory, nutty
시원해요	siwonhaeyo	refreshing
비려요	biryeoyo	fishy, gamey
떫어요	tteolbeoyo	pucker-y: a "taste" that makes your mouth pucker, with(out) sourness

GRAMMAR NOTE Verbs in noun-modifying form with -는 -neun in a relative clause

To describe a noun with a whole phrase, the verb at the end needs to be in the correct noun-modifying form, with suffix -는 **-neun** attached to the verb root. No matter how long the modifying clause is, it always comes *before* the modified noun in Korean:

In Korea, we eat Chinese food on <u>moving</u> day.
Hangugeseoneun <u>isahaneun nar</u>e jung.gug eumsigeul meogeoyo.
한국에서는 <u>이사하는 날</u>에 중국 음식을 먹어요.

<u>People who dislike shopping</u> can save money.
<u>Syoping.eul sireohaneun saram</u>eun doneul jeolyakal ssu isseoyo.
<u>쇼핑을 싫어하는 사람</u>은 돈을 절약할 수 있어요.

PATTERN PRACTICE 4

Practice the following sentences with verbs in noun-modifying forms.

1. I usually stay at home on <u>my days off</u> (days when I "rest").
   Swineun narenun botong jibe isseoyo. 쉬는 날에는 보통 집에 있어요.
2. That restaurant (is <u>a restaurant that) makes good *jjamppong*</u>.
   Jeo sikdang.un jjamppong.eul jal haneun sikdang.ieyo.
   저 식당은 짬뽕을 잘 하는 식당이에요.
3. In Korea, people eat Chinese food on <u>moving day</u>.
   Han.gugeseoneun <u>isahaneun nare</u> Jung.guk eumsigeul meogeoyo.
   한국에서는 이사하는 날에 중국 음식을 먹어요.
4. Take the <u>subway that takes you toward the city</u>.
   Sicheong jjogeuro ganeun jihacheoreun yeogiseo taseyo.
   시청쪽으로 가는 지하철은 여기서 타세요.

GRAMMAR NOTE Self-directed announcement with -다 *-da*

The suffix **-da** -다 serves two functions. Attached to the root of a verb, it creates a dictionary form: **ilkda** 읽다 "to read," **jakda** 작다 "to be small." With adjectives (and only with adjectives), it has the effect of exclamation or self-talk, almost as if making an announcement to yourself. It is frequently repeated with a regular **eo-** 어- conjugated adjective for emphasis:

Hungry! **Baegopeuda!** 배고프다!
Brrrrr! Soooo cold! **Chupda, chuwo!** 춥다, 추워!

PATTERN PRACTICE 5

Practice the following self-directed announcements with **-da** -다 .

1. Ah, it's hot! **A, deopda!** 아, 덥다!
2. I am hungry! **Baegopeuda!** 배고프다!
3. It is really delicious! **Jeongmal masitda!** 정말 맛있다!
4. I want to see my mom... (I miss my mom.) **Eomma bogo sipda... .**
   엄마 보고 싶다….

GRAMMAR NOTE 하 *ha* and 되 *doe* "Can, possible"

Most Sino-Korean verbs, especially those roots that use the 하 **ha** suffix, can use the **doe** 되 suffix for a passive meaning close to "possible" or "can." It also sometimes means that something has been arranged or come to be a certain way.

Can you deliver now? **Jigeum baedaldoejyo?** 지금 배달돼요?

It is an item that can pressure-cook as well.
Amnyeokdo doeneun jepumieyo. 압력도 되는 제품이에요.

When you get off at the Kwanghwamun Station, it's connected.
Gwanghwamunyeog.eseo naerimyeon yeon.gyeoldoe.eo isseoyo.
광화문역에서 내리면 연결되어 있어요.

PATTERN PRACTICE 6

Practice the following conversations with −하다 **-hada** and −되다 **-doeda**.

1. A: Is the Internet working now? **Jigum inteonet dwaeyo?**
       지금 인터넷 돼요?
    B: No, it's not working. **Aniyo, an dwaeyo.** 아니요, 안 돼요.
2. A: Today's meeting has been canceled.
       Oneul miting.i chwisodwaesseumnida. 오늘 미팅이 취소됐습니다.
    B: I beg your pardon? Who cancelled the meeting?
       Ne? Nuga chwisohaesseumnikka? 네? 누가 취소했습니까?
3. A: Can you deliver a bowl of *jjajangmyeon*?
       Jjajangmyeon han geureut baedaldwaeyo?
       짜장면 한 그릇 배달돼요?
    B: Yes, we can. **Ne, baedaldoemnida.** 네, 배달됩니다.
4. A: Are you ready? **Junbidwaesseoyo?** 준비됐어요?
    B: Yes, I'm ready. **Ne, junbiga da dwaesseoyo.** 네, 준비가 다 됐어요.

GRAMMAR NOTE 거 *Geo* **as a filler word**

Geo 거 (or its full form **geot** 것) means "thing" or "stuff," but it is also used as a filler word. You have seen its use in two endings **-(eu)l kkeoyeyo** -(으)ㄹ 거에요 "be going to," and **-(eu)l kkeo gatayo** -(으)ㄹ 거 같아요 "it seems." Sometimes it is used as a filler word after the fact because Koreans, in general, like to say the most important thing first.

I need a bag—a big one.
Gabang.i keun geo hana piryohaeyo. 가방이 큰 거 하나 필요해요.
(said as often as **Keun gabang.i hana piryohaeyo.**)
(큰 가방이 하나 필요해요.)

One small *tangsuyuk*.
Tangsuyuk jageun geo hanayo. 탕수육 작은 거 하나요.
(said more often than **Jageun tangsuyuk hanayo.**)
(작은 탕수육 하나요.)

CULTURE NOTE Delivery and dining

There is a great variety of cuisines available for delivery in the cities in Korea, often (but not only) with a Korean twist, such as **bulgogi** 불고기 피자 pizza and **gimchi** 김치 햄버거 hamburgers. Well-known US fast-food chains also have stores and delivery in Korea. Generally speaking, restaurant, delivery and street vender food is less expensive in Korea than in the US, so eating outside the home is quite common, and healthy and savory. You don't have to tip in Korea, and your tax is already included in the bill.

At a restaurant sit-down meal, food is often shared family-style at the table, where everyone eats from a large dish and meats are ordered as one large plate (e.g., 4 servings = **sainbun** 사인분) and grilled at the table. This communal eating is more common than ordering one's own individual meal, and to many, eating alone seems sad, although the **honbap** 혼밥 (eating a meal alone) and **honsul** 혼술 (drinking alone) culture has emerged and is spreading in Korea.

CULTURE NOTE Drinking rituals

Wherever they serve drinks, there is food in Korea (**anju** 안주—snacks and dishes accompanying alchoholic beverages). When getting together for dinner, people usually end up drinking together, too. A company outing, **hoesik** 회식, usually expects the members to participate in a free dinner and follow-up "bar hopping." The second stop or the "second round," **icha** 이차, is for drinks after a shared meal or for *noraebang*. (The first stop is called **ilcha** 일차.) The rounds can continue on with added numbers (**samcha** 삼차, **sacha** 사차) for more drinking and singing.

CULTURE NOTE Traditional foods

If you ask Koreans about special foods eaten on particular days, you may get various answers depending on the region or family they grew up in. Some popular foods for rainy days include **makkeolli** 막걸리 (unfiltered rice wine) and **buchim** 부침 (savory pancakes, also called **jeon** 전) or **bindaeddeok** 빈대떡 (mungbean pancake). Roasted chestnuts or sweet potatoes from a street vendor are popular on a cold winter day, and **naengmyeon** 냉면 (cold noodles), **momilguksu** 모밀국수 (buckwheat noodles), or **bingsu** 빙수 (red-bean and shaved ice sundae) on a hot day. Traditional party entrées prepared at home typically include **japchae** 잡채 (sweet potato noodles mixed with vegetables and beef) and **bulgogi** 불고기 (sweet-marinated beef).

If you ask about "traditional foods" you'll get answers about foods you should eat on special occasions, holidays (**myeongjeol** 명절) and celebrations. For example, every Korean will agree that **miyeokguk** 미역국 (seaweed soup) is what you eat on your birthday. It's given to new mothers as it restores iron and general health just after giving birth. Some foods Koreans eat have symbolic meanings and are good for your health.

dongjinnal (dongji) 동짓날 (동지)	Winter solstice (around December 22 or 23)
Eat: **patjuk** 팥죽 sweet red bean porridge	Because: The color red was believed to scare off evil spirits or fight off diseases. Eating red beans also boosts one's Yang (bright, positive) energy on this shortest day of the year when Yin (dark, negative) energy is strongest.
On *seollal* 설날	New Year's Day (solar or lunar calendar)
Eat: **tteokguk** 떡국 rice cake soup	Because: Long, log-shaped rice cake (sliced into the soup) represents wishes for longevity.
At *chuseok* 추석	Full moon at autumn harvest time (8/15 by the lunar calendar)
Eat: **songpyeon** 송편 half-moon-shaped, sweet rice dumplings with pine needle flavoring and various fillings (sesame seed butter, sweet red beans, honey, chestnut butter, sweet potato)	Because: The dumplings represent the shape of the moon and its cycle, symbolizing the cycle of life.
On *daeboreum* 대보름	First full moon of the lunar year
Eat: **bureom** 부럼 specific nuts eaten at this time: chestnuts, peanuts, walnuts, gingko nuts, pine nuts; and **ogok** 오곡 five (cooked) grains—rice, barley, beans, two kinds of millet—and **namul** 나물 sautéed vegetables (especially fern fiddleheads, sweet potato leaves, pepper leaves, bell flower root)	Because: Breaking the hard shell of nuts scares away evil spirits for the coming year. (Also eaten because they reduce itching and inflammation.) The other foods build health for the coming year.
On *bongnal* 복날	The three hottest days of summer (calculated using traditional astrological calendars)
Eat: **samgyetang** 삼계탕 chicken porridge with ginseng, and **jang.eo** 장어 eel	Because: Koreans say **iyeolchiyeol** 이열치열 "quell heat with heat": drinking hot soup with heat-building ginseng is said to ultimately cool you down. Eel is also traditionally considered a "hot" (heat-inducing or Yang-energy) food.

Food traditions include serving noodles to guests at weddings and generously giving out **patsirutteok** 팥시루떡 (steamed rice cake topped with red beans) to neighbors on the day you move in. Noodles could easily feed the whole town, and also symbolized the bride and groom's long life together. Although not everyone serves noodles at weddings these days, the expression "**Guksu eonje meokge haejul kkeoya?**" "국수 언제 먹게 해줄 거야?" "When will you let me eat noodles?" is still very commonly-used as a round-about way to to urge people to get married or to poke fun at friends whose romantic life seems to be going well.

EXERCISE 4

Introduce your friends below, and describe what kind of person each is, using the noun-modifying form -는 **-neun**.

Minjoon 민준	**Jeohago gachi ilhaeyo.** 저하고 같이 일해요.
Emma 엠마	**Maeil keopireul se jan masyeoyo.** 매일 커피를 세 잔 마셔요.
Aiden 에이든	**Hyojadong.e sarayo.** 효자동에 살아요.
Eunbi 은비	**Han.gung nyeonghwareul jaju bwayo.** 한국 영화를 자주 봐요.

Minjoon: **Jeohago gachi ilhaneun sarameun Minjun ssiyeyo.**
민준: 저하고 같이 일하는 사람은 민준 씨예요.

1. Emma 엠마: _____
2. Aiden 에이든: _____
3. Eunbi 은비: _____

EXERCISE 5

Try making self-directed announcements using the given information.
1. Wow, this *jjamppong* is really spicy! (wow: 와! **Wa!**)
2. Oof. I am so tired! (oof: 에휴… **Ehyu…**)
3. Phew! It's done. (phew: 휴! **Hyu!**)
4. Oy, my head hurts! (oy: 아이고! **Aigo!**)
5. Ugh, it is too hot today! (ugh: 에구… **Egu…**)

EXERCISE 6

You and Aiden are preparing a surprise party for Emma. Ask Aiden if everything is ready, using -되다 **-doeda**.
1. You: Has the food been delivered?
   Aiden: Yes, it has.
2. You: Has the room been cleaned?
   Aiden: Yes, it has. (to clean: 청소하다 **cheongsohada**)
3. You: Has the present been prepared?
   Aiden: Yes, it has. (present: 선물 **seonmul**; to prepare: 준비하다 **junbihada**)

LESSON 12
Getting a Haircut

 **DIALOGUE 1** I'm trying to get a haircut.

Emma makes an appointment for a haircut.

Emma: Hello. I'm trying to get a haircut. Can I get it cut today?
Annyeonghaseyo. Meori jom jareuryeogo haneundeyo. Oneul doelkkayo?
안녕하세요. 머리 좀 자르려고 하는데요. 오늘 될까요?

Manager: Hello. Welcome, come right in. Will you be getting a perm or color treatment today?
Eoseo oseyo! Pamahasil kkeoyeyo, animyeon yeomsaekasil kkeoyeyo?
어서 오세요! 파마하실 거예요, 아니면 염색하실 거예요?

Emma: I just need a trim.
Meoriman yakgan dadeumeuryeogo haeyo.
머리만 약간 다듬으려고 해요.

Manager: Just a minute, please. We are full until the afternoon. Can you come back after 1 or 2?
Jamsimanyo. Ohukkaji sigani an doeneundeyo. Han sina du si ihue dasi osigesseoyo?
잠시만요. 오후까지 시간이 안 되는데요. 한 시나 두 시 이후에 다시 오시겠어요?

Emma: Yes, that's fine.
Ne. Algesseoyo.
네. 알겠어요.

Manager: Would you like me to give you a reminder call or text message?
Jeonhwana munjja deurilkkayo?
전화나 문자 드릴까요?

Emma: No, thank you. I'll just come back around a quarter to 2 or stop by again tomorrow morning.
Anieyo, gwaenchanayo. Du si shibo bun jeonjjeume dasi ogeona naeil ojeone dasi deulleulkkeyo.
아니에요, 괜찮아요. 2 시 15 분 전쯤에 다시 오거나 내일 오전에 다시 들를게요.

Manager: OK.
Ne.
네.

VOCABULARY AND EXPRESSIONS

파마*	pama	a perm
염색*	yeomsaek	dye, dyeing
문자*	munjja	text, texting
매니저	maenijeo	manager, receptionist
전	jeon	before
오전	ojeon	AM/before noon
아니면	animyeon	or, if not
약간	yakgan	a little bit, kind of
다시	dasi	again
자르려고 (자르-)	jareuryeogo (jareu-)	trying to (have it) cut
다듬으려고 (다듬-)	dadeumeuryeogo (dadeum-)	trying to (have it) trimmed
들를게요 (들르-)	deulleulkkeyo (deulleu-)	stop by

VOCABULARY PRACTICE 1

Give the Korean terms for the words described below.
1. the person in charge of a shop: _____
2. to make your hair a different color: _____
3. before noon: _____
4. a quick message sent digitally: _____

Supplementary Vocabulary
Useful time adverbs

옛날에	yennare	in the olden days, long time ago
(예)전에	(ye)jeone	before, some time ago
과거에	gwageo.e	in the past
아까	akka	a while ago (today)
조금 전에	jogeum jeone	a little while ago (today)
전에	jeone	before (not today)
이제	ije	now (unlike before)
지금	jigeum	now (at this point in time)
벌써	beolsseo	already
아직(도)	ajik(do)	not yet, still not
이따(가)	itta(ga)	(a little while) later (today)
나중에	najung.e	(some time) later
훗날에	hunnare	some (other) day in the future
장래에	jangnae.e	in the days to come
미래에	mirae.e	in the future

GRAMMAR NOTE Revisiting the intention suffix -(으)려고 그러, -(으)려고 하 *-(eu)ryeogo geureo, -(eu)ryeogo ha*

You learned that the connector suffix -(으)려고 *-(eu)ryeogo* expresses that one is about to or intending to do something. With the helping verb **ha** 하 or **geureo** 그러, it can be used as the main verb of the sentence.

I'm trying to get a haircut. **Meori jom jareuryeogo geureoneundeyo.**
머리 좀 자르려고 그러는데요.

I'm just going to trim my hair a bit. **Meori yakgan dadeumeuryeogo haeyo.**
머리 약간 다듬으려고 해요.

The bus is about to leave. **Beoseuga tteonaryeogo geuraeyo.**
버스가 떠나려고 그래요.

I am going to close the door because I am cold.
Chuwoseo mun dadeuryeogo haeyo.
추워서 문 닫으려고 해요.

PATTERN PRACTICE 1
Practice saying your intentions using -(으)려고 그러 *-(eu)ryeogo geureo*.
1. I am going to eat sushi for lunch today.
   Oneureun jeomsime seusireul meogeuryeogo haeyo.
   오늘은 점심에 스시를 먹으려고 해요.
2. I am trying to get a perm tomorrow. **Naeil pamareul haryeogo haneundeyo.**
   내일 파마를 하려고 하는데요.
3. I am about to leave. **Jigeum nagaryeogo haeyo.**
   지금 나가려고 해요.

GRAMMAR NOTE Using the marker -만 *-man* "only," "just"

The marker **-man** -만 means "only," but it is also used to soften requests or commands, e.g., "just a minute please." **Jamsimanyo.** 잠시만요.

I just need to have my bangs trimmed.
Ammeoriman yakgan dadeumeuryeogo haeyo.
앞머리만 약간 다듬으려고 해요.

PATTERN PRACTICE 2
Practice the following -만 *-man* sentences.
1. Wait a minute please. **Jamkkanman gidaryeo juseyo.**
   잠깐만 기다려 주세요.

2. I just need to have my hair trimmed on the sides.
   Yeommeoriman yakgan dadeumeuryeogo haeyo.
   옆머리만 약간 다듬으려고 해요.

3. I eat only vegetables because I am a vegetarian.
   Chaesikju-uijaraseo chaesoman meokseumnida.
   채식주의자라서 채소만 먹습니다.

GRAMMAR NOTE Offering to do something for someone (honored) -어 드릴까요? *-eo deurilkkayo?* "Shall I ... for you?"

You learned that **juseyo** 주세요 is added to verbs (in the **-eo** -어 form) to make a polite request for a favor ("for me"). There are a few ways to offer to do something: **-eo julkkeyo** -어 줄게요 "I will ... for you" if done more or less for a peer, or **-eo deurilkkayo** -어 드릴까요? for someone in an honored position, such as a customer or elder. **Deuri** 드리 is a humble version of **ju** 주 "to give." That is, it is used when giving "upwards" (to someone of higher status or honor).

Would you like me to give you a reminder call or text message?
Jeonhwana munjja deurilkkayo? 전화나 문자 드릴까요?

How would you like your hair cut? **Eotteoke jalla deurilkkayo?**
어떻게 잘라 드릴까요?

PATTERN PRACTICE 3
Practice the following conversations using, "Shall I... for you?" -어 드릴까요? **-eo deurilkkayo?**

1. A: When would you like me to give you a call?
      Eonje jeonhwahae deurilkkayo? 언제 전화해 드릴까요?
   B: Around 8 PM tonight please.
      Oneul bam yeodeol sijjeum jeonhwahae juseyo.
      오늘 밤 여덟 시쯤 전화해 주세요.

2. A: Is there anything I can help? **Mwo dowa deurilkkayo?**
      뭐 도와 드릴까요?
   B: Please help me lift this box. **I sangja deuneun geo jom dowa juseyo.**
      이 상자 드는 거 좀 도와 주세요.

3. A: Would you like me to hold your bag? **Gabang deureo deurilkkayo?**
      가방 들어 드릴까요?
   B: No, I am fine. **Aniyo. Gwaenchanseumnida.**
      아니요. 괜찮습니다.

EXERCISE 1

You are in Seoul to work and are visiting many places today. Respond to what people say with -으려고 하다 **-(eu)ryeogo hada**, based on the given information.

1. Hair Salon Manager: **Eoteoke osyeosseoyo?** 어떻게 오셨어요?
   You: I am trying to get a haircut.
2. Real Estate Agent: **Eoteoke osyeosseoyo?** 어떻게 오셨어요?
   You: I am trying to find a studio.
3. Sales Clerk at a Clothing Store: **Mwo chajeuseyo?** 뭐 찾으세요?
   You: I am trying to buy t-shirts.
4. Sales Clerk at an Electronics Store: **Mwo chajeuseyo?** 뭐 찾으세요?
   You: I am trying to buy a small rice cooker.

EXERCISE 2

Guess what the hairdresser might have said. Use -어 드릴까요 **-eo deurilkkayo?** in the question.

1. Hairdresser: How much would you like me to trim it?
   You: **Jogeumman dadeumeo juseyo.** 조금만 다듬어 주세요.
2. Hairdresser: Would you like me to wash your hair?
   You: **Ne, meorireul gamgyeo juseyo.** 네, 머리를 감겨 주세요.
3. Hairdresser: Would you like me to send you a text message?
   You: **Ne, munjahae juseyo.** 네, 문자해 주세요.

DIALOGUE 2 How would you like your hair cut?

Aiden gets his hair cut.

Hairdresser:	Come this way. Have a seat. I'll wash your hair first. Do you have a perm?
	Ijjogeuro oseyo. Yeogi anjeuseyo. Meori meonjeo gamgyeo deurigesseumnida. Pamahasyeosseoyo?
	이쪽으로 오세요. 여기 앉으세요. 머리 먼저 감겨 드리겠습니다. 파마하셨어요?
Aiden:	No, my hair is naturally curly.
	Anieyo. Wollae gopseulmeoriyeyo.
	아니에요. 원래 곱슬머리예요.
Hairdresser:	Oh, you are lucky! You have nice hair. How would you like your hair cut?
	Uni jo.eusineyo. Meorigyeoldo aju joayo. Eotteoke jalla deurilkkayo?
	운이 좋으시네요. 머리결도 아주 좋아요. 어떻게 잘라 드릴까요?

Aiden:	I am trying to grow it out so please just trim it a bit.	

Aiden: I am trying to grow it out so please just trim it a bit.
Meorireul jom gireuryeogo hanikka yakganman dadeumeo juseyo.
머리를 좀 기르려고 하니까 약간만 다듬어 주세요.

Hairdresser: Oh, yes. Long hairstyles are trendy these days. Shall I leave the bangs long and just cut the back and sides like in this photo?
Ne. Yojeum gin meoriga yuhaeng.ieyo. Ammeorineun geunyang gilge dugo i sajincheoreom dwinmeorihago yeommeoriman jalladeurilkkayo?
네. 요즘 긴 머리가 유행이에요. 앞머리는 그냥 길게 두고 이 사진처럼 뒷머리하고 옆머리만 잘라드릴까요?

Aiden: Hmmm, I don't know. Please don't cut the back and sides too short, either.
Geulsseyo. Yeommeorirang dwinmeorido mani kkakji maseyo.
글쎄요. 옆머리랑 뒷머리도 많이 깎지 마세요.

Hairdresser: Then, how about this look?
Geureom ireon seutaireun eotteoseyo?
그럼 이런 스타일은 어떠세요?

Aiden: Yes, that's nice. How long will it take to cut?
Ne, jonneyo. Jareuneun de eolmana geollyeoyo?
네, 좋네요. 자르는 데 얼마나 걸려요?

Hairdresser: It will likely take about an hour. Shall I do it like this?
Han siganjjeum geollil kkeo gatayo. Geureom ireoke jalla deuryeoyo?
한 시간쯤 걸릴 거 같아요. 그럼 이렇게 잘라 드려요?

Aiden: Yes, please do.
Ne.
네.

VOCABULARY AND EXPRESSIONS

운	**un**	luck
머리결	**meorikkyeol**	hair (texture)
유행(*)	**yuhaeng**	trend, *trendy
앞머리	**ammeori**	bangs
사진	**sajin**	photo
뒷머리	**dwinmeori**	hair in the back
옆머리	**yeommeori**	hair on the sides
스타일	**seutail**	style
원래	**wollae**	originally, by nature
약간	**yakgan**	a little bit
요즘	**yojeum**	these days
그냥	**geunyang**	as is; just because

-처럼	**cheoreum**	like (noun marker)
-게	**ge**	complement suffix
긴 (길-)	**gin (gil-)**	long
이런 (이렇-)	**ireon (ireoh-)**	this kind
자르는 데 (자르-)	**jareuneun de (jareu-)**	to cut, in cutting
기르려고 (기르-)	**gireuryeogo (gireu-)**	trying to grow (out)
두고 (두-)	**dugo (du-)**	leave it and
걸려요 (걸리-)	**geollyeoyo (geolli-)**	takes (time)
감겨 드리겠습니다 (감기-, 드리-)	**gamgyeo deurigesseumnida. (gamgi-, deuri-)**	I will wash (your hair).
잘라 드릴까요? (자르-, 드리-)	**jalla deurilkkayo? (jareu-, deuri-)**	should I cut (it for you)?
다듬어 주세요 (다듬-, 주-)	**dadeumeo juseyo (dadeum-, ju-)**	trim it, please.
깎지 마세요 (깎-, 말-)	**kkakji maseyo (kkakk-, mal-)**	don't shave (/cut it short), please.
걸릴 거 같아요 (걸리-, 같-)	**geollil kkeo gatayo (geolli-, gat-)**	will likely take (time)

VOCABULARY PRACTICE 2

Give the Korean terms for the words described below.

1. something that is currently popular: _____
2. what you get from a camera: _____
3. the hair above your forehead: _____
4. My hair is _____ straight, but I have a perm to make it wavy.

Supplementary Vocabulary
Useful locations

post office	우체국	**ucheguk**
bank	은행	**eunhaeng**
police station	경찰서	**gyeongchalseo**
fire station	소방서	**sobangseo**
restaurant	식당	**sikdang**
convenience store	편의점	**pyeonuijeom**
gas station	주유소	**juyuso**
vet	동물 병원	**dongmul byeongwon**
barber shop/hairdresser	이발소/미용실	**ibalso/miyongsil**
nail salon	네일샵	**neilsyap**
car rental place	렌터카	**renteoka**
sauna	찜질방, 사우나	**jjimjilbang, sauna**
subway	지하철	**jihacheol**
library	도서관	**doseogwan**

National Health Insurance Services	건강보험 관리공단 (You get your foreigner's insurance here.)	Geongang boheom gwalligongdan
Korea immigration service	출입국 사무소	Chulipguk samuso

GRAMMAR NOTE *"Please do not..." -지 마세요 -ji maseyo*

To make a polite negative request, add **-ji maseyo** -지 마세요 to the verb root. The verb **malda** 말다 means "not do," and is used only in commands.

Please don't cut the back too much. **Dwinmeorineun mani jareuji maseyo.**
뒷머리는 많이 자르지 마세요.

Please don't sit there. **Geogi anjji maseyo.**
거기 앉지 마세요.

PATTERN PRACTICE 4

Practice the following negative polite commands with -지 마세요 **-ji maseyo**.
1. Please do not cut my bangs. **Ammeorineun jareuji maseyo.**
   앞머리는 자르지 마세요.
2. Please do not talk loudly here. **Yeogieseo keuge yaegihaji maseyo.**
   여기에서 크게 얘기하지 마세요.
3. Please do not wear shoes inside the house.
   Jibaneseo sinbareul sinji maseyo. 집안에서 신발을 신지 마세요.

GRAMMAR NOTE *"How long does it take?" -는 데 얼마나 걸려요? –Neun de eolmana geollyeoyo?*

To talk about the time it takes to do something, use the set expression: [action] **-neun** -는 데 (amount of time) ... **geollyeoyo** ... 걸려요. To ask, use **eolmana** 얼마나 "how (long)."

How long does it take to get a haircut?
Meori jareuneun de eolmana geollyeoyo?
머리 자르는 데 얼마나 걸려요?

How long does it take to go from City Hall to Hongdae?
Sicheong.eseo hongdaekkaji ganeun de eolmana geollyeoyo?
시청에서 홍대까지 가는 데 얼마나 걸려요?

To talk about the cost of something, use the same phrase with a different verb: [action] **-neun de** -는 데 [expense] ...**deureoyo** ... 들어요. To ask, use the same word **eolmana** 얼마나 "how (much)."

How much does it cost to get my hair cut?
Meori jareuneun de eolmana deureoyo?
머리 자르는 데 얼마나 들어요?

PATTERN PRACTICE 5
Practice the following conversations using "how long/much does it take?" -는 데 얼마나 걸려요/들어요? **-neun de eolmana geollyeoyo/deureoyo?**
1. A: How much does it cost to rent a car per day?
    Chareul billineun de harue eolmana deureoyo?
    차를 빌리는 데 하루에 얼마나 들어요?
    B: It will be about 20,000 won. **Iman wonjjeum deul kkeoyeyo.**
    이만 원쯤 들 거예요.
2. A: How long does it take from home to work by subway?
    Jibeseo hoesakkaji jihacheollo eolmana geollyeoyo?
    집에서 회사까지 지하철로 얼마나 걸려요?
    B: It takes about 30 minutes. **Samship bunjjeum geollyeoyo.**
    삼십 분쯤 걸려요.
3. A: How long does it take from New York to Incheon by air?
    Nyuyogeoseo Incheonkkaji bihaenggiro eolmana geollyeoyo?
    뉴욕에서 인천까지 비행기로 얼마나 걸려요?
    B: Maybe about 13 hours. **Ama yeolse siganjjeum geollil kkeoyeyo.**
    아마 열세 시간쯤 걸릴 거예요.

GRAMMAR NOTE **Manner suffix -게** *ge*
The suffix **ge** -게 tells you the manner of *how* something is done. The English equivalent usually uses an adjective to express this.

Please leave the bangs <u>long</u> (as is). **Ammeorineun geunyang <u>gilge</u> duseyo.**
앞머리는 그냥 <u>길게</u> 두세요.

<u>Enjoy</u> your food. **<u>Masitge</u> deuseyo.** <u>맛있게</u> 드세요.
(*Literally*, eat delicious(ly).)

Please speak <u>louder</u>. **<u>Deo keuge</u> malsseumhae juseyo.**
더 <u>크게</u> 말씀해 주세요.

PATTERN PRACTICE 6

Practice the following sentences with the adverbial suffix -게 **-ge**.

1. Please turn down the volume. **Sorireul jom jakge hae juseyo.**
   소리를 좀 작게 해 주세요.
2. Big smile, please. **Keuge useuseyo.** 크게 웃으세요.
3. Please cut my hair shorter. **Meorireul jjalpge jalla juseyo.**
   머리를 짧게 잘라 주세요.

CULTURE NOTE   Tipping

Generally speaking, tipping is not expected in Korea. Some fancy restaurants and hotels add a mandatory 10% service charge to the bill in addition to the 10% VAT. If you would like to tip a taxi driver, you can just say "keep the change!" (**Geoseureum tton geunyang duseyo** 거스름돈 그냥 두세요.). There is a fairly new trend of giving a tip in high-brow *kalbi* restaurants or famed beauty salons that have upscale or foreign clientele, so it's worth researching this beforehand. Valet parking is not free and a flat rate will be charged.

CULTURE NOTE   Tattooing and body piercing

Currently, tattooing is considered a medical procedure in Korea and is illegal if the tattooist does not hold a medical license. Tattooing has become a wildly popular summer activity, though its origins are a social enigma to many. Some Koreans also use a pseudo-tattoo service to tint their eyebrows and lip lines at beauty parlors. With the exception of celebrities, the only "accepted" body piercings are on the ear lobes by woman.

EXERCISE 3

You are sharing an apartment with a new Korean roommate and want to make the following requests (commands) in Korean. Use -지 마세요 **-ji maseyo**.

1. Please do not sit on my chair.
2. Please do not use my computer.
3. Please do not watch TV at night.
4. Please do not bring your friends to the apartment. (to bring someone: 데리고
   오다 **derigo oda**)

EXERCISE 4

Practice asking questions using −는 데 얼마나 걸려요/들어요? **-neun de eolmana geollyeoyo/deureoyo?**

1. You: How long does it take from here to the hair salon?
   Friend: **Jihacheollo samsip bunjjeum geollyeoyo.**
           지하철로 30분쯤 걸려요.
2. You: How much does it cost to get a haircut?
   Friend: **Samman wonjjeum deureoyo.** 30,000원쯤 들어요.
3. You: How much does it cost to get a perm?
   Friend: **Simman wonjjeum deureoyo.** 100,000원쯤 들어요.
4. You: How long does it take to get a haircut?
   Friend: **Han siganjjeum geollyeoyo.** 한 시간쯤 걸려요.

EXERCISE 5

Use the manner suffix -게 **-ge** to make the following requests.

1. 잘 안 들려요. _____ 얘기해 주세요. (loudly)
   Jal an deullyeoyo. ... yaegihae juseyo.
2. 저는 매운 음식을 못 먹어요. 좀 _____ 해 주세요. (bland)
   Jeoneun mae.un eumsigeul mon meogeoyo. Jom ... hae juseyo.
3. 순두부를 만들었어요. _____ 드세요. (deliciously)
   Sundubureul mandeureosseoyo. ... deuseyo.
4. 음악이 좀 시끄러워요. 소리를 _____ 해 주세요. (softly/"small")
   Eunmagi jom sikkeureowoyo. Sorireul ... hae juseyo.

Visiting a Dry Sauna Spa

DIALOGUE 1 Have you ever been to a *jjimjilbang*?

Eunbi and Emma talk about a dry sauna spa.

Emma: I'm so tired. I want a rest.
          A, pigonhada. Jom swigo simneyo.
          아, 피곤하다. 좀 쉬고 싶네요.

Eunbi: How about a spa tonight then? Have you ever been to a dry sauna spa?
          Geureom oneul bame jjimjilbang eottaeyo? Jjimjilbang.e ga bon jeok isseoyo?
          그럼 오늘 밤에 찜질방 어때요? 찜질방에 가 본 적 있어요?

Emma: A dry sauna spa? I've never been (*Literally*, I have not tried going).
          Jjimjilbang.iyo? Han beondo an ga bwasseoyo.
          찜질방이요? 한번도 안 가 봤어요.

Eunbi: It's a lot of fun. You can take a bath, take a dry or wet sauna, and
          even have good food. They also have a book café and a movie room.
          **Aju jaemiisseoyo. Mogyokdo hago jjimjildo hago masinneun
          eumsikdo meogeul ssu isseoyo. Tto bukkapedo itgo yeonghwa
          gamsangsildo isseoyo.**
          아주 재미있어요. 목욕도 하고 찜질도 하고 맛있는 음식도 먹을
          수 있어요. 또 북카페도 있고 영화 감상실도 있어요.

Emma: I want to get some sleep... Can you sleep in the sauna room?
          Jom jago sipeunde... jjimjilbang.eseo jado dwaeyo?
          좀 자고 싶은데... 찜질방에서 자도 돼요?

Eunbi: Of course. You can stay up to 12 AM at the spa.
          Geureomyo. Yeoldu sigkkaji jjimjilbang.e isseul ssu isseoyo.
          그럼요. 열두 시까지 찜질방에 있을 수 있어요.

Emma: How much (does it cost)?
          Eolmayeyo?
          얼마예요?

Eunbi: Just a sec. Let me look it up on Naver. Well, 12,000 won on weekdays
          and 14,000 won on weeknights, it seems. Weekends and holidays
          14,000 won. It seems like weekdays are the cheapest.
          **Jamkkan! Neibeo-eseo chaja bolkkeyo. Eum... Pyeong.il
          juganeun manicheon won, Pyeong.il yaganeun mansacheon
          wonin geo gatayo. Jumal mit gonghyuireun man sacheon
          woniyo. Pyeong.il jugani jeil ssan geo ganneo.**

잠깐! 네이버에서 찾아 볼게요. 음... 평일 주간은 12,000원, 평일 야간은 14,000원인 거 같아요. 주말 및 공휴일은 14,000원이요. 평일 주간이 제일 싼 거 같네요.

Emma: Then let's go tonight at 7.
Geureom oneul jeonyeog ilgop sie gayo.
그럼 오늘 저녁 7시에 가요.

Eunbi: Good! I'll buy you a broiled egg and *sikhye*.
Joayo! Naega gu.un gyeranhago sikyereul sa julkkeyo!
좋아요! 내가 구운 계란하고 식혜를 사 줄게요!

Emma: I like *sikhye*! I'll see you at 6:30 at the company lobby then.
Jeo sikye joahaeyo! Geureom yeoseos si bane hoesa robieseo mannayo.
저 식혜 좋아해요! 그럼 6시 반에 회사 로비에서 만나요.

VOCABULARY AND EXPRESSIONS

목욕*	**mogyok**	bathing, showering, *to take a bath
찜질*	**jjimjil**	sauna, steam bath, *to take a sauna
찜질방	**jjimjilbang**	dry sauna spa, dry sauna room
북카페	**bukkape**	book café, portable library
영화	**yeonghwa**	movie
감상실	**gamsangsil**	viewing room, listening room
평일	**pyeong.il**	weekdays
주간	**jugan**	during the daytime
야간	**yagan**	at night time
공휴일	**gonghyuil**	holidays
반	**ban**	half
로비	**robi**	lobby
계란	**gyeran**	egg
식혜	**sikye**	sweet rice drink
한번 (← 한 번)	**hanbeon (← han beon)**	a trial (from "one time, once")
및	**mit**	and, as well as, also
제일 (= 가장)	**jeil (=gajang)**	the most
구운 (굽-)	**gu.un (gup-)**	baked, roasted, broiled
피곤하다 (피곤하-)	**pigonhada (pigonha-)**	tired
쉬고 싶네요 (쉬-, 싶-)	**swigo simneyo (swi-, sip-)**	want to rest, take a break!

가 본 적 있어요? (가-, 보-, 있-)	**ga bon jeok isseoyo?** **(ga-, bo-, iss-)**	have you been to, have you gone to?
안 가 봤어요 (가-, 보-)	**an ga bwasseoyo** **(ga-, bo-)**	have not been to
찾아 볼게요 (찾-, 보-)	**chaja bolkkeyo** **(chaj-, bo-)**	I'll look (up, for)
싼 거 같아요 (싸-, 같-)	**ssan geo gatayo** **(ssa-, gat)**	seems cheap
맛있는 (있-)	**masinneun (iss-)**	delicious
사 줄게요 (사-, 주-)	**sa julkkeyo (sa-, ju-)**	I'll buy for you, my treat

VOCABULARY PRACTICE 1

Give the Korean terms for the words described below.
1. washing your body: _____
2. a story acted and recorded on video: _____
3. Monday through Friday: _____
4. days when no one has to work: _____

GRAMMAR NOTE "Good" vs. "Like"

The adjective 좋아요 (좋-) **joayo (joh-)** "good" expresses one's on-the-spot likes (or dislikes, in the negative).

Good! **Joayo!** 좋아요!

(This) coffee is no good. *OR* I don't like (this) coffee.
Keopiga an joayo. 커피가 안 좋아요.

Joahaeyo (joaha-) 좋아해요 (좋아하-) "like" is an *active* verb (not an adjective) and it is *transitive*, so it has to be paired with an object (which would be marked with **-eul/reul** -을/를 in written Korean). But since markers are frequently dropped in spoken Korean, you will see sentences with **joayo** 좋아요 and **joahaeyo** 좋아해요 that look nearly the same. **Joahaeyo** 좋아해요 expresses one's general or lasting likes.

| (I would like *sikhye!*)
Jeo sikye joayo!
저 식혜 좋아요! | vs. | I like *sikhye!*
Jeo sikye joahaeyo!
저 식혜 좋아해요! |

If confusion might arise, use appropriate markers:

Sikhye is (a) good (idea as a choice.)		I like *sikhye*/I enjoy *sikhye*.
Jeoneun sikyega joayo!	vs.	**Jeoneun sikyereul joahaeyo.**
저는 식혜가 좋아요.		저는 식혜를 좋아해요.

PATTERN PRACTICE 1

Practice the following sentences with -좋아요 **-joayo** and -좋아해요 **-joahaeyo**.

1. I like that (particular) *jjimjilbang*. (*Lit.*, As for me, that *jjimjilbang* is good.)
   Jeoneun geu jjimjilbang.i joayo. 저는 그 찜질방이 좋아요.
2. Jason (usually) likes *jjimjilbang*. **Jeiseuneun jjimjilbang.eul joahaeyo.**
   제이슨은 찜질방을 좋아해요.

GRAMMAR NOTE "Have experienced" -(으)ㄴ 적 있어요 *-(eu)n jeog isseoyo*

-(Eu)n jeog isseoyo -(으)ㄴ 적 있어요 means "there has been a time when," or simply "have done (something)." It attaches to a verb root. To highlight the "trying out" part, **-eo bo** -어 보 can be added, to get **-eo bon jeog isseoyo** -어 본 적 있어요 "have tried." Since **jeok** 적 is a noun, the markers **i** 이, **eun** 은, and **do** 도 can be added to it.

I once got lost around here.
I geuncheo.eseo gireul han beon ireun jeogi isseoyo.
이 근처에서 길을 한 번 잃은 적이 있어요.

Have you ever been to a dry sauna? **Jjimjilbang ga bon jeog isseoyo?**
찜질방 가 본 적 있어요?

PATTERN PRACTICE 2

Practice conversations with "have experienced" -(으)ㄴ 적 있어요 **-(eu)n jeog isseoyo**.

1. A: Have you ever been to Jeju Island? **Jejudo.e ga bon jeog isseoyo?**
      제주도에 가 본 적 있어요?
   B: Yes, I've been to Jeju Island last year. **Ne, jangnyeone ga bwasseoyo.**
      네, 작년에 가 봤어요.
2. A: Have you had a haircut at Best Hair?
      Beseuteu he.eo.eseo meorireul jalla bon jeogi isseoyo?
      베스트 헤어에서 머리를 잘라 본 적이 있어요?
   B: No, I haven't. **Aniyo, eopseoyo.** 아니요. 없어요.
3. A: Have you taken Korean Air?
      Daehanhanggong bihaenggireul tan jeogi isseoyo?
      대한항공 비행기를 탄 적이 있어요?

B: No, but I've taken Asiana Air.
Aniyo. Geureonde Asiana bihaenggireul tan jeogeun isseoyo.
아니요. 그런데 아시아나 비행기를 탄 적은 있어요.

GRAMMAR NOTE -(으)ㄴ 거 같아요 *-(eu)n geo gatayo* "it seems like..."

You learned in Lesson 9 that you can use **-(eu)l kkeo gatayo** -(으)ㄹ 거 같아요 (it seems like) to be non-committal or less assertive. This ending consists of two elements: **-(eu)l** -(으)ㄹ, which is about the unknown (an element shared by the future plan ending **-(eu)l kkeoyeyo** -(으)ㄹ 거예요), and **kkeo gatayo** 거 같아요, which says "it's like" or "it's similar to." You can use **-(eu)n geo gatayo** -(으)ㄴ 거 같아요 to be similarly non-committal with present *descriptions* (in adjectives) and *past* actions (in verb forms).

It's 14,000 won during weeknights, it seems. It seems like weekdays are the cheapest. **Pyeong.il yaganeun man.sacheon won<u>in</u> geo gatayo. Pyeong.il jugani jeil <u>ssan</u> geo ganneyo.** 평일 야간은 14,000원<u>인</u> 거 같아요. 평일 주간이 제일 <u>싼</u> 거 같네요.

I've tried lots of other things in Korea, but it doesn't seem like I've ever tried a hot steam room. **Han.gugeseo dareun geon mani haebwanneunde jjimjilbang.eun han beondo an ga <u>bon</u> geo gatayo.** 한국에서 다른 건 많이 해봤는데 찜질방은 한 번도 안 가 <u>본</u> 거 같아요.

PATTERN PRACTICE 3

Practice making less assertive statements with -(으)ㄴ 거 같아요 **-(eu)n geo gatayo**.
1. The volume seems to be a bit loud. **Soriga jom keun geo gatayo.**
   소리가 좀 큰 거 같아요.
2. I don't think I've ever tried Korean rice punch.
   Sikyeneun han beondo an meogeo bon geo gatayo.
   식혜는 한 번도 안 먹어 본 거 같아요.
3. That hair salon is a bit expensive. **Geu miyongsireun jom bissan geo gatayo.**
   그 미용실은 좀 비싼 거 같아요.

GRAMMAR NOTE Time words

You have learned these time words so far:

시간 **sigan**	time hour	시간 있어요? Do you have time? **Sigan isseoyo?** 한 시간 걸렸어요. It took an hour. **Han sigan geollyeosseoyo.**

시 si	o'clock	지금 몇 시예요? What time is it now? **Jigeum myeot siyeyo?**
번 beon	times	거기 두 번 가 봤어요. I've been there twice. **Geogi du beon ga bwasseoyo.**
때 ttae	the time when	바쁠 때 잘 못 먹어요. I don't/can't eat well when I'm busy. **Bappeul ttae jal mon meogeoyo.**

In addition to the time words above, **jeog** 적 is another time-related word you may hear. If not used in its typical phrase **-(eu)n jeok isseoyo** -(으)ㄴ 적 있어요 "have done, have been," it means "some time in the past."

Rollerblading was popular when I was young.
Naega eoril jeogeneun rolleobeulleideuga yuhaeng.ieosseoyo.
내가 어릴 적에는 롤러블레이드가 유행이었어요.

Once upon a time… **Yennalyetjeoge…** 옛날옛적에…

EXERCISE 1
Ask Emma the following questions about her life in Korea.
1. Have you lived in Busan?
2. Have you ever been to a *noraebang*?
3. Have you eaten baked eggs at *jjimjilbang*?
4. Have you walked at Hangang Park (Han River Park)? (Hangang Park: 한강 공원 **Han.gang Gongwon**)

EXERCISE 2
Eunbi is asking some questions, and you are not sure about the answer. Respond appropriately using -(으)ㄴ 거 같아요 **-(eu)n geo gatayo.**
1. Eunbi: **Oneul nalssiga eottaeyo?** 오늘 날씨가 어때요?
    You: (I'm not sure, but) it seems to be cold.
2. Eunbi: **Nae meori seutairi eottaeyo?** 내 머리 스타일이 어때요?
    You: (I'm not sure, but) it seems to be a little short.
3. Eunbi: **Iri eottaeyo?** 일이 어때요?
    You: (I'm not sure yet, but) it seems fun.
4. Eunbi: **Bibimbabi eottaeyo?** 비빔밥이 어때요?
    You: It seems a little spicy.

DIALOGUE 2 It sounds too hot for me.

Eunbi and Emma visit the dry sauna.

Eunbi: Two adults.
        Daein du myeong.iyo.
        대인 두 명이요.

C. Staff: Twenty-eight thousand won, please.
        Ne, imanpalcheon wonimnida.
        네, 28,000 원입니다.

Eunbi: OK. Here is 28,000 won.
        Ne. Yeogi imanpalcheon won isseumnida.
        네. 여기 28,000 원 있습니다.

C. Staff: Thank you. Here are the towels, clothes, and the keys.
        Gamsahamnida. Yeogi sugeonhago, ot, ki isseumnida.
        감사합니다. 여기 수건하고, 옷, 키 있습니다.

Emma: Are these locker keys?
        Ojjang kiyeyo?
        옷장 키예요?

C. Staff: Yes. Use your locker key in the spa whenever you use the services
        and any facilities. Any expenses you have accrued (using the services
        and facilities) get charged when you leave.
        **Ne, geurigo seupa an modeun budaesiseoreul iyonghasil ttae
        rakeo kireul iyonghaseyo. Iyonghasin geumaegeun toejanghasil
        ttae hubullo jeongsandoemnida.**
        네, 그리고 스파 안 모든 서비스나 부대시설을 이용하실 때
        락커 키를 이용하세요. 이용하신 금액은 퇴장하실 때 후불로
        정산됩니다.

Emma: I see.
        A, geuraeyo?
        아, 그래요?

C. Staff: Leave your valuables at the counter.
        Gwijungpumeun kaunteo.e matgiseyo.
        귀중품은 카운터에 맡기세요.

Emma, Eunbi:
        OK. Got it.
        Ne, algesseumnida.
        네, 알겠습니다.

Eunbi and Emma have changed into their spa clothes and are deciding where to
go next.

Emma:	Where to?	
	Eodiro galkkayo?	
	어디로 갈까요?	
Eunbi:	Shall we go to the pine tree fire-sauna room?	
	"Sonamu bulhanjeungmag"e galkkayo?	
	"소나무 불한증막"에 갈까요?	
Emma:	Fire-sauna? It sounds too hot for me.	
	"Bulhanjeungmak"? Geu bang.eun neomu tteugeoul kkeot	
	gatayo.	
	"불한증막"? 그 방은 너무 뜨거울 것 같아요.	
Eunbi:	Let's go to the forest bath room then.	
	Geureom "samnimyokbang"e gayo.	
	그럼 "삼림욕방"에 가요.	
Emma:	"Forest bath"?	
	"Samnimyog"iyo?	
	"삼림욕"이요?	
Eunbi:	It's a tree room. It feels like you are in a forest in that room.	
	Namubang.ieyo. Geu bang.e isseumyeon supe inneun geot	
	gatayo.	
	나무방이에요. 그 방에 있으면 숲에 있는 것 같아요.	
Emma:	Sounds good. Let's try that first, then!	
	Jo.eundeyo. Geogibuteo gajiyo!	
	좋은데요. 거기부터 가지요!	

VOCABULARY AND EXPRESSIONS

퇴장*	**toejang**	leaving, *to walk out (of a stage)
정산*	**jeongsan**	balancing, adjusting, *to add up
대인	**daein**	adult
옷	**ot**	clothes
키	**ki**	key
옷장	**otjang**	closet, cabinet, locker
스파	**seupa**	spa
안	**an**	inside
부대시설	**budaesiseol**	additional facilities
라커	**rakeo**	locker
금액	**geumaek**	amount
후불	**hubul**	expenses to be charged later
귀중품	**gwijungpum**	valuables

카운터	kaunteo	counter
소나무	sonamu	pine tree
불한증막	bulhanjeungmak	"fire-hot" sauna
삼림욕	samnimyok	forest bath
나무방	namubang	tree room, wood room
숲	sup	forest
명	myeong	counter for people
등	deung	etc.
거기	geogi	there
모든	modeun	all, every
-지요	-jiyo	why not … (suggestion)
맡기세요 (맡-)	matgiseyo (mat-)	drop off, leave, entrust
뜨거울 것 같아요 (뜨겁-, 같-)	tteugeo.ul kkeot gatayo (tteugeop-, gat-)	seems like it will be too hot

VOCABULARY PRACTICE 2

Give the Korean terms for the words described below.

1. items that are worth lots of money (or sentimental value): _____
2. a grown person: _____
3. where clothing is stored: _____

GRAMMAR NOTE -지요 *-jiyo* "Why don't you...?"

In questions, **-jiyo** -지요 signals that the listener knows what you are talking about and you are trying to confirm it. Used as a non-question, **-jiyo** -지요 is more of an urging invitation, with the idea that the suggestion made is definitely a good idea.

Let's try that first, then! **Geogibuteo gajiyo!** 거기부터 가지요!

Why not just rest at home today? **Oneureun geunyang jibeseo swijiyo.** 오늘은 그냥 집에서 쉬시지요.

PATTERN PRACTICE 4

Practice the following suggestion/invitation using -지요 **-jiyo.**

1. Let's have Chinese food for dinner today.
   Oneul jeonyeogeneun Jung.guk eumsigeul meokjiyo.
   오늘 저녁에는 중국 음식을 먹지요.
2. Why don't you sit here? **Yeogi anjeusijiyo.** 여기 앉으시지요.
3. Please come this way. **Ijjogeuro osijiyo.** 이쪽으로 오시지요.

GRAMMAR NOTE Making non-committal statements with -는 거 같아요 *-neun geo gatayo*

The ending for less assertive statements changes slightly yet again for habitual actions, where **-neun geo gatayo** -는 거 같아요 is the form. A good translation is "I think…"

I think they eat Chinese food on moving day in Korea.
Han.gugeseoneun isahaneun nare Jung.guk eumsigeul meongneun geo gatayo. 한국에서는 이사하는 날에 중국 음식을 먹는 거 같아요.

The ending is also used in its sense of "seems like" or "feels like" for an activity that's going on now.

It feels like you are in a forest in that room.
Geu bang.e isseumyeon supe inneun geot gatayo.
그 방에 있으면 숲에 있는 것 같아요.

Here is a summary chart for the non-committal endings:

	WHEN TO USE	EXAMPLES
-는 거 같아요 **-neun geo gatayo.**	habitual, repeated	매일 중국 음식을 먹는 거 같아요. **Maeil Jung.guk eumsigeul meongneun geo gatayo.** It seems like we eat Chinese food every day.
	progressive action	지금 비 오는 거 같아요. **Jigeum bi oneun geo gatayo.** I think it's raining now.
-(으)ㄴ 거 같아요 **-(eu)n geo gatayo.**	past (completed) action	그 사람 아직 안 온 거 같아요. **Geu saram ajik an on geo gatayo.** I think he is not here yet. (He hasn't come yet.)
	present descriptive	오늘 추운 거 같아요. **Oneul chu.un geo gatayo.** (I'm not sure but) I think it's cold today.
	WHEN TO USE	EXAMPLES
-(으)ㄹ 거 같아요 **-(eu)l kkeo gatayo.**	guess	내일 추울 거 같아요. **Naeil chu.ul kkeo gatayo.** I think it's going to be cold tomorrow.
		밖이 추울 거 같아요. **Bakki chu.ul kkeo gatayo.** (I don't know but) I think it's cold outside now.

PATTERN PRACTICE 5

Practice making statements showing your reservation, using -는 거 같아요 **-neun geo gatayo**.

1. I think that the *jjimjilbang* does not open on Mondays.
   Geu jjimjilbang.eun woryoireneun an yeoneun geo gatayo.
   그 찜질방은 월요일에는 안 여는 거 같아요.

2. Korean people do not eat rice cake soup for Chuseok.
   Han.guk saramdeureun Chuseogeneun tteokgugeul an meongneun geo gatayo.
   한국 사람들은 추석에는 떡국을 안 먹는 거 같아요.

3. It feels like I am by the ocean. **Badatga.e inneun geo gatayo.**
   바닷가에 있는 거 같아요.

GRAMMAR NOTE The relative clause: Completed action verbs in noun-modifying form -(으)ㄴ *-(eu)n*

You have learned that an adjective takes the ending **-(eu)n** -(으)ㄴ to come before a noun and modify it (e.g., **jo.eun chin.gu** 좋은 친구 "a good friend"). To describe a noun using a *sentence* (e.g., "the person who (does)…"), the verb at the end gets the suffix **-neun** -는 if it is in the present tense. If the descriptive phrase is about something that happened in the past or has been completed, then the verb needs **-(eu)n** -(으)ㄴ. (This is also the ending used for modifying adjectives.)

Give me the book(s) you have finished reading, please.
Da ilgeun chaegeun jeoreul juseyo.
다 읽은 책은 저를 주세요.

Who is the person who was here (literally, who came) a while ago?
Akka on sarami nuguyeyo?
아까 온 사람이 누구예요?

Any expenses you accrued using the (services and facilities) get adjusted when you leave. **Iyonghasin geumaegeun toejanghasil ttae hubullo jeongsandoemnida.** 이용하신 금액은 퇴장하실 때 후불로 정산됩니다.

PATTERN PRACTICE 6

Practice the past noun-modifying form -(으)ㄴ **-(eu)n**.

1. The hair that was permed yesterday **Eoje pamahan meori**
   어제 파마한 머리

2. The song that Emma sang a while ago **Emmaga akka bureun norae**
   엠마가 아까 부른 노래

3. The news that I just heard **Banggeum deureun nyuseu** 방금 들은 뉴스

GRAMMAR NOTE Sino-Korean words in public spaces

One of the reasons why Sino-Korean words are common in the public sphere is their brevity. It's more efficient to use these Sino-Korean words in their limited linguistic constructions so you can do away with the markers for politeness and honorifics. This lesson introduces many Sino-Korean words. Try to remember as many as you can.

Sino-Korean	Native Korean	Meaning
대인 **daein**	어른 **eoreun**	adult
귀중품 **gwijungpum**	중요한 물건 **jung.yohan mulgeon**	valuables
식음료 **sigeumnyo**	먹을 것하고 마실 것 **meogeul kkeothago masil kkeot**	food and beverages

CULTURE NOTE The public bath—*Jjimjilbang*

Koreans have a history of **jjimjilbang** 찜질방 as public baths, but these days it has more to do with taking a break and taking care of one's health by relaxing and keeping warm. **Jjimjilbang** 찜질방 refers to the heated rooms, dry sauna rooms with different herbs, minerals, or soils as detoxifiers, relaxants and tonics for various stresses and ailments. These spa establishments separate men and women. For each gender there are usually lockers, a common bathing area (with shampoo and soap), jacuzzis or hot tubs of different temperatures (including a cold-plunge tub), and the various dry and sometimes wet sauna hot-rooms, some reaching 170 degrees Fahrenheit (77 degrees Celsius). One should disrobe and store items in a locker, then bathe thoroughly before entering a hot tub (nude) or a sauna room (usually in the provided robes). Some **jjimjilbang** 찜질방 offer other services such as massage, manicure and pedicure, masks, and the famous body scrub (**sesin** 세신), where a specialist removes all the dead skin (**ttae** 때). There is also usually a restaurant (which you enter in your spa clothes or robe), so one can truly make a day of going to the **jjimjilbang** 찜질방.

Families and friends chat, watch TV, sleep and/or relax together while eating signature **jjimjilbang** 찜질방 foods such as **maekbanseok gyeran** 맥반석 계란 (baked eggs), **sikye** 식혜 (Korean rice punch) and **miyeokguk** 미역국 (seaweed soup).

EXERCISE 3

Respond to your friends using the urging suffix -지(요) **-ji(yo)**.
1. Friend: **Oneul mwo halkkayo?** 오늘 뭐 할까요?
   You: Let's go to the *jjimjilbang*!
2. Friend: **Baega gopeundeyo.** 배가 고픈데요.
   You: Let's eat baked eggs at the *jjimjilbang*.

3. Friend: **Hyeon.geumi isseoyo?** 현금이 있어요?
   You: No. Let's just use a credit card.
4. Friend: **Eodie anjeulkkayo?** 어디에 앉을까요?
   You: Let's sit here.

EXERCISE 4

You don't know the exact answer to the questions your friends are asking, but that shouldn't stop you from giving them your well-informed guesses. Respond using -는 거 같아요 **-neun geo gatayo.**

1. Friend: **Emma ssineun eonje undonghaeyo?** 엠마 씨는 언제 운동해요?
   You: I think she exercises on weekends.
2. Friend: **Minjun ssineun museun eumageul deureoyo?**
             민준 씨는 무슨 음악을 들어요?
   You: I think he listens to classical music. (classical music: 클래식 음악
             keullaesik eumak)
3. Friend: **Eideun ssineun nuguhago teniseureul chyeoyo?**
             에이든 씨는 누구하고 테니스를 쳐요?
   You: I think he plays tennis with Minjoon.
4. Friend: **Eunbi ssineun tellebijeoneul bwayo?**
             은비 씨는 텔레비젼을 봐요?
   You: I don't think she watches TV.

EXERCISE 5

Use -(으)ㄴ **-(eu)n** to explain who's who by their actions.

Minjoon 민준	**Akka jeohago mannasseoyo.** 아까 저하고 만났어요.
Emma 엠마	**Migugeseo wasseoyo.** 미국에서 왔어요.
Aiden 에이든	**Eoje jeohago keopireul masyeosseoyo.** 어제 저하고 커피를 마셨어요.
Jason 제이슨	**Eoje meorireul jallasseoyo.** 어제 머리를 잘랐어요.
Hyeonjin 현진	**Jinan jue yeonghwareul bwasseoyo.** 지난 주에 영화를 봤어요.

1. Minjoon:
   Akka jeohago mannan sarameun Minjun ssiyeyo.
   아까 저하고 만난 사람은 민준 씨예요.
   The person who met with me a little while ago is Minjoon.
2. Emma:
3. Aiden:
4. Jason:
5. Hyeonjin:

저기 옷 가게 있다.
There is a clothing store over there.

블라우스도 파네요.
They sell blouses, too!

어디 한번 들어가 보자.
Let's go in there and see.

이것들 좀 봐요.
Look at these.

예쁘네!
They're so cute!

아저씨!
Excuse me! (Sir!)

빨간 블라우스 사이즈 44나 55 있어요?
Do you have a red blouse in size 44 or 55?

빨간 거는 스몰이랑 미디움 사이즈가 현재 다 나갔는데요.
As for the red ones, all medium and small sizes are currently out of stock.

라지는 있어요.
We do have large ones.

요즘은 좀 크게 입는 게 유행인데.
It's trendy to wear looser clothes these days.

66짜리 보여드려요?
Do you want me to show you one in 66?

네.
Yes.

LESSON 14
Shopping and Haggling

🔘 **DIALOGUE 1** **May I try them on?**

Eunbi and Emma have become close friends and they are going shopping. They began to drop the -요 **-yo** ending occasionally and use informal casual forms to show intimacy, and they are mixing in "self-talk."

Eunbi:	There is a clothing store over there. They sell blouses, too! Let's go in there and see.
	Jeogi ot gage itda. Beullauseudo paneyo. Eodi hanbeon deureoga boja.
	저기 옷 가게 있다. 블라우스도 파네요. 어디 한번 들어가 보자.
Emma:	Look at these. They're so cute! Excuse me! (Sir!) Do you have a red blouse in size 44 or 55?
	Igeotteul jom bwayo. Yeppeune! Ajeossi! Ppalgan beullauseu sasana o.o oshibo isseoyo?
	이것들 좀 봐요. 예쁘네! 아저씨! 빨간 블라우스 사이즈 44나 55 있어요?
Shopkeeper:	As for the red ones, all medium and small sizes are currently out of stock. We do have large ones. It's trendy to wear looser clothes these days. Do you want me to show you one in 66?
	Ppalgan geoneun seumorirang midium saijeuga hyunjae da naganneundeyo. Lajineun isseoyo. Yojeumeun jom keuge imneun ge yuhaeng.inde. Yukyukjjari boyeodeuryeoyo?
	빨간 거는 스몰이랑 미디움 사이즈가 현재 다 나갔는데요. 라지는 있어요. 요즘은 좀 크게 입는 게 유행인데. 66짜리 보여드려요?
Eunbi:	Yes.
	Ne.
	네.

The shopkeeper finds and hands a red blouse to Emma.

Emma:	It looks a bit big for me; can I try it on?
	Nahante jom keo boineunde, ibeo bwado dwaeyo?
	나한테 좀 커 보이는데, 입어 봐도 돼요?

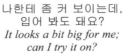

나한테 좀 커 보이는데,
입어 봐도 돼요?
*It looks a bit big for me;
can I try it on?*

치마는 입어 보셔도
되지만 블라우스는
화장이 묻기 때문에
입으시면 안 됩니다.
*You can try on skirts but
not blouses because you
may get your make-up
(smudged) on them.*

더러워지면 팔기
힘들어서요.
*It's because it's
difficult to sell them
when they get dirty.*

그럼 됐어요.
It's okay then.
더 돌아보고 올게요.
*I'll look around more
(other places) first.*

Shopkeeper: You can try on skirts but not blouses because you may get your make-up (smudged) on them. It's because it's difficult to sell them when they get dirty.

Chimaneun ibeo bosyodo doejiman beulauseunun hwajang.i mutgi ttaemune ibeusimyeon an doemnida. Deoreowojimyeon palgi himdeureoseoyo.

치마는 입어 보셔도 되지만 블라우스는 화장이 묻기 때문에 입으시면 안 됩니다. 더러워지면 팔기 힘들어서요.

Emma: It's okay then. I'll look around more (other places) first.

Geureom dwaesseoyo. Deo dorabogo olkkeyo.

그럼 됐어요. 더 돌아보고 올게요.

VOCABULARY AND EXPRESSIONS

옷	**ot**	clothes
가게	**gage**	store
블라우스	**beullauseu**	blouse
어디	**eodi**	where, also used with a suggestion (어디 한번 **eodi hanbeon**)
이거들	**igeodeul**	these
주인	**Ju.in**	owner
아저씨	**ajeossi**	uncle, sir (calling someone's attention)
스몰	**seumol**	small (size)
미디엄†	**midium**	medium (size)
라지	**laji**	large (size)
사이즈	**saijeu**	size
현재	**hyeonjae**	now, at the present time, presently
화장	**hwajang**	make-up
정도 (= -쯤)	**jeongdo (= jjeum)**	about that much
-짜리	**jjari**	X's worth
-밖에	**bakke**	merely, only, just
-한테	**hante**	to, for someone
-지만	**jiman**	but, however (with verb roots)
팔아 (팔-)	**para (pal-)**	sell
들어가 (들어가-)	**deuleogal (deuleoga-)**	enter
보자 (보-)	**boja (bo-)**	let's see
예쁘네 (예쁘-)	**yeppeune (yeppeu-)**	pretty, eh?
빨간 (빨갛-)	**ppalgan (ppalgah-)**	red
나갔는데요 (나가-)	**naganneundeyo (naga-)**	went out; gone, sold out

크게 (크-)	**keuge (keu-)**	big
커 보이는데 (크-, 보이-)	**keo boineunde (keu-, boi-)**	it looks a little big...
입어봐도 돼요? (입-, 되-)	**ibeobwado dwaeyo? (ip-, doe-)**	can I try them on?
입으시면 안 됩니다 (입으시-, 되-)	**ibeusimyeon an deomnida. (ip-, doe-)**	you may not put it on.
묻기 때문에 (묻-)	**mutgi ttaemune (mut-)**	because (you can) get (something smudged) on it
됐어요 (되-)	**dwaesseoyo (doe-)**	it's alright, that's OK
돌아보고 (돌-, 보-)	**dorabogo (dol-, bo-)**	look around and then

†The dictionary "standard" form is 미디엄 **midi.eom**, but nobody in real life pronounces the word that way, so we listed it as 미디움 **midium.**

VOCABULARY PRACTICE 1

Give the Korean terms for the words described below.
1. the first color of the rainbow; the color of cherries and apples: _____
2. how you call a man of a certain age: _____
3. the owner of a shop or store: _____
4. to try on clothes: _____

Supplementary Vocabulary
Clothing items

윗도리, 상의 **witdori, sang.ui**	shirts, tops	바지 **baji**	pants
티셔츠 **tishyeocheu**	t-shirt	청바지 **cheongbaji**	jeans
와이셔츠 **waishyeocheu**	shirt with buttons	반바지 **banbaji**	shorts
스웨터 **seuweteo**	sweater	치마 **chima**	skirt
재킷 **jaekit**	jacket	원피스 **wonpiseu**	dress
코트 **koteu**	coat	운동복, 추리닝 **undongbok, churining**	sweatsuit
패딩 **paeding**	padded/down jacket	(양복) 정장 (**yangbok**) **jeongjang**	(men's dress) suit
폴라티, 터틀넥 **pollati, teoteulnek**	turtleneck shirt	배꼽티, 탱크탑 **baekkopti, taengkeutap**	tank top
속옷 **sogot**	underwear	양말 **yangmal**	socks
(털)모자 (**teol**) **moja**	(wool) hat	구두 **gudu**	dress shoes
잠옷, 파자마 **jamot, pajama**	pajamas	운동화 **undonghwa**	sports shoes

수영복 **suyeongbok**	swimsuit	신발 **sinball**	shoes
넥타이 **nektai**	tie	조끼 **jokki**	vest
반지 **banji**	ring	목도리 **mokdori**	winter scarf
목걸이 **mokgeori**	necklace	스카프 **seukapeu**	(dress) scarf
팔찌 **paljji**	bracelet	시계 **sigye**	watch
한복 **hanbok**	traditional Korean clothes		

GRAMMAR NOTE Informal casual suggestion: -자 *-ja* "Let's!"

When making an invitation or suggestion between friends and to young children, you use the suffix **-ja** -자. The word **hanbeon** 한번 is often used together to mean "a little" or "some time," although it literally means "once." Some people may even use **eodi** 어디 "where" to emphasize the sense of giving something a try. The suffix can also be used for self-talk "Let me..."

Let's take a look!/Let me take a look! **Eodi hanbeon boja!**
어디 한번 보자!

Let's go to the *jjimjilbang* one of these days! **Jjimjilbang.e hanbeon gaja!**
찜질방에 한번 가자!

PATTERN PRACTICE 1
Practice the informal casual suggestion using -자 **-ja**.
1. Let's walk together. **Gachi geotja** 같이 걷자.
2. Let's meet at 10 AM tomorrow. **Naeil achim yeol sie mannaja.**
   내일 아침 열 시에 만나자.
3. Let's try wearing the red sneakers. **Ppalgan undonghwareul sineo boja.**
   빨간 운동화를 신어 보자.

GRAMMAR NOTE "Just," "only," "merely" -밖에 *-bakke* with a negative verb

The suffix **-man** -만 means "only" or "just," but it is also used as a conversational softener. To emphasize the limited *number* or *amount* you are talking about, however, use **-bakke** -밖에 with a *negative verb* to mean "(not/nothing) besides..."

I'll just do this and (then I'll) go. **Igeonman hago galkkeyo.**
이것만 하고 갈게요.

I only had breakfast today. **Oneureun achimbakke mon meogeosseoyo.**
오늘은 아침밖에 못 먹었어요.

So far only one person has come. **Ajik han myeongbakke oji anasseoyo.**
아직 한 명밖에 오지 않았어요.

We only have up to (size) 250 in the red ones.
Ppalgan geoneun ibaegoshipkkajibakke eomneundeyo.
빨간 거는 250까지밖에 없는데요.

CULTURE NOTE Clothing and shoes sizes

Clothing size: Women

Korea	44	55	66	77	88
US	00-0	2-4	6-8	10-12	14-16

Clothing size: Men

Korea chest (cm)	90	95	100	105	110
US	XS	S	M	L	XL

Shoes size: Women

Korea (mm)	220	225	230	235	240	245	250	255	260
US	5	5.5	6	6.5	7	7.5	8	8.5	9

Shoes size: Men

Korea (mm)	245	250	255	260	265	270	275	280	285
US	6.5	7	7.5	8	8.5	9	9.5	10	10.5

PATTERN PRACTICE 2

Practice the following sentences with -밖에 **-bakke.**

1. I only had ramen today. **Oneul ramyeonbakke mon meogeosseoyo.**
   오늘 라면밖에 못 먹었어요.
2. Only three people came to the meeting yesterday.
   Eoje hoe.ui.e se myeongbakke an wasseoyo.
   어제 회의에 세 명밖에 안 왔어요.
3. It's only 7 o'clock now. **Jigeum ilgop sibakke an dwaesseoyo.**
   지금 일곱 시밖에 안 됐어요.

GRAMMAR NOTE 되 *doe* (돼 *dwae*)

The verb **doe** 되 is quite versatile. Its basic meaning is "to become" in sentences like **Hanaga uisaga dwaesseoyo** 하나가 의사가 됐어요 "Hannah has become a doctor." More frequently, **doe** 되 means "to be okay/fine/work out."

A: How did it go?
Geu il eotteoke dwaesseoyo?
그 일 어떻게 됐어요?

B: It turned out okay.
Jal dwaesseoyo.
잘 됐어요.

In the past tense, **dwaet** 됐 can be used to decline an invitation ("I have enough; I am fine; I do not need what you are offering"). It can sound a little blunt, and **gwaenchanayo** 괜찮아요 is a slightly more polite alternative.

A: Would you like more coffee?
Keopi deo masillae?
커피 더 마실래?

B: No, I'm fine.
Ani, dwaesseo/gwaenchana.
아니, 됐어/괜찮아.

Doe 되, as a helping verb, is also used in phrases about permission, obligation, and necessity.

A: May I come in?
Deureogado dwaeyo?
들어가도 돼요?

B: No, you should/may not come in.
Ani, deureo.omyeon an dwaeyo.
아니, 들어오면 안 돼요.

A: I have to speak Korean better.

Han.gugeo deo jal haeya dwaeyo
한국어 더 잘 해야 돼요.

B: All you need to do is to make a Korean friend.

Hanguk chin.gureul sagwimyeon. dwaeyo.
한국 친구를 사귀면 돼요.

Finally, for most Sino-Korean 하 **ha** words, 되 **doe** provides a passive, involuntary version of the verb.

A: Contact your sister.

Nunahante yeollakae.
누나한테 연락해.

B: I can't get a hold of/get in touch with her.

Nunahante yeollak an dwae.
누나한테 연락 안 돼.

GRAMMAR NOTE "Becoming" -어지 *-eoji* vs. 되 *doe*

There are two ways to say "become" in Korean. With adjectives that describe a (change of) state, you use **-eoji** -어지. With nouns, you need to say it as if one "turns into" the other, using the verb **doe** 되.

It's difficult to sell them when they get dirty.
Deoreowojimyeon palgi himdeureoseoyo. 더러워지면 팔기 힘들어서요.

You have gotten prettier since I saw you last!
Geugan deo yeppeojyeonneyo! 그간 더 예뻐졌네요!

The baby (of the family) has become a doctor.
Mangnaega uisaga dwaesseoyo. 막내가 의사가 됐어요.

PATTERN PRACTICE 3

Practice the following sentences using the appropriate 되 **doe** expression.
1. It turned out well. **Iri jal dwaesseoyo.** 일이 잘 됐어요.
2. May I drink this water? **I mul masyeodo dwaeyo?** 이 물 마셔도 돼요?
3. No, you cannot go in there. **Geogi deureogamyeon an dwaeyo.**
   거기 들어가면 안 돼요.

CULTURE NOTE | **Shopping**

There are many venues for shopping in Seoul, with specialty stores all throughout
the city, in every neighborhood, from **hanbok** 한복 (traditional Korean clothing)
specialty shops to international name-brand fashion boutiques to shops for
inexpensive loungewear or luggage.

Major **baekwajeom** 백화점 (department stores) such as Sinsegye 신세계,
Lotte 롯데 and Hyeondae 현대 sell a wide repertoire of items from electric fans to
baby goods. The layout of the stores is usually like this: groceries and food courts
on the basement floors, housewares, clothing and other goods on the upper floors,
and restaurants and culture centers on the top floor.

Some of the most famous shopping areas are: Itaewon 이태원 catering to
foreigners with European-style (so called "Western") goods, groceries, restaurants
and bars as well as souvenirs and luggage; Apgujeong 압구정 and Cheongdam
청담, located in the affluent Gangnam 강남 area, more ritzy shopping areas
with international *haute couture* and high design items; Namdaemun 남대문 a
popular open market; Insadong 인사동 with a long street of traditional shops and
restaurants; and Myeongdong 명동, the heart of old Seoul, known for street foods,
cosmetic brand stores and trendy clothing stores.

Haggling is not done in most stores, especially not in **baekwajeom** 백화점,
but you can often haggle with street vendors in Itaewon and Namdaemun.

EXERCISE 1

You want to do something with your friend this weekend. Give the following
suggestions using the informal casual suggestion form -자 **-ja**.
1. Let's go shopping.
2. Let's watch a movie.

3. Let's get a perm.
4. Let's walk at the park.

EXERCISE 2

You are at a shoe store, and the clerk is answering your questions as follows, using the particle -밖에 **-bakke**. Translate what the clerk says.

1. You: **Ppalgansaek gudu isseoyo?** 빨간색 구두 있어요?
    Clerk: All we have are black and white ones.
2. You: **Saijeu ibaek sasibo isseoyo?** 사이즈 245 있어요?
    Clerk: All we have are sizes 240 and 250.
3. You: **I gudu eolmayeyo?** 이 구두 얼마예요?
    Clerk: They are only 20,000 won.
4. You: **Sinyong kadeureul badeuseyo?** 신용 카드를 받으세요?
    Clerk: We only take cash.

EXERCISE 3

Answer your friends' questions using -돼요 **-dwaeyo** or -됐어요 **-dwaesseoyo**.

1. Friend: **Iri eotteoke dwaesseoyo?** 일이 어떻게 됐어요?
    You: It turned out okay.
2. Friend: **Bap deo meogeullaeyo?** 밥 더 먹을래요?
    You: No, I'm fine.
3. Friend: **Jjimjilbang.eseo jal ssu isseoyo?** 찜질방에서 잘 수 있어요?
    You: Yes, you may sleep at the *jjimjilbang*.
4. Friend: **Naeil mannallaeyo?** 내일 만날래요?
    You: Sorry. I have to work.

🔘 DIALOGUE 2 **Can you lower the price a bit?**

Emma wants to buy a suitcase. She and Eunbi head to Namdaemun Market to buy a suitcase. They are still mixing polite and informal casual speech forms.

Emma: I have to buy a carry-on suitcase. I only have my big one.
        Ginaeyong yeohaenggabang.eul hana saya doeneunde. Keun geobakke eopgeodeunyo.
        기내용 여행가방을 하나 사야 되는데. 큰 거밖에 없거든요.
Eunbi: Yes, you need a smaller one for the Jeju trip. There are a couple luggage shops down this way. Be sure to haggle with the owner (*Lit.*, ask the owner to lower the price).
        Maja. Jejudo garyeomyeon jageun ge hana piryohal kkeoyeyo. Ijjogeuro gamyeon gabang gagega han du gunde isseunikka ju.inhante kkok kkakkadallago haeya dwaeyo.

맞아. 제주도 가려면 작은 게 하나 필요할 거예요. 이쪽으로
가면 가방 가게가 한 두 군데 있으니까 주인한테 꼭
깎아달라고 해야 돼요.

Emma: Got it…

Arasseoyo…
알았어요…

Shopkeeper: Fifty-thousand won each for carry-ons! Hundred thousand for
a set! Trendy cartoon luggage! Ladies! What suitcase are you
looking for? (*Lit.*, what suitcases should I show you?)

**Ginaeyong gabang oman won! Seteu-e simmanwoniyo!
Yuhaenghaneun manhwa gabangdo isseoyo.o~! Agassideul!
Gabang mwollo boyeo deurilkkayo?**
기내용 가방 50,000 원! 세트에 100,000 원이요! 유행하는
만화가방도 있어요오~! 아가씨들! 가방 뭘로 보여 드릴까요?

Eunbi: Do you have black carry-on luggage?

Ajeossi, ginaeyong gabang kkamansaek isseoyo?
아저씨, 기내용 가방 까만색 있어요?

Shopkeeper: Everyone has a black bag, don't they? How about this green one?

Kkamansaek gabang.eun da itjanayo. Choroksaegi eottaeyo?
까만색 가방은 다 있잖아요. 초록색이 어때요?

Emma: The color is okay, but it seems too expensive.

Saegkkareun gwaenchaneunde neomu bissaneyo.
색깔은 괜찮은데 너무 비싸네요.

Shopkeeper: What do you mean (it's) expensive? Where can you find a 50,000
won bag? It's like free!

**Bissagineunyo! Yojeum oman wonjjari gabang.i, eodisseoyo?
Wanjeon geojeoyeyo.**
비싸기는요! 요즘 50,000 원짜리 가방이 어딨어요? 완전
거저예요.

Emma: Free?! It's still too expensive. Come on, come down on the price a
bit more.

**Geojeoraniyo. Geuraedo neomu bissayo. Jom deo kkakka
juseyo.**
거저라니요. 그래도 너무 비싸요. 좀 더 깎아 주세요.

Shopkeeper: Okay, I will give it to you for 45,000 won.

Arasseoyo. Samanocheon wone deurilkkeyo.
알았어요. 45,000 원에 드릴게요.

Emma: Make it 40,000, please?

Saman wone hae juseyo.
40,000 원에 해 주세요.

Shopkeeper: You ladies are killing me! Okay, okay. 40,000 won. Here is your luggage. Happy travels. Please come again!
Agassideul kkakjaeng.ida. Saman won joayo. Gabang yeogi isseoyo. Yeohaeng jal haseyo. Tto oseyo!
아가씨들 깍쟁이다. 40,000 원 좋아요. 가방 여기 있어요. 여행 잘 하세요. 또 오세요!

VOCABULARY AND EXPRESSIONS

중간	**junggan**	mid-size, medium, middle
가방	**gabang**	bag, luggage
여행	**yeohaeng**	travel, trip
제주도	**Jejudo**	Jeju Island
군데	**gunde**	spot, location (dependent noun, used only when modified by counting words)
만화	**manhwa**	cartoon, comic strip, animation, graphic novel
기내용	**ginaeyong**	carry-on (*Lit.*, for in-flight purposes)
세트	**seteu**	set
아가씨들	**agassideul**	ladies
까만색	**kkamansaek**	black
초록색	**choroksaek**	green
돈	**don**	money
거저 (= 공짜)	**geojeo (= gongjja)**	bargain, give-away, for free
깍쟁이	**kkakjaeng.i**	haggler, city slicker
(작은) 게	**(jageun) ge**	(a small) one (거 **geo** "thing" with a subject marker)
뭘로	**mwollo**	by what (뭐 **mwo** "what" with a choice marker)
꼭	**kkok**	for sure, definitely, without fail
완전	**wanjeon**	completely, absolutely
그래도	**geuraedo**	still, even so
-거든	**geodeun**	you know (I forgot to tell you)
-잖아요	**janayo**	you know (you probably/should know this)
-기는요	**gineunyo**	What do you mean ___! (used with verb roots)
-(이)라니	**-(i)rani**	What do you mean ___! (used with nouns)
맞아 (맞-)	**majayo (maj-)**	correct, right; (get) hit, hit the target
깎아달라고 해 (깎-, 하-)	**kkakkadallago hae (kkakk-, ha-)**	(You) ask for a discount
드릴게요 (드리-)	**deurilkkeyo (deuri-)**	I'll give (humble)

VOCABULARY PRACTICE 2

Give the Korean terms for the words described below.
1. something you don't have to pay for is: _____
2. going away from home to visit or tour: _____
3. how you refer to young women: _____
4. stories told with drawings (especially popular among youth): _____

GRAMMAR NOTE Adding an explanation with -거든(요) –geodeun(yo) "You see (I forgot to tell you/you may not know this)"

Many Korean suffixes and endings convey what might be expressed in English just by intonation (changing the tone of your voice). -**Geodeun(yo)** -거든(요) is such an ending, similar to saying "it's because" or "you see... ."

I have to go home early today. Mom is coming from the States, you see.
Jibe iljjik deureogaya dwae. Migugeseo eommaga osigeodeun.
집에 일찍 들어가야 돼. 미국에서 엄마가 오시거든.

I have to buy a mid-size or smaller suitcase because I only have my big one, you see. **Junggan saijeuna jom jageun yeohaenggabang.eul hana saya dwae. Keun geobakke eopgeodeun.**
중간 사이즈나 좀 작은 여행가방을 하나 사야 돼. 큰 거밖에 없거든요.

PATTERN PRACTICE 4

Practice adding on an explanation using -**geodeun(yo)** -거든(요).
1. A: Why do you have to go home early? **Wae jibe iljjik gaya dwaeyo?**
      왜 집에 일찍 가야 돼요?
   B: It's my mom's birthday, you see. **Oneul eomma saengsin.igeodeunyo.**
      오늘 엄마 생신이거든요.
2. A: Would you like to try seafood scallion pancake?
      Haemul pajeoneul meogeo bollaeyo? 해물 파전을 먹어 볼래요?
   B: No, I cannot eat seafood. I am allergic, you see.
      Aniyo. Jeoneun haemureul mon meogeoyo. Allereugiga itgeodeunyo.
      아니요. 저는 해물을 못 먹어요. 알레르기가 있거든요.
3. A: Shall we go to the department store to buy clothes?
      Ot sareo baekwajeome galkkayo? 옷 사러 백화점에 갈까요?
   B: Let's go to Dongdaemun Shopping Complex. It's cheaper there, you see.
      Dongdaemun syopingtaune gayo. Geogiga deo ssageodeunyo.
      동대문 쇼핑타운에 가요. 거기가 더 싸거든요.

GRAMMAR NOTE Asserting ideas and getting agreement
with -잖아(요) *-jana(yo)* "Right? (you know)"

-Jana(yo) -잖아(요) adds a nuance very similar to **-geodeun(yo)** -거든(요), but
you assume the listener knows what you are talking about:

Everyone has a black bag, right? How about green?
Kkamansaek gabang.eun da itjanayo. Choroksaegi eottaeyo?
까만색 가방은 다 있잖아요. 초록색이 어때요?

Oh, you are wondering about why the road is not jammed/backed up? Well,
it's Sunday.
Giri an makindagoyo? Iryoirijanayo. 길이 안 막힌다고요? 일요일이잖아요.

PATTERN PRACTICE 5
Practice asserting ideas and getting agreement using -잖아(요) **-jana(yo)**.
1. A: Should I buy the blue skirt? **Paran chimareul salkkayo?**
    파란 치마를 살까요?
    B: Buy the yellow one. You already have a blue one, right?
    Noran geollo sa. Paran geon beolsseo itjana.
    노란 걸로 사. 파란 건 벌써 있잖아.
2. A: I am sleepy, so let's have coffee. **Jollinde keopi masija.**
    졸린데 커피 마시자.
    B: Well, it's pretty late (to drink coffee). Just go to sleep.
    Keopi masigi.e neomu neujeotjana. Geunyang ja.
    커피 마시기에 너무 늦었잖아. 그냥 자.
3. A: We are late! Let's take a taxi. **Neujeotda! Taeksi taja.**
    늦었다! 택시 타자.
    B: Let's take subway. It's rush hour now, right?
    Jihacheol taja. Jigeum chultoegeun siganijana.
    지하철 타자. 지금 출퇴근 시간이잖아.

GRAMMAR NOTE Challenging others' statements: -기는(요)
-gineun(yo) and -(이)라니요 *-(i)raniyo* "What do
you mean?"

To challenge or counter what the other person says, add **-gineun(yo)** -기는(요) to
the verb root to say the colloquial version, equivalent to something like "whaddaya
mean?!," e.g., What do you mean it's expensive? **Bissagineunyo!** 비싸기는요!

Hungry!? (No way!) I ate too much.
Baegopeugineun. Neomu mani meogeosse.
배고프기는. 너무 많이 먹었어.

To contest the item (a noun) that is brought up, use **-(i)raniyo** -(이)라니요.

Fake leather? What are you talking about?
Gajja gajugirani! Museun malsseumieyo!
가짜 가죽이라니! 무슨 말씀이에요!

PATTERN PRACTICE 6
Practice responding to what you just heard using -기는(요) **-gineun(yo)** or -(이)
라니요 **-(i)raniyo**.
1. A: The room is too hot. **Bang.i neomu deowoyo.** 방이 너무 더워요.
   B: Hot?! It's rather cold. **Deopgineunyo! Jom chuundeyo.**
   덥기는요! 좀 추운데요.
2. A: Is Best Hair good at haircuts? **Beseuteu he.eoga meorireul jal jallayo?**
   베스트 헤어가 머리를 잘 잘라요?
   B: Good (cutting)?! They are terrible.
   Jal jareugineunyo! Jeongmal mot jallayo.
   잘 자르기는요! 정말 못 잘라요.
3. A: Isn't this fake leather?
   Igeo gajja gajuk anieyo? 이거 가짜 가죽 아니에요?
   B: Fake?! It's real leather. **Gajjaraniyo! Jinjja gajugieyo.**
   가짜라니요! 진짜 가죽이에요.

GRAMMAR NOTE Topic first
There are many sentences like **Gabang mwollo boyeo deurilkkayo?** 가방 뭘로
보여 드릴까요? "What kind of bag should I show you?" in Korean where the
main idea of discussion is said first, e.g., **gabang** 가방 "bag." **-Ro** -로 here is a
choice marker and is used to specify "of all these bags, which one(s)." Here are a
couple more examples for you to savor.

When is good for you? (Time—when is good?)
Sigan eonjega joayo? 시간 언제가 좋아요?

What shall we have for lunch? (Lunch—what shall we have?)
Jeosim mwollo meogeulkka? 점심 뭘로 먹을까?

GRAMMAR NOTE "-worth" or "-sized" -짜리 *-jjari*
The suffix **-jjari** -짜리 means "worth," but it is usually not translated in English.

Where can you find a 50,000-won bag these days?
Yojeum oman wonjjari gabang.i eodisseoyo?
요즘 오만 원짜리 가방이 어딨어요?

For a two-year old, this child is big.
Du saljjari aiga kiga keuneyo. 두 살짜리 아이가 키가 크네요.

EXERCISE 4
Answer Aiden's questions in Korean using -거든(요) **-geodeun(yo).**
1. Aiden: **Wae yeohaeng gabang.eul saryeogo haeyo?**
   왜 여행 가방을 사려고 해요?
   You: I am going to Jeju next weekend, you see.
2. Aiden: **Wae usani eopseoyo?** 왜 우산이 없어요?
   You: I lost my umbrella, you see. (to lose: 잃어버리다 **ireobeorida**).
3. Aiden: **Wae jeomsimeul an meogeoyo?** 왜 점심을 안 먹어요?
   You: I am too busy now, you see.
4. Aiden: **Wae patie an wasseoyo?** 왜 파티에 안 왔어요?
   You: I was sick, you see.

EXERCISE 5
Respond to what your friend says using -잖아(요) **-jana(yo).**
1. Friend: **Gabang.eul hana saryeogo haeyo.** 가방을 하나 사려고 해요.
   You: You bought a suitcase last week, didn't you?
2. Friend: **Meorireul jom dadeumeuryeogo haeyo.**
   머리를 좀 다듬으려고 해요.
   You: You cut your hair two weeks ago, didn't you?
3. Friend: **Undonghaeya dwaeyo.** 운동해야 돼요.
   You: You are sick today, aren't you?
4. Friend: **Jumare chin.guhago mannal kkeoyeyo.**
   주말에 친구하고 만날 거예요.
   You: You decided to watch a movie with me this weekend, right?

EXERCISE 6
Respond to Eunbi's comments using -기는(요) **-gineun(yo).**
1. Eunbi: **Gabang.i neomu bissayo.** 가방이 너무 비싸요.
   You: What do you mean too expensive?
2. Eunbi: **Gabang.i neomu keoyo.** 가방이 너무 커요.
   You: What do you mean too big?
3. Eunbi: **Gabang.i neomu mugeowoyo.** 가방이 너무 무거워요.
   You: What do you mean too heavy? (heavy: 무겁다 **mugeopda**)
4. Eunbi: **Saegi neomu ppalgaeyo.** 색이 너무 빨개요.
   You: What do you mean too red?

LESSON 15

Going Out With Friends

DIALOGUE 1 It's been such a long time!

Eunbi is reuniting with her college friends, and Emma and Aiden are joining them.

Hayoung: Eunbi, come on over! Great to see you! It's been such a long time!
Sit here.
**Eunbiya, yeogi! Eoseo wa! Bangapda! Jinjja oraenmanida!
Yeogi anjara.**
은비야, 여기! 어서 와! 반갑다! 진짜 오랜만이다! 여기 앉아라.

Eunbi: Wow, Hayoung Seonbae! You're here already! It's been such a long
time! Great to see you!
**Wa, hayeong seonbae. Beolsseo osyeotgunyo! Jeongmal
oraeganmanine. Jinjja ban.gawayo!**
와, 하영 선배, 벌써 오셨군요! 정말 오래간만이네. 진짜
반가워요!

Oh, Yejin—you are here, too. Good to see you. So, hey, these are my
friends from work, Emma and Aiden.
**Eo, Yejini neodo watguna. Bangapda. Cham, ijjogeun nae jikjang
chin.gu Emma ssihago Eideun ssi.**
어, 예진이 너도 왔구나. 반갑다. 참, 이쪽은 내 직장 친구 엠마
씨하고 에이든 씨.

Introduce yourselves.
Insadeul haeyo.
인사들 해요.

Hayoung: Oh, nice to meet you. I'm Hayoung Shin.
A, ban.gawoyo. Sinhayeong.ieyo.
아, 반가워요. 신하영이에요.

Yejin: Hello! I'm Yejin Park.
Annyeonghaseyo? Jeon bagyejinirago haeyo.
안녕하세요? 전 박예진이라고 해요.

Emma: Nice to meet you. My name is Emma.
Ban.gawoyo. Emmarago haeyo.
반가워요. 엠마라고 해요.

Aiden: I'm Aiden. How do you do?
Eideunimnida. Jal butakdeuryeoyo.
에이든입니다. 잘 부탁드려요.

Eunbi:	Have you guys ordered (anything)?
	Mwo sikyeosseo?
	뭐 시켰어?
Yejin:	No, not yet.
	Ani, ajik.
	아니, 아직.
Eunbi:	Then, let's order a few bottles of beer and some side dishes. What do you want for side dishes?
	Geureom maekju myeot byeonghago anju myeot gae sikija. Anju mwo hallae?
	그럼 맥주 몇 병하고 안주 몇 개 시키자. 안주 뭐 할래?
Yejin:	Let's order chicken. And you, Emma and Aiden?
	Chikin sikija. Emma ssihago eideun ssineunyo?
	치맥! 치킨 시키자. 엠마 씨하고 에이든 씨는요?
Aiden:	Chicken is good for me, too. And fries, too!
	Chikin jeodo joayo. Gamjatwigimdoyo!
	치킨 저도 좋아요. 감자튀김도요!
Hayoung:	OK. Excuse me! (*Literally*, here!)
	Geurae. Yeogiyo!
	그래. 여기요!
Waitress:	Yes. Would you like to order?
	Ne, jumunhasigesseoyo?
	네, 주문하시겠어요?
Yejin:	We would like 4 draft beers, 500 cc each, and an order of seasoned fried chicken, one fries, please. An order of spicy seasoned whelk, too, please.
	Yeogi saengmaekju obaek ssissi ne gaehago yangnyeom chikin hana, gamjatwigim hana juseyo. Golbang.i muchimdo hanayo.
	여기 생맥주 500 cc 네 개하고 양념 치킨 하나, 감자튀김 하나 주세요. 골뱅이 무침도 하나요.
Hayoung:	Make it (the chicken) spicy, please.
	Maeun maseuro juseyo.
	매운 맛으로 주세요.
Waitress:	OK. Right away.
	Ne, geumbang gatdadeurigesseumnida.
	네, 금방 갖다드리겠습니다.
Yejin:	It's on us today so, guests, eat up!
	Oneureun jeohuiga naeneun geonikka sonnimeun manideul deuseyo.
	오늘은 저희가 내는 거니까 손님은 많이들 드세요.
Eunbi:	Really? Thanks! We'll pay next time.
	Jeongmal? Gomawo. Da.eumeneun uriga salgkke!
	정말? 고마워. 다음에는 우리가 살게!

Emma, Aiden: Thanks! (*Literally*, I will eat deliciously.)
Jal meogeulkkeyo.
잘 먹을게요.

VOCABULARY AND EXPRESSIONS

인사*	insa	greeting
오래(간)만	orae(gan)man	a long time (since)
선배	seonbae	senior colleagues/co-workers/schoolmates
진짜 (= 정말)	jinjja (= jeongmal)	really
너	neo	you (informal casual, addressed to minors, childhood friends)
내	nae	my (informal casual)
전 (= 저는)	jeon (= jeoneun)	I-topic (humble)
직장	jikjang	job, workplace
이쪽 (= 여기)	ijjok (= yeogi)	this side, this person
인턴	inteon	intern
안주	anju	side-dishes that accompany alcoholic beverages
치킨	chikin	(cooked) chicken
감자튀김	gamjatwigim	French fries, fried potatoes
웨이터	weiteo	waiter
생맥주	saengmaekju	draft beer
양념	yangnyeom	seasoning, seasoned (before nouns)
골뱅이 무침	golbaeng.i muchim	red pepper and vinegar-seasoned whelk
맛	mat	taste
손님	sonnim	guest
-아	a	marker used with a child(hood friend)'s name ending in a consonant
-야	ya	marker used with a child(hood friend)'s name ending in a vowel
-이	i	marker used after children's or childhood friends' names ending in a consonant
-들	deul	plurality marker
-군요	gunnyo	Eh! Ah! suffix (suffix for noticing/confirming; used with verb roots)
벌써	beolsseo	already
어서	eoseo	hurriedly, now
참	cham	oh, by the way
아직	ajik	not yet, still
금방	geumbang	right away, just now
같은 (같-)	gateun (gat-)	same, alike
매운 (맵-)	maeun (maep-)	spicy

VOCABULARY PRACTICE 1

Give the Korean terms for the words described below.
1. someone who started at work or school before you: _____
2. the place where you work: _____
3. I haven't finished _____ (yet), but will finish _____ (right away).
4. side dishes to eat alongside alcoholic drinks: _____

GRAMMAR NOTE Informal casual command addressing minors -어라/아라 -eora/ara

-Eora -어라 (or **-ara** -아라) is a suffix used in casual, informal situations to those who are younger than you or peers who are childhood friends. With verbs, it works as a command.

Sit here. **Yeogi anjara.** 여기 앉아라.
Don't go there. **Geogi gaji mara.** 거기 가지 마라.

When attached to adjectives, it works as an exclamation suffix.

Yikes, so hot! **Egu, deowora!** 에구, 더워라!

PATTERN PRACTICE 1

Practice the informal casual command form with -어라/아라 **-eora/ara**.
1. Eat this. **Igeo meogeora.** 이거 먹어라.
2. Don't cut your hair. **Meori jareuji mara.** 머리 자르지 마라.
3. Use this toothbrush. **i chissol sseora.** 이 칫솔 써라.

GRAMMAR NOTE The plurality marker -들 -deul

Korean does not use a plural marker like the English "s." Instead you have to glean the number of items from the context or by number words, e.g., "Three people will come." **Se sarami ol kkeoyeyo.** 세 사람이 올 거예요.

When the plurality marker **-deul** -들 is used, it is to let the listener know that the statement (or question) is about more than one *person*. **-Deul** -들 can be attached to objects or adverbs, as well as subjects.

There will be a lot of people there. **Saramdeuri mani ol kkeoyeyo.**
사람들이 많이 올 거예요.

You guys greet (each other). **Insadeul haseyo.** 인사들 하세요.

Where are you guys going? **Eodideul ga?** 어디들 가?

PATTERN PRACTICE 2

Practice using -들 **deul** in the following contexts.
1. My friends came. **Chin.gudeuri wasseoyo.** 친구들이 왔어요.
2. Please sit down (all). **Yeogideul anjeuseyo.** 여기들 앉으세요.
3. Please have some coffee (you all). **Keopideul deuseyo.** 커피들 드세요.

GRAMMAR NOTE Use of question words for indefinite ideas

Question words ("who, what, where, how many" etc.) used in statements are used for indefinite items like "a few" or "someone."

There is <u>someone</u> (*Lit.*, There who it is). Let's ask him.
Jeogi <u>nuga</u> inne. Jeo saramhante mureoboja.
저기 <u>누가</u> 있네. 저 사람한테 물어보자.

Stop by <u>sometime</u> to play.
<u>Eonje</u> hanbeon nolleo oseyo. <u>언제</u> 한번 놀러 오세요.

I gotta eat <u>something</u>. **Mwo jom meogeoyagetta.** 뭐 좀 먹어야겠다.

Something will happen (to resolve this issue., e.g., somehow it will all turn out well.) **<u>Eotteke</u> doel kkeoya.** 어떻게 될 거야.

Let's order <u>a few</u> bottles of beer.
Maekju <u>myeot</u> byeong sikija. 맥주 <u>몇</u> 병 시키자.

The restaurant is big but with only <u>a few</u> waiters, so the service is slow.
Sikdang.eun keunde weiteoga <u>myeot</u> myeongbakke eopseoseo seobiseuga neuryeo.
식당은 큰데 웨이터가 <u>몇</u> 명밖에 없어서 서비스가 느려.

One sentence can have two meanings, so listen carefully to the speaker's intonation. For example, **Mwo sikyeosseo** 뭐 시켰어? can mean both "What have you ordered?" and "Have you ordered anything?" If the intonation is smooth throughout, then the meaning is the first. If there's a break after the question word, and then a subsequent higher pitch at the end of the sentence, then the meaning is the latter.

What have you ordered? **Mwo sikyeosseo?** 뭐 시켰어?
Have you guys ordered anything/something? **Mwo sikyeosseo?** 뭐　시켰어?

PATTERN PRACTICE 3

Practice the following with the indefinite ideas "something," "someone," and "somewhere."

1. I am hungry… Shall we eat something? **Bae gopeunde mwo meogeulkka?** 배 고픈데 뭐 먹을까?
2. Someone came? **Nuga wasseoyo?** 누가 왔어요.
3. A: Are you going somewhere? **Eodi gaseyo?** 어디 가세요?
   B: Yes, I am going somewhere. **Ne, eodi jom gayo.** 네, 어디 좀 가요.

| CULTURE NOTE | **Negotiating politeness and intimacy**

In the first dialogue, Eunbi calls out her greeting to her upper-classman, Hayoung, and drops the politeness suffix **-yo** -요. Throughout the conversation she often drops the suffix. This is a tactic that Koreans often adopt when speaking to someone whom they are close to but who is older by a few years (or people of the same age who haven't established a firm casual relationship with their listener). By occasionally dropping **-yo** -요. Eunbi is showing that she and Hayoung are closer than casual acquaintances. Observe how Koreans manage the art of linguistic balancing without coming across as rude and then you, too, can adopt this.

EXERCISE 1

You've gotten together with Eunbi and Yejin, who are your juniors (후배 **hubae**). Make informal casual commands to them using -어라/아라 **-eora /ara**.

1. Eunbi, sit here.
2. Eunbi, try eating this chicken.
3. Yejin, order fries.
4. Yejin, call me tomorrow.

EXERCISE 2

Complete the conversations using question words as indefinite words. Ask them out loud using the right intonation.

1. You: Are you going somewhere?
   Minjoon: **Ani, wae?** 아니, 왜?
2. You: Let's drink something.
   Emma: **Jo.a! Keopi masija.** 좋아! 커피 마시자.
3. You: Let's have coffee together sometime!
   Eunbi: **Ne, joayo!** 네, 좋아요.
4. You: Let's do something together this weekend.
   Aiden: **Mian, ibeon jumare jom bappa.** 미안, 이번 주말에 좀 바빠.

EXERCISE 3

You are at a pub with your friends. How would you place the following orders in Korean?

Waiter: **Jumunhasigesseoyo?** 주문하시겠어요?

1. Two draft beers, 500 cc each, please.
2. Three orders of seasoned fried chicken, please.
3. An order of spicy seasoned whelk, please.
4. Please get us three more draft beers.

DIALOGUE 2 I'll take you to an 8-person room.

Everyone goes to a *noraebang* after dinner.

Noraebang Staff:	Hi! How many?
	Eoseo oseyo. Modu myeot buniseyo?
	어서 오세요. 모두 몇 분이세요?
Eunbi:	Do you have a room for 5 people?
	Daseot myeong deureogal bang isseoyo?
	다섯 명 들어갈 방 있어요?
Noraebang Staff:	OK. Just a second. How long will you stay?
	Ne, jamkkanman gidaryeo juseyo. Eolmana gyesil kkeoyeyo?
	네, 잠깐만 기다려 주세요. 얼마나 계실 거예요?
Eunbi:	About two hours.
	Du siganjjeumiyo.
	2 시간쯤이요.
Noraebang Staff:	We don't have a 5-person room now. I'll take you to a 8-person room.
	Jigeum o innyong bang.i eopseoseoyo. Palinnyong bang-euro annaehae deurilkkeyo.
	지금 5인용 방이 없어서요. 8인용 방으로 안내해 드릴게요.
Eunbi:	How much is it for the 8-person room?
	Palinnyong bang.eun eolmandeyo?
	8인용 방은 얼만데요?
Noraebang Staff:	It's 15,000 won.
	Manocheon wonimnida.
	15,000 원입니다.
Eunbi:	How about for 5 people?
	O.inyoung.eunyo?
	5인용은요?
Noraebang Staff:	It's 10,000 won. But, I'll give you an extra 10 minutes.
	Man wonieyo. Daesin seobiseu ship bun deurilkkeyo.
	10,000 원이에요. 대신 서비스 10분 드릴게요.

Eunbi:	What shall we do? Do you guys feel OK about the 8-person room? Shall we go out to look for a cheaper place?

Eotteoke halkka? Palinnyong bang.e gado gwaenchana? Deo ssan de chajeureo naga bolkka?

어떻게 할까? 8인용 방에 가도 괜찮아? 더 싼 데 찾으러 나가 볼까?

Aiden:	We may not find a room in other places, either; it's the weekend.

Jumarira dareun de gado jariga eopseuljji molla.

주말이라 다른 데 가도 자리가 없을지 몰라.

Emma:	It's okay. I'll pay.

Gwaenchana. Ibeoneneun naega naelkkeyo!

괜찮아. 이번에는 내가 낼게요!

Eunbi:	Really? OK, we'll take that room then. Do we pay now (in advance)?

Geurae? Geureom geu bang.euro halkkeyo. Seonburieyo?

그래? (To the worker) 그럼 그 방으로 할게요. 선불이에요?

Noraebang Staff:	No, you pay afterwards. This way, please.

Aniyo, yogeumeun huburimnida. Ijjogeuro oseyo.

아니. 요금은 후불입니다. 이쪽으로 오세요.

VOCABULARY AND EXPRESSIONS

안내*	annae	guide, *to guide
분	bun	counter for people
시간	sigan	time, hours
5인용	o.inyong	for use by 5 people
서비스	seobiseu	service (as an extra, complimentary service)
데	de	place, location (used only after a modifier)
자리	jari	spot, space, available seating or room
요금	yogeum	fee, fare
선불	seonbul	paying in advance
후불	hubul	paying after use/afterwards
대신	daesin	instead, in exchange
이번	ibeon	this time
얼마나	eolmana	approximately how (long, much, etc.)
계실 거예요? (계시-)	gyesil kkeoyeyo? (gyesi-)	will you stay? (honorific)
주말이라 (주말이-)	jumarira (jumali-)	since it's the weekend
낼게 (내-)	naelkke (nae-)	I'll pay

VOCABULARY PRACTICE 2

Give the Korean terms for the words described below.

1. when a merchant or service-provider adds something on for free: _____
2. what you have to pay for a service or use: _____
3. If you're buying lunch, then _____ (in exchange/in return) I'll buy coffee.
4. when you get on a bus or subway, you look for this so you can sit down:

_____

GRAMMAR NOTE Goal suffix -(으)러 -(eu)reo "in order to"

The suffix **-(eu)reo** -(으)러 is very similar to **-(eu)ryeo** -(으)려, but it is more goal-oriented, and it can only be used with verbs of moving such as "go, come, enter, exit" to express the purpose of the movement. Use **-reo** -러 with verbs that end in a vowel or ㅣㄹ.

Let's go and have lunch together. **Gachi jeomsim meogeureo gaja.**
같이 점심 먹으러 가자.

I'm here to pick up (look for) my pants. **Baji chajeureo wasseoyo.**
바지 찾으러 왔어요.

Shall we go out to look for a cheaper place?
Deo ssan de chajeureo naga bolkka? 더 싼 데 찾으러 나가 볼까?

PATTERN PRACTICE 4

Practice expressing your goal using -(으)러 **-(eu)reo**.

1. I am going to a hair salon to get a haircut.
   Meorireul jareureo miyongsire gal kkeoyeyo.
   머리를 자르러 미용실에 갈 거예요.
2. A: How can I help you? (What brought you here?) **Eotteke osyeosseoyo?**
   어떻게 오셨어요?
   B: I am here to meet Manager Park. **Bak Bujangnimeul boereo wasseumnida.**
   박 부장님을 뵈러 왔습니다.
3. A: Come on in, Ma'am/Sir! **Eoseo oseyo, sonnim!**
   어서 오세요, 손님!
   B: I came to pick up my coat that I brought in for dry cleaning last week.
   Jinan jue deurai matgin koteu chajeureo wanneundeyo.
   지난 주에 드라이 맡긴 코트 찾으러 왔는데요.

GRAMMAR NOTE -(으)ㄹ지(도) 몰라 -*(eu)l jji(do) molla* "It may be the case; you never know"

The ending **-(eu)l jji(do) molla** -(으)ㄹ지(도) 몰라 expresses a tentative attitude or warning. **Jji** 지 is always pronounced strongly.

Emma might not be able to come today. **Emmaneun mot ol jji molla.**
엠마는 못 올지 몰라.

We may not find a room in other places, either.
Dareun de gado jariga eopseul jjido molla.
다른 데 가도 자리가 없을지도 몰라.

PATTERN PRACTICE 5

Practice saying the following sentences with -(으)ㄹ지도 몰라 **-(eu)l jji(do) molla**.
1. I may be busy tomorrow. **Naeireun bappeul jjido mollayo.**
내일은 바쁠지도 몰라요.
2. Today's event may be canceled due to the rain.
Oneul haengsaneun bi ttaemune chwisodoel jjido mollayo.
오늘 행사는 비 때문에 취소될지도 몰라요.
3. It might be cold if you don't wear a coat.
Koteu an ibeumyeon chu.ul jjido mollayo. 코트 안 입으면 추울지도 몰라.

GRAMMAR NOTE Relative clause: modifying nouns with yet-to-happen events -(으)ㄹ -*(eu)l* "a (noun) to/that will..."

Phrases that end in **-(eu)l** -(으)ㄹ modify nouns with the sense of "to (do)" (or sometimes, "someone/something that will do…"). The lax consonants **g** ㄱ, **d** ㄷ, **b** ㅂ, **s** ㅅ, **j** ㅈ are always pronounced strongly after this **-(eu)l** -(으)ㄹ.

I have nothing more <u>to say</u>. **Deo <u>hal</u> mal eopseo.** 더 <u>할</u> 말 없어.

Do you have a room <u>for four people (to go into)</u>?
<u>Ne myeong deureogal</u> ppang isseoyo? 네 명 <u>들어갈</u> 방 있어요?

Is there anyone <u>who will help me</u>?
<u>Na dowajul</u> ssaram isseo? <u>나 도와줄</u> 사람 있어?

PATTERN PRACTICE 6

Practice asking the following questions with -(으)ㄹ **-(eu)l**.
1. (Is there) a place to sit down?
Jom anjeul ttega isseulkkayo? 좀 앉을 데가 있을까요?

2. Is there anyone who will go fishing with me?
   Nahago naksihareo gachi gal ssaram? 나하고 낚시하러 같이 갈 사람?
3. Do you have a room for five? **Daseon myeong.i deureogal ppang isseoyo?**
   다섯 명이 들어갈 방 있어요?

GRAMMAR NOTE Contracted pronouns

Pronouns (or other small words) and markers are often contracted in everyday speech. We give some examples here, but once you understand how the system works—we suggest saying them out loud—you can apply them for the rest of the pronouns.

내 (= 나의)	**nae (= na.ui)**	I (familiar)-possessive marker
전 (= 저는)	**jeon (= jeoneun)**	I (humble)-topic marker
그건 (= 그것은)	**geugeon (= geugeoseun)**	that/it-topic marker
그걸 (= 그것을)	**geugeol (= geugeoseul)**	that/it-object marker
그게 (= 그것이)	**geuge (= geugeosi)**	that/it-subject marker
우린 (= 우리는)	**urineun (= urineun)**	us (familiar)-subject marker
우릴 (= 우리를)	**uril (= urireul)**	us (familiar)-object marker
뭘 (= 무얼, 무엇을)	**mwol (= mueol, mueoseul)**	what-object marker
여긴 (= 여기는)	**yeogin (= yeogineun)**	here, this place-topic marker

GRAMMAR NOTE Reviewing -는/-(으)ㄹ/-(으)ㄴ 거 같아요 *-neun/(eu) l/(eu)n geo gatayo*

As a shorthand, the **-neun** -는 vs. **-(eu)l** -(으)ㄹ distinction in verb endings can be thought of as "present" and "future," in the concept of on-going/happening vs. unknown/yet-to-happen. This distinction will help you catch a subtle nuance difference.

I think Minjoon is coming, too. **Minjun ssido <u>oneun</u> geo gatayo.**
민준 씨도 <u>오는</u> 거 같아요.

I think Minjoon will be coming/is going to come, too.
Minjun ssido <u>ol</u> kkeo gatayo.
민준 씨도 <u>올</u> 거 같아요.

In the same vein, **-(eu)l** -(으)ㄹ is less certain while **-(eu)n** -(으)ㄴ is more fact-based with adjectives. Either way, you are trying to avoid sounding too direct. You may or may not have tasted the food in the first case below, and you definitely haven't in the second situation:

I think this is a little spicy for me.
Igeo jeohante jom <u>maeun</u> geo gatayo. 이거 저한테 좀 <u>매운</u> 거 같아요.

I think this will be a little spicy for me.
Igeo jeohante jom <u>maeul</u> kkeo gatayo. 이거 저한테 좀 매울 거 같아요.

CULTURE NOTE **Korean names**

Almost all Korean last names are one-syllable long (like Gim/Kim 김 金 and I/Lee 이 李) and first names are two-syllables (like **Suhyeon** 수현 秀賢 and **Junho** 준호 峻浩). These two-syllable names are normally created based on Chinese characters, although pure Korean names, such as **haneul** 하늘 (sky) and **bada** 바다 (sea), are becoming more common nowadays. In fact, Korean people rarely use Chinese characters to write their names except on some official documents such as their family registry. It can be difficult to get a feel for the aesthetics of male and female names in Korean as it depends on the combination of syllables as well as the meanings of the characters. Some same-sounding syllables are found in both genders' names (the associated Chinese character may be the same or different). So a woman's name may be **HaJiwon** 하지(智)원, and a man's name may be **SoJiseop/SoJisup** 소지(志)섭, where **Ji** 지 is found in both names. (There is a standard way to write Korean names in new, government-developed romanization, but some people choose to spell their names differently.)

It used to be that masculine names had more hard 받침 batchim (e.g. **Dong-uk** 동욱) and feminine names had more sonorous sounds and open syllables (**Yejin** 예진), but the latter are common in popular boys' names today as well, so some names (such as **Suhyeon** 수현 and **Jiwon** 지원) can be either male or female. There are also trends in the popularity of name-syllables, sometimes based on entertainers' names.

In more traditional households, siblings share a name-syllable of that particular generation so the younger brother's name may be **Hyeongjin** 형진, while the older brother's name is **Dongjin** 동진, for example. These name-syllables are called **dollimjja** 돌림자 (a shared (*Lit.*, "circulating")) character.

CULTURE NOTE **Who pays?**

Just as in many Asian countries, Koreans often fight to be the one to pay the bill when they eat out with their peers and close friends. They will try tricks like pretending to go to the restroom (and pay behind the scenes) or physically wrestle to get the bill out of each other's hands. Eventually, the agreement usually comes that whoever loses or gives in agrees to pay the next time they go out or to pay for the next "round" of drinks, dessert or *noraebang*. Traditionally, the bill is virtually *never* split, and individuals' choice of dishes or drinks is of no concern. (Remember that meals are generally meant to be communal.)

There are also customs as to who pays in certain situations: the birthday boy or girl usually treats their friends, and the older person or the person with a job usually pays for the other. The most senior person or the person with the highest rank pays the bill. However, **deochipei** 더치페이 (paying bills separately) culture is spreading nowadays and is aided by the proliferation of apps like Toss and Kakao Pay, where money can be easily transferred from one person to another, without needing the party's banking details.

EXERCISE 4

Complete the conversations in Korean using -(으)러 가다/오다 -**(eu)reo gada/ oda**.

1. Receptionist: 어떻게 오셨어요? **Eotteoke osyeosseoyo?**
   What can I do for you? (*Lit.*, How did you come here?)
   You: I came here to meet Mr. Minjoon Kim.
2. Colleague: 선배님 어디 계셔? 누가 만나러 오셨어.
   Seonbaenim eodi gyesyeo? Nuga mannareo osyeosseo.
   You: He went to Gangnam to see his client (클라이언트 **keullai. eonteu**)
3. Friend: 오늘 집에 있어? **Oneul jibe isseo?**
   You: Yes, my mother will come to give me *kimchi*.
4. Friend: 이번 주말에 뭐 해? **Ibeon jumare mwo hae?**
   You: I will go to Bukhan Mountain to hike.

EXERCISE 5

Complete the conversations using -(으)ㄹ 지(도) 몰라(요) -**(eu)l ji(do) molla(yo)**.

1. Friend: 이 재킷 입고 나갈까? **I jaekit ipgo nagalkka?**
   You: Wear a coat. It might be cold today.
2. Friend: 이 가방 살까? **I gabang salkka?**
   You: Don't buy it. It might go on sale next week.
3. Friend: 엠마는 오늘 안 와? **Emmaneun oneul an wa?**
   You: Emma might not be able to come.
4. Friend: 엠마한테 전화할까? **Emmahante jeonhwahalkka?**
   You: Emma might not pick up the phone. She is busy today.

EXERCISE 6

Eunbi is waiting for you to meet her at the *noraebang*. Complete the conversations using a phrase in -(으)ㄹ -**(eu)l** to describe a noun.

1. Eunbi: 노래방으로 빨리 와. **Naraebang.euro ppalli wa.**
   You: Is there something to eat?
2. Eunbi: 응. 감자튀김하고 골뱅이 무침 있어.
   Eung. Gamjatwigimhago golbaeng.i muchim isseo.
   You: Is there something to drink?
3. Eunbi: 응. 맥주하고 콜라가 있어. **Eung. Maekjuhago kollaga isseo.**
   You: Okay, I also have something to give you.
   Eunbi: 좋아! 빨리 와! **Joa! Ppalli wa!**

예진 씨, 은비가 그러던데 테니스 선수라면서요?
Yejin, Eunbi says you are quite the tennis player. Is that right?

하하. 네.
Haha. Yes.
지난 달부터 우리 회사 테니스 팀을 위해 뛰고 있지요.
I started playing for my company's tennis team last month.

그런데 에이든 씨, 이제 우리도 말 놓을까요?
By the way, Aiden, shall we use informal speech?
친한 친구의 친구도 친구고, 우리 나이도 동갑이니까.
A good friend's friend is also a friend, and since we are the same age, too.

그럴까? 좋아!
Shall we? OK!
그럼 이제부터 반말 한다!
Then I'm going to use casual speech, starting now!

LESSON 16
Talking Casually

DIALOGUE 1 Do you know how to play tennis?

Aiden and Yejin are the same age. They met through Eunbi and have gotten to know each other well. They are chatting about their hobbies today.

Aiden: Yejin, Eunbi says you are quite the tennis player. Is that right?
         Yejin ssi, Eunbiga geureodeonde teniseu seonsuramyeonseoyo?
         예진 씨, 은비가 그러던데 테니스 선수라면서요?

Yejin: Haha. Yes. I started playing for my company's tennis team last month.
         Haha. Ne. Jinan dalbuteo uri hoesa teniseu timeul wihae ttwigo itjiyo.
         하하. 네. 지난 달부터 우리 회사 테니스 팀을 위해 뛰고 있지요.
         By the way, Aiden, shall we use informal speech? A good friend's friend is also a friend, and since we are the same age, too.
         Geureonde Eideun ssi, ije urido mal no.eulkkayo? Chinhan chin. gu.ui chin.gudo chin.gugo, uri naido donggabinikka.
         그런데 에이든 씨, 이제 우리도 말 놓을까요? 친한 친구의 친구도 친구고, 우리 나이도 동갑이니까.

Aiden: Shall we? OK! Then I'm going to use casual speech, starting now!
         Geureolkka? Joa! Geureom ijebuteo banmal handa!
         그럴까? 좋아! 그럼 이제부터 반말 한다!
         OK! By the way, how long have you been playing tennis? How come you play tennis so well?
         Geunde, neon teniseu bae.un ji eolmana dwaesseo? Eotteoke geureoke teniseureul jal chyeo?
         근데, 넌 테니스 배운 지 얼마나 됐어? 어떻게 그렇게 테니스를 잘 쳐?

Yejin: I may not look like much, but I've been playing since I was on the intramural tennis team for my junior high school.
         Irae bwaedo, junghakgyo ttaebuteo teniseubu seonsuyeotta!
         이래 봐도, 중학교 때부터 테니스부 선수였다!

Aiden: Awesome!
         Goengjanghande!
         굉장한데!

Yejin: Do you (know how to) play tennis?
         Neon teniseu chil jjul ani?
         넌 테니스 칠 줄 아니?

Aiden: I just started learning last year.
Naneun il lyeon jeonbuteo teniseureul bae.ugi sijakaesseo.
나는 일 년 전부터 테니스를 배우기 시작했어.

Yejin: How do you like it?
Teniseu chineun geo eottae?
테니스 치는 거 어때?

Aiden: I'm just a beginner, but it's a lot of fun.
Ajik chobojiman aju jaemiisseo.
아직 초보지만 아주 재미있어.

Yejin: Let's play together some time.
Geureom eonje duri hanbeon gachi chija.
그럼 언제 둘이 한번 같이 치자.

Aiden: OK! I'm a little nervous, but I'll learn a lot, I think.
Joa! Jogeum tteollijiman mani bae.ul ssu isseul kkeo gatda.
좋아! 조금 떨리지만 많이 배울 수 있을 거 같다.

VOCABULARY AND EXPRESSIONS

테니스	**teniseu**	tennis
선수	**seonsu**	professional athlete, athletic team member
달	**dal**	moon, month (only when modified)
팀	**tim**	team
반말*	**banmal**	informal, casual speech, *speak casually with no polite endings
나이	**na.i**	age
동갑	**donggap**	same age
중학교	**junghakgyo**	middle school, junior high school
일 년	**il lyeon**	one year
전	**jeon**	before, ago
초보	**chobo**	novice, beginner
둘	**dul**	the two, both
그렇게	**geureoke**	like that, like so
이래 봬도	**irae bwaedo**	I/this might not look like much, but
-부	**bu**	club (used after club name)
-지만 (-이지만)	**-jiman (-ijiman)**	however (if attached to nouns, the verb **i**- is used)
-을/를 위해	**eul/reul wihae**	for (the benefit of, sake of)
그러던데	**geureodeonde**	I heard (someone) say
선수라면서요	**seonsuramyeonseoyo**	(professional) athlete, I hear.
뛰고 있지요 (뛰-, 있-)	**ttwigo itjiyo (ttwi-, iss-)**	playing (*lit.*, running), you know
말 놓을까요? (놓으-)	**mal no.eulkkayo? (noheu-)**	shall we use casual speech?
친한 (친하-)	**chinhan (chinha-)**	close, intimate

그럴까? (그러-)	Geureolkka? (geureo-)	Shall we?
배운 지 (배우-)	bae.un ji (bae.u-)	since you began to learn
굉장한데! (굉장하-)	goengjanghande! (goengjangha-)	Amazing! Great!
칠 줄 아니? (치-, 알-)	chil jjul ani? (chi-, al-)	do you (know how to) play (e.g., tennis)?
지난 (지나-)	jinan (jina-)	last, past
배우기 (배우-)	bae-ugi (baeu-)	learning
힘든데 (힘들-)	himdeunde (himdeul-)	difficult, tough but
떨리지만 (떨리-)	tteollijiman (tteolli-)	nervous

VOCABULARY PRACTICE 1

Give the Korean terms for the words described below.
1. what's in the sky at night, besides stars: _____
2. someone who plays a sport: _____
3. before you can be an expert, you have to be a _____
4. how many years you have lived since your birth* is your _____
*In Korea, an additional year is counted in one's age, and years are counted at the turn of the new calendar year as opposed to on your actual birthday

GRAMMAR NOTE Confirming statements with -면서(요)? -myeonseo(yo)

When you want to confirm the validity of what you have heard—whether from a third party or the person you are speaking with—you can use the question phrase **-myeonseo(yo)?** -면서(요)?

You two are good friends, I hear?
Duri joeun chin.guramyeonseoyo? 둘이 좋은 친구라면서요?

Didn't you say your house is in front of Hongdae?
Jibi Hongdae ape itdamyeonseo? 집이 홍대 앞에 있다면서?

Use **-((i)ramyeonseo(yo)** -(이)라면서(요) after a noun, and **-da** -다 or **-n/neundamyeonseo(yo)** -ㄴ/는다면서(요) after verbs. See the table below for conjugation specifics.

TENSE	FORM	EXAMPLES
Past	었/았다면서(요)? **eot/atdamyeonseo(yo)?**	갔다면서(요)? **Gatdamyeonseo(yo)?** I hear you went..?
Present	Adjective stem + 다면서(요)? **damyeonseo(yo)?**	예쁘다면서(요)? **Yeppeudamyeonseo(yo)?** I hear they are pretty?
	있 + 다면서(요)? **iss + damyeonseo(yo)?**	시간 있다면서(요)? **Sigan itdamyeonseo(yo)?** Didn't you say you had time?
	Verb stem + ㄴ/는다면서(요)? **n/neundamyeonseo(yo)?**	간다면서(요)? **Gandamyeonseo(yo)?** Didn't you say you go?
		먹는다면서(요)? **Meongneundamyeonseo(yo)?** Didn't you say you eat...?
	Noun + (이)라면서(요)? **(i)ramyeonseo(yo)?**	친구라면서(요)? **Chin.guramyeonseo(yo)?** I hear you guys are friends?
Future	(으)ㄹ 거라면서(요)? **(eu)l kkeoramyeonseo(yo)?**	갈 거라면서(요)? **Gal kkeoramyeonseo(yo)?** I hear you will be going?

PATTERN PRACTICE 1

Practice confirming what you heard using -면서요? **-myeonseoyo**.

1. Samsung is a Korean brand. Is it true?
   Samseong.i Han.guk braendeuramyeonseoyo?
   삼성이 한국 브랜드라면서요?

2. It is going to rain tomorrow, I heard.
   Nae.il biga ol kkeoramyeonseoyo? 내일 비가 올 거라면서요?

3. Aiden plays ping-pong well. Is that true?
   Eideuni takgureul jal chindamyeonseoyo?
   에이든이 탁구를 잘 친다면서요?

4. It snowed in Boston yesterday, I heard.
   Eoje Boseuteone nuni watdamyeonseoyo?
   어제 보스턴에 눈이 왔다면서요?

GRAMMAR NOTE "Know how to" (have specific knowledge and skill) -(으)ㄹ 줄 알다/모르다 *-(eu)l jjul alda/ moreuda*

Instead of saying "Do you do X?" Koreans may ask "Do you know how to do X?" if there is learning involved or a perceived challenge in the activity. **Al-** 알- means "to know" and **moreu-** 모르- means "to not know" and conjugates irregularly as **molla(yo)** 몰라(요).

Do you (know how to) play tennis? **Neo teniseu chil jjul ani?**
너 테니스 칠 줄 아니?

You (know how to) eat *kimchi*? **Kimchi meogeul jjul aseyo?**
김치 먹을 줄 아세요?

PATTERN PRACTICE 2
Practice talking about specific skills and abilities using -(으)ㄹ 줄 알다/모르다 **(eu)l jul alda/moreuda**.

1. A: Do you know how to ride a bicycle? **Jajeon.geo tal jjul arayo?**
      자전거 탈 줄 알아요?
   B: No, I don't. **Aniyo. Mollayo.** 아니요. 몰라요.
2. A: Do you know how to use Excel?
      Eksel sseul jjul amnikka? 엑셀 쓸 줄 압니까?
   B: Yes, I do. **Ne, sseul jjul amnida.** 네, 쓸 줄 압니다.
3. A: Do you know any foreign languages?
      Oegugeo hasil jjul asimnikka? 외국어 하실 줄 아십니까?
   B: Yes, I can speak Chinese and English.
      Ne, Jung.gugeohago Yeong.eoreul hal ssu isseumnida.
      네, 중국어하고 영어를 할 수 있습니다.

GRAMMAR NOTE Using -(으)ㄴ 지 (얼마나) 됐어요? *-(eu)n ji (eolmana) dwaesseoyo?* for "it's been [how long] since …"

Eolmana dwaesseoyo? 얼마나 됐어요? asks the question "how long has it been," and is linked to a preceding phrase with **-(eu)n ji** -(으)ㄴ 지. It asks "how long has it been since (you did something)" or "since (you) started (doing something)?"

How long has it been since you came to Korea?
Han.guge on ji eolmana dwaesseoyo? 한국에 온 지 얼마나 됐어요?

When did you start learning Korean?
Han.gugeo bae-un ji eolmana dwaesseo? 한국어 배운 지 얼마나 됐어?

To make a statement, e.g., "it's been [amount of time] since I last drank wine," replace the question word **eolmana** 얼마나 with an expression of time.

It's been five minutes since the bus left.
Geu beoseu tteonan ji o bun dwaesseo. 그 버스 떠난 지 오 분 됐어.

It's been ages since I've had pork belly.
Samgyepsal meogeun ji jeongmal orae dwaetda!
삼겹살 먹은 지 정말 오래 됐다!

It's been 6 months since I came to Korea, and I haven't gotten out of the city until now! **Han.guge on ji yuk gaewol dwaenneunde gyo.oero naogineun cheo-eumiya!** 한국에 온 지 육 개월 됐는데 교외로 나오기는 처음이야!

PATTERN PRACTICE 3
Practice the following dialogues with -(으)ㄴ지 (얼마나) 됐어요? **-(eu)n ji olmana dwaesseoyo.**
1. A: When did you start working here?
      Yeogieseo ilhan ji eolmana dwaesseoyo?
      여기에서 일한 지 얼마나 됐어요?
    B: About six months. **Yuk gaewoljjeum dwaesseoyo.**
      육 개월쯤 됐어요.
2. A: It's been 30 minutes since we ordered food.
      Eumsik jumunhan ji samsip bunina dwaenneundeyo.
      음식 주문한 지 30분이나 됐는데요.
    B: I am sorry. I will check and get back to you.
      Joesonghamnida. Ara bogo malsseumdeurilkkeyo.
      죄송합니다. 알아 보고 말씀드릴게요.
3. A: It's been three months since I had a haircut.
      Meori jareun ji se dari dwaesseo. 머리 자른 지 세 달이 됐어.
    B: Let's go get a hair cut tomorrow. **Naeil gachi meori jareureo gaja.**
      내일 같이 머리 자르러 가자.

GRAMMAR NOTE "To play"
For general "hanging out," Koreans use the verb 놀 **nol-**, and for computer or card games, **hada** 하다. But for musical instruments and different sports types, they use the verbs repeatedly involved in the playing, e.g., "blowing" for wind instruments like the flute and "striking" for tennis, bowling, and playing the piano. If the sport involves various movements, they use the general verb for musical instruments **yeonjuhada** 연주하다.

ACTIVITIES	VERBS TO USE
테니스 **teniseu** "tennis," 탁구 **takgu** "ping-pong," 볼링 **boling** "bowling"	치다 **chida** "to strike"
기타 **gita** "guitar," 피아노 **piano** "piano," 드럼 **deureom** "drum"	
피리 **piro** "recorder," 플룻 **peullut** "flute," 단소 **danso** "traditional short flute"	불다 **bulda** "to blow"
바이올린 **baiolin** "violin," 첼로 **chello** "cello"	켜다 **keyoda** "to play (bow instruments)"

Do you want to play a computer game? **Keompyuteo geim hallae?**
컴퓨터 게임 할래?

Let's play tennis! **Teniseu chija!** 테니스 치자!

Someone is playing the flute. **Nuga peulluseul bulgo isseo.**
누가 플룻을 불고 있어.

Do you know how to play the violin? **Baiollin kyeol jjul ani?**
바이올린 켤줄 아니?

GRAMMAR NOTE The informal casual speech style

When speaking to minors, childhood friends, or close peers one can be casual with, Koreans use an informal, casual speech style called **banmal** 반말. The simplest way to use **banmal** 반말 is to drop **-yo** -요 from the informal polite forms for statements, questions, suggestions, and commands, but there are other endings in **banmal** 반말 that would be good to learn, which we introduce below.

Statements
For statements, the ending is **-da** -다 for adjectives, which means it looks the same as the dictionary form.

It's really cold today. **Oneul jeongmal chupda.** 오늘 정말 춥다.

For the present tense, use **-neunda** -는다 for verbs that end in a consonant, and **-nda** -ㄴ다 for verbs that end in a vowel or in ㅣㄹ, which is then dropped.

I'm going to use blunt-talk starting now, alright? **Ijebuteo banmal handa!**
이제부터 반말 한다!

They sell *tteokbokki* over there! **Jeogieseo tteokbokki panda!**
저기에서 떡볶이 판다!

Use -었/았다 **-eotda/atda** for the past tense, and for the future tense the **-(eu)l kkeoda** -(으)ㄹ 거다 suffix. The **-da** -다 **banmal** endings are typically used to make an announcement.

I was a tennis club captain in junior high school!
Junghakkyo ttae teniseubu kaeptini.eotda!
중학교 때 테니스부 캡틴이었다!

It will rain tomorrow. **Nae.il bi ol kkeoda.** 내일 비 올 거다.

Questions
Questions in this speech style use the ending **-ni** -니 (or a little more tomboyish version, **-nya** -냐), but this form is especially endearing and most often used toward those who are younger than you or really close friends.

Do you (know how to) play tennis?
Neon teniseu chil jjul ani? 넌 테니스 칠 줄 아니?

Suggestions & Commands
For suggestions, the ending is **-ja** -자, and for commands, it is the less commonly-used **-eora/ara** -어라/아라.

Let's play tennis together. **Tenis gachi chija.** 테니스 같이 치자.
OK. Good bye, now! (*Lit.*, "go well") **Geurae. Jal gara!** 그래. 잘 가라!

PATTERN PRACTICE 4
Practice the informal speech style.
1. A: Let's go exercise tomorrow.
      Naeil undonghareo gaja.
      내일 운동하러 가자.
   B: Good. Let's meet at Hangang Park.
      Joa. Han.gang Gongwoneseo manjanja.
      좋아. 한강 공원에서 만나자.
2. A: Are you busy today?
      Oneul bappeuni?
      오늘 바쁘니?
   B: No, I am not busy.
      Ani, an bappa.
      아니, 안 바빠.
3. A: It's cold today. Put on a coat!
      Oneul chupda. khoteu ibeora.
      오늘 춥다. 코트 입어라!

B: Yes.
    Eung, ibeulkke.
    응, 입을게.

EXERCISE 1
Confirm what you just heard using -면서요 **-myeonseoyo.**
1. You heard: **Eunbihago Eideuni dong.gabieyo.**
    은비하고 에이든이 동갑이에요.
2. You heard: **Eideunirang Joiga oneul deungsan gayo.**
    에이든이랑 조이가 오늘 등산가요.
3. You heard: **Naeil nuni ol kkeoyeyo.** 내일 눈이 올 거예요.
4. You heard: **Jigeum nalssiga deowoyo.** 지금 날씨가 더워요.
5. You heard: **Emmahago Eideuni japchaereul mandeureosseoyo.**
    엠마하고 에이든이 잡채를 만들었어요.

EXERCISE 2
Find out what each person knows how to do. Complete the following conversations using -(으)ㄹ 줄 알다 **-(eu)l jjul alda.**
1. You: Do you know how to play tennis?
    Yejin: **Eung, teniseu jal chyeo.** 응, 테니스 잘 쳐.
2. You: Do you know how to drive?
    Emma: **Eung, unjeon jal hae.** 응, 운전 잘 해.
3. You: Do you know how to make *bulgogi*?
    Eunbi: **Aniyo, mon mandeureoyo.** 아니요, 못 만들어요.
4. You: Do you (know how to) eat *kimchi*?
    Aiden: **Ne, jal meogeoyo.** 네, 잘 먹어요.

EXERCISE 3
Complete the following conversations using -(으)ㄴ 지 얼마나 됐어요 **-(eu)n ji olmana dwaesseoyo?**
1. A: How long has it been since you came to Korea?
    B: **O nyeon dwaesseoyo.** 오 년 됐어요.
2. A: When did you start learning Korean?
    B: **I nyeon dwaesseoyo.** 이 년 됐어요.
3. A: How long have you worked at the company?
    B: **Se dal dwaesseoyo.** 세 달 됐어요.
4. A: When did you start to play piano?
    B: **Sa nyeon dwaesseoyo.** 사 년 됐어요.

EXERCISE 4

Change the following dialogues using 반말 banmal.

1. A: **Uri nae.il gachi jeonyeok meogeulkkayo?**
   우리 내일 같이 저녁 먹을까요?

   B: **Joayo.**
   좋아요.

2. A: **Myeot siga joayo?**
   몇 시가 좋아요?

   B: **Ohu du sineun eottaeyo?**
   오후 두 시는 어때요?

3. A: **Gwaenchanayo. Eodiseo mannallaeyo?**
   괜찮아요. 어디서 만날래요?

   B: **Naega masinneun sikdang arabogo munjahalgeyo.**
   내가 맛있는 식당 알아보고 문자할게요.

4. A: **Geureom naeil achime munjjahaseyo.**
   그럼 내일 아침에 문자하세요.

   B: **Ne, geureom naeil mannayo.**
   네. 그럼 내일 만나요.

DIALOGUE 2 It says they are open at night, too.

Aiden and Yejin arrange a tennis game for tomorrow.

Aiden: Yejin, I have time tomorrow. Do you want to play tennis together?
Yejina, naeil sigani inneunde gachi teniseu chillae?
예진아, 내일 시간이 있는데 같이 테니스 칠래?

Yejin: Aren't they saying it will rain tomorrow?
Naeil bi an ondae?
내일 비 안 온대?

Aiden: No, I hear the weather is good tomorrow.
Ani, naeil nalssiga jotae.
아니, 내일 날씨가 좋대.

Yejin: Let me check the forecast. Oh, tomorrow's high is 33 degrees (about 91 degrees Fahrenheit).
Ilgiyebo chekeuhae bolkke. A... Naeil choego gioni samsipsam done.
일기예보 체크해 볼게. 아... 내일 최고 기온이 33도네.

Aiden: Do you think it's too hot?
Jom deounga?
좀 더운가?

Yejin:	I don't really like exercising in the heat…
	Nan deoun nalssie bakkeseo undonghaneun geo byeollo an joahaneunde…
	난 더운 날씨에 밖에서 운동하는 거 별로 안 좋아하는데…
Aiden:	Oh, right.
	Geureokuna.
	그렇구나.
Yejin:	If the tennis courts are open at night, how about playing tonight? Let's see. Right. It says they are open at night, too.
	Teniseujang.i bamedo yeolmyeon oneul ppame chimyeon eottae? Eodi boja… Eung. Bamedo yeondae.
	테니스장이 밤에도 열면 오늘 밤 치면 어때? 어디 보자… 응. 밤에도 연대.
Aiden:	That's an idea! What time would you like?
	Geuge joketda! Myeot siga jo.eunde?
	그게 좋겠다! 몇 시가 좋은데?
Yejin:	Let's meet around 8:00 after dinner. I'll text you the map to the tennis court.
	Jeonyeong meokgo yeodeol sijjeum mannaja. Teniseujang jidoreul munjjaro bonaejulkke.
	저녁 먹고 8시쯤 만나자. 테니스장 지도를 문자로 보내줄게.
Aiden:	Got it. See you later tonight then.
	Arasseo. Geureom ittaga bame manna.
	알았어. 그럼 이따가 밤에 만나.

VOCABULARY AND EXPRESSIONS

체크*	chekeu	check; (double-)checking, confirming
운동*	undong	sports; exercising
말*	mal	language; talking
비	bi	rain
날씨	nalssi	high school
일기예보	ilgiyebo	weather forecast
최고	choego	best, highest
기온	gion	temperature (of the weather)
도	do	degree (of temperature, used as a unit word)
테니스장	teniseujang	tennis court
지도	jido	map
문자	munjja	text
별로	byeollo	much, all that, particularly (used with a negative/not)

온대? (오-)	**ondae? (o-)**	do they say it is coming/it will come?
이따가	**ittaga**	later today
좋대 (좋-)	**jotae (joh-)**	they say it is good
더운가? (덥-)	**deounga? (deop-)**	Is it hot, I wonder?
더운 (덥-)	**deoun (deop-)**	hot
그렇구나 (그렇-)	**geureokuna (geureoh-)**	oh, really? Oh, right.
열면 (열-)	**yeolmyeon (yeol-)**	if open
치면 (치-)	**chimyeon (chi-)**	if play (of musical instruments, sports that involve striking)
치면 어때? (치-, 어떻-)	**chimyeon eottae? (chi-, eotteoh-)**	how about it (we) play (of musical instruments, sports that involve striking)
그게 좋겠다! (좋-)	**geuge joketda! (joh-)**	that would be great! That sounds great!

VOCABULARY PRACTICE 2

Give the Korean terms for the words described below.
1. moving your body to keep fit: _____
2. a graphic representation of an area's geography that helps you find your way: _____
3. #1 best: _____
4. to check what the weather is going to be like, find the: _____

Supplementary Vocabulary

Weather/Season words

맑아요	**malgayo**	clear (skies)
흐려요	**heuryeoyo**	overcast
해가 나요	**haega nayo**	the sun is out
구름이 꼈어요	**gureumi kkyeosseoyo**	cloudy
바람이 불어요	**barami bureoyo**	windy
안개가 꼈어요	**an.gaega kkyeosseoyo**	foggy
비가 와요	**biga wayo**	rainy
눈이 와요	**nuni wayo**	snowy
더워요	**deowoyo**	hot
추워요	**chuwoyo**	cold
따뜻해요	**ttatteutaeyo [ttadeutaeyo]**	warm
시원해요	**siwonhaeyo**	cool, refreshing
해가 떴어요/나요	**haega tteosseoyo/nayo**	the sun is up/out

해가 져요	haega jyeoyo	the sun is setting
봄	bom	spring
여름	yeoreum	summer
가을	ga.eul	autumn
겨울	gyeoul	winter
(사)계절	(sa)gyejeol	(four) seasons
기상청	gisangcheong	national weather service
미세먼지 주의	misemeonji ju.ui	fine dust caution
폭풍경보	pokpung kyeongbo	storm warning
황사현상	hwangsa hyeonsang	yellow dust phenomenon (in the spring)

GRAMMAR NOTE Transmitting information with adjectives:
-다고 하/-대 *-dago ha/-dae* "They say..."

If you are reporting what you have heard or read and want to make sure your listeners know you are transmitting information or hearsay, you can use the suffix **-daeyo** -대요 (short for **-dago haeyo** -다고 해요) after adjectives, and **-(i)raeyo** -(이)래요 (short for **-(i)rago haeyo** -(이)라고 해요) after nouns.

I hear it's cold tomorrow. **Naeil chupdago haeyo.** OR **Naeil chupdaeyo.**
내일 춥다고 해요. OR 내일 춥대요.

I hear the weather is bad tomorrow.
Naeil nalssiga nappeudae. 내일 날씨가 나쁘대.

PATTERN PRACTICE 5

Practice passing on the information with adjectives.

1. I hear that Jeju Island is beautiful all four seasons.
   Jejudoneun sagyejeori da areumdapdaeyo.
   제주도는 사계절이 다 아름답대요.
2. I heard Kim sunbae is a little busy tomorrow.
   Gim seonbaenimi naeil jom bappeusidaeyo.
   김 선배님이 내일 좀 바쁘시대요.
3. I heard housing prices in Gangnam are very high.
   Gangnamui jipgapsi aju bissadaeyo. 강남의 집값이 아주 비싸대요.

GRAMMAR NOTE "They say..." -는다고 하 *-neundago ha/*-ㄴ다고 하 *-ndago ha* and -는대 *-neundae/*-ㄴ대 *ndae*

If you're relaying information containing an *action*, i.e., "closing down," attach **-neundae** -는대 (short for **-neundago hae** -는다고 해) to a verb root if it ends in a consonant and **-ndae** -ㄴ대 if the verb ends in a vowel or ㅣㄹ (the ㅣㄹ in the verb root is dropped). Verbs conjugate for this "reportative" ending exactly the same way as for informal casual speech.

That store is closing (down) yet again, I hear.
Jeo gage mun tto danneundago haeyo. 저 가게 문 또 닫는다고 해요.

I hear Tobi can't play tennis. **Tobineun teniseu mot chindae.**
토비는 테니스 못 친대.

It says the tennis court is open at night, too. **Teniseujang bamedo yeondae.**
테니스장 밤에도 연대.

Use **-tdae** -ㅆ대 for descriptions in the past and **-(eu)l kkeorae** -(으)ㄹ 거래 for future.

I read it snowed there yesterday. **Eoje geogi nun watdae.**
어제 거기 눈 왔대.

I hear it's going to rain tomorrow. **Naeil biga ol kkeorae.**
내일 비가 올 거래.

They say it's going to be hot tomorrow. **Naeil nalssiga deoul kkeorae.**
내일 날씨가 더울 거래.

PATTERN PRACTICE 6

Practice passing on the information with verbs.
1. I hear that Sam Park can speak Chinese.
   Bak Saem ssiga Junggugeoreul hal jjul andaeyo.
   박 샘 씨가 중국어를 할 줄 안대요.
2. I heard that Jamie sent a fax to the client yesterday.
   Jeimi ssiga eoje keullai.eonteuhante paekseureul bonaetdaeyo.
   제이미 씨가 어제 클라이언트한테 팩스를 보냈대요.
3. I heard that a new Korean restaurant will be opening soon around here.
   I geuncheo.e sae Han.guk sikdang.i muneul yeol kkeoraeyo.
   이 근처에 새 한국 식당이 문을 열 거래요.

GRAMMAR NOTE "Well, then... I wonder?/maybe?" -(으)ㄴ가, -나/-는가 -*(eu)n.ga, –na/–neun.ga*

-(Eu)lkkayo -(으)ㄹ까요 is a question ending that expresses wondering in general. In contrast, this ending **-(eu)n.ga,** -(으)ㄴ가, expresses wondering about a current, more certain situation. This ending also allows you to ask questions indirectly and politely. The form **-(eu)n.ga** -(으)ㄴ가 is used with adjectives.

Isn't it a bit hot, I wonder?/Don't you think it's too hot? **Jom deoun.gayo?**
좀 더운가요?

With verbs, you can use **-na** -나 or **-neun.ga** -는가, where **-neun.ga** -는가 is a little older or bookish sounding. **-Na** -나 is also used for past tense.

Where are you going? (polite question) **Eodi ganayo?**
어디 가나요?

Have you finished eating? (polite question) **Da deusyeonnayo?**
다 드셨나요?

For the future, **-(eu)l kkeon.ga** -(으)ㄹ 건가 is used. This ending asks about more a specific plan or situation than **-(eu)lkkayo** -(으)ㄹ까요, which is for more general wondering.

When will you give (her) a call?	I wonder when she will call.
Eonje jeonhwahasil kkeon.gayo? vs.	**Eonje jeonhwahasilkkayo?**
언제 전화하실 건가요?	언제 전화하실까요?

PATTERN PRACTICE 7
Practice asking questions with -가/나 **-ga/na.**
1. A: How's the food? **Eumsik masi eotteon.gayo?** 음식 맛이 어떤가요?
   B: It's good! **Aju masinneundeyo!** 아주 맛있는데요!
2. A: Is it raining now? **Jigeum biga onayo?** 지금 비가 오나요?
   B: No, it isn't. **Aniyo. An wayo.** 아니요. 안 와요.
3. A: Did Manager Jeong come? **Jeong Bujangnim osyeonnayo?**
   정 부장님 오셨나요?
   B: No, but I heard that he is coming shortly. **Aniyo. Got osindaeyo.**
   아니요. 곧 오신대요.

GRAMMAR NOTE 계시- *gyesi-*, honorific "there is"

Gyesi- 계시-, the honorific version of the existence verb for **iss-** 있- "(there) is," can come with any of the wondering suffixes. The same phrase "Are you home/is she home, perhaps?" can be said in three different ways.

Jigeum daege gyesinayo? 지금 댁에 계시나요?
Jigeum daege gyesineun.gayo? 지금 댁에 계시는가요?
Jigeum daege gyesin.gayo? 지금 댁에 계신가요?

CULTURE NOTE Hobbies

Koreans love hobbies (**chwimi** 취미) like tennis, running, biking, hiking, and video or virtual reality games as well as martial arts, art, and music. **Manhwa** 만화 (graphic novels) have been popular since the 1970s in Korea, but the traditional **manhwabang** 만화방 (reading shop) is now a thing of the past. It was replaced by **PC bang** 피씨방 (computer-gaming centers) although these may also become increasingly obsolete as technology and digital entertainment become more portable.

Many Koreans love hiking. Seventy percent of the Korean peninsula is mountains and hills. According to a 2014 Gallup survey, mountain climbing/hiking (**deungsan** 등산) and listening to music (**eumak gamsang** 음악감상) were found to be the top two most popular hobbies in Korea. Koreans in their 40s and 50s listed reading (**dokseo** 독서), golf, and fishing (**naksi** 낚시) as their favorite activities while people in their 20s and 30s preferred playing video games or soccer (**chukku** 축구) and watching movies (**yeonghwa gwallam** 영화 관람) as their favorite pastimes.

EXERCISE 5

Follow the example and pass on what you just heard to your friend using -대/래요 -dae/rae(yo).

You heard: **Nae.il nalssiga aju deowo.** 내일 날씨가 아주 더워.
You say: **Nae.il nalssiaga aju deopdaeyo.** 내일 날씨가 아주 덥대요.

1. You heard: **Oneul ohu du sie hoe.uiga isseo.**
   오늘 오후 2시에 회의가 있어.
   You say:
2. You heard: **Eideuni gam.gie geollyeoseo apa.**
   에이든이 감기에 걸려서 아파.
   You say:
3. You heard: **Geuraeseo Eideuni oneul hoesa.e an wasseo.**
   그래서 에이든이 오늘 회사에 안 왔어.
   You say:

4. You heard: **Gunae sikdang.i oneul dada.**
   구내 식당이 오늘 닫아.

   You say:

5. You heard: **Naeil hoesa.e jung.yohan keullai.eonteuga wa.**
   내일 회사에 중요한 클라이언트가 와.
   (important client: 중요한 클라이언트 **jung.yohan keullai. eonteu**)

   You say:

EXERCISE 6

Make the following questions more indirect and polite, using the -(으)ㄴ가 **-(eu) n.ga** or -나/는가 **-na/neun.ga** ending.

1. **I sikdang.eun cheo.eumieyo?** 이 식당은 처음이에요?
2. **Han.guk eumsigeun mworeul joahaeyo?** 한국 음식은 뭐를 좋아해요?
3. **Tteokbokkireul meogeo bwasseoyo?** 떡볶이를 먹어 봤어요?
   (spicy rice cake dish: 떡볶이 **tteokbokki**)
4. **Gimchiga neomu maewoyo?** 김치가 너무 매워요?

엠마 씨!
Emma!

오늘 저녁에 우리 집에서 같이 요리하는 거 안 잊어버렸지?
You didn't forget we are cooking together at my place tonight, right?

잡채 만들려고 하거든.
I'm thinking of having us make japchae.

에이든도 오는 거 잊지 마!
Aiden, you too, don't forget to come!

잊어버리기는.
Forget!
잔뜩 기대하고 있어.
We are so looking forward to it.

알았어.
Got it.
꼭 갈게!
I am definitely coming.

모두 내 아파트로 6 시 반까지 와서 같이 요리해요.
So, everyone, come to my apartment at about 6:30, and let's cook together.

갈 때 디저트를 가져갈게.
I'll bring a dessert when I come.

일곱 시까지 막걸리 가지고 갈게.
I'll be there by 7:00. I'll bring makkeoli.

응, 알았어.
OK, got it.
집 근처에 오면 전화해.
Call me when you get near my place.

Hanging Out at a Friend's House

Don't forget to come!

Eunbi, Emma and Aiden talk about their plans to cook together at Eunbi's house.

Eunbi: Emma! You didn't forget we are cooking together at my place tonight, right? I'm thinking of having us make *japchae*. Aiden, you too, don't forget to come!

Emma ssi! Oneul jeonyeoge uri jibeseo gachi yorihaneun geo an ijeobeoryeotji? Japchae mandeullyeogo hageodeun. Eideundo onun geo itji ma!

엠마 씨! 오늘 저녁에 우리 집에서 같이 요리하는 거 안 잊어버렸지? 잡채 만들려고 하거든. 에이든도 오는 거 잊지 마!

Emma: Forget! We are so looking forward to it.

Ijeobeorigineun. Jantteuk gidaehago isseo.

잊어버리기는. 잔뜩 기대하고 있어.

Aiden: Oh. Today is the party? Got it. I am definitely coming.

A. Oneuri patiya? Arasseo. Kkok galkke!

아. 오늘이 파티야? 알았어. 꼭 갈게!

Eunbi: So, everyone, come to my apartment at about 6:30, and let's cook together.

Modu nae apateuro yeoseot si bankkaji waseo gachi yorihaeyo.

모두 내 아파트로 6 시 반까지 와서 같이 요리해요.

Emma: I have my Taekwondo practice so I'll be a little late, but I'll be there by 7:00. I'll bring *makkeoli*.

Nan Taekkwondo yeonseubi isseoseo jogeum neujeul kkeoye. Ilgop sikkaji makkeolli gajigo galkke.

난 태권도 연습이 있어서 조금 늦을 거야. 일곱 시까지 막걸리 가지고 갈게.

Aiden: I can come on time. I'll bring a dessert when I come.

Naneun je sigane gal ssu isseo. Gal ttae dijeoteureul gajyeogalkke.

나는 제 시간에 갈 수 있어. 갈 때 디저트를 가져갈게.

Eunbi: OK, got it. Call me when you get near my place.

Eung, arasseo. Jip geuncheo.e omyeon jeonhwahae.

응, 알았어. 집 근처에 오면 전화해.

Aiden:	Before I leave, I will call (to see) whether you need anything else (for me to bring).
	Gagi jeone dareun piryohan geo inneunji jeonhwahalkke.
	가기 전에 다른 필요한 거 있는지 전화할게.
Eunbi:	Okay, see you later! Emma, too, see you later!
	Eung, najung.e boja. Emma ssido ittaga bwa!
	응, 나중에 보자. 엠마 씨도, 이따가 봐!

VOCABULARY AND EXPRESSIONS

기대*	gidae	expecting, anticipating
요리*	yori	cooking
연습*	yeonseup	practice
파티	pati	party
잡채	japchae	savory clear noodle dish with many cooked vegetables
디저트	dijeoteu	dessert
태권도	Taekkwondo	Taekwondo
막걸리	makgeolli	unrefined rice liquor
늦을 거야 (늦-)	neujeul kkeoya (neut-)	will be late
제	je	right, proper, appropriate, pre-set
잔뜩	jantteuk	to the gills, fully
응	eung	yes (informal casual)
나중에	najung.e	later
이따(가)	ittaga	later (the same day)
잊어버렸지? (잊어버리-)	ijeobeoryeotji (ijeobeoli-)	forgot, right?
(가지-, 가-)	(gaji-, ga-)	I will bring (it)

VOCABULARY PRACTICE 1
Give the Korean terms for the words described below.
1. "I can't wait!": _____
2. sweets eaten after a meal: _____
3. Korean martial art involving much kicking and bare hands: _____
4. to get better at anything you have to do this: _____

GRAMMAR NOTE Informal, casual "to be" -(이)야 -*(i)ya*

The formal **imnida** 입니다 and the informal **yeyo/ieyo** 예요/이에요 become -(i)ya -(이)야 when you speak casually with your close friends or children. The ending **-(eu)l kkeoyeyo** -(으)ㄹ 거예요 for your predictions or future plans changes to **-(eu)l kkeoya** -(으)ㄹ 거야.

What's your name? **Ireumi mwoya?** 이름이 뭐야?

This is a sea urchin. **Igeon seong.geya.** 이건 성게야.

I have my Taekwondo practice so I'll be late.
Taekkwondo yeonseubi isseoseo neujeul kkeoya.
태권도 연습이 있어서 늦을 거야.

PATTERN PRACTICE 1
Practice the following sentences using -(이)야 -(i)ya.
1. A: What is the name of the new intern who came yesterday?
      Eoje saero on inteon ireumi mwoya?
      어제 새로 온 인턴 이름이 뭐야?
   B: It's Alison Tyler. **Tailleo Alliseoniya.** 타일러 알리슨이야.
2. A: When are you coming back today? **Oneul eonje ol kkeoya?**
      오늘 언제 올 거야?
   B: I will be late because I have to go to a company dinner outing.
      Oneul hoesige gaya dwaeseo jom neujeul kkeoya.
      오늘 회식에 가야 돼서 좀 늦을 거야.

GRAMMAR NOTE "Before ...ing" -기 전(에) *-gi jeon(e)*
Jeon 전 means "before," so **-gi jeon(e)** -기 전(에) attached to a verb root means "before doing something."

I'll call before coming over. **Gagi jeone jeonhwahalkke.**
가기 전에 전화할게.

Let's eat before going to the movie.
Yeonghwa boreo gagi jeone bam meokja. 영화 보러 가기 전에 밥 먹자.

PATTERN PRACTICE 2
Practice the following sentences with -기 전 **-gi jeon**.
1. Write the names of the sender and receiver before you send a fax.
   Paekseu bonaegi jeone bonaeneun saramhago badeul saram ireumeul sseuseyo. 팩스 보내기 전에 보내는 사람하고 받을 사람 이름을 쓰세요.
2. Before you leave the room, please turn off the lights.
   Bang.eul nagagi jeone bureul kkeuseyo. 방을 나가기 전에 불을 끄세요.
3. Before you cut the vegetables, please rinse them.
   Chaesoreul jareugi jeone ssiseuseyo. 채소를 자르기 전에 씻으세요.

GRAMMAR NOTE "Whether (or not)" -는지 *-neunji/*-(으)ㄴ지 *-(eu)njinji*

To ask a grammatically indirect question (e.g., "I don't know <u>whether you like this</u>" or "Tell me <u>where you are</u>"), you can add **-neunji** -는지 to the verb root. The suffix takes on the form **-(eu)nji** -(으)ㄴ지 for adjectives and the identity verb **i** 이. The verb **i** 이 usually drops out in spoken Korean.

I will call (to see) <u>whether there is anything you need</u>.
Piryohan geo inneunji jeonhwahalkke. <u>필요한 거 있는지</u> 전화할게.

Do you know <u>where this is/where we are</u>? **Yeogi eodinji (eodiinji) aseyo?**
<u>여기 어딘지 (어디인지)</u> 아세요?

Put the shoes on and see <u>if the shoes are (too) small</u>.
Sinbari jageunji hanbeon sineo bwa. <u>신발이 작은지</u> 한번 신어 봐.

PATTERN PRACTICE 3

Practice the following embedded question forms with -는지 **-neunji**.

1. A: Do you know where the power button is on this laptop?
   I laeptabui jeonwon beoteuni eodie inneunji aseyo?
   이 랩탑의 전원 버튼이 어디에 있는지 아세요?
   B: It is on the upper right side of the keyboard.
   Kibodeu oreun jjok wi.e isseoyo. 키보드 오른 쪽 위에 있어요.
2. A: Do you know how to get to Shinchon from here?
   Yeogieseo Sinchonkkaji eotteoke ganeunji aseyo?
   여기에서 신촌까지 어떻게 가는지 아세요?
   B: Take subway line 2. **Jihacheol ihoseoneul taseyo.**
   지하철 이호선을 타세요.

GRAMMAR NOTE Using -는 거 *-neun geo* vs. -는지 *–nunji:* "that," "whether"

The two endings **-neun geo** -는거 and **-neunji** -는지 can sometimes be used interchangeably. The main difference is whether what you are talking about is an established fact (then use **-neun geo** -는 거) or something you are trying to find out (then use **-neunji** -는지).

You didn't know (that) I was hungry? **Na baegopeun geo mollasseo?**
나 배고픈 거 몰랐어?

You didn't know whether I was hungry or not? **Na baegopeunji mollasseo?**
나 배고픈지 몰랐어?

EXERCISE 1

You and Eunbi are talking about tonight's party. Change the following conversations into the informal casual style.

1. You: **Patiga myeot siyeyo? 파티가 몇 시예요?**
   Eunbi: **Oneul jeonyeok yeoseot si banieyo. 오늘 저녁 여섯 시 반이에요.**
2. You: **Jip jusoga mwoyeyo? 집 주소가 뭐예요?**
   Eunbi: **Dongjakgu Haengbok apateu samdong palbaeksibo hoyeyo.**
           동작구 행복 아파트 3동 815 호예요.
3. You: **Mwo mandeul kkeoyeyo? 뭐 만들 거예요?**
   Eunbi: **Japchaereul mandeul kkeoyeyo. 잡채를 만들 거예요.**
4. You: **Japchaega mwoyeyo? 잡채가 뭐예요?**
   Eunbi: **Han.guge janchi eumsigieyo. 한국의 잔치 음식이에요.**
           (잔치 음식 **janchi eumsik** party food)

EXERCISE 2

You and Aiden are talking about the cooking party tonight. Complete the following exchanges using -기 전에 **-gi jeone**.

1. You: I have to go to my Taekwondo practice before going to the party.
   Aiden: **Eung, arasseo. 응, 알았어.**
2. You: Buy dessert before you come to Eunbi's place.
   Aiden: **Eung, geureol kkeoya. 응, 그럴 거야.**
3. You: We are going to make *japchae* together. Don't eat (anything) before you come.
   Aiden: **Eung, geureolkke. 응, 그럴게.**
4. You: Let's make rice before we make 잡채 *japchae*.
           (to make/cook rice: 밥을 하다 **babeul hada**)
   Aiden: **Eung, geureoja. 응, 그러자.**

EXERCISE 3

You want to send the following text messages to Aiden (your close, same-age friend) before you join him at Eunbi's house. Write the messages in Korean.
1. Do you know if Yejin is coming?
2. Do you know whether Eunbi likes beer?
3. Do you know whether Eunbi is good at cooking? (*Lit.*, Eunbi cooks well?)
4. Do you know whether there is anything Eunbi needs?

🔘 DIALOGUE 2 Come up to the 8th floor.

Aiden helps Eunbi with cooking at her house before Emma arrives.

Eunbi: OK, Aiden. Come this way. I cooked the meat first and put it aside.
Eideun, ijjogeuro wa bwa. Naega gogireul junbihae nwasseo.
에이든, 이쪽으로 와 봐. 내가 고기를 준비해 놨어.

Aiden: OK. What shall I do to help?
Naega mwol dowa jumyeon doeji?
내가 뭘 도와 주면 되지?

Eunbi: Let's wash and julienne the vegetables. I'll wash and you chop.
Chaesoreul ssiseoseo chae sseoreoya dwae. Naega ssiseul tenikka niga sseoreo jwo.
채소를 씻어서 채 썰어야 돼. 내가 씻을 테니까 네가 썰어 줘.

Aiden: How shall I chop the green onions? Is it okay if I do it like this?
Yangpareul eotteoke sseolji? Ireoke hamyeon dwae?
양파를 어떻게 썰지? 이렇게 하면 돼?

Eunbi: I'll finish chopping them and give them to you. You sauté the vegetables with the meat. Oh, wait. Emma seems to be here. (*On the phone*) Yes, take the elevator and come to the 8th floor. It's unit 815.
Naega sseoreoseo julkke. Gogireul bokkeun dae-ume yangpareul bokka jwo. A, jamkkanman. Emma ssiga on geo gata. (Jeonhwaro) Eung, ellebeiteo tago pal cheung.euro olla wa. Palbaeksibo hoyeyo.
내가 썰어서 줄게. 고기를 볶은 다음에 양파를 볶아 줘. 아, 잠깐만. 엠마 씨가 온 거 같아. (전화로) 응, 엘레베이터 타고 팔 층으로 올라와. 815 호야.

Emma is in the apartment now.

Eunbi: Aiden is sautéing the vegetables and the meat; they are about done.
Eideuni gogirang chaesoreul bokkgo inneunde geo-ui da dwaesseo.
에이든이 고기랑 채소를 볶고 있는데 거의 다 됐어.

Emma: The rice is ready. Shall I toss it?
Babi da dwaenneunde, hanbeon hwik jeo.eulkka?
밥이 다 됐는데, 한번 휙 저을까?

Eunbi: Yes. And then please serve it in bowls in about 3 minutes. And, if you know even that, you've truly become Korean!
Eung. geu da.eum sambun ittaga peo jweo. Geunde geureon geotkkajido aneun geol bonikka jinjja Han.guksaram da dwaenne!
응. 그 다음 삼분 이따가 그릇에 퍼 줘. 근데 그런 것까지도 아는 걸 보니까 진짜 한국사람 다 됐네!

VOCABULARY AND EXPRESSIONS

고기	gogi	meat
채소	chaeso	vegetables
양파	yangpa	onion
밥	bap	cooked rice
그릇	geureut	bowl
그런 것	geureon geot	that (sort of) thing
내가	naega	I (informal casual form with the subject marker)
네가	nega	you (informal casual form with the subject marker)
거의	geo.ui	almost
휙	hwik	quickly, hastily, lightly
도와 주면 (돕-, 주-)	dowa jumyeon (dop-, ju-)	if (someone) helps out
채썰어야 돼 (썰-, 되-)	chaesseoleoya dwae (sseol-, doe-)	need to julienne
씻을 테니까 (씻-)	ssiseul tenikka (ssis-)	will wash so then
썰어 (썰-)	sseoreo (sseol-)	chop
썰어서 (썰-)	sseoleoseo (sseol-)	having chopped
볶아 (볶-)	bokka (bokk-)	sauté
온 거 같아 (오-, 같-)	on geo gata (o-, gat-)	seems to have come
저을까 (젓-)	jeo.eulkka (jeos-)	should I stir it?
퍼 줘 (푸-, 주-)	peo jweo (pu-, ju-)	scoop it out/serve it, please
아는 걸 (알-)	aneun geol (al-)	that you know, what you know (with the object marker)

VOCABULARY PRACTICE 2

Give the Korean terms for the words described below.

1. _____: but not quite
2. a mainstay grain of Korean cuisine, served at virtually every meal (cooked): _____
3. if you are vegetarian, you don't eat this: _____
4. to clean something by hand in water: _____

GRAMMAR NOTE "Get something done for future" use -어/아 놓아 *-eo/a noa*

To express doing something in advance or leaving it that way for future use, use the helping verb **nwa** 놔 (shortened from the written form **noh.a** 놓아) after the main verb in its **-eo/a** -어/아 form. In polite (e.g., honorific) speech and in written Korean, the full form is used.

I got the meat ready. **Gogireul junbihae nwasseo.** 고기를 준비해 놨어.

Leave the door open. **Mun yeoreo nwa.** 문 열어 놔.
Please leave the light on. **Bul kyeo no.euseyo.** 불 켜 놓으세요.

PATTERN PRACTICE 4

Practice the following sentences with -어/아 놓다 -eo/a nohta.
1. Please clean the place and order food before the party.
   Pati jeone cheongsoreul hago eumsigeul jumunhae no.euseyo.
   파티 전에 청소를 하고 음식을 주문해 놓으세요.
2. Please cut up the vegetables before cooking.
   Yorihagi jeone chaesoreul sseoreo no.euseyo.
   요리하기 전에 채소를 썰어 놓으세요.
3. Please leave the light off because we will be throwing a surprise party.
   Kkamjjak patireul hal kkeonikka bureul kkeo no.euseyo.
   깜짝 파티를 할 거니까 불을 꺼 놓으세요.

GRAMMAR NOTE "Future" connector -(으)ㄹ 테니까 -(eu)l tenikka

The future tense is not used very often when you connect clauses in Korean. If
you do need to, use either **-(eu)l kkeo** -(으)ㄹ 거—for more definite instances
like "I'll wash the vegetables and you chop them"—or **-(eu)l te** -(으)ㄹ 테 (with
the verb **-i** enmeshed with it), for probable situations that may arise, e.g., "it will
probably rain so you should bring an umbrella."

I'll wash and you chop. **Naega ssiseul tenikka nega sseoreo.**
내가 씻을 테니까 네가 썰어.
OR
I will wash and *you* chop. **Naega ssiseul kkeonikka nega sseoreo.**
내가 씻을 거니까 네가 썰어.

It will probably rain so take your umbrella. **Biga ol tenikka usan gajgo ga.**
비가 올 테니까 우산 갖고 가.
OR
It's going to rain (as forecast) so let's close the windows.
Biga ol kkeonikka changmun datja. 비가 올 거니까 창문 닫자.

PATTERN PRACTICE 5

Practice the following sentences with the future connector, -(으)ㄹ 테니까 **-(eu)
l tenikka**.
1. I will pay for beverages and party supplies, so you pay for the food.
   **Naega eumnyosuhago pati yongpum gapseul nael tenikka eumsikgapseun
   niga nae.** 내가 음료수하고 파티 용품 값을 낼 테니까 음식값은 네가 내.
2. I am going to clean, so please open the windows.
   Cheongsohal tenikka changmun jom yeoreo jwo. 청소할 테니까 창문 좀
   열어 줘.

3. It will be cold today, so wear a hat and gloves.
   Oneul chuul tenikka moja sseugo janggapdo kkyeo.
   오늘 추울 테니까 모자 쓰고 장갑도 껴.

GRAMMAR NOTE "after doing..." -(으)ㄴ 후에 -*(eu)n hue*/다음에 *da.eume*

The word **hu** 후 means "after" and **daeum** 다음 means "next." To say "after doing (something)" in Korean, pair what has already been done with the noun-modifying (relative clause) ending for completed verbs, e.g., **-(eu)n** -(으)ㄴ to get **-(eu)n hu** -(으)ㄴ 후 or **-(eu)n da.eum** -(으)ㄴ 다음. Another way is to use the connector **-go naseo** -고 나서, which means "and then."

After you (have) sauté(ed) the meat, sauté the vegetables.
Gogireul bokkeun da.eume yangpareul bokka juseyo.
고기를 볶은 다음에 양파를 볶아 주세요. (more casual)

Gogireul bokkeun hue yangpareul bokka juseyo.
고기를 볶은 후에 양파를 볶아 주세요. (more formal)

After you (have) clean(ed) (the house/area), start cooking please.
Cheongsoreul han da.eume yorireul sijakaseyo.
청소를 한 다음에 요리를 시작하세요.

Aiden wants to work in Korea after he graduates from college.
Eideuneun daehakkyoreul joreopan hue Han.gugeseo ilhago sipeohamnida.
에이든은 대학교를 졸업한 후에 한국에서 일하고 싶어합니다.

PATTERN PRACTICE 6
Practice the following sentences with -(으)ㄴ 후/다음에 **-(eu)n hue/da.eume**.
1. Please stir-fry the onions after you slice them.
   Yangpareul sseon da.eume peuraipaene bokka juseyo.
   양파를 썬 다음에 프라이팬에 볶아 주세요.
2. Please make a copy of this report and then send it to Aiden.
   I bogoseoreul boksareul han da.eume Eideun ssihante bonaeseyo.
   이 보고서를 복사를 한 다음에 에이든 씨한테 보내세요.
3. Please save the file and close it. **Paireul jeojanghan hue dadeuseyo.**
   파일을 저장한 후에 닫으세요.

GRAMMAR NOTE Pronouncing *e* 네

There are different ways to pronounce 네 **e**, depending on its usage.

ne 네 "yes"	→	[ne]
ne 네 "your"	→	[ni]
nega 네가 "you-subject marker"	→	[niga]
ne geo 네 거 "your thing; yours"	→	[ni kkeo]

The **e** ㅔ in **be.eosseo** 베었어 "I got a cut" and **de.eosseo** 데었어 "I burned myself" is also pronounced as **i** ㅣ, as **bi.eosseo** 비었어 and **di.eosseo** 디었어.

CULTURE NOTE Cultural psychology of Koreans

There are some Korean cultural concepts that are a little tough for foreigners to "get." Some of the most common ones are **chemyeon** 체면, **gibun** 기분, and **nunchi** 눈치 trio. **Chemyeon** is very important if you care about what others think of you or how they judge you. It is sometimes translated as "face," thus if Eunbi cares about her "face," she would clean her house, decorate it nicely and prepare plenty of food and dessert so she won't "lose face" in front of her guests.

Gibun is how you feel about the situation at a particular moment. If the evening is going particularly well, those who are swayed by their **gibun** might treat the whole group to dinner and drinks. You can hang out with these people for free food, but you'd have to ensure that they stay in a good mood. To ensure that happens, you need **nunchi**, a quick wit with the ability to gauge how others feel.

Very often, the group's harmony is considered more important than individuals' moods in Korean society. From the group's point of view, that sense of harmony is called **hwahap** 화합, and from an individual member's point of view, it is called **uiri** 의리, a sense of loyalty.

EXERCISE 4

You and Emma are preparing for a big party tonight. Ask Emma to get the following things done using -어/아 놓다 **-eo/a nohta**.
1. Please buy meat and vegetables (ahead of time) at the market.
2. Please slice up the meat.
3. Please wash the vegetables (and have them ready).
4. Please have the vegetables and meat sautéed (and ready).

EXERCISE 5

You and Emma are preparing for a big party tonight. Suggest who does what using -(으)ㄹ 테니까 **-(eu)l tenikka**.
1. I will go grocery shopping, so you cook *japchae*.
2. I will wash the vegetables, so you get the meat ready.
3. I will chop the vegetables, so you sauté them.
4. I will serve rice, so you put 잡채 *japchae* in the dish. (to put something in a dish. 그릇에 담다 **geureuse damda**)

EXERCISE 6

Tell Emma what to do using -(으)ㄴ 다음/후에 **-(eu)n da.eum/hue**.
1. After you wash the vegetables, please slice them.
2. After you sauté the meat, please sauté the vegetables.
3. After you serve rice in bowls, please serve soup in bowls. (soup: **guk**)
4. After you eat (the meal), please eat dessert.

일곱 시 표로 한 장 주세요.
Please give me the 7:00 one, please.

창측 좌석 드릴까요, 내측 좌석 드릴까요?
Do you want it by the window or by the aisle?

창측으로 주세요.
By the window, please.
신용카드로 지불할게요.
I'll pay with a card.

전주에서 할 만한 게 뭐가 있나요?
What's worth doing in Jeonju?

먹을 게 많겠지요?
There's probably a lot of good food.

음식도 음식이지만 한옥 마을에서 한복을 빌려서 한복을 입고 관광도 할 수 있어요.
Yes, the food. But you can also tour around in a hanbok *that you rent from the Hanok Village.*

LESSON 18

Getting Out of Town

 **DIALOGUE 1** Is there a bus to Jeonju at noon?

Aiden buys a ticket at the Inter-city bus terminal.

Ticket Officer:	Welcome!
	Eoseo oseyo.
	어서 오세요.
Aiden:	Is there a bus to Jeonju at noon?
	Jeong.o.e Jeonju ganeun beoseu innayo?
	정오에 전주 가는 버스 있나요?
Ticket Officer:	Yes. There is premium and express. (Both depart) every 30 minutes.
	Ne, udeungdo itgo gosokdo isseumnida. Samship bunmada han daessik isseumnida.
	네, 우등도 있고 고속도 있습니다. 30분마다 한 대씩 있습니다.
Aiden:	How much is it for the ticket?
	Pyoga eolmayeyo?
	표가 얼마예요?
Ticket Officer:	Round-trip or one-way?
	Wangbok pyoyo? Pyeondo pyoyo?
	왕복 표요? 편도 표요?
Aiden:	Round-trip, please.
	Wangbogiyo.
	왕복이요.
Ticket Officer:	The premium bus is 20,800 won and the express is 14,200 won for round-trip.
	Udeung.eun wangboge imanpalbaek wonigo gosogeun wangboge mansacheonibaek wonimnida.
	우등은 왕복에 20,800원이고 고속은 왕복에 14,200원입니다.
Aiden:	Then give me an express ticket for 6:30, please.
	Geureom gosogeuro yeoseos si ban pyo han jang juseyo.
	그럼 고속으로 여섯 시 반 표 한 장 주세요.
Ticket Officer:	Oh, sorry. The 6:30 ones are sold out. There are still tickets for 7:00.
	A, joesonghamnida. Yeoseos si ban pyoneun maejinineyo. Ilgop sineun pyoga isseumnida.
	아, 죄송합니다. 여섯 시 반 표는 매진이네요. 일곱 시는 표가 있습니다.

Aiden: Ummm, then I will have to take a 7:00 bus. Please give me the 7:00 one.

A... geureom ilgop si beoseureul tayagenneyo. Ilgop si pyoro han jang juseyo.

아... 그럼 일곱 시 버스를 타야겠네요. 일곱 시 표로 한 장 주세요.

Ticket Officer: Do you want it by the window or by the aisle?

Changcheuk jwaseok deurilkkayo, naecheuk jwaseok deurilkkayo?

창측 좌석 드릴까요, 내측 좌석 드릴까요?

Aiden: By the window, please. I'll pay with a card.

Changcheugeuro juseyo. Sinyongkadeuro jibulhalkkeyo.

창측으로 주세요. 신용카드로 지불할게요.

Ticket Officer: Thank you. Let me process the card for you.

Gamsahamnida. Gyeoljje dowa deurigesseumnida.

감사합니다. 결제 도와 드리겠습니다.

Aiden: What's worth doing in Jeonju? There's probably a lot of good food.

Jeonjueseo hal manhan ge mwoga innayo? Meogeul kke manketjiyo?

전주에서 할 만한 게 뭐가 있나요? 먹을 게 많겠지요?

Ticket Officer: Yes, the food. But you can also tour around in a *hanbok* that you rent from the Hanok Village.

Eumsikdo eumsigijiman hanok ma.eureseo hanbogeul billyeoseo hanbogeul ipgo gwan.gwangdo hal ssu isseo.

음식도 음식이지만 한옥 마을에서 한복을 빌려서 한복을 입고 관광도 할 수 있어요.

Aiden: I see. Thank you.

Geureokunnyo. Gamsahamnida.

그렇군요. 감사합니다.

VOCABULARY AND EXPRESSIONS

정오	jeong.o	noon
우등	udeung	premium, top-notch
고속	gosok	express, high speed
표	pyo	ticket
왕복	wangbok	round-trip
편도	pyeondo	one-way
매진	maejin	sold out
그럼	geureom	well then
창측	changcheuk	by the window
좌석	jwaseok	seat
내측	naecheuk	aisle

신용카드	**sinyongkadeu**	credit card
터미널	**teomineol**	terminal
시내버스	**sinaebeoseu**	intra-city bus
대	**dae**	counter for machinery
장	**jang**	counter for sheets
-도	**do**	both
-씩	**ssik**	each (used like an adverb after a number expression)
거기(에)서부터는	**geogi(e)seo buteoneun**	(starting) from there
지불할게요	**jibulhalkkeyo (jibulha-)**	I'll pay

VOCABULARY PRACTICE 1

Give the Korean terms for the words described below.

1. a ticket to go and come back: _____
2. no tickets left: _____
3. the middle of the day: _____
4. buy one of these to get into a show or onto a train, bus, subway, etc.: _____

GRAMMAR NOTE Using -도 *-do*

The suffix **-do** -도 usually means "also," but it can also signal the listener that other options are going to be listed:

We have both premium and express.
Udeungdo itgo gosokdo isseumnida. 우등도 있고 고속도 있습니다.

They didn't come either yesterday or today.
Eojedo an ogo oneuldo an wanne. 어제도 안 오고 오늘도 안 왔네.

Keep both this and that.
Igeotdo gatgo geugeotdo gajyeo. 이것도 갖고 그것도 가져.

PATTERN PRACTICE 1

Practice the following sentences using -도 **-do**.

1. I am planning on going to both Gyeongju and Busan.
   Gyeongjudo gago Busando garyeogo haeyo.
   경주도 가고 부산도 가려고 해요.
2. We have both shrimp fried rice and kimchi fried rice.
   Sae.u bokkeumbapdo itgo gimchi bokkeumbapdo isseumnida.
   새우 볶음밥도 있고 김치 볶음밥도 있습니다.

GRAMMAR NOTE Using -어야겠 -*eoyaget* to express that something should be done

Use **-eoyaget** -어야겠, a shortened form of **-eoya doe** -어야 되 (have to, should) plus **-get** -겠, to say that someone—including yourself—should do something.

I'd better hurry and do my homework.
Ppalli sukjehaeyagesseo. 빨리 숙제해야겠어.

I'd better ask that person.
Jeo saramhante mureobwayagetda. 저 사람한테 물어봐야겠다.

I should meet her and see. **Geu saram hanbeon mannabwayagesseumnida.**
그 사람 한번 만나봐야겠습니다.

PATTERN PRACTICE 2
Practice the following sentences using -어야겠 **-eoyaget**.
1. We should buy tickets before they are sold out.
   Maejindoegi jeone pyoreul sayagesseoyo.
   매진되기 전에 표를 사야겠어요.
2. I should exercise more to be healthy.
   Geon.ganghaejigi wihae deo un.dong.eul haeyagesseoyo.
   건강해지기 위해 더 운동을 해야겠어요.
3. I'd better make a note before I forget. **Ijeo beorigi jeone sseo nwayagesseoyo.**
   잊어 버리기 전에 써 놔야겠어요.

GRAMMAR NOTE "Worth ...ing" -(으)ㄹ 만해요 -*(eu)l manhaeyo*

-(Eu)l manhaeyo -(으)ㄹ 만해요 attaches to a verb to express that "it is worth it" to do that action. **(Eu)l man han** (으)ㄹ 만한, before a noun, can be used to describe something that is worth doing the action *to* (or *with*).

Is that book worth reading? **Geu chaek ilgeul manhaeyo?**
그 책 읽을 만해요?

The museum is small but worth visiting.
Bangmulgwani jageunde bangmunhal manhae.
박물관이 작은데 방문할 만해.

What is worth seeing around here?
I geuncheo.e bol manhan ge mwoga isseoyo?
이 근처에 볼 만한 게 뭐가 있어요?

PATTERN PRACTICE 3

Practice the following sentences with -(으)ㄹ 만해요 **-(eu)l manhaeyo**.

1. It is worth visiting N Seoul Tower in Seoul.
   Seo.uleseo N Seo.ul Tawoga gal manhaeyo.
   서울에서 N서울 타워가 갈 만해요.
2. A: How is the soup? Does it taste okay? **Gugi meogeul manhaeyo?**
   국이 먹을 만해요?
   B: It is very delicious. **Aju masinneundeyo.** 아주 맛있는데요.
3. A: I heard that Section Manager Kim has been promoted to Manager, right?
   Gimgwajangnimi bujangnimeuro seungjinhasyeotdamyeonseo?
   김과장님이 부장님으로 승진하셨다면서?
   B: He worked so hard, so he deserves the promotion.
   Seungjinhasil manhae. Jeongmal yeolsimhi ilhasyeotgeodeun.
   승진하실 만해. 정말 열심히 일하셨거든.

GRAMMAR NOTE Giving a one-word answer politely

To avoid sounding curt and extremely rude when you are giving a one-word answer, add **(i)yo** -(이)요, especially if you're not talking to your family members or close friends. If you connect **i(e)yo/yeyo** 이(에)요/예요 to a noun, it is considered a complete sentence. If the word is an adverb, adding just **-yo** -요 is fine.

Round-trip.   vs.   It's a round-trip.
Wangbogiyo. 왕복이요.   **Wangbokiyeyo.** 왕복이에요.

Quickly, please.
Ppalliyo. 빨리요.

EXERCISE 1

You are making New Year's resolutions. Complete the following resolutions using -어야겠어(요) **-eoyagesseo(yo)**.

1. I'd better exercise every day.
2. I'd better study Korean more diligently. (diligently: 열심히 **yeolsimhi**)
3. I'd better eat healthy. (to eat healthy: 건강하게 먹다 **geon.ganghage meokda**)
4. I'd better spend more time with my family: (to spend time with family: 가족과 시간을 보내다 **gajokgwa siganeul bonaeda**)

EXERCISE 2

You are telling a friend where she should visit and what to do in Korea. Complete the sentences using -(으)ㄹ 만해요 -(eu)l manhaeyo.

1. 서울 **Seoul** – 한강 공원 **Han.gang Gongwon**, 걷다 **geotda**
   → 서울에서는 한강 공원이 걸을 만해요. **Seo.ureseoneun Han.gang Gongwoni georeul manhaeyo.**
2. 서울 **Seoul** – N서울타워 (N Seoul Tower), 구경하다 **gugyeonghada** (to look around)
3. 한국 **Han.guk** – 제주도 **Jejudo** (Jeju Island), 관광하다 **Gwan.gwanghada** (to sightsee)
4. 제주도 **Jejudo** – 용두암 **Yongdu.am** (Youngduam Rock), 가보다 **gaboda**

🔘 DIALOGUE 2 You'll see Mural Village on the left.

Emma and Eunbi visit the tourist information center to ask for directions.

Eunbi: Let's first go to the tourist information center since we're meeting Aiden there.
Eideunirang gwan.gwang annaeso apeseo mannagiro haesseunikka uri geogibuteo ja.
에이든이랑 관광 안내소 앞에서 만나기로 했으니까 우리, 거기부터 가자.

Emma: OK, let's. Hmmm. I can't figure it out even with the map. I'd better ask.
Geurae. Eum... jidoreul bwado jal moreugenne. Hanbeon mureobwayagesseoda.
그래. 음... 지도를 봐도 잘 모르겠네. 한번 물어봐야겠다.

Eunbi: I'll ask. (to a passerby) Excuse me. May I ask a question?
Naega mureo bolkke. Jeogiyo. Malsseum jom mutgesseumnida.
내가 물어 볼게. 저기요. 말씀 좀 묻겠습니다.

Passerby: Yes. Go ahead.
Ne. Malsseumhaseyo.
네. 말씀하세요.

Eunbi: How do I get to the tourist information center from here?
Yeogieseo gwan.gwang annaesokkaji garyeomyeon eotteoke gaya dwaeyo?
여기에서 관광 안내소까지 가려면 어떻게 가야 돼요?

Passerby: Oh, you see the Jeondong Cathedral there on the left? Walk along the opposite way, and you'll see the center.
A, jeogi oenjjoge Jeondong seongdang boisijyo? Geogi.e geonneopyeoneuro jjuk georeogaseyo. Geureom gwan.gwang annaesoga boil kkeoyeyo.

	아, 저기 왼쪽에 전동 성당 보이시죠? 거기의 건너편으로 쭉 걸어가세요. 그럼 관광 안내소가 보일 거예요.
Eunbi:	Thank you! **Gamsahamnida!** 감사합니다!

At the information center...

Emma:	Hello! Could we please have a map of the Jeonju Hanok Village? **Annyeonghaseyo? Jeonju hanok ma.eul jido han jang eodeul ssu isseulkkayo?** 안녕하세요? 전주 한옥 마을 지도 한 장 얻을 수 있을까요?
*ICO:	Certainly. Here you are. **Ne, geureomyo. Yeogi isseumnida.** 네, 그럼요. 여기 있습니다.
Emma:	What else should we see other than Hanok Village here? **Yeogi hanok ma.eul malgo tto bol manhan ge mwoga isseulkkayo?** 여기 한옥 마을 말고 또 볼 만한 게 뭐가 있을까요?
ICO:	There is the Mural Village, and the filming site of the drama "Sungkyunkwan Scandal" that many go to see. **Byeokwa ma.euldo itgo Seonggyun.gwan Seukaendeuriraneun deurama chwaryeongjido manideul gaseyo.** 벽화 마을도 있고 성균관 스캔들이라는 드라마 촬영지도 많이들 가세요.
Eunbi:	How do I get to the Mural Village? **Byeokwa ma.eureun eotteoke gayo?** 벽화 마을은 어떻게 가요?
ICO:	(Pointing at the map) When you leave here, walk straight until you see the three-way intersection. Turn right at the intersection and walk a bit. You'll see the Mural Village on the left. **Jeohi gwan.gwangannaeso.eseo nagasyeoseo jjuk georeusimyeon samgeoriga nawayo. Geogieseo oreunjjogeuro doseyo. Geurigo jom georeogasimyeonseo oenjjoge byeokwa ma.euri boil kkeoyeyo.** 저희 관광안내소에서 나가셔서 쭉 걸으시면 삼거리가 나와요. 거기에서 오른쪽으로 도세요. 그리고 좀 걸어가시면서 왼쪽에 벽화 마을이 보일 거예요.

*ICO = Information Center Office

Eunbi: Thank you!
            Gamsahamnida!
            감사합니다!

Emma: I see Aiden there. Aiden!
            Jeogi Eideuni boine. Eideun!
            저기 에이든이 보이네. 에이든!

VOCABULARY AND EXPRESSIONS

관광	**Gwan.gwang**	tourism
안내소	**annaeso**	information center/booth
저기요	**Jeogiyo**	Excuse me! (calling for someone's help)
까지	**kkaji**	up to, until (and including)
왼쪽	**oenjjok**	left side
전동 성당	**Jeondong Seongdang**	Jeondong Cathedral
건너편	**geonneopyeon**	opposite side, across
마을	**Ma.eul**	village
장	**jang**	counter for paper, flat items
벽화	**byeokwa**	mural, fresco
성균관	**Seonggyungwan**	Korea's top educational institution in the royal court during the Joseon Dynasty
스캔들	**seukaendeul**	scandal
드라마	**deurama**	drama
촬영지	**chwaryeongji**	filming site
삼거리	**samgeori**	three-way intersection
오른쪽	**oreunjjok**	right-hand side
쭉	**jjuk**	directly, all the way, all along
-의	**ui/e**	's, of (possessive marker)
거기부터 가요 (가-)	**geogibuteo gayo (ga-)**	let's start from there, let's go there first
말씀 좀 묻겠습니다 (묻-)	**malsseum jom mutgesseumnida. (mut-)**	May I ask a question? (to a passerby)
가려면 (-가려고 하면) (가-)	**garyeomyeon (-garyeogo hamyeon) (ga-)**	if I want to go, if I'm trying to go
보이시죠? (보이-)	**boisijyo? (boi-)**	you see it, right? (honorific)
얻을 수 있을까요? (얻-)	**eodeul ssu isseulkkayo? (eot-)**	may I get/obtain (one)?
도세요 (돌-)	**doseyo (dol-)**	turn (honorific)
걸어가시면서 (걷-, 가-)	**georeogasimyeonseo (geot-, ga-)**	while walking (honorific)

VOCABULARY PRACTICE 2

Give the Korean terms for the words described below.

1. the opposite side of the road: _____
2. when you go to visit a new place and explore, enjoy, and learn about it: _____
3. left side: _____ and right side: _____
4. smaller than a city or a town: _____

GRAMMAR NOTE Communicating what's visible/audible with passives: -이/가 보이 *-i/ga boi* "you can see/hear..."

Korean passive verbs are created using **middle suffixes** (that come before speech style endings, past tense, etc.). Verbs of the senses, such as **-bo** -보 "to see" and **-deut** -듣 "to hear" are often used in the passive (**-boi** -보이 and **-deulli** -들리, respectively) to mean "(something) *can be* seen/heard." (A more natural English translation is "(you) can see/hear it.") The thing that can be seen or heard gets the *subject* marker **-i/ga** -이/가.

As/while you are walking, you will see Mural Village on the left.
Georeogasimyeonseo oenjjoge byeokwa ma.eul boil kkeoyeyo.
걸어가시면서 왼쪽에 벽화 마을이 보일 거예요.

Can you hear that sound/noise from your apartment?
Geu soriga apateu.eseo deullyeoyo? 그 소리가 아파트에서 들려요?

PATTERN PRACTICE 4

Practice the following sentences with -이/가 보이다/들리다 **-i/ga boida/deullida**.

1. Can you hear me? **Nae moksoriga deullyeoyo?** 내 목소리가 들려요?
2. Can you see the subway station on your right?
   Oreunjjoge jihacheol lyeogi boyeoyo? 오른쪽에 지하철 역이 보여요?
3. If you turn left, you will see the café where I am now.
   Oenjjogeuro dolmyeon naega inneun kapega boil kkeoyeyo.
   왼쪽으로 돌면 내가 있는 카페가 보일 거예요.

GRAMMAR NOTE Polite request: -(으)ㄹ 수 있을까요? *-(eu)l ssu isseulkkayo?* "Might I..."

-(Eu)l ssu isseulkkayo -(으)ㄹ 수 있을까요 is used as a very polite way to ask for permission or make a request. It also demonstrates how suffixes can stack up in Korean, especially in polite speech. It consists of **-(eu)l ssu iss** -(으)ㄹ 수 있 "can," **(eu)lkka** (으)ㄹ까 "I wonder," and the polite ending **-yo** -요.

Could we get a map of the Jeonju Hanok Village?
Jeonju hanok ma.eul jido han jang eodeul ssu isseulkkayo?
전주 한옥 마을 지도 한 장 얻을 수 있을까요?

Where might I be able to buy a bus ticket?
Beoseupyoreul eodieseo sal ssu isseulkkayo?
버스표를 어디에서 살 수 있을까요?

PATTERN PRACTICE 5

Practice the following polite requests with -(으)ㄹ 수 있을까요 **-(eu)l ssu isseulkkayo**.

1. Could I talk to you for a minute? **Jamkkan yaegi jom hal ssu isseulkkayo?**
   잠깐 얘기 좀 할 수 있을까요?
2. Where can I buy a subway ticket?
   Jihacheol pyoreul eodieseo sal ssu isseulkkayo?
   지하철 표를 어디에서 살 수 있을까요?
3. Could I use your phone please? My phone battery ran out.
   Jeonhwa jom sseul ssu isseulkkayo? Je haendeupon baetteoriga nagaseoyo. 전화 좀 쓸 수 있을까요? 제 핸드폰 배터리가 나가서요.

GRAMMAR NOTE Simultaneous actions: -(으)면서 *-(eu)myeonseo* "while ...ing"

-(Eu)myeonseo -(으)면서 connects two simultaneous actions by the same person.

I read the news (while) eating breakfast.
Achimeul meogeumyeonseo sinmuneul ilgeosseoyo.
아침을 먹으면서 신문을 읽었어요.

While you are walking, you'll see the Mural Village on the left.
Georeogasimyeonseo oenjjoge byeokwa ma.eureul bosil su isseul geoyeyo.
걸어가시면서 왼쪽에 벽화 마을을 보실 수 있을 거예요.

-(Eu)myeonseo -(으)면서 cannot be used if the subjects of the two verbs are different (as in "<u>I</u> sing while <u>my friend</u> plays the piano"). For different people engaging in simultaneous actions, use **-neun dongan** -는 동안.

I read the news while my brother was making breakfast.
Dongsaeng.i achimbabeul mandeuneun dong.an naneun sinmuneul ilgeosseoyo. 동생이 아침밥을 만드는 동안 나는 신문을 읽었어요.

It snowed while I was sleeping. **(Naega) janeun dong.an nuni wasseoyo.**
(내가) 자는 동안 눈이 왔어요.

PATTERN PRACTICE 6

Practice describing simultaneous actions with -(으)면서 **-(eu)myeonseo**.

1. Don't text while driving. **Unjeonhamyeonseo munjjahaji maseyo.**
   운전하면서 문자하지 마세요.
2. My older sister laughed while watching TV.
   Eonnineun tellebijyeoneul bomyeonseo useosseoyo.
   언니는 텔레비전을 보면서 웃었어요.
3. Aiden became interested in Korea while traveling in Korea.
   Eideuneun Han.gung nyeohaeng.eul hamyeonseo Han.guge gwansimeul gajige dwaetda.
   에이든은 한국 여행을 하면서 한국에 관심을 가지게 됐다.

GRAMMAR NOTE **The versatile marker -까지 –kkaji**

Be aware that **-kkaji** -까지 is a versatile marker that can be interpreted in many different ways.

Even *you* are going? **Neokkaji ga?** 너까지 가?

Please come by 3 o'clock. **Se sikkaji oseyo.** 세 시까지 오세요.

We played until late into the night. **Bamneutgekkaji norasseoyo.**
밤늦게까지 놀았어요.

I'll go with you up to that point only. **Geogikkajiman gachi galkke.**
거기까지만 같이 갈게.

CULTURE NOTE **Korean history and historical sites**

There are many beautiful and historical sites throughout Korea. Some of the gates that used to surround the Joseon Dynasty palaces can still be seen in Seoul. These palaces were carefully planned out by auspicious geomancy with respect to nearby mountains and rivers in the city. More than seventy percent of Korea's land is mountainous, and there are some thirty mountains north of the Han river and nearly forty mountains south of the river—and that's just within Seoul. The mountains often house Buddhist temples, which were driven out of the inner cities during the Joseon Dynasty. Before Christianity was introduced to Korea in modern times, and before Confucianism took over as the political ideals of Joseon, Buddhism had long been the religion of the land since the time it was introduced to Goguryeo in the fourth century. For this reason, many tourist sites include Buddhist temples as well as royal palaces and mountain fortresses.

Of the many kingdoms and dynasties, Unified Silla and Joseon are the "winners" in history, so to speak, so the royal tombs and most historical relics are from these eras. Goguryeo's territory went far beyond the current North and South Korean peninsula combined, and Goryeo was once such a developed nation that its name "**Goryeo** 고려 (Korea)" was known to its neighbors, but few records remain although some of its world renowned relics (e.g. Goryeo celadons) can be found in museums. Here is an overview of Korean historical eras (that is, the eras of countries that historically existed on the Korean peninsula).

Gojoseon 고조선 ? – 108 BC
Pre-Three Kingdoms Buyeo 부여 (2 BC–494 BC) Goguryeo백제 (37 BC–668 AD) Okjeo 옥저 Dongye 동예 Three Hans 삼한 **Samhan** (**Mahan** 마한, **Byeonhan** 변한, **Jinhan** 진한)
Three Kingdoms 삼국시대 Goguryeo 고구려 Baekje 백제 (18 BC–660 AD) Silla 신라 (57 BC–935 AD) Gaya confederacy: **Gaya yeonmaeng** 가야연맹 (42 AD–562 AD)
Unified Silla Tong-il Silla 통일신라 and **Balhae** 발해 (698–926)
Goryeo: 고려 (918–1392)
Joseon: 조선 (1392–1897)
Korean Empire Daehanjeguk 대한제국 (1897–1910)
Colonial Japanese rule: **Iljje Gangjeomgi** 일제 강점기 (1910–1945) Provisional Government: **Imsijeongbu** 임시정부 (1919–1948)
Military Governments: **Gunjeongbu** 군정부 (1945–1948)
South Korea Namhan 남한 (1948–) (= Republic of Korea **Daehanmin.guk** 대한민국) **North Korea Bukan** 북한 (1948–) (= Democratic People's Republic of Korea **Joseon Minjujuui Inmin Gonghwaguk** 조선 민주주의 인민공화국)

| CULTURE NOTE | **Korean history and K-dramas**

While some Korean dramas represent the Three Kingdoms period (e.g. *Queen Seon Deok* **Seondeok Yeowang** 선덕여왕, *Ju Mong* 주몽, and *Emperor Wang Gun* **Taejo WangGun** 태조왕건) and some Unified Silla (e.g., *Emperor of the Sea Haesin* 해신) or Goryeo (e.g., *Empress Ki* **Ki Hwanghu** 기황후), the most famous historic dramas and movies depict the Joseon period, which allows a relatively detailed look into the lives of Koreans of that time with more written records. Some must-see Joseon period dramas include *Deep-rooted Tree* **Ppuri Gipeun Namu** 뿌리깊은 나무, *Jewel in the Palace* **Daejanggeum** 대장금, *Sungkyunkwan Scandal* 성균관 스캔들, *Huh Joon* 허준, *Slave Hunter* **Chuno** 추노, and *The Moon that Embraces the Sun* **Haereul Pumeun Dal** 해를 품은 달, but the list continues to grow as new movies and dramas come out.

EXERCISE 3

You have a very nice view from your place. Describe what you can see using -이/가 보이다 **-i/ga boida**.
1. I can see N Seoul Tower (서울 타워 **Seoul Tawo**) from my room.
2. I can see Han River (한강 **Han.gang**) from my apartment.
3. I can see Gyeongbok Palace (경복궁 **Gyeongbokgung**) from my office.

EXERCISE 4

You are visiting a tourist information center in 전주 Jeonju. Complete the following conversations using -(으)ㄹ 수 있을까요 **-(eu)l ssu isseulkkayo**.
1. You: Could I get a map of 전주 *Jeonju*?
   Guide: **Ne, yeogi isseumnida.** 네, 여기 있습니다.
2. You: Where can I see the mural?
   Guide: **Samgeorieseo oreunjjogeuro doseyo.**
             삼거리에서 오른쪽으로 도세요.
3. You: Where can I eat delicious *bibimbap*?
   Guide: **Jeonju sikdang.e gaseyo.** 전주 식당에 가세요.
4. You: Where might I be able to buy a bus ticket?
   Guide: **Beoseu teomineoreseo saseyo.** 버스 터미널에서 사세요.

EXERCISE 5

Say what Emma or her friends do simultaneously using -(으)면서 **-(eu) myeonseo**.
1. Aiden: walk while listening to music
2. Emma: cook while watching TV
3. Eunbi: eat while reading a book
4. Minjoon: text while talking

엠마 씨!
Emma!
와 줘서 고마워요.
Thanks for coming.

아니에요.
No, no.
초대해 주셔서 감사합니다.
Thank YOU for inviting me.

근데, 누나 그림 진짜 멋있던데요!
And your sister's paintings are really great!

그렇지요?
I know, right?
저도 우리 민희 누나 그림 아주 좋아해요.
I really like my sister Minhee's paintings, too.

엠마 씨, 잠깐 여기 앉아서 기다려 줄래요?
Emma, do you want to sit and wait here for a sec?
이 전화 좀 받고 올게요.
I need to take this call.

LESSON 19
Talking Respectfully

 **DIALOGUE 1** I'll be troubling you today.

Emma visits Minjoon's sister's art exhibit, then joins his family at the gallery café.

Minjoon: Emma! Thanks for coming.
            Emma ssi! Wa Jwoseo gomawo.
            엠마 씨! 와 줘서 고마워요.
Emma: No, no. Thank YOU for inviting me. And your sister's paintings are
            really great!
            **Anieyo. Chodaehae jusyeoseo gamsahamnida. Geunde, nuna
            geurim jinjja meositdeondeyo!**
            아니에요. 초대해 주셔서 감사합니다. 근데, 누나 그림 진짜
            멋있던데요!
Minjoon: I know, right? I really like my sister Minhee's paintings, too.
            Geureochiyo? Jeodo uri Minhui nuna geurim aju joahaeyo.
            그렇지요? 저도 우리 민희 누나 그림 아주 좋아해요.

Minjoon's cell phone rings.

Minjoon: Emma, do you want to sit and wait here for a sec? I need to take this call.
            **Emma ssi, jamkkan yeogi anjaseo gidaryeo jullaeyo? I jeonhwa
            jom batgo olkkeyo.**
            엠마 씨, 잠깐 여기 앉아서 기다려 줄래요? 이 전화 좀 받고 올게요.
            Auntie, this is a designer at work. We'll be working together for
            another year.
            **Imo, jeohui heosa dija.ineo.inde apeuro il lyeon deo gachi ilhage
            dwaesseoyo.**
            이모, 저희 회사 디자이너인데 앞으로 일 년 더 같이 일하게
            됐어요.
Emma: May I sit here?
            Yeogi anjado doegesseumnikka?
            여기 앉아도 되겠습니까?
Minjoon's Aunt: Of course. Have a seat.
            Mullonijiyo. Anjeuseyo.
            물론이지요. 앉으세요.

Emma: Hello. It's nice to meet you. I am Emma Curtis, and I work with Mr. Kim.
          **Annyeonghaseyo. Cheo.eum boekkesseumnida. Jeoneun
          Keotiseu Emmarago hamnida. Gim timjangnimhago gateun
          jikjang.eseo ilhago isseumnida.**
          안녕하세요. 처음 뵙겠습니다. 저는 커티스 엠마라고 합니다. 김
          팀장님하고 같은 직장에서 일하고 있습니다.

Aunt: Wow! Your Korean is so good! I am Minjoon's aunt.
          Ayu! Hang.gungmal cham jal hasineyo. Naneun Minjuni imoyeyo.
          아유! 한국말 참 잘 하시네요. 나는 민준이 이모예요.

Emma: Oh gosh, no. I have a long way to go, really.
          Anieyo. Ajik jinjja meoreosseoyo.
          아니에요. 아직 진짜 멀었어요.

Aunt: Oh, Minjoon's grandmother is here. Mom! We are over here!
          A, jeogi Minjuni halmeoni osineyo. Eomma! Ijjogieyo!
          아, 저기 민준이 할머니 오시네요. 엄마! 이쪽이에요!

Emma: Would you like to sit here, Ma'am?
          Yeogi anjeusigesseoyo?
          여기 앉으시겠어요?

Grandmother: Yes. Thank you. Yonghee, all the children are alright?
          Geuraeyo. Gomawoyo. Yonghuiya, aedeureun da jal itji?
          그래요. 고마워요. 용희야, 애들은 다 잘 있지?

Aunt: Yes, yes. They are all studying hard. This is Emma. She is a
          colleague at Minjoon's company and they are working together now,
          so I've been told.
          **Ne, ne. Gongbu jaldeul hago isseoyo. Ijjogeun Emma ssiyeyo.
          Minjuni hoesa dongnyoinde il lyeon deo gachi ireul hage dwael
          kkeoraeyo.**
          네, 네. 공부 잘들 하고 있어요. 이쪽은 엠마 씨예요. 민준이 회사
          동료인데 앞으로 일 년 더 같이 일을 하게 될 거래요.

Emma: Hello! Nice to meet you.
          Annyeonghasimnikka? Jal butakdeurimnida.
          안녕하십니까? 잘 부탁드립니다.

Grandmother: Is that right? You speak Korean so well! Is Minjoon good to you?
          **Geuraeyo? Hangungmareul eojjeomyeon ireoke jalhaeyo? Uri
          Minjuniga jalhaejwoyo?**
          그래요? 한국말을 어쩌면 이렇게 잘해요? 우리 민준이가
          잘해줘요?

Emma: Yes. I'm so indebted to him. I am inconveniencing you today, too.
          **Ne. Timjangnimhante sinse mani jigo isseoyo. Oneuldo pye jom
          kkichigessumnida.**
          네. 팀장님한테 신세 많이 지고 있어요. 오늘도 폐 좀
          끼치겠습니다.

Grandmother: What inconvenience? I hope you are having a good time today.
Pyeneun museun. Oneul jaemiitge nolda gaseyo.
폐는 무슨. 오늘 재미있게 놀다 가세요.

She turns to her daughter.

Grandmother: Oh, what about Minhee?
Cham, Minhuineun?
참, 민희는?

Aunt: Right. She said she'd come right away after thanking the visitors.
Ne. Sonnimdeulkke insadeurigo geumbang ol kkeoraeyo.
네. 손님들께 인사드리고 금방 올 거래요.

VOCABULARY AND EXPRESSIONS

초대*	chodae	inviting
그림	geurim	picture, painting
누나	nuna	older sister (to a male sibling)
이모	imo	maternal aunt
동료	dongnyo	colleague, co-worker
할머니	halmeoni	grandmother
잠깐 (=잠시)	jamkkan (= jamsi)	for a moment, short time
앞으로	apeuro	from now on, in the future
재미있게 (재미있-)	jaemiitge (jaemi iss-)	enjoying (fun)
참	cham	quite, very
잘(들)	jal(deul)	well (for everyone involved)
손님	sonnim	guests, customers, visitors
-께	kke	to, for someone (exalting the recipient)
어쩌면 이렇게/그렇게	eojjeomyeon ireoke/ geureoke	how come this/that much, how could it be that
멋있던데요 (멋있-)	meositdeondeyo (meosiss-)	it looked great (first-hand account)
기다릴래 (기다리-)	gidarillae (gidari-)	going to/want to wait
받고 (받-)	batgo (bat-)	receive/take and
일하게 됐어요 (일하-, 되-)	ilhage dwaesseoyo (ilha-, deo-)	have come to work (currently working, will start working)
앉으시겠어요? (앉-)	Anjeusigesseoyo? (anj-)	Would you like to sit? (honorific)
잘해줘요? (잘해주-)	jalhaejeoyo (jalhaeju-)	good to you/take care of you
신세 지고 있어요 (지-)	sinse jigo isseoyo (ji-)	I am being a burden, being indebted for the trouble
폐 좀 끼치겠습니다 (끼치-)	pye jom kkichigesseumnida (kkichi-)	I am imposing; causing inconvenience

놀다 가세요 (놀-, 가-)	**nolda gaseyo (nol-, ga-)**	have a good time/short rest
인사드리고 (인사드리-)	**insadeurigo (insadeuri-)**	say hello/pay respects and

VOCABULARY PRACTICE 1

Give the Korean terms for the words described below.

1. asking someone if they'd like to come to a party or outing (with you):
   _____

2. someone who works with you: _____
3. graphic/visual representation of something: _____
4. people who are invited to your home or party: _____

GRAMMAR NOTE Recalling your personal experience with -던데요 *-deondeyo*

The suffix **-deondeyo** -던데요 underscores that what you are describing or stating is based on your own personal observation.

(I saw them and) the paintings were really great!
Geurim jinjja meositdeondeyo! 그림 진짜 멋있던데요!

I didn't find that restaurant all that great.
Geu jip byeollo mad eopdeondeyo. 그 집 별로 맛 없던데요.

I found out (for myself) that Emma wasn't/isn't in today.
Emmaga oneul an watdeondeyo. 엠마가 오늘 안 왔던데요.

PATTERN PRACTICE 1

Practice the following conversations using -던데요 **-deondeyo**.

1. The food was so great! **Eumsigi jeongmal masitdeondeyo!**
   음식이 정말 맛있던데요!
2. I found that Aiden was really fluent in Korean!
   Eideun ssiga Han-gugeoga jeongmal yuchanghadeondeyo!
   에이든 씨가 한국어가 정말 유창하던데요!
3. Jeonju Hanok Village was worth visiting!
   Jeonju.ui hanok ma.euri ga bol manhadeondeyo!
   전주의 한옥 마을이 가 볼 만하던데요!

GRAMMAR NOTE Expressing a development over the course of time: -게 됐 *ge dwaet* "It turns out" or "It has come to be that"

Previously, you learned that the suffix **-ge** -게, when attached to adjectives, conveys *how* things are experienced or done. When attached to verb roots and used with the verb **doe** 되, it shows what something has come to be.

(It has come to be that) we will be working together from now on.
Apeuro gachi ilhage dwaesseoyo. 앞으로 같이 일하게 됐어요.

It turns out I am going to Korea in the spring!
Bome Han.guge gage dwaesseo! 봄에 한국에 가게 됐어!

How did you two come to know each other?
Duri eotteke alge dwaesseoyo? 둘이 어떻게 알게 됐어요?

PATTERN PRACTICE 2

Practice expressing a development in the course of time with -게 됐 **-ge dwaet**.

1. A: It turns out I will be on a business trip to Japan next week.
   Da.eum jue Ilbone chuljang gage dwaesseoyo.
   다음 주에 일본에 출장 가게 됐어요.
   B: Have a safe trip to Japan!
   Ilbone jal danyeo oseyo! 일본에 잘 다녀 오세요!
2. A: How did you two come to know each other?
   Duri eotteoke alge dwaesseoyo? 둘이 어떻게 알게 됐어요?
   B: We came to know each other while taking a Korean class together.
   Han.gugeo sueobeul deutdaga seoro alge dwasseoyo.
   한국어 수업을 같이 듣다가 서로 알게 됐어요.

GRAMMAR NOTE -(으)ㄹ 거래요 *-(Eu)l kkeoraeyo* "They say they will..."

When you are relaying someone else's plan, use the ending **-(eu)l kkeoraeyo** -(으)ㄹ거래요 (shortened from **-(eu)l kkeorago haeyo** -(으)ㄹ 거라고 해요) to mean "they say that (they) will...."

They say it will rain tomorrow. **Naeil biga ol kkeoraeyo.**
내일 비가 올 거래요.

I hear they'll be working on the same project from now on.
Apeuro gateun ireul hage doel kkeoraeyo.
앞으로 같은 일을 하게 될 거래요.

She said she'd come after thanking the visitors.
Sonnimdeulkke insadeurigo ol kkeoraeyo.
손님들께 인사드리고 올 거래요.

PATTERN PRACTICE 3

Practice passing on information with -(으)ㄹ 거래요 **-(eu)l kkeoraeyo**.

1. I hear the bus to Jeonju will be departing soon.
   Jeonju ganeun beoseuga got chulbalhal kkeoraeyo.
   전주 가는 버스가 곧 출발할 거래요.
2. He said that he would call me when he arrived.
   Dochak hamyeon yeollakal kkeoraeyo. 도착하면 연락할 거래요.
3. I hear that tickets to Busan will be sold out shortly.
   Busan ganeun pyoga geumbang maejindoel kkeoraeyo.
   부산 가는 표가 금방 매진될 거래요.

GRAMMAR NOTE To do something "to/for" someone

-Hante -한테 means "to," as in "give or do something To someone," and it can only be used with animate beings like humans and animals (but not plants). **-Ege** -에게 is its formal, written version. **-Kke** -께 is used with people who need to be honored.

Tell me everything. I'll hear you out/I'll make it happen.
Nahante da malhae. Da deureojulkke. 나한테 다 말해. 다 들어줄게.

Give me death if not bread!
Na.ege ppang.i animyeon jugeumeul! 나에게 빵이 아니면 죽음을!

You need to greet the guests.
Sonnimdeulkke insadeuryeoyaji. 손님들께 인사드려야지.

GRAMMAR NOTE "Would you (like to) ...?" -(으)시겠어요? *-(eu) sigesseoyo?*

-(Eu)sigesseoyo? -(으)시겠어요? is a useful ending that will make your Korean sound refined and your personality warm and charming. Use it as much as you can!

Would you like to sit here?
Yeogi anjeusigesseoyo? 여기 앉으시겠어요?

Would you like to try this?
Igeo deusyeo bosigesseoyo? 이거 드셔 보시겠어요?

PATTERN PRACTICE 4

Practice saying polite requests with -(으)시겠어요 **-(eu)sigesseoyo**.
1. A: What would you like to order?
       Mwo jumunhasigesseoyo? 뭐 주문하시겠어요?
    B: I'd like to have *kimchi sundubu*.
       Gimchi sundubu juseyo. 김치 순두부 주세요.
2. A: Would you like to come this way, please?
       Ijjogeuro osigesseoyo? 이쪽으로 오시겠어요?
    B: Yes. **Ne.** 네.

EXERCISE 1

You are talking to Hayoung about the trip that you went with Emma and Eunbi.
Complete the following conversations using -던데요 **-deondeyo**.
1. Hayoung: **Jeonju eottaesseoyo?** 전주 어땠어요?
    You: It was great, indeed!
2. Hayoung: **Jeonju bibimbap eottaesseoyo?** 전주 비빔밥 어땠어요?
    You: It was delicious, indeed!
3. Hayoung: **Gosok beoseu eottaesseoyo?** 고속 버스 어땠어요?
    You: It was convenient, indeed!
4. Hayoung: **Hanong ma.eul eottaesseoyo?** 한옥 마을 어땠어요?
    You: It was beautiful, indeed!
                (beautiful: 아름답다 **areumdapda** *p*-irregular)

EXERCISE 2

Complete the following conversations using -게 됐어요 **-ge dwaesseoyo**.
1. Bella: I did not like *kimchi* at first, but I (have come to) like it now.
2. George: I did not speak Korean well, but now I speak Korean well.
3. Matthew: I could not eat spicy food, but I have come to be able to eat it (well)
              now. (spicy: 맵다 **maepda** (*p*-irregular))
4. Aisha: I did not walk much when I lived in the United States, but it turns
              out that I walk every day while living in Seoul.

EXERCISE 3

Tell Emma what Eunbi said using -거래요 **-kkeoraeyo**.
1. (Eunbi said) it will be cold tomorrow.
2. (Eunbi said) she will not go hiking tomorrow.
3. (Eunbi said) she will be staying home tomorrow.
4. (Eunbi said) she will text you tomorrow afternoon.

DIALOGUE 2 The city is modern, but the culture is ancient.

Minjoon's grandmother and Emma exchange thoughts about Korean culture.

Grandmother: Emma, what do you think of Korea? Do you like your neighborhood?

Emma ssineun Han.gugi eottaeyo? Saneun dongneneun mame deulgo?

엠마 씨는 한국이 어때요? 사는 동네는 맘에 들고?

Emma: I love it!

Neomu joayo!

너무 좋아요!

Grandmother: How do you like the food? Korean food is good for your health, but isn't it spicy?

Eumsigeun ibe majayo? Momeneun jo.eunde neomu maepji?

음식은 입에 맞아요? 몸에는 좋은데 너무 맵지?

Emma: Korean food is just right for my taste because I like spicy food.

Hanguk eumsigi je ibe ttang majayo. Jega mae.un eumsigeul joahageodeunyo.

한국 음식이 제 입에 딱 맞아요. 제가 매운 음식을 좋아하거든요.

Aunt: How about the city? The stores and public transportation are very convenient, right?

Seo.ureun eottaeyo? Syopinghagido pyeonhago daejunggyo-tongdo pyeollihaji?

서울은 어때요? 쇼핑하기도 편하고 대중교통도 편리하지?

Emma: Yes, the city is very modern and convenient. And, Korea also has really beautiful traditional culture as well.

Ne. Dosiga aju hyeondaejeogigo pyeollihaeyo. Hangugeun jeontong munhwado aju areumdaun geot gatayo.

네. 도시가 아주 현대적이고 편리해요. 그리고 한국은 전통 문화도 정말 아름다운 것 같아요.

Grandmother: That is nice to hear. Sometimes I think the younger generation is forgetting their traditions.

Deutgi jonneyo. Jeolmeun saramdeureun jeontong.eul swipge ijeobeorindago saeng.gakaenneunde.

듣기 좋네요. 젊은 사람들은 전통을 쉽게 잊어버린다고 생 각했는데.

Emma: Trees with deep roots do not suffer from drought, don't they say?

Ppuri gipeun namuga gamumeul an tandagodo hajanayo.

뿌리 깊은 나무가 가뭄을 안 탄다고도 하잖아요.

One cannot easily cut off the traditional culture that runs so deep, if I may say so.

Jeontongmunhwareul jeobeorigineun himdeuldago saeng-gakaeyo.

전통문화를 저버리기는 힘들다고 생각해요.

Aunt: The city is modern, but the culture is ancient.

Dosineun hyeondaehwadwaetjiman munhwaneun oraedwa-esseunikkayo.

도시는 현대화됐지만 문화는 오래됐으니까요.

That's why I hope the youth are enthusiastic about maintaining good traditional culture.

Jeolmeunideuri bal beotgo naseoseo joeun jeontongmun-hwareul jikyeosseumyeon jokesseoyo.

젊은이들이 발 벗고 나서서 좋은 전통문화를 지켰으면 좋 겠어요.

Grandmother: Indeed! If you are determined, there is nothing you can't do.

Geureochi! Ma.eumeul meokgo haryeogo hamyeon mot hal kke eopji.

그렇지! 마음을 먹고 하려고 하면 못 할 게 없지.

VOCABULARY AND EXPRESSIONS

동네	dongne	neighborhood
맘 (= 마음)	mam (= ma.eum)	mind, heart
입	ip	mouth
딱	ttak	exactly, abruptly
대중교통	daejunggyotong	public transportation
전통	jeontong	tradition
문화	munhwa	culture
어른들	eoreundeul	adults, elders
뿌리	ppuri	root
젊은이	jeolmeuni	youth, young people
발	bal	foot
도시	dosi	city
현대화	hyeondaehwa	modernization
들어 (들-)	deuleo (deul-)	(come/go) in
맞아요 (맞-)	majayo (maj-)	fit, right, correct
맘에 들 (들-)	mame deul (deul-)	pleases you; is to your liking
입에 맞아요? (맞-)	Ibe majayo? (maj-)	Is the (food) to your liking?
몸에는 좋은데 (좋-)	momeneun jo.eunde (joh-)	is good for your health, so...
편리하지요? (편리하-)	pyeollihajiyo? (pyeonriha-)	it's convenient, right?
현대적이고 (현대적이-)	hyeondaejeogigo (hyeondaejeoki-)	modern and

아름다워요 (아름답-)	areumdawoyo (areumdap-)	beautiful
듣기 (듣-)	deutgi (deut-)	listening
쉽게 (쉽-)	swipge (swip-)	easily
잊어버린다고 (잊어버리-)	ijeobeorindago (ijeobeori-)	that one forgets
생각했는데 (생각하-)	saenggakhaessneunde (saenggakha-)	(I) thought
깊은 (깊-)	gipeun (gip-)	deep
저버리기 (저버리-)	jeobeorigi (jeobeori-)	abandoning, deserting
오래됐으니까요 (되-)	oraedwaesseunikkayo (doe-)	because it's old
벗고 (벗-)	beotko (beot-)	taking (shoes/socks) off and
나서서 (나서-)	naseoseo (naseo-)	step up/out and
지켰으면 (지키-)	jikyeosseumyeon (jiki-)	if one kept, protected

Supplementary Vocabulary
Body Part Phrases

If you put your **mind** to it, there is nothing you can't do.
Ma.eum meokgo haryeomyeon mot hal kke eopji.
마음 먹고 하려면 못 할 게 없지.

The youth will **jump** into it.
Jeolmeuniga balbeotgo naseoseo hal kkeoyeyo.
젊은이가 발벗고 나서서 할 거예요.

Is the food to your (**palate's**) liking?
Eumsigi ibe majayo? 음식이 입에 맞아요?

Elders' advice rubs them the wrong way.
Eoreundeuri haneun maldo gwie geoseullyeo hago.
어른들이 하는 말도 귀에 거슬려 하고.

Good medicine is bitter (in your **mouth**), don't they say?
Ibe sseun yagi mome jotajanayo.
입에 쓴 약이 몸에 좋다잖아요.

VOCABULARY PRACTICE 2
Give the Korean terms for the words described below.
1. if the water is above your chest, it is getting: _____
2. the vicinity around where one lives: _____
3. traditions, beliefs, and ways of living: _____
2. people of the younger generation: _____

GRAMMAR NOTE Ending a sentence with a connector

You can use the connector suffix **-go** -고 at the end of your sentence (plus **-yo** -요) to signal the listener that you are starting a topic of conversation, and that there is more to be said on the subject.

My name is Maya and... (and what else?)
Je ireumeun maya<u>go</u>yo. 제 이름은 마야<u>고요</u>.

You like your neighborhood and... other things?
Saneun dongneneun mame deul<u>go</u>? 사는 동네는 맘에 <u>들고</u>?

They don't like what elders have to say (and stuff like that).
Eoreundeuri haneun maldo gwie geoseullyeo ha<u>go</u>.
어른들이 하는 말도 귀 거슬려 <u>하고</u>.

PATTERN PRACTICE 5

Practice ending the sentence using -고 **-go**.
1. My name is Sara, and I am living in Seoul now.
   Je ireumeun Saera<u>go</u>yo. Jigeum Seo.ureseo sarayo.
   제 이름은 사라고요. 지금 서울에 살아요.
2. So, you are doing well (and ...)? **Geurae, jal jinae<u>go</u>?** 그래, 잘 지내고?
3. And your parents are well too (and ...)?
   Bumonimdo annyeonghasi<u>go</u>? 부모님은 안녕하시고?

GRAMMAR NOTE Create a sentence within a sentence with
-고 *-go*

You can embed a sentence within another, e.g., "Good medicine might be bitter to your tongue" in the longer sentence "They say that good medicine might be bitter to your tongue" with the suffix **-go** -고. It functions as the connector "that," usually accompanied by verbs like "say" **(mal)ha-** (말)하- or "think" **saeng. gakha-** 생각하-.

I think that it would be difficult for people to abandon their traditional culture.
Saramdeuri jeontongmunhwareul jeobeorigineun himdeulda<u>go</u> saenggakaeyo. 사람들이 전통문화를 저버리기는 힘들다<u>고</u> 생각해요.

I heard that Maya is not coming today.
Mayaga oneul an onda<u>go</u> deureosseoyo.
마야가 오늘 안 온다<u>고</u> 들었어요.

(People say that) it might be a little difficult (to make it a reality).
Saramdeuri geugeon jom himdeul kkeora<u>go</u> haeyo.
사람들이 그건 좀 힘들 거라<u>고</u> 해요.

PATTERN PRACTICE 6

Practice saying the following sentences with the embedding suffix -고 **-go**.

1. I heard that Aki is busy today.
   Aki ssineun oneul bappeudago deureosseoyo.
   아키 씨는 오늘 바쁘다고 들었어요.

2. I think winter is not a good time to visit Seattle.
   Siaetteureun gyeoure yeohaenghagi an jotago saenggakaeyo.
   시애틀은 겨울에 여행하기 안 좋다고 생각해요.

3. Well, they say that the early bird catches the worm, right?
   Iljjik ireonaneun saega beollereul jamneundagodeul malhajanayo.
   일찍 일어나는 새가 벌레를 잡는다고들 말하잖아요.

GRAMMAR NOTE Expressing wishes: -(으)면 좋겠 *-(eu)myeon joket* "it would be great if...," "I wish..."

When your wishes are for others' actions or are not in your control, you can express them with **-(eu)myeon joket** -(으)면 좋겠 "it would be great if... ." The "past tense" version **-(ess)eumyeon joket** -었으면 좋겠 suggests a smaller chance of the actions happening, the equivalent of "if one had (done something)."

I really hope I can get tickets for that concert.
Konseoteu tikeseul sal ssu iss(eoss)eumyeon joketda.
콘서트 티켓을 살 수 있(었)으면 좋겠다.

I wish that fellow would stop smoking already.
Jeo saram dambae jom geuman piwosseumyeon jokesseoyo.
저 사람 담배 좀 그만 피웠으면 좋겠어요.

PATTERN PRACTICE 7

Practice expressing wishes using -(었)으면 좋겠다 **-(eoss)eumyeon joketda**.

1. I hope we go to Jeju Island this summer.
   Ibeon yeoreume Jejudoe gamyeon jokesseoyo.
   이번 여름에 제주도에 가면 좋겠어요.

2. I hope I can find an apartment to move into soon.
   Ppalli isagal apateureul chajasseumyeon jokesseoyo.
   빨리 이사갈 아파트를 찾았으면 좋겠어요.

3. I hope we can maintain good traditional culture.
   Jo.eun jeontong munhwareul jikyeosseumyeon jokesseoyo.
   좋은 전통 문화를 지켰으면 좋겠어요.

CULTURE NOTE **Responding to a compliment**

When your friend's parents or grandparents compliment you with **Han.gungmal jal hane** 한국말 잘 하네 "You speak Korean well," for a more sophisticated answer, try **Ajing meoreosseoyo** 아직 멀었어요 "I'm far off/have a long way to go" or **Hwolssin deo mani baewoya dwaeyo** 훨씬 더 많이 배워야 돼요 "I need to learn far more."

CULTURE NOTE **Korean traditional culture**

Stately palaces, colorful temples and shrines co-exist with high-rise and techno-artsy structures in modern-day Korea, showing the country's hybrid culture. But the "traditional culture" of Korea also includes intangible customs and rituals, genres of art, styles of architecture, and even its ways of bowing or setting a table. Koreans' love for festive gathering, singing and dancing—you know this if you've ever visited a *noraebang* or are a fan of K-POP idols—dates as far back as the second century BC, as attested by **Samguksagi** 삼국사기, *The Annals of the Three Kingdoms*, the oldest Korean historical record. People on the Korean Peninsula performed rituals to various deities and sang and danced over food and drink.

Since Korea was a monarchy until the turn of the 20th century, some traditional rituals and entertainment practices were restricted to aristocrats and others to the royal palace alone, while the majority of Koreans enjoyed "folk" customs. For example, aristocrats played **baduk** 바둑 (similar to Japanese *go*), whereas the commoners enjoyed **jang.gi** 장기 (known as Chinese chess in the west). While **seonbi** 선비, the classical scholars were reciting poetry over music played by **gisaeng** 기생, women trained in music and educated in art and poetry, the king and his vassals appreciated fan dances accompanied by somber, slow-paced palace music.

Traditional visual art includes **minhwa** 민화, which depicted the daily lives of the commoners, as well as **mukhwado** 묵화도, black and white ink brush painting that aspires to capture the down-to-earth grandeur of nature and noble men's abstract philosophy.

As for sports, **taekgyeon** 택견 (an older variety of the contemporary national sport **taekwondo** 태권도) was practiced by **hwarang** 화랑 the "flower youths" during the **Shilla** 신라 Kingdom. **Gungdo** 궁도 archery is an event that still brings ample Olympic gold medals to Korea and has been around for centuries as evidenced in 5th century cave murals (e.g. **Goguryeo suryeopdo** 고구려 수렵도). The cave murals also show traditional wrestling **ssireum** 씨름, which was imported to Japan and later developed into their sumo wrestling.

The culture of commoners, most of whom were peasants, was always colorful and lively. During agricultural lulls **nong.han.gi** 농한기 or after the harvesting season, families got together with townsmen to share food and music, playing **samulnori** 사물놀이, a percussion quartet. Traveling clowns would wow spectators with tightrope walking as well as mask dancing **talchum** 탈춤 or traditional "cantastoria" **pansori** 판소리, reinforcing the moral values of the time or criticizing the malaise of the caste system. On dreary winter days, people played **yunnori** 윷놀이, and in more recent days since the early 20th century, **hwatu** 화투, a game of cards with colorful and whimsical paintings, established itself as a fun family game. Traditional life was, and still is, profoundly influenced by **pungsu** 풍수 (feng shui) and oriental medicine as well. Most of these traditions remain part of life in modern days, as pastimes or entertainment, if not skills or hobbies to pick up.

EXERCISE 4

Emma and her friends have expressed their opinions about Korea and its traditional culture. Use -다고 생각하다 **-dago saenggakada** to convey what they have said.
1. Emma: **Han.gugeun salgiga pyeonhaeyo.** 한국은 살기가 편해요.
2. Hayoung: **Han.gugeseo Jejudoga ga bol manhaeyo.**
             한국에서 제주도가 가 볼 만해요.
3. Aiden: **Han.guk jeontong munhwaneun aju areumdawoyo.**
             한국 전통 문화는 아주 아름다워요.
4. Eunbi: **Jeontong munhwareul jikyeoya dwaeyo.**
             전통 문화를 지켜야 돼요.

EXERCISE 5

Use -었으면 좋겠다 **-eosseumyeon joketda** and the given information to share what everyone has wished for.
1. Emma: **Han.gugeseo (orae salda)**
             한국에서 (오래 살다)
2. Minjoon: **Emmahago Eideuni hoesa saenghwareul (himdeureohaji anhda)** 엠마하고 에이든이 회사 생활을 (힘들어하지 않다)
3. Aiden: **Han.gugeseo yeohaeng.eul (mani hada)**
             한국에서 여행을 (많이 하다).
4. Eunbi: **Jeontong munhwareul (jal jikida)** 전통 문화를 (잘 지키다).

English–Korean Dictionary

A

A.T.M. **hyeon.geuminchulgi** 현금인출기

abandoning, deserting **jeobeorigi (jeobeori-)** 저버리기 (저버리-)

about that much **jeongdo (= jjeum)** 정도 (= -쯤)

about, approximately **jjeum** -쯤

about, on (used before a noun) **e daehan** -에 대한

act of doing (subject marker) **-neun ge** -는 게; (topic marker) **-neun geon** -는 건; (what one does) **-neun geo** -는 게

act of eating; what one eats **meongneun geon (meok-)** 먹는 건 (먹-)

act of going out, honorific **nagasineun ge (naga-)** 나가시는 게 (나가-)

additional facilities **budaesiseol** 부대시설

adult **daein** 대인

adults, elders **eoreundeul** 어른들

after (it) ends **kkeunnago (kkeutna-)** 끝나고 (끝나-)

after a meal **siku** 식후

again **dasi** 다시

age **nai** 나이

air conditioner, air conditioning **e.eokeon** 에어컨

aisle seat **naecheuk** 내측

alcohol, booze, liquor **sul** 술

all together **modu** 모두

altogether, everyone, everything **jeonbu** 전부

all, every **modeun** 모든

almost **geo.ui** 거의

alone, by oneself **honja** 혼자

already **beolsseo** 벌써

also, as well, too (noun marker) **do** -도

AM/before noon **ojeon** 오전

Amazing! Great! **Goengjanghande! (goengjangha-)** 굉장한데! (굉장하-)

America; U.S.; United States **Miguk** 미국

American (person) **Miguk saram** 미국사람

amount **geumaek** 금액

and **geurigo** 그리고; (noun connector, formal) **hago** 하고; (noun connector for nouns ending in consonants) **irang** -이랑; (for nouns ending in vowels) **rang** -랑;

(used with verb roots) **go** -고; as well as, also, (comes) with **mit** 및

animal **mari** 마리

another, different **dareun (dareu-)** 다른(다르)-

any (used with negatives and questions) **amu** 아무

apartment **apateu** 아파트

apple **sagwa** 사과

approximately how (long, much, etc.) **eolmana** 얼마나

April **Sawol** 사월

arrival point **dochakji** 도착지

as is; just because **geunyang** 그냥

Asian pear **bae** 배

assistant manager **Daerinim** 대리님

at **e** -에

at (point of activity), from **eseo** -에서

at Christmas time **Keuriseumaseuttae** 크리스마스때

at dinner time **jeonyeokttae** 저녁때

at lunch time **jeomsimttae** 점심때

at night time **yagan** 야간

at that time **geuttae** 그때

at the time of, on the occasion when **ttae** 때

at vacation time **banghakttae** 방학때

August **Parwol** 팔월

Australia **Hoju** 호주

awfully, greatly **goengjanghi** 굉장히

B

baby **agi** 아기

bag (plastic, paper) **bongji** 봉지

bag, luggage **gabang** 가방

baked, roasted, broiled **guun (gup-)** 구운 (굽-)

balancing, to add up **jeongsan** 정산

bangs **ammeori** 앞머리

barbecued (beef) ribs **galbi** 갈비

barbecued beef **bulgogi** 불고기

bargain, give away for free **geojeo (= gongjja)** 거저 (= 공짜)

basement **jiha** 지하

bathing, showering **mogyok** 목욕

bathroom (for taking a shower) **yoksil** 욕실

be—after consonant-ending nouns (informal polite) **ieyo** -이에요; after vowel-ending nouns **yeyo** -예요

be (am, is, are, formal) **imnida** -입니다
be called—after consonant-ending nouns,
  informal polite **irago haeyo** -이라고해요;
  after vowel-ending nouns **rago haeyo**
  -라고해요
beautiful **areumdawoyo (areumdap-)**
  아름다워요
  (아름답-)
because of (something) **ttaemune** 때문에
bedroom **chimsil** 침실
beef **sogogi** 소고기
beef rib soup **galbitang** 갈비탕
beer **maekju** 맥주
before **jeon** 전
before (not today) **jeone** 전에; ago **jeon**
  전; some time ago **(ye)jeone** (예)전에
beginning, to start **sijak** 시작
belly, stomach **bae** 배
best, highest **choego** 최고
beverage **eumnyosu** 음료수
big **keun (keu-)** 큰 (크-); **keo boineunde**
  (keu-, boi-) 커 보이는데 (크-, 보이-);
  keuge (keu-) 크게 (크-)
Big, eh? **Keuneyo (keu-)** 크네요 (크-)
Big, I see. **Keugunyo (keu-)** 크군요 (크-)
black **kkamansaek** 까만색
blouse **beullauseu** 블라우스
body **mom** 몸
book **chaek** 책; counter for books: **gwon** 권
book café, portable library **bukkape** 북카페
both **do** -도; **dul** 둘
bottle **byeong** 병
bowl **geureut** 그릇
box **sangja** 상자
braised (beef) rib **galbijjim** 갈비찜
breaded, glazed sweet-and-sour pork
  tangsuyuk 탕수육
budget **yesan** 예산
building **bilding (= geonmul)** 빌딩
  (= 건물)
business card **myeongham** 명함
but (used with verb roots) **jiman** -지만;
  however **geunde**
  (= **geureonde**) 근데 (= 그런데);
  geureochiman (= **hajiman**) 그렇지만
  (=하지만)
by what **mwollo** 뭘로

C
cabbage **yangbaechu** 양배추

cake **keikeu** 케이크
calculation, paying, to calculate **gyesan** 계산
came (honorific-formal) **osyeosseum-**
  nikka (o-) 오셨습니까 (오-); (honorific,
  polite) **osyeosseoyo (o-)** 오셨어요 (오-);
  (informal, polite) **wasseoyo (o-)** 왔어요
  (오-)
Can I try them on? **Ibeobwado dwaeyo?**
  (ip-, doe-) 입어봐도 돼요? (입-, 되-)
can receive, get **badeul su isseoyo (bat-,**
  iss-) 받을 수 있어요
Canada **Kaenada** 캐나다
can't **mot** 못
can't sleep **jal suga eopseoyo (ja-,**
  eops-) 잘 수가 없어요 (자-, 없-)
carry-on (*Lit.*, for in-flight purposes)
  ginaeyong 기내용
cartoon, comic strip, animation, graphic novel
  manhwa 만화
cash **hyeon.geum** 현금
cell phone **hydaepon** 휴대폰
cheap **ssan (ssa-)** 싼 (싸-)
check; (double-)checking, confirming
  chekeu 체크
chicken **dakgogi** 닭고기
China **Jung.guk** 중국
choice marker after a noun ending in a
  consonant **euro** -으로; after a noun ending
  in a vowel or ㄹ **lo** -로
chop **sseoleo (sseol-)** 썰어 (썰-)
chopsticks **jeotgarak** 젓가락
Chungjeong Road, Chungjeong Street
  Chungjeongno 충정로
city **dosi** 도시
City Hall **Sicheong** 시청
clam **jogae** 조개
clear noodle with seasoned vegetables
  jabchae 잡채
close, intimate **chinhan (chinha-)** 친한
  (친하-)
close, nearby **gakkawoyo (gakkap-)**
  가까워요 (가깝-)
closet, cabinet, locker **otjang** 옷장
clothes **os** 옷
club (used after club's name) **bu** -부
coffee **keopi** 커피
cola **kolla** 콜라
cold, flu **gamgi** 감기
cold noodles in soup **mulnaengmyeon**
  물냉면

colleague, co-worker **dongnyo** 동료
colleagues, co-workers **dongnyodeul** 동료들
color **saek** 색
come **wayo (o-)** 와요 (오-)
come and… (honorific) **osyeoseo (o-)**
오셔서 (오-)
come/go in **deuleo (deul-)** 들어 (들-)
come out and **nago (na-)** 나고 (나-)
company **hoesa** 회사
company chief **sajangnim** 사장님
complement suffix **ge** -게
completely, absolutely **wanjeon** 완전
connected **yeon.gyeoldoe.eo (yeon.
gyeoldoe-)** 연결되어 (연결되-)
continually, constantly **gyesok** 계속
convenience store **pyeonuijeom** 편의점
convenient, comfortable **pyeonhaeyo
(pyeonha-)** 편해요 (편하-)
cooked chicken **chikin** 치킨
cooked rice **bap** 밥
cooking **yori** 요리
correct, right; (get) hit, hit the target **majayo
(maj-)** 맞아 (맞-)
cough **gichim** 기침
counter **kaunteo** 카운터
counter for paper, flat items **jang** 장
counter for people **myeong** 명; (honorific,
used after numbers) **bun** 분
counter for "machinery" **dae** 대
counter for "sheets" **jang** 장
country **nara** 나라
credit card **sinyongkadeu** 신용카드
credit card processing **gyeolje** 결제
cucumber **oi** 오이
culture **munhwa** 문화

D
Daum (search portal) **Da.eum** 다음
day **nal** 날
day after tomorrow, in two days **more** 모레
December **Shibiwol** 십이월
decided to go **gagiro haesseoyo (ga-,
ha-)** 가기로 했어요 (가-, 하-)
decided to meet, are going to meet
mannagiro haesseoyo (manna-, ha-)
만나기로 했어요 (만나-,하-)
deep **gipeun (gip-)** 깊은 (깊-)
deeply, sufficiently **puk** 폭
degree (of temperature, used as a unit word)
do 도

delicious **masinneun (iss-)** 맛있는 (있-);
masisseoyo (iss-) 맛있어요 (있-)
delivering, to deliver **baedal** 배달
Denmark **Denmakeu** 덴마크
departing point **chulbalji** 출발지
department chief **bujangnim** 부장님
dessert **dijeoteu** 디저트
diarrhea **seolsa** 설사
difficult **eoryeowoyo (eoryeop-)**
어려워요 (어렵-); tough but **himdeunde
(himdeul-)** 힘든데 (힘들-)
directly **jikjeop** 직접
directly, all the way, all along **jjuk** 쭉
directly, right away, straight(ly) **baro** 바로
Do they say it is coming/it will come?
Ondae? (o-) 온대? (오-)
Do you (know how to) play (e.g., tennis)?
Chil jjul ani? (chi-, al-) 칠 줄 아니?
(치-, 알-)
Do you have/is there? (honorific, polite)
isseusimnikka? (iss-) 있으십니까? (있-)
do you need (honorific, polite) **piryohaseyo? (piryoha-)** 필요하세요? (필요하-)
doctor **uisa** 의사
does **haeyo (ha-)** 해요 (하-)
does not exist, does not have (formal)
eopseumnida (eop-) 없습니다 (없-)
don't, not **an** 안
Don't shave (cut it short), please. **Kkakji
maseyo (kkakk-, mal-)** 깎지마세요
(깎-,말-)
Don't worry. **Geokjeong maseyo (mal-).**
걱정 마세요 (말-)
draft beer **saengmaekju** 생맥주
drama **deurama** 드라마
drawer **seorap** 서랍
dresser **seorapjang** 서랍장
drop me off, let me out (honorific) **naeryeo
juseyo (naeri-, ju-)** 내려주세요 (내리-,
주-)
drop off, leave, entrust **matgiseyo (mat-)**
맡기 세요 (맡-)
drop you off, let you out (humble) **naeryeo
deuryeoyo (naeri-, deuri-)** 내려드려요
(내리-, 드리-)
drug store, pharmacy **yakguk** 약국
dry sauna spa, room **jjimjilbang** 찜질방
duration of time **sigan** 시간
during the daytime **jugan** 주간
dye, dying **yeomsaek** 염색

E

each (used like an adverb after a number expression) **ssik** -씩
easily **swipge (swip-)** 쉽게 (쉽-)
eats **meogeoyo (meok-)** 먹어요 (먹-)
egg **gyeran** 계란
Eh! Ah! suffix (suffix for noticing/confirming; used with verb roots) **-gunnyo** -군요
eight **pal** 팔; **yeodeol** 여덟
eighteen **yeolyeodeol** 열여덟
electric **jeon.gi** 전기
electronics, car (counter) **dae** 대
elevator **ellibeiteo** 엘리베이터
eleven **sibil** 십일; **yeolhana; yeolhan** 열하나; 열한 (before a noun)
enjoying (fun) **jaemiitge (jaemi iss-)** 재미있게 (재미있-)
enter **deuleogal (deuleoga-)** 들어갈 (들어가-)
etc. **deung** 등
even if/although you sing/call out **bulleodo (bureu-)** 불러도 (부르-)
evening (dinner time) **jeonyeok** 저녁
every(one), every(thing), all **da** 다
every, each **-mada** -마다
exactly, abruptly **ttak** 딱
Excuse me (formal) **Sillyehamnida (sillyeha-)** 실례합니다 (실례하-); (calling for someone's help) **jeogiyo** 저기요
exercise **undong** 운동
exercises **undonghaeyo (undongha-)** 운동해요 (운동하-)
exists, there is (What do you think..?) **inneundeyo (iss-)** 있는데요 (있-)
expecting, anticipating **gidae** 기대
expenses to be charged later **hubul** 후불
expensive so, **bissaseo (bissa-)** 비싸서 (비싸-)
express, high speed **gosok** 고속

F

Facebook **Peiseubuk, pebuk** 페이스북, 페북
fair, not bad, OK, no big deal **gwaen-chaneundeyo (gwaenchanh-)** 괜찮은데요 (괜찮-); **gwaenchanneyo (gwaenchanh-)** 괜찮네요 (괜찮-)
fast **ppallayo (ppareu-)** 빨라요 (빠르-)
February **Iwol** 이월
fee, fare **yogeum** 요금

feel cold **chuwoyo (chup-)** 추워요 (춥-)
fever **yeol** 열
fifty **sibo** 십오
filming site **chwaryeongji** 촬영지
fire station **sobangseo** 소방서
first time **cheo.eum** 처음
first, before others **meonjeo** 먼저
fish **saengseon** 생선
fit, right, correct **majayo (maj-)** 맞아요 (맞-)
five **o** 오; **daseot** 다섯
flower **song.i** 송이
food **eumsik** 음식
food and beverages **sigeumnyo** 식음료
foot **bal** 발
for (marker for duration) **-gan (= dong.an)** -간 (= 동안); (the benefit of, sake of) **eul/reul wihae** -을/를 위해
for a minute, for a second **jamsiman (= jamkkanman)** 잠시만 (= 잠깐만)
for a moment, short time **jamkkan (= jamsi)** 잠깐 (= 잠시)
for sure, definitely, without fail **kkok** 꼭
forest **sup** 숲
forest bath **samnimyok** 삼림욕
Forgot, right? **Ijeobeoryeotji (ijeobeoli-)** 잊어버렸지? (잊어버리-)
four **sa** 사; **net; ne** 넷; 네 (before a noun)
France **Peurangseu** 프랑스
French fries, fried potatoes **gamjatwigim** 감자튀김
Friday **Geumyoil** 금요일
fried rice **bokkeumbap** 볶음밥
friend **chin.gu** 친구
from **eseo** -에서
from now on, in the future **apeuro** 앞으로
fruit **gwail** 과일

G

garlic **maneul** 마늘
Gee, ... hmm! (suffix used with verb roots to express emotion) **neyo** -네요
Germany **Dogil** 독일
get directions, finding one's way around **gilchatgi** 길찾기
ginger **saenggang** 생강
glass, cup **jan** 잔
Go ahead and ask (informal, honorific) **Mureoboseyo (mureobo-)** 물어보세요 (물어보-)
go and... **gaseo (ga-)** 가서 (가-)

going out/moving out so/but/and…
naganeunde (naga-) 나가는데 (나가-)
going to/want to wait **gidarillae (gidari-)**
기다릴래 (기다리-)
good **joayo (joh-)** 좋아요 (좋-)
Goodbye (to the one staying) **Annyeonghi
gyeseyo (gyesi-)** 안녕히계세요
(안녕히계시-)
good to you/take care of you **jalhaejeoyo
(jalhaeju-)** 잘해줘요 (잘해주-)
good, but **jo.eunde (joh-)** 좋은데
good, fine; fair, not bad, OK, no big deal
gwaenchanayo (gwaenchanh-)
괜찮아요 (괜찮-)
Got it (humble, formal) **Algesseumnida
(al-)** 알겠습니다 (알-)
grandma, grandmother, ma'am (to an older
woman) **Halmeoni** 할머니
grandpa, sir (to an older man) **Halabeoji**
할아버지
grape **podo** 포도
green **choroksaek** 초록색
greeting **insa** 인사
grilled fish **saengseon gui** 생선 구이
grows **keoyo (keu-)** 커요(크-)
guest **sonnim** 손님
guest(s), customer(s), visitor(s); client
sonnim 손님
guide, to guide **annae** 안내
Gwanghwamun branch store **Gwanghwamunjeom** 광화문점

H

haggler, city slicker **kkakjaeng.i** 깍쟁이
hair (texture) **meorigyeol** 머리결
hair in the back **dwinmeori** 뒷머리
hair on the sides **yeommeori** 옆머리
half **ban** 반
Happy (to meet you). (informal, polite)
**(Mannaseo) ban.gawoyo (manna-,
bangap-)** (만나서) 반가워요 (만나-,
반갑-)
hard liquor **yangju** 양주
has invited **chodaehaesseoyo
(chodaeha-)** 초대했어요 (초대하-)
have a good time/rest for a short while **nolda
gaseyo (nol-, ga-)** 놀다 가세요 (놀-, 가-)
have come to work (currently working, will
start working) **ilhage dwaesseoyo
(ilha-, deo-)** 일하게 됐어요 (일하-, 되-)

have not been to **an ga bwasseoyo (ga-,
bo-)** 안 가 봤어요 (가-, 보-)
have to transfer **garataya (gal-, ta-)**
갈아타야 (갈-, 타-)
Have you been to, have you gone to? **Ga
bon jeok isseoyo (ga-, bo-, iss-)**
가 본 적 있어요? (가-, 보-, 있-)
having chopped **sseoleoseo (sseol-)**
썰어서 (썰-)
having passed **jinaseo (jina-)** 지나서 (지나-)
having sat (honorific) **anjeusyeoseo (anj-)**
앉으셔서 (앉-)
head, hair **meori** 머리
heated stone floor **ondol** 온돌
hello (on the phone) **Yeoboseyo** 여보세요;
How are you? (formal, honorific)
Annyeonghasimnikka? 안녕하십니까?;
(informal, honorific, polite)
Annyeonghaseyo? 안녕하세요?
here (where I am) **yeogi** 여기
high school **nalssi** 날씨
hmmm… **heum…** 흠…
holidays **gonghyuil** 공휴일
Hong Kong **Hong Kong** 홍콩
hospital **byeongwon** 병원
hot **deoun (deop-)** 더운 (덥-)
hot pepper paste **gochujang** 고추장
hour (on the clock; time of day) **si** 시
house, home **jip** 집
how **eotteoke** 어떻게
how (long, much) **eolmana** 얼마나
how come this/that much, how could it be that
eojjeomyeon ireoke/geureoke 어쩌면
이렇게/그렇게
How is it (can you tell me)? **Eotteondeyo?
(eotteoh-)** 어떤데요? (어떻-)
How is/how do you like…? **Eoteoseyo?
(eotteoh-)** 어떠세요? (어떻-)
How is…? **Eeottaeyo (eotteoh-)?** 어때요
(어떻-)?
how long something will likely take **geollil
kkeo gatayo geolli-, gat-** 걸릴 거
같아요 걸리-, 같-
how many **myeot** 몇
how much (price only) **eolma** 얼마
How much is it/are they? (informal, polite)
Eolmayeyo? (eolmai-) 얼마예요? (이-)
however (if attached to nouns, the verb 이- is
used) **jiman (ijiman)** -지만 (-이지만)
hundred **baek** 백

hungry **baegopeuda (baegopeu-)**
배고프다 (배고프-)

hurriedly, now **eoseo** 어서

I

I (humble form) **jeo** 저; (informal casual
form with the subject marker) **naega** 내가

I am being a burden, being indebted for the
trouble **Sinse jigo isseoyo (ji-)** 신세
지고 있어요 (지-)

I am imposing; causing inconvenience
Pye kkichigesseumnida (kkichi-)
폐 끼치겠습니다 (끼치-)

I am sorry (formal) **Joesonghamnida
(joesongha-)** 죄송합니다 (하-)

I have heard a lot about you. (formal)
Malsseum mani deureosseumnida
말씀많이들었습니다

I heard (someone) say **Geureodeonde**
그러던데

I know, right? **Aljiyo (al-)** 알지요? (알-)

I thought **Saenggakhaessneunde
(saenggakha-)** 생각했는데 (생각하-)

I understand; got it (formal)
Algesseumnida (al-) 알겠습니다 (알-)

I want to/would like to eat... **Meokgo
sipeundeyo (meok-, sip-)** 먹고
싶은데요

I will bring (it) **Gajigo galkke**
가지고 갈게

I will help you (humble, formal) **Dowa.
deurigesseumnida (dop-, deuri-)**
도와드리겠습니다 (돕-, 도와드리-)

I will pay (informal) **Naelgeyo (nae-)**
낼게요 (내-)

I-topic (humble) **jeon** (= **jeoneun**) 전
(= 저는)

I.D. **aidi, sinbunjeung** 아이디, 신분증

ice cream **aiseukeurim** 아이스크림

identification card **sinbunjeung** 신분증

if help (out) **dowa jumyeon (dop-, ju-)**
도와주면 (돕-, 주-)

if I want to go, if I'm trying to go
garyeomyeon (= **garyeogo hamyeon**)
(ga-) 가려면 (= 가려고 하면) (가-)

if one kept, protected **jikyeosseumyeon
(jiki-)** 지켰으면 (지키-)

if open **yeolmyeon (yeol-)** 열면 (열-)

if you go out (honorific) **nagasimyeon
(naga-)** 나가시면 (나가-)

if you open (honorific) **yeosimyeon
(yeol-)** 여시면 (열-)

information booth receptionist; guide
annaewon 안내원

in front of **ap** 앞

in the building, facilities affiliated with X
gunae 구내

in the days to come **jangnae.e** 장래에

in the future **mirae.e** 미래에

in the middle of the night **hanbamjung**
한밤중

in the olden days, long time ago **yennare**
옛날에

in the past **gwageo.e** 과거에

inconvenient, uncomfortable
bulpyeonhaeyo (bulpyeonha-)
불편해요 (불편하-)

individual, private **gaein** 개인

informal, casual speech, speak casually with
no polite endings **banmal** 반말

information center/booth **annaeso** 안내소

inside **an** 안

Instagram **Inseutageuraem** 인스타그램

instead, in exchange **daesin** 대신

insurance card **uiryoboheomjeung**
의료보험증

intern **inteon** 인턴

intra-city bus **sinaebeoseu** 시내버스

inviting **chodae** 초대

is blocked up/congested and **makigo
(makhi-)** 막히고 (막히-)

is good for your health, so... **momeneun
joeunde (joh-)** 몸에는 좋은데 (좋-)

is growing **keugo isseoyo (keu-, iss-)**
크고 있어요 (크-, 있-)

is in, has in it (informal, polite) **deureo
isseoyo (deul-, iss-)** 들어 있어요 (들-,
있-)

Is it hot, I wonder? **Deounga? (deop-)**
더운가? (덥-)

is living **salgo isseoyo (sal-, iss-)**
살고 있어요 (살-, 있-)

is looking for **chatgo isseoyo (chaj-,
iss-)** 찾고 있어요 (찾-, 있-)

Is that right? Is that so? **Geuraeyo?
(geureoh-)** 그래요? (그렇-)

Is the (food) to your liking? **Ibe majayo?
(maj-)** 입에 맞아요? (맞-)

it is the case so **iraseo = ieoseo (i-)**
이라서=이어서 (이-)

It goes without saying; of course!
Mullo-nijyo 물론이죠
it is so; yes, please **geuraeyo (geureoh-)**
그래요 (그렇-)
it looked great (and I saw it personally)
meositdeondeyo (meosiss-)
멋있던데요 (멋있-)
it looks like it will take (time) **geollil geo
gasseumnida (geolli-, gat-)**
걸릴 거 같습니다 (걸리-, 같-)
it will be blocked up, congested **makil
geoyeyo (makhi-, i-)** 막힐 거예요 (막히-,
이-)
Italy **Itallia, Itaeri** 이탈리아,이태리
item **gae** 개
it's alright, that's OK **dwaesseoyo (doe-)**
됐어요 (되-)
It's been a long time! **Oraenmanieyo
(oraenmani-)** 오랜만이에요 (오랜만이-)
It's convenient, right? **Pyeollihajiyo?
(pyeonriha-)** 편리하지요? (편리하-)
it's OK, it works **dwaeyo (doe-)** 돼요 (되-)
it's on sale so… **seilhaeseo (seilha-)**
세일해서 (세일하-)
I'll buy for you, my treat. **Sa julkkeyo (sa-,
ju-).** 사줄게요 (사-, 주-).
I'll get/bring (it to you) (humble) **Gatda
deurilkkeyo (gaj-, deuri-)**
갖다 드릴게요 (갖-, 드리-)
I'll give (humble) **Deurilkkeyo (deuri-)**
드릴게요 (드리-)
I'll look (up, for) **Chaja bolkkeyo (chaj-,
bo-).** 찾아 볼게요 (찾-, 보-).
I'll pay **Jibulhalkkeyo (jibulha-)**
지불할게요; **Naelkke (nae-)** 낼게 (내-)
I'm in your care. Please take care of me.
(formal) **Jal butakdeurimnida.**
잘 부탁드립니다.
I'm so sorry **joesonghamnida** 죄송합니다

J
January **Irwol** 일월
Japan **Ilbon** 일본
Jeju Island **Jejudo** 제주도
Jeondong Cathedral **Jeondong
Seongdang** 전동성당
job, workplace **jikjang** 직장
juice **juseu** 주스
July **Chirwol** 칠월
June **Yuwol** 유월

K
Kakao Story (social media) **Kakao Seutoli**
카카오스토리
Kakao Talk (instant messaging application)
Kakao Tok 카카오톡; **Katok** 카톡
karaoke room, singing room **noraebang**
노래방
key **ki** 키
kimchi **gimchi** 김치
knew it, got it **arasseoyo (al-)** 알았어요
(알-)
knows (formal, humble) **algesseumnida
(al-)** 알겠습니다 (알-)
Korea **Han.guk** 한국
Korean food **hansik** 한식
Korean melon **chamoe** 참외
Korea's top educational institution in the
royal court during the Joseon Dynasty
Seonggyungwan 성균관

L
ladies **agassideul** 아가씨들
language; talking **mal** 말
large (size) **laji** 라지
last, past **jinan (jina-)** 지난 (지나-)
later **najung.e** 나중에; later (the same day)
ittaga 이따 (가)
learning **bae.ugi (baeu-)** 배우기 (배우-)
leave it and **dugo (du-)** 두고 (두-)
leaving, to walk out (of a stage) **toejang**
퇴장
left side **oenjjok** 왼쪽
let me ask (someone honored, older)
yeojjwobolgeyo (yeojjwobo-)
여쭤볼게요 (여쭤보-)
let's go (semi-formal) **gapsida (ga-)**
갑시다 (가-)
let's see **boja (bo-)** 보자 (보-)
let's see each other (formal) **bopsida (bo-)**
봅시다 (보-)
Let's start from there, let's go there first
geogibuteo gayo (ga-) 거기부터 가요
(가-)
let's text, text (me) **munjjahaeyo
(munjjaha-)** 문자해요 (문자하-)
like (noun marker) **cheoreum** -처럼
like that, like so **geureoke** 그렇게
likes **joahaeyo (joh-aha-)** 좋아해요
(좋아하-)
Line #X **X-hoseon** X-호선

Line (instant messaging application) **Lain** 라인

listening **deutgi (deut-)** 듣기 (듣-)

little (conversational softener), a **jom** (= **jogeum**) 좀 (= 조금)

little bit, kind of **yakgan** 약간

little while ago (today), a **jogeum jeone** 조금전에

little while later (today), a **itta (ga)** 이따 (가)

lives **sarayo (sal-)** 살아요 (살-)

living, to live **salgi (sal-)** 살기 (살-)

lobby **robi** 로비

locker **rakeo** 라커

long **gin (gil-)** 긴 (길-)

look around and then **dorabogo (dol-, bo-)** 돌아보고 (돌-, 보-)

look for, looking for (honorific, polite) **chajeuseyo (chaj-)** 찾으세요? (찾-)

looks/seems good (polite) **joa boineyo (joh-, boi-)** 좋아 보이네요 (좋-, 보이-)

long time (since) **orae(gan)man** 오래 (간)만

lot, much, many **mani** 많이

lot, plenty **manayo (manh-)** 많아요 (많-)

luck **un** 운

lunch, lunch time **jeomsim** 점심

M

main gate, main entry **jeongmun** 정문

make-up **hwajang** 화장

manager, receptionist **maenijeo** 매니저

mandarin orange **gyul** 귤

map **jido** 지도

March **Samwol** 삼월

marker of the direct object of the sentence (used after nouns ending in consonants) **-eul** -을; (used after nouns ending in vowels) **-reul** -를

marker used after children's or childhood friends' names ending in a consonant **-i** -이; name ending in a consonant **-a** -아; a child(hood friend)'s name ending in a vowel **-ya** -야

maternal aunt **imo** 이모

matter, job, business, to work **il** 일

May **Owol** 오월

May I ask a question? (to a passer-by) **Malsseum jom mutgesseumnida (mut-)** 말씀 좀 묻겠습니다 (묻-)

May I get/obtain (one)? **Eodeul ssu isseulkkayo? (eot-)** 얻을 수 있을까요? (얻-)

ma'am (to a woman over 40) **ajumma** 아줌마; (more polite) **ajummeoni** 아주머니

meal, to have a meal **siksa** 식사

meal, cooked rice **bap** 밥

meat **gogi** 고기

medical exam and treatment, to give a medical exam **jillyo** 진료

medicine, drug **yak** 약

medium (size) **midium** 미디엄+

meeting **miting** (= **hoe-ui**) 미팅 (= 회의)

meeting room **hoe.uisil** 회의실

meets **mannayo (manna-)** 만나요 (만나-)

memory; to remember **gieok** 기억

merely, only, just **bakke** 밖에

Mexico **Meksiko** 멕시코

mid-size, medium, middle **junggan** 중간

middle school, junior high school **junghakgyo** 중학교

mind, heart **mam** (= **ma-eum**) 맘 (= 마음)

miss, young lady **Agassi** 아가씨

modern **hyeondaesigigo (hyeondaesigi-)** 현대식이고 (현대식이-)

modern and **hyeondaejeogigo (hyeondaejeoki-)** 현대적이고 (현대적이-)

modernization **hyeondaehwa** 현대화

Monday **Woryoil** 월요일

money **don** 돈

monthly installment **halbu** 할부

moon, month (only when modified) **dal** 달

more **deo** 더

morning **achim** 아침; AM **ojeon** 오전

mouth **ip** 입

movie **yeonghwa** 영화

moving **isa** 이사

moving (day) **isahaneun (nal) (isaha-)** 이사하는 (날) (이사하-)

Mr./Ms. (used after first or full name in formal situations) **ssi** 씨

much, all that, particularly (used with a negative/not) **byeollo** 별로

mural, fresco **byeokwa** 벽화

my (humble form) **je** 제; (informal casual) **nae** 내

my house (*Lit.*, "our house") **uri jip** 우리집

N

name **ireum** 이름; (formal, official, honorific) **seongham** 성함

nappa cabbage **baechu** 배추

Naver (a Korean search engine) **Neibeo** 네이버

Naver Band (mobile community application) **Neibeo baendeu** 네이버밴드

nearly **geo.ui** 거의

need to julienne **chaesseoleoya dwae (sseol-, doe-)** 채썰어야돼 (썰-, 되-)

neighborhood **dongne** 동네

nervous **tteollijiman (tteolli-)** 떨리지만 (떨리-)

Netherlands **Nedeollandeu** 네덜란드

new product **sinjepum** 신제품

New Zealand **Nyujillaendeu** 뉴질랜드

next (time, one) **da.eum** 다음

next time (around) **da.eumen (= da.eumeneun)** 다음엔 (= 다음에는)

next to, beside **yeop** 옆

next week **da.eum ju** 다음주

Nice to meet you. (formal, humble) **Cheo.eum.boekesseumnida** 처음뵙겠습니다.; (formal) **Mannaseo bangapseumnida.** 만나서반갑습니다.

nine **ahop; gu** 아홉 구

nineteen **yeolahop** 열아홉 19

ninety-nine **gusipgu** 구십구

no (informal polite) **aniyo** 아니요

noodles with black bean sauce **jjajangmyeon** 짜장면

noon **jeong.o** 정오

nose **ko** 코

not **an** 안

not (formal, used with verb roots) **ji anayo (ji anh-)** -지않아요

not be (informal polite) **anieyo (ani-)** 아니에요 (아니-)

not sure, I don't know **geulsseyo** 글쎄요

not yet, still **ajik** 아직; still not **ajik (do)** 아직 (도)

November **Shibirwol** 십일월

novice, beginner **chobo** 초보

now (at this point in time) **jigeum** 지금; (unlike before) **ije** 이제; at the present time, presently **hyeonjae** 현재

number **beonho** 번호

nurse **ganhosa** 간호사

O

object marker after a noun that ends in a consonant **eul** -을; after a noun that ends in a vowel **reul** -를

October **Shiwol** 시월

of course, certainly, sure! (polite) **geureomnyo** 그럼요

Oh! **A!** 아!

oh, by the way **cham** 참!

Oh, I see. **Geureokunyo (geureoh-).** 그렇군요 (그렇-).

Oh, really? Oh, right. **Geureokuna (geureoh-).** 그렇구나 (그렇-).

OK, it is so, let's do **geuraeyo (geureoh-)** 그래요 (그렇-)

older brother (said by females) **oppa** 오빠; (said by males) **hyung** 형

older sister (of a female, said by females) **eonni** 언니; (said by males or of a male sibling) **nuna** 누나

one **il** 일; **hana; han** 하나;한 (before a noun) one thousand **cheon** 천; one year **il lyeon** 일년

one-room, studio **wonrum** 원룸

one-time pay/pay all at once **ilsibul** 일시불

one-way **pyeondo** 편도

onion **yangpa** 양파

only (noun marker) **man** -만

opposite side, across **geonneopyeon** 건너편

or (after consonant-ending nouns) **ina** -이나; (after vowel-ending nouns) **na** -나; (attached to verb roots) **geona** -거나; if not **animyeon** 아니면

ordering, to order **jumun** 주문

originally, by nature **wollae** 원래

outside **bakk** 밖

over there **jeogi** 저기

owner **ju.in** 주인

P

pack, sealed package **paek** 팩

paper, thin object **jang** 장

party **pati** 파티

patient (honorific) **hwanjabun** 환자분

paying after use/afterwards **hubul** 후불

paying in advance **seonbul** 선불

peach **bogsung.a** 복숭아

pencil, pen **jaru** 자루

per **e** -에

perhaps, probably **ama** 아마
perm **pama** 파마
persimmon **gam** 감
person **saram** 사람; **myeong** 명; (honorific) **bun** 분
phone **jeonhwa** 전화
phone/computer application **aep** 앱
photo **sajin** 사진
picture, painting **geurim** 그림
pine tree **sonamu** 소나무
place, location (used only after a modifier) **de** 데
play and (then) **nolgo (nol-)** 놀고 (놀-)
playing (literally, running) **ttwigo itjiyo (ttwi-, iss-)** 뛰고 있지요 (뛰-, 있-)
plays, hits **chyeoyo (chi-)** 쳐요 (치-)
Please come! (honorific, polite) **Oseyo! (o-)** 오세요! (오-)
please get off (e.g., the subway) **naeriseyo (naeri-)** 내리세요 (내리-)
please get/bring (X to) me (honorific) **gatda juseyo (gaj-, ju-)** 갖다 주세요 (갖-, 주-)
please give (honorific, polite) **juseyo (ju-)** 주세요 (주-)
please go down(stairs) (formal) **naeryeogasipsio (naeryeoga-)** 내려가십시오 (내려가-)
please rest (honorific) **swiseyo (swi-)** 쉬세요 (쉬-)
please take a look (honorific) **boseyo (bo-)** 보세요 (보-)
please wait (honorific-formal) **gidaryeo juseyo (gidari-, ju-)** 기다려 주십시오 (기다리-, 주-)
please write down (honorific-polite) **jeogeo juseyo (jeok-, ju-)** 적어주세요 (적-,주-)
please, may I ask that you (humble, formal) **butak deurigeseumnida (deuri-)** 부탁드리겠습니다 (부탁드리-)
pleases you; is to your liking **mame deul (deul-)** 맘에들 (들-)
plurality marker **-deul** -들
police station **gyeongchalseo** 경찰서
pork **dwaejigogi** 돼지고기
potato **gamja** 감자
practice **yeonseup** 연습
premium, top-notch **udeung** 우등
prescribing, to prescribe **cheobang** 처방
prescription (note) **cheobangjeon** 처방전

pressure **amnyeok** 압력
Pretty, eh? **Yeppeune (yeppeu-)** 예쁘네 (예쁘-)
price **gagyeok** 가격
problem **munje** 문제
product, sales item **jepum** 제품
professional athlete, athletic team member **seonsu** 선수
promise, appointment **yaksok** 약속
public transportation **daejunggyotong** 대중교통

Q

quickly, hastily, lightly (onomatopeia of quickly passing) **hwik** 휙
quickly, hurriedly **ppalli** 빨리
quite **kkwae** 꽤
quite, very **cham** 참
quitting time (when people get off work) **toegeun sigan** 퇴근시간

R

radish **mu** 무
radish kimchi **kkagdugi** 깍두기
rain **bi** 비
really **jinjja (= jeongmal)** 진짜 (= 정말)
receipt **yeongsujeung** 영수증
receive, take, get (honorific) **badeuseyo (bat-)** 받으세요 (받-)
receive/take and **batgo (bat-)** 받고 (받-)
red **ppalgan (ppalgah-)** 빨간 (빨갛-)
red pepper and vinegar-seasoned whelk **golbaeng.i muchim** 골뱅이무침
refrigerator **naengjanggo** 냉장고
rent (money) **bangse** 방세
restaurant **sikdang** 식당
restaurant that serves Korean food only **hansikdang** 한식당
restroom **hwajangsil** 화장실
rice cooker **bapsot** 밥솥
rice mixed with vegetables and hot sauce **bibimbap** 비빔밥
rides and **tago (ta-)** 타고 (타-)
right away, just now **geumbang** 금방
right now, this moment, these days **jigeum** 지금
right side **oreunjjok** 오른쪽
right, proper, appropriate, pre-set **je** 제
road, street, way **gil** 길
roasted seaweed **gim** 김

room **bang** 방
root **ppuri** 뿌리
round-trip **wangbok** 왕복
Russia **Reosia** 러시아

S
salesclerk **jigwon** 직원
salt **sogeum** 소금
salty stew **jjigae** 찌개
same age **donggap** 동갑
same, alike **gateun (gat-)** 같은 (같-)
Saturday **Toyoil** 토요일
sauna, steam bath **jjimjil** 찜질
sauté **bokka (bokk-)** 볶아 (볶-)
savory clear noodle dish with many cooked
   vegetables **japchae** 잡채
say hello/pay respects and **insadeurigo**
   (insadeuri-) 인사드리고 (인사드리-)
scallion, green onion **pa** 파
scandal **seukaendeul** 스캔들
scoop it out/serve it, please **peo juseyo**
   (pu-, ju-) 퍼 주세요 (푸-, 주-)
seafood **haemul** 해물
seafood scallion pancake **(haemul) pajeon**
   (해물) 파전
seasoned fried chicken **yangnyeom chikin**
   양념 치킨
seasoned steamed vegetable **namul** 나물
seasoning, seasoned (before nouns)
   yangnyeom 양념
seat **jwaseok** 좌석
section chief **Gwajangnim** 과장님
seems cheap **ssan geo gatayo (ssa-, gat)**
   싼 거 같아요 (싸-, 같-)
seems like it will be too hot **tteugeo.ul**
   kkeot gatayo (tteugeop-, gat-)
   뜨거울 것 같아요 (뜨겁-, 같-)
seems to have come **on geo gata (o-, gat-)**
   온 거 같아 (오-, 같-)
sees, watches **bwayo (bo-)** 봐요 (보-)
self-assembly, Do-it-yourself **joripsik** 조립식
sell **para (pal-)** 팔아 (팔-)
senior colleagues/co-workers/ schoolmates
   seonbae 선배
separately **ttaro** 따로
September **Guwol** 구월
service (as an extra, complimentary service)
   seobiseu 서비스
service window **sunapcheo** 수납처
sesame oil **chamgireum** 참기름

set **seteu** 세트
seven **chil** 칠; **ilgop** 일곱
seventy **chilsip** 칠십
severe, so... **simhaeseo (simha-)** 심해서
   (심하-)
Shall I give (humble, polite) **Deurilkkayo**
   (deuri-) 드릴까요 (드리-)
Shall we look? **Bolkkayo? (bo-)** 볼까요?
   (보-)
Shall we use casual speech? **Mal**
   no-eulkkayo? (noh) 말 놓을까요? (놓)
Shall we? **Geureolkka? (geureo-)**
   그럴까? (그러-)
Shilla (Kingdom) **Silla** 신라
Should I cut (it for you)? **Jalla**
   deurilkkayo? (jareu-, deuri-) 잘라
   드릴까요? (자르-, 드리-)
Should I stir it? **Jeo.eulkkayo (jeos-)?**
   저을까요 (젓-)?
Should I/we order? **Sikilkkayo? (siki-)**
   시킬까요? (시키-)
shrimp **sae.u** 새우
sick/hurt so... **apaseo (apeu-)** 아파서 (아프-)
side **jjok** 쪽
side dishes **banchan** 반찬
side dishes that accompany alcoholic
   beverages **anju** 안주
signature **seomyeong** 서명
since **buteo** 부터
since it's the weekend **jumarira (jumali-)**
   주말이라 (주말이-)
since you began to learn **bae-un ji (bae-u-)**
   배운 지 (배우-)
Singapore **Singgaporeu** 싱가포르
singing **norae** 노래
sir, mister **Ajeossi** 아저씨
six **(r)yuk** 육; **yeoseot** 여섯
size **saijeu** 사이즈
sleep and (honorific) **jumusigo (jumusi-)**
   주무시고 (주무시-)
sleeping **jam** 잠
small **jageun (jak-)** 작은 (작-)
small (size) **seumol** 스몰
small one, small size **sojja** 소자
snack chips, crackers, cookies **gwaja** 과자
so **geuraeseo** 그래서
social media **Eseueneseu** SNS
socks, shoes **kyeolle** 켤레
soft tofu (stew) **sundubu (jjigae)** 순두부
   (찌개)

soju **soju** 소주
sold out **maejin** 매진
some (other) day in the future **hunnare**
훗날에
some time later **najung.e** 나중에
something that came out **naon nao-** 나온나오-
song **gok** 곡
Sounds (like) fun. **Jaemiitgenneyo**
(jaemiiss-) 재미있겠네요 (재미있-)
soup **guk** 국
soy bean paste **doenjang** 된장
soy sauce **ganjang** 간장
spa **seupa** 스파
Spain **Seupein** 스페인
spicy **maeun (maep-)** 매운 (맵-)
spicy cold noodles **bibimnaengmyeon**
비빔냉면
spicy seafood noodle soup **jjamppong** 짬뽕
spoon(s) **sutgarak** 숟가락
spoon(s) and chopsticks **sujeo** 수저
sports; exercising **undong** 운동
spot, location (dependent noun, used only
when modified by counting words) **gunde**
군데
spot, space, available seating or room **jari**
자리
Sprite **Saida** 사이다
squid **ojing.eo** 오징어
starting with (a point), starting from, since
buteo -부터
starting from there **geogieseo buteoneun**
거기에서부터는
step up/out and **naseoseo (naseo-)**
나서서 (나서-)
still, even so **geuraedo** 그래도
stir-fried squid **ojing.eo bokkeum**
오징어볶음
stop by **deulleulgeyo (deulleu-)**
들를게요 (들르-)
store **gage** 가게
strawberry **ttalgi** 딸기
student, kid (preschool to college)
haksaeng 학생
style **seutail** 스타일
subject marker after a noun that ends in a
consonant **i** -이; after a noun that ends in a
vowel **ga** -가
subway **jihacheol** 지하철
suffix often used with Chinese restaurants
banjeom 반점

sugar **seoltang** 설탕
Sunday **Iryoil** 일요일
sweet potato **goguma** 고구마
sweet rice drink **sikye** 식혜
symptom **jeungsang** 증상

T
T(ransit)-card **ti kadeu** 티카드
table **teibeul** 테이블
Taekwondo **Taekkwondo** 태권도
take it with you and (honorific) **gajyeo**
gasyeoseo (gaji-, ga-) 가져가셔서
(가지-,가-)
takes (time) **geollyeoyo (geolli-)** 걸려요
(걸리-)
taking (shoes/socks) off and **beotko (beos-)**
벗고 (벗-)
taste **mat** 맛
taxi driver **taeksi gisa** 택시기사
tea **cha** 차
teach, inform **gareuchyeo (gareuchi-)**
가르쳐 (가르치-)
teacher, doctor **Sunsaengnim** 선생님
team **tim** 팀
team captain **timjang(nim)** 팀장(님)
temperature (weather) **gion** 기온
temporary noun-making suffix (usually for
idiomatic expressions; used with verb roots)
gi -기
ten **ship** 십; **yeol** 열 10
ten thousand **man** 만
tennis **teniseu** 테니스
tennis court **teniseujang** 테니스장
terminal **teomineol** 터미널
text **munjja** 문자
-th floor (in a building) **cheung** 층
Thank you **Gomawoyo (gomap-)**
고마워요 (고맙-); (formal)
Gamsahamnida (gamsaha-)
감사합니다 (감사하-)
Thank you (to a service provider)
Sugohaseyo (sugoha-) 수고하세요
(수고하-)
that (sort of) thing **geureon geos** 그런것
that one forgets **ijeobeorindago**
(ijeobeori-) 잊어버린다고 (잊어버리-)
that one, that thing **geugeo** 그거
that side over there **jeojjok** 저쪽
That would be great! That sounds great!
Geuge joketda! (joh-) 그게 좋겠다 (좋-)

that you know, what you know (with the object marker) **aneun geol (al-)** 아는 걸 (알-)
the most **jeil** (= **gajang**) 제일 (= 가장)
there **geogi** 거기
there is, one has (informal) **isseoyo (iss-)** 있어요 (있-)
there will be (formal) **isseul geoyeyo (iss-, i-)** 있을거예요 (있-,이-)
these **igeodeul** 이거들
these days **yojeum** 요즘
they say it is good **jotae (joh-)** 좋대 (좋-)
thirty minutes **samsip bun** 삼십분
this (needs a noun after) **i** 이
this kind **ireon (ireoh-)** 이런 (이렇-)
this month **ibeon dal** 이번 달
this side, this person **ijjok** (= **yeogi**) 이쪽 (= 여기)
this time **ibeon** 이번
this time (around) **ibeonen** (= **ibeonenun**) 이번엔 (= 이번에는)
this week **ibeon ju** 이번 주
three **sam** 삼; **set; se** 셋; 세 (before a noun)
three days **saheul** 사흘
three-way intersection **samgeori** 삼거리
Thursday **Mokyoil** 목요일
ticket **pyo** 표
time, hours **sigan** 시간
tired **pigonhada (pigonha-)** 피곤하다 (피곤하-)
to **e** -에
to cut, in cutting **jareuneun de (jareu-)** 자르는데 (자르-)
to, for someone **hante** -한테; (exalting the recipient) **kke** -께
to the gills, fully **jantteuk** 잔뜩
to, towards, by way of (after a noun that ends in a consonant) **euro** -으로; (after a noun that ends in a vowel or ㄹ) **lo** -로
today **oneul** 오늘
tofu stew (spicy) **sundubu** 순두부
together **gachi** 같이
together with, and (connects two nouns) **hago** -하고; (used after a noun that ends in a consonant) **irang** -이랑; (used after a noun that ends in a vowel) **rang** -랑
tomorrow **naeil** 내일
too, overly **neomu** 너무
topic marker after a noun that ends with a consonant **eun** -은; after a noun that ends with a vowel **neun** -는

tourism **gwan.gwang** 관광
tradition **jeontong** 전통
traditionally wood-floored living room, space between/connecting rooms **maru** 마루
train station **yeok** 역
travel, trip **yeohaeng** 여행
tree room, wood room **namubang** 나무방
trend, trendy **yuhaeng** 유행
trial (from "one time, once") **hanbeon (han beon)** 한번 (한 번)
Trim it, please. **Dadeumeo juseyo (dadeum-, ju-)** 다음어 주세요 (다듬-, 주-)
truth, really **jeongmal** 정말
trying to (have it) cut **jareuryeogo (jareu-)** 자르려고 (자르-)
trying to (have it) trimmed **dadeumeuryeogo (dadeum-)** 다듬으려고 (다듬-)
trying to grow (out) **gireuryeogo (gireu-)** 기르려고 (기르-)
trying to look at, intending to see **boryeogoyo (bo-)** 보려고요 (보-)
Tuesday **Hwayoil** 화요일
turn (honorific) **doseyo (dol-)** 도세요 (돌-)
twelve **yeoldul; yeoldu** 열둘; 열두 (before a noun)
Twitter **Teuwiteo** 트위터
two **i** 이; **dul; du** 둘; 두 (before a noun)

U

uncle, sir (calling someone's attention) **ajeossi** 아저씨
United Kingdom **Yeong.guk** 영국
unrefined rice liquor **makgeolli** 막걸리
up to (and including), up until (a point), by **kkaji** -까지
up to, until (and including) **kkaji** 까지
use; to use **iyong** 이용
usually, in general **botong** 보통

V

valuables **gwijungpum** 귀중품
vegetable **chaeso** 채소
vegetables **chaeso** 채소
very **aju** 아주
vicinity, nearby **geuncheo** 근처
Vietnam **Wollam, Beteunam** 월남, 베트남
viewing room, listening room **gamsangsil** 감상실

village **ma.eul** 마을
vomitting **guto** 구토

W

wait, please (honorific, polite)
gidaryeojuseyo (gidari-, ju-)
기다려주세요 (기다리-, 주-)
waiter **weiteo** 웨이터
want to go, feel like going **gasillaeyo (ga-)**
가실래요 (가-)
want to rest, take a break **swigo simneyo
(swi-, sip-)** 쉬고 싶네요 (쉬-, 싶-)
washing machine **setakgi** 세탁기
watermelon **subak** 수박
we both know/right **-jiyo** -지요
we, our (humble) **jeohui** 저희
we, us **uri** 우리
weather forecast **ilgiyebo** 일기예보
Wednesday **Suyoil** 수요일
weekdays **pyeong.il** 평일
weekend **jumal** 주말
Welcome/Come on in! (honorific, polite)
Eoseo oseyo! (o-) 어서 오세요! (오-)
well **jal** 잘
well (for everyone involved) **jal (deul)**
잘 (들)
well, often **jal** 잘
went out; gone, sold out **naganneundeyo
(naga-)** 나갔는데요 (나가-)
well then **geureom** 그럼
what **mwo** 뭐
What do you mean ___! (used with nouns)
-(i)rani -(이)라니; (used with verb roots)
gineunyo -기는요
what else, who else, and; again **tto** 또
what kind of/what for **museun** 무슨; what
sort (modifier) **eotteon (eotteoh-)** 어떤
(어떻-)
what month **myeot wol** 몇월
What time? **Myeot si?** 몇시
What's the date? **Myeochirieyo?**
며칠이에요?
when (I) call **bureul ttae (bureu-)**
부를 때 (부르-)
when, sometime **eonje** 언제
where **eodi** 어디
where to drive/take (you) (humble)
mosilkkayo (mosi-) 모실까요 (모시-)
where, also used with a suggestion (어디 한번
eodi hanbeon) **eodi** 어디

which **eoneu** 어느
while ago (today) **aakka** 아까
while walking (honorific)
georeogasimyeonseo (geot-, ga-)
걸어가시면서 (걷-, 가-)
white (used before a noun) **hayan (hayah-)**
하얀 (하얗-)
who (as the subject)/non-subject **nuga/nugu**
누가/누구
why **wae** 왜
why not … (suggestion) **jiyo** -지요
will be late **neujeul kkeoya** 늦을 거야;
will get late **neujeojil geoyeyo
(neujeoji-, i-)** 늦어질 거예요 (늦어지-,
이-)
will bring/take (offer, promise) **gajyeo
galgeyo (gaji-, ga-)** 가져갈게요 (가지,
-가-)
will go (promise, offer) **galgeyo (ga-)**
갈게요(가-)
will prepare **junbihalgeyo (junbiha-)**
준비할게요 (준비하-)
will see (formal, humble) **boekesseumnida
(boep-)** 뵙겠습니다 (뵙-)
will wash so then **ssiseul tenikka (ssis-)**
씻을테니까 (씻-)
Will you stay? (honorific) **Gyesil
kkeoyeyo? (gyesi-)** 계실거예요? (계시-)
window seat **changcheuk** 창측
with/by that choice **geollo (= geoseuro)**
걸로 (= 것으로)
words, stories (honorific) **malsseum** 말씀
World Cup **WoldeuKeop** 월드컵
worrying, to worry **geokjeong** 걱정
would you (honorific, polite)
hasigesseoyo (ha-) 하시겠어요 (하-)
would you like to eat (honorific)
deusigesseoyo (deusi-) 드시겠어요
(드시-)
Would you like to sit (honorific)
Anjeusigesseoyo? (anj-) 앉으시겠어요?
(앉-)
Wow! **Wa!** 와!

X

X life, life as a…, life in … (usually after a
descriptive noun) **saenghwal** 생활
X's worth **X jjari** X -짜리

Y

Yay! Hooray! **Yaho** 야호
yes (humble form; also written and
   pronounced as 예 **(ye) ne** 네
yes (informal casual) **eung** 응
(You) ask for a discount **kkakkadallago
   hae (kkakk-, ha-)** 깎아달라고 해 (깎, 하-)
you (informal casual form with the subject
   marker) **nega** 네가
you (informal casual, addressed to minors,
   childhood friends) **neo** 너
you have to wait (honorific-formal) **gidarisyeoya doemnida (gidari-, doe-)**
   기다리셔야 됩니다 (기다리-, 되-)

you know (I forgot to tell you) **geodeun**
   -거든; you probably/should know this
   janayo -잖아요
You may not put it on. **Ibeusimyeon an
   deomnida. (ip-, doe-)** 입으시면 안
   됩니다 (입으시-, 되-)
younger brother **namdongsaeng** 남동생
younger sister **yeodongsaeng** 여동생
youth, young people **jeolmeuni** 젊은이

Z

zero **gong/yeong** 공/영
zucchini, pumpkin **hobak** 호박

Korean–English Dictionary

A

-a marker used with a child(hood friend)'s name ending in a consonant -아

A! Oh! 아!

achim morning 아침

aep phone/computer application 앱

Agassi miss, young lady 아가씨

agassideul ladies 아가씨들

agi baby 아기

ahop; gu nine 아홉

aidi, sinbunjeung I.D. 아이디, 신분증

aiseukeurim ice cream 아이스크림

Ajeossi sir, mister 아저씨

ajeossi uncle, sir (calling someone's attention) 아저씨

ajik not yet, still 아직

ajik(do) not yet, still not 아직 (도)

aju very 아주

ajumma ma'am (to a woman over 40) 아줌마; **ajummeoni** (more polite) 아주머니

akka a while ago (today) 아까

algesseumnida (al-) I understand/I got it/ knows (humble, formal) 알겠습니다 (알-)

aljiyo al- I know, right? 알지요? 알-

ama perhaps, probably 아마

ammeori bangs 앞머리

amnyeok pressure 압력

amu any (used with negatives and questions) 아무

an don't; inside; not 안

an ga bwasseoyo (ga-, bo-) have not been to 안가봤어요 (가-, 보-)

aneun geol (al-) that you know, what you know (with the object marker) 아는걸 (알-)

anieyo (ani-) not be (informal polite) 아니에요 (아니-)

animyeon or, if not 아니면

aniyo no (informal polite) 아니요

Anjeusigesseoyo? (anj-) Would you like to sit (honorific)? 앉으시겠어요? (앉-)

anjeusyeoseo (anj-) having sat (honorific) 앉으셔서 (앉-)

anju side-dishes that accompany alcoholic beverages 안주

annae guide, to guide 안내

annaeso information center/booth 안내소

annaewon information booth receptionist; guide 안내원

Annyeonghaseyo? Hello!/How are you? (informal, honorific, polite) 안녕하세요?

Annyeonghasimnikka? Hello!/How are you? (formal, honorific) 안녕하십니까?

Annyeonghi gyeseyo (gyesi-) Goodbye (to the one staying) 안녕히계세요 (안녕히계시-)

ap in front of 앞

apaseo (apeu-) sick/hurt so… 아파서 (아프-)

apateu apartment 아파트

apeuro from now on, in the future 앞으로

arasseoyo (al-) knew it, got it 알았어요 (알-)

areumdawoyo (areumdap-) beautiful 아름다워요 (아름답-)

B

badeul su isseoyo (bat-, iss-) can receive, get 받을 수 있어요 (받-)

badeuseyo (bat-) receive, take, get (honorific) 받으세요 (받-)

bae Asian pear; belly, stomach 배

bae han sangja one box of pears 배한상자

bae-ugi (baeu-) learning 배우기 (배우-)

bae-un ji (bae-u-) since you began to learn 배운지 (배우-)

baechu nappa cabbage 배추

baedal delivering, to deliver 배달

baegopeuda (baegopeu-) hungry 배고프다 (배고프-)

baek hundred 백

bakk outside 밖

bakke merely, only, just 밖에

bal foot 발

ban half 반

banchan side dishes 반찬

bang room 방

banghakttae at vacation time 방학때

bangse rent (money) 방세

banjeom suffix often used with Chinese restaurants 반점

banmal informal, casual speech, speak casually with no polite endings 반말
bap cooked rice, meal 밥
bapsot rice cooker 밥솥
baro directly, right away, straight(ly) 바로
batgo (bat-) receive/take and 받고 (받-)
beolsseo already 벌써
beonho number 번호
beotko (beot-) taking (shoes/socks) off and 벗고(벗-)
beullauseu blouse 블라우스
bi rain 비
bibimbap rice mixed with vegetables and hot sauce 비빔밥
bibimnaengmyeon spicy cold noodles 비빔냉면
bilding (= geonmul) building 빌딩 (= 건물)
bissaseo (bissa-) expensive so, 비싸서 (비싸-)
bogsung.a peach 복숭아
Boisijyo? (boi-) 보이시죠? (보이-) You see it, right? (honorific)
boja (bo-) let's see 보자 (보-)
bokka (bokk-) sauté 볶아 (볶-)
bokkeumbap fried rice 볶음밥
Bolkkayo? (bo-) Shall we look? 볼까요? (보-)
bongji bag (plastic, paper) 봉지
bopsida (bo-) let's see each other (formal) 봅시다 (보-)
boryeogoyo (bo-) trying to look at, intending to see 보려고요 (보-)
boseyo (bo-) Please take a look (honorific) 보세요 (보-)
botong usually, in general 보통
bu club (used after club name) -부
budaesiseol additional facilities 부대시설
Bujangnim Department Chief 부장님
bukkape book café, portable library 북카페
bulgogi barbecued beef 불고기
bulleodo (bureu-) even if/although you sing/call out 불러도 (부르-)
bulpyeonhaeyo (bulpyeonha-) inconvenient, uncomfortable 불편해요 (불편하-)
bun counter for people (honorific, used after numbers); person (honorific) 분
bureul ttae (bureu-) when (I) call 부를때 (부르-)

Butak deurigeseumnida (deuri-) Please, may I ask that you (humble, formal) 부탁드리겠습니다 (부탁드리-)
buteo since; starting with (a point); starting from 부터
bwayo (bo-) sees, watches 봐요 (보-)
boekesseumnida (boep-) will see (formal, humble) 뵙겠습니다 (뵙-)
byeokwa mural, fresco 벽화
byeollo much, all that, particularly (used with a negative/not) 별로
byeong bottle 병
byeongwon hospital 병원

C
cha tea 차
chaek han gwon one book 책 한 권
chaeso vegetable; vegetables 채소
chaesseoleoya dwae (sseol-, doe-) need to julienne 채썰어야 돼 (썰-, 되-)
chaja bolkkeyo (chaj-, bo-) I'll look (up, for) 찾아 볼게요 (찾-, 보-)
chajeuseyo (chaj-) look for, looking for (honorific, polite) 찾으세요? (찾-)
Cham Oh, by the way; quite, very 참!
chamgireum sesame oil 참기름
chamoe Korean melon 참외
changcheuk by the window 창측
chatgo isseoyo (chaj-, iss-) is looking for 찾고 있어요 (찾-, 있-)
chekeu check; (double-)checking, confirming 체크
cheo.eum first time 처음
Cheo.eum boekesseumnida. Nice to meet you. (formal, humble) 처음뵙겠습니다.
cheobang prescribing, to prescribe 처방
cheobangjeon prescription (note) 처방전
cheon one thousand 천
cheoreum like (noun marker) -처럼
cheung th floor (in a building) 층
chikin cooked chicken 치킨
chil seven 칠
Chil jjul ani? (chi-, al-) Do you (know how to) play (e.g., tennis)? 칠 줄 아니? (치-, 알-)
chilsip seventy 칠십
chimsil bedroom 침실
chimyeon (chi-) if play (of musical instruments, sports that involve striking) 치면 (치-)

Chimyeon eottae? (chi-, eotteoh-) How about (we) play (musical instruments, sports that involve striking)? 치면 어때? (치-, 어떻-)

chin.gu friend 친구

chinhan (chinha-) close, intimate 친한 (친하-)

Chirwol July 칠월

chobo novice, beginner 초보

chodae inviting 초대

chodaehaesseoyo (chodaeha-) has invited 초대했어요 (초대하-)

choego best, highest 최고

choroksaek green 초록색

chulbalji departing point 출발지

Chungjeongno Chungjeong Road, Chungjeong Street 충정로

chuwoyo (chup-) feel cold 추워요 (춥-)

chwaryeongji filming site 촬영지

chyeoyo (chi-) plays, hits 쳐요 (치-)

D

da every(one), every(thing), all 다

Da-eum Daum (search portal) 다음

da-eum ju next week 다음주

da-eumen (= **da-eumeneun**) next time (around) 다음엔 (= 다음에는)

da.eum next (time, one) 다음

Dadeumeo juseyo (dadeum-, ju-) Trim it, please. 다듬어주세요 (다듬-, 주-)

dadeumeuryeogo (dadeum-) trying to (have it) trimmed 다듬으려고 (다듬-)

dae counter for "machinery"; electronics, 대

daein adult 대인

daejunggyotong public transportation 대중교통

Daerinim assistant manager 대리님

daesin instead, in exchange 대신

dakgogi chicken 닭고기

dal moon, month (only when modified) 달

dareun (dareu-) another, different 다른 (다르-)

daseot five 다섯

dasi again 다시

de place, location (only after modifiers) 데

Denmakeu Denmark 덴마크

deo more 더

deoun (deop-) hot 더운 (덥-)

Deounga? (deop-) Is it hot, I wonder? 더운가? (덥-)

-deul plurality marker -들

deul come/go in 들

deuleogal (deuleoga-) enter 들어가 (들어가-)

deulleulgeyo (deulleu-) stop by 들를게요 (들르-)

deung etc. 등

deurama drama 드라마

deureo isseoyo (deul-, iss-) is in, has in it (informal, polite) 들어 있어요 (들-, 있-)

deurilkkayo (deuri-) Shall I give (humble, polite) 드릴까요 (드리-)

deurilkkeyo (deuri-) I'll give (humble) 드릴게요 (드리-)

deusigesseoyo (deusi-) would you like to eat (honorific) 드시겠어요 (드시-)

deutgi (deut-) listening 듣기(듣-)

dijeoteu dessert 디저트

Do both; also, as well, too (noun marker) -도

do degree (of temperature, as a unit word) 도

dochakji arriving point 도착지

doenjang soy bean paste 된장

Dogil Germany 독일

don money 돈

donggap same age 동갑

dongne neighborhood 동네

dongnyo colleague, co-worker 동료

dongnyodeul colleagues, co-workers 동료들

dongsaeng han myeong one younger brother 동생 한 명

dorabogo (dol-, bo-) look around and then 돌아보고 (돌-, 보-)

doseyo (dol-) turn (honorific) 도세요 (돌-)

dosi city 도시

dowa jumyeon (dop-, ju-) if help (out) 도와주면 (돕-, 주-)

dowadeurigesseumnida (dop-, deuri-) I will help you (humble, formal) 도와드리겠습니다 (돕-, 도와드리-)

dugo (du-) leave it and 두고 (두-)

du; dul two (before a noun); both 두; 둘

dwaejigogi pork 돼지고기

dwaesseoyo (doe-) it's alright, that's OK 됐어요 (되-)

dwaeyo (doe-) it's OK, it works 돼요 (되-)

dwinmeori hair in the back 뒷머리

E

e at; per; to -에

e daehan about, on (used before a noun) -에 대한

e.eokeon air conditioner, air conditioning 에어컨

Eeottaeyo (eotteoh-) How is...? 어때요 (어떻-)

ellibeiteo elevator 엘리베이터

eo-ryeowoyo (eo.ryeop-) difficult 어려워요 (어렵-)

Eodeul ssu isseulkkayo? (eot-) May I get/obtain (one)? 얻을 수 있을까요? (얻-)

eodi where; also used with a suggestion 어디

eojjeomyeon ireoke/geureoke how come this/that much, how could it be that 어쩌면 이렇게/그렇게

eolma how much (price only) 얼마

eolmana approximately how (long, much, etc.) 얼마나

Eolmayeyo? (eolmai-) How much is it/are they? (informal, polite) 얼마예요? (이-)

eoneu which 어느

eonje when, sometime 언제

eonni older sister (said by females; of a female) 언니

eopseumnida (eop-) does not exist, does not have (formal) 없습니다 (없-)

eoreundeul adults, elders 어른들

eoseo hurriedly, now 어서

Eoseo oseyo! (o-) Welcome/Come on in! (honorific, polite) 어서오세요! (오-)

Eoteoseyo (eotteoh-) How is/how do you like...? 어떠세요 (어떻-)

eotteoke how 어떻게

eotteon (eotteoh-) what sort/kind of (modifier) 어떤 (어떻-)

Eotteondeyo? (eotteoh-) How is it (can you tell me)? 어떤데요? (어떻-)

eseo at (point of activity); from -에서

Eseueneseu social media SNS

eul marker of the direct object of the sentence (used after nouns ending in consonants) -을

eul/reul wihae for (the benefit of, sake of) -을/를 위해

eumnyosu beverage 음료수

eumsik food 음식

eun topic marker after a noun that ends with a consonant -은

eung yes (informal casual) 응

euro choice marker after a noun ending in a consonant; to, towards, by way of (after a noun ending in a consonant) -으로

G

ga subject marker after a noun that ends in a vowel -가

Ga bon jeok isseoyo (ga-, bo-, iss-) Have you been to, have you gone to? 가 본 적 있어요? (가-, 보-, 있-)?

gabang bag, luggage 가방

gachi together 같이

gae item 개

gaein individual, private 개인

gage store 가게

gagiro haesseoyo (ga-, ha-) decided to go 가기로 했어요 (가-, 하-)

gagyeok price 가격

gajigo galkke I will bring (it) 가지고 갈게

gajyeo galkkeyo (gaji-, ga-) will bring/take (offer, promise) 가져 갈게요 (가지-, -가-)

gajyeo gasyeoseo (gaji-, ga-) take it with you and (honorific) 가져 가셔요 (가지-, 가-)

gakkawoyo (gakkap-) close, nearby 가까워요 (가깝-)

galbi barbecued (beef) ribs 갈비

galbijjim baised (beef) rib 갈비찜

galbitang beef rib soup 갈비탕

galgeyo (ga-) will go (promise, offer) 갈게요 (가-)

gam persimmon 감

gamgi cold, flu 감기

Gamgyeo deurigesseumnida (gamgi-, deuri-). I will wash (your hair). 감겨 드리겠습니다 (감기-, 드리-)

gamja potato 감자

gamjatwigim French fries, fried potatoes 감자튀김

Gamsahamnida (gamsaha-). Thank you (formal). 감사합니다 (감사하-)

gamsangsil viewing room, listening room 감상실

-gan (= dong.an) for (marker for duration) -간 (= 동안)

ganhosa nurse 간호사

ganjang soy sauce 간장

gapsida (ga-). let's go (semi-formal) 갑시다 (가-).

gapsida (ga-) Let's go. 갑시다(가-)

garataya (gal-, ta-) have to transfer
갈아타야 (갈-, 타-)

gareuchyeo (gareuchi-) teach, inform
가르쳐 (가르치-)

garyeomyeon (= **garyeogo hamyeon**)
(ga-) if I want to go, if I'm trying to go
가려면 (= 가려고하면) (가-)

gaseo (ga-) go and… 가서 (가-)

gasillaeyo (ga-) want to go, feel like going
가실래요? (가-)

Gatda deurilkkeyo (gaj-, deuri-).
I'll get/bring (it to you) (humble)
갖다 드릴게요 (갖-, 드리-).

Gatda juseyo (gaj-, ju-). Please get/bring
(X to) me (honorific). 갖다 주세요 (갖-, 주-)

gateun (gat-) same, alike 같은 (같-)

ge complement suffix -게

geo-ui almost; nearly 거의

geodeun you know (I forgot to tell you)
-거든

geogi there 거기

Geogibuteo gayo (ga-) Let's start from
there, let's go there first. 거기부터 가요
(가-).

geogieseobuteoneun starting from there
거기에서부터는

geojeo (= **gongjja**) bargain, give-away, for
free 거저 (= 공짜)

geokjeong worrying, to worry 걱정

geokjeong maseyo (mal-) Don't worry
걱정마세요 (말-)

geollil geo gasseumnida (geolli-, gat-)
it looks like it will take (time) 걸릴 거
같습니다 (걸리-, 같-)

geollil kkeo gatayo geolli-, gat- time
something will likely take 걸릴 거 같아요
걸리-, 같-

geollo (= **geoseuro**) with/by that choice
걸로 (= 것으로)

geollyeoyo (geolli-) takes (time) 걸려요
(걸리-)

geona or (attached to verb roots) -거나

geonneopyeon opposite side, across
건너편

georeogasimyeonseo (geot-, ga-)
while walking (honorific) 걸어가시면서
(걷-, 가-)

Geuge joketda! (joh-) That would be
great! That sounds great! 그게 좋겠다 (좋-)

geugeo that one, that thing 그거

geulsseyo not sure, I don't know 글쎄요

geumaek amount 금액

geumbang right away, just now 금방

Geumyoil Friday 금요일

geuncheo vicinity, nearby 근처

geunde (= **geureonde**) but, however
근데 (= 그런데)

geunyang as is; just because 그냥

geuraedo still, even so 그래도

geuraeseo so 그래서

geuraeyo (geureoh-) it is so; yes, please;
okay, let's do 그래요 (그렇-)

Geuraeyo? (geureoh-) Is that right? Is
that so? 그래요? (그렇-)

geureochiman (= **hajiman**) but, however
그렇지만 (= 하지만)

geureodeonde I heard (someone) say
그러던데

geureoke like that, like so 그렇게

Geureokuna (geureoh-) Oh, really? Oh,
right. 그렇구나 (그렇-)

Geureokunyo (geureoh-) Oh, I see.
그렇군요 (그렇-)

Geureolkka? (geureo-) Shall we?
그럴까? (그러-)

geureom well then 그럼

geureomnyo of course, certainly, sure!
(polite) 그럼요

geureon geos that (sort of) thing 그런 것

geureonde (= **geunde**) by the way;
however 그런데 (= 근데)

geureus bowl 그릇

geurigo and 그리고

geurim picture, painting 그림

geuttae at that time 그때

gi temporary noun-making suffix (usually
for idiomatic expressions; used with verb
roots) -기

gichim cough 기침

gidae expecting, anticipating 기대

gidarillae (gidari-) going to/want to wait
기다릴래 (기다리-)

Gidarisyeoya doemnida (gidari-, doe-)
ㅇ딛ㅅㄷ ㅔ ㄷ갸ㅐㅇ You have to wait
(honorific-formal). 기다리
셔야 됩니다 (기다리-, 되-)

Gidaryeojuseyo (gidari-, ju-) Wait,
please (honorific, polite). 기다려주세요
(기다리-, 주-)

gieok memory; to remember 기억

gil road, street, way 길
gilchatgi get directions, finding one's way around 길찾기
gim roasted seaweed 김
gimchi kimchi 김치
gin (gil-) long 긴 (길-)
ginaeyong carry-on (literally, for in-flight purposes) 기내용
Gineunyo What do you mean (used with verb roots)...! 기는요
gion temperature (weather) 기온
gipeun (gip-) deep 깊은 (깊-)
gireuryeogo (gireu-) trying to grow (out) 기르려고 (기르-)
go and (used with verb roots) -고
gochujang hot pepper paste 고추장
Goengjanghande! (goengjangha-) Amazing! Great! 굉장한데! (굉장하-)
goengjanghi awfully, greatly 굉장히
gogi meat 고기
goguma sweet potato 고구마
gok song 곡
golbaeng.i muchim red pepper and vinegar-seasoned whelk 골뱅이무침
gomawoyo (gomap-) thank you 고마워요 (고맙-)
gonghyuil holidays 공휴일
gosok express, high speed 고속
goyang.i han mari one cat 고양이한마리
gudu han kyeolle one pair of dress shoes 구두한켤레
guk soup 국
gunae in the building, facilities affiliated with X 구내
gunde spot, location (dependent noun, used only when modified by counting words) 군데
-gunnyo Eh! Ah! suffix (suffix for noticing/confirming;used with verb roots) -군요
gusipgu ninety-nine 구십구
guto vomiting 구토
guun (gup-) baked, roasted, broiled 구운 (굽-)
Guwol September 구월
gwaenchanayo (gwaenchanh-) good, fine; fair, not bad, OK, no big deal 괜찮아요 (괜찮-)
gwaenchaneundeyo, gwaenchanneyo (gwaenchanh-) fair, not bad, OK, no big deal 괜찮은데요, 괜찮네요 (괜찮-)

gwageo.e in the past 과거에
gwail fruit 과일
gwaja snack chips, crackers, cookies 과자
Gwajangnim section chief 과장님
gwan-gwang tourism 관광
Gwanghwamunjeom Gwanghwamun branch store 광화문점
gwijungpum valuables 귀중품
gwon book 권
gyeolje credit card processing 결
Gyeoljehae.deuryeosseumnida (gyeoljeha-, deuri-) I have processed (it) for you (humble, formal) 결제해드렸습니다 (결제하-, 드리-)
gyeongchalseo police station 경찰서
gyeran egg 계란
gyesan calculation, paying, to calculate 계산
gyesil kkeoyeyo? (gyesi-) Will you stay? (honorific) 계실거예요? (계시-)
gyesok continually, constantly 계속
gyul mandarin orange 귤

H
haemul seafood 해물
(haemul) pajeon seafood scallion pancake (해물) 파전
haeyo (ha-) does 해요 (하-)
hago together with, and (connects two nouns) -하고
Haksaeng student, kid (from preschool to college) 학생
Halabeoji grandpa, sir (to an older man) 할아버지
halbu monthly installment 할부
Halmeoni grandma; grandmother, ma'am (to an older woman) 할머니
Han-guk Korea 한국
hana; han one (before a noun) 하나; 한
hanbamjung in the middle of the night 한밤중
hanbeon (han beon) a trial (from "one time, once") 한번(한번)
hansik Korean food 한식
hansikdang restaurant that serves Korean food only 한식당
hante to, for someone -한테
hasigesseoyo (ha-) would you (honorific, polite) 하시겠어요 (하-)
hayan (hayah-) white (used before a noun) 하얀 (하얗-)

heum... hmmm... 흠...

himdeunde (himdeul-) difficult, tough but 힘든데 (힘들-)

hoe.uisil meeting room 회의실

hoesa company 회사

Hoju Australia 호주

Hongkong Hong Kong 홍콩

honja alone, by oneself 혼자

hubul expenses to be charged later; paying after use 후불

hunnare some (other) day in the future 훗날에

hwajang make-up 화장

hwajangsil restroom 화장실

hwanjabun patient (honorific) 환자분

Hwayoil Tuesday 화요일

hwik quickly, hastily, lightly (onomatopeia of quickly passing) 휙

hydaepon cell phone 휴대폰

hyeon.geum cash 현금

hyeon.geuminchulgi ATM 현금인출기

hyeondaehwa modernization 현대화

hyeondaejeogigo (hyeondaejeoki-); hyeondaesigigo (hyeondaesigi-) modern and 현대적이고 (현대적이-); 현대식이고 (현대식이-)

hyeonjae now, at the present time, presently 현재

hyung older brother (said by males; of a male) 형

I

-i marker used after children's or childhood friends' names ending in a consonant -이

i subject marker after a noun that ends in a consonant; this (needs a noun after); two 이

Ibe majayo? (maj-) Is the (food) to your liking? 입에 맞아요? (맞-)

Ibeobwado dwaeyo? (ip-, doe-) Can I try them on? 입어봐도 돼요? (입-, 되-)

ibeon this time 이번

ibeon dal this month 이번 주

ibeon ju this week 이번 주

ibeonen (= ibeonenun) this time (around) 이번엔 (= 이번에는)

Ibeusimyeon an deomnida. (ip-, doe-). You may not put it on. 입으시면 안 됩니다 (입으시-, 되-).

ieyo be—after consonant-ending nouns (informal polite) -이에요

igeodeul these 이거들

iil the 2nd 이일

ije now (unlike before) 이제

ijeobeorindago (ijeobeori-) that one forgets 잊어버린다고 (잊어버리-)

ijeobeoryeotji (ijeobeoli-) forgot, right? 잊어버렸지? (잊어버리-)

ijjok (= yeogi) this side, this person 이쪽 (= 여기)

il matter, job, business, to work; one 일

il lyeon one year 일년

Ilbon Japan 일본

ilgiyebo weather forecast 일기예보

ilgop seven 일곱

ilhage dwaesseoyo (ilha-, deo-) have come to work (currently working, will start working) 일하게 됐어요 (일하-, 되-)

ilsibul one-time pay/pay all at once 일시불

imnida be (am, is, are)—verb of identity (formal) -이에요

imo maternal aunt 이모

ina or (after consonant-ending nouns) -이나

inneundeyo (iss-) exists, there is (What do you think..?) 있는데요 (있-)

insa greeting 인사

insadeurigo (insaderi-) say hello/pay respects and 인사드리고 (인사드리-)

Inseutageuraem Instagram 인스타그램

inteon intern 인턴

ip mouth 입

irae bwaedo I/this might not look like much, but 이래봬도

irago haeyo be called—after consonant-ending nouns (informal polite) -이라고 해요

irang together with; and (used after a noun that ends in a consonant, more colloquial)— 이랑

-(i)rani What do you mean...! (used with nouns) -(이) 라니

iraseo = ieoseo i- it is the case so 이라서 = 이어서 이-

ireon (ireoh-) this kind 이런 (이렇-)

ireum name 이름

iril the 1st (day) of the month 일일

Irwol January 일월

Iryoil Sunday 일요일

isa moving 이사

isa moving, to move 이사

isahaneun (nal) (isaha-) moving (day) 이사하는 (날) (이사하-)

isipsamil the 23rd 이십삼일
isseoyo (iss-) there is, one has (informal) 있어요 (있-)
isseul geoyeyo (iss-, i-) there will be (formal) 있을 거예요 (있-, 이-)
isseusimnikka? (iss-) Do you have/is there? (honorific-polite) 있으십니까? (있-)
Itallia, Itaeri Italy 이탈리아, 이태리
itta(ga) a little while later (today) 이따 (가)
Iwol February 이월
iyong use; to use 이용

J

jabchae clear noodle with seasoned vegetables 잡채
jaemiitge (jaemi iss-) enjoying (fun) 재미있게 (재미있-)
jaemiitgenneyo (jaemiiss-) Sounds (like) fun. 재미있겠네요 (재미있-)
jageun (jak-) small 작은 (작-)
jal well, often 잘
Jal butakdeurimnida. I'm in your care. Please take care of me. (formal) 잘 부탁드립니다.
jal suga eopseoyo (ja-, eops-) can't sleep 잘 수가 없어요 (자-, 없-)
jal(deul) well (for everyone involved) 잘 (들)
jalhaejeoyo (jalhaeju-) good to you/take care of you 잘해줘요 (잘해주-)
Jalla deurilkkayo? (jareu-, deuri-) Should I cut (it for you)? 잘라 드릴까요? (자르-, 드리-)
jam sleeping 잠
jamkkan (= jamsi) for a moment, short time 잠깐 (= 잠시)
jamsiman (= jamkkanman) for a minute, for a second 잠시만 (= 잠깐만)
jan glass, cup 잔
janayo you know (you probably/ should know this) -잖아요
jang paper, thin object 장
jangmi han song.i one rose stem 장미 한 송이
jangnae.e in the days to come 장래에
jantteuk to the gills, fully 잔뜩
japchae savory clear noodle dish with many cooked vegetables 잡채
jareuneun de (jareu-) to cut, in cutting 자르는데 (자르-)

jareuryeogo (jareu-) trying to (have it) cut 자르려고 (자르-)
jari spot, space, available seating or room 자리
jaru pencil, pen 자루
je my (humble form); right, proper, appropriate, pre-set 제
jeil (= gajang) the most 제일 (= 가장)
Jejudo Jeju Island 제주도
Jeo I (humble form) 저
Jeo.eulkkayo (jeos-)? Should I stir it? 저을까요 (젓-)
jeobeorigi (jeobeori-) abandoning, deserting 저버리기 (저버리-)
Jeogeo juseyo (jeok-, ju-) Please write down (honorific-polite) 적어 주세요 (적-, 주-)
jeogi over there 저기
Jeogiyo Excuse me! (calling for someone's help) 저기요
jeohui we, our (humble) 저희
jeojjok that side over there 저쪽
jeomsim lunch, lunch time 점심
jeomsimttae at lunch time 점심때
jeon before 전
jeon (= jeoneun) I-topic (humble) 전 (= 저는)
jeon.gi electric 전기
jeonbu altogether, everyone, everything 전부
Jeondong Seongdang Jeondong Cathedral 전동성당
jeone before (not today) 전에
jeong.o noon 정오
jeongdo (= jjeum) about that much 정도 (= -쯤)
jeongmal truth, really 정말
jeongmun main gate, main entry 정문
jeongsan balancing, adjusting, to add up 정산
jeonhwa phone 전화
jeontong tradition 전통
jeonyeok evening (dinner time) 저녁
jeonyeokttae at dinner time 저녁때
jeotgarak chopsticks 젓가락
jepum product, sales item 제품
jeungsang symptom 증상
ji anayo (ji anh-) not (formal, used with verb roots) -지않아요?
Jibulhalkkeyo (jibulha-) I'll pay 지불할게요

jido map 지도
jigeum now (at this point in time); right now; this moment; these days 지금
jigwon salesclerk 직원
jiha basement 지하
jihacheol subway 지하철
jikjang job, workplace 직장
jikjeop directly 직접
jikyeosseumyeon (jiki-) if one kept, protected 지켰으면 (지키-)
jillyo medical exam and treatment, to give a medical exam 진료
jiman but; however (used with verb roots; if attached to nouns, use the verb 이-) -지만
jinan (jina-) last, past 지난 (지나-)
jinaseo (jina-) having passed 지나서 (지나-)
jinjja (= **jeongmal**) really 진짜 (= 정말)
jip house, home 집
jiyo why not … (suggestion); we both know, right -지요
jjajangmyeon noodles with black bean sauce 짜장면
jjamppong spicy seafood noodle soup 짬뽕
jjari X's worth -짜리
jjeum about, approximately -쯤
jjigae salty stew 찌개
jjimjil sauna, steam bath, to take a sauna 찜질
jjimjilbang dry sauna spa, dry sauna room 찜질방
jjok side 쪽
jjuk directly, all the way, all along 쭉
jo.eunde (joh-) good, but 좋은데
joa boineyo (joh-, boi-) looks/seems good (polite) 좋아보이네요 (좋-, 보이-)
joahaeyo (joh-aha-) likes 좋아해요 (좋아하-)
joayo (joh-) good 좋아요 (좋-)
Joesonghamnida (joesongha-) I am sorry (formal) 죄송합니다 (하-)
jogae clam 조개
jogeum jeone a little while ago (today) 조금전에
jom (= **jogeum**) a little (conversational softener) 좀 (= 조금)
joripsik self-assembly, do-it-yourself 조립식
jotae (joh-) they say it is good 좋대 (좋-)
ju.in owner 주인
jugan during the daytime 주간

juin owner, master 주인
jumal weekend 주말
jumarira (i-) since it's the weekend 주말이라 (이-)
jumun ordering, to order 주문
jumusigo (jumusi-) sleep and (honorific) 주무시고 (주무시-)
junbihalgeyo (junbiha-) will prepare 준비할게요 (준비하-)
junggan mid-size, medium, middle 중간
Jung.guk China 중국
junghakgyo middle school, junior high school 중학교
juseu juice 주스
juseyo (ju-) Please give (honorific, polite) 주세요 (주-)
jwaseok seat 좌석

K
Kaenada Canada 캐나다
Kakao seutoli Kakao Story (social media) 카카오스토리
Katok Kakao Talk (Korean messaging application) 카톡
kaunteo counter 카운터
keikeu cake 케이크
keo boineunde (keu-, boi-) big(ly), in big manners, ways, sizes, etc. 커 보이는데 (크-, 보이-)
keopi coffee 커피
keoyo (keu-) grows 커요 (크-)
keuge (keu-) big(ly), in big manners, ways, sizes, etc. 크게(크-)
keugo isseoyo (keu-, iss-) is growing 크고 있어요 (크-, 있-)
keugunyo (keu-) big, I see. 크군요 (크-)
keun (keu-) big 큰 (크-)
Keuneyo (keu-)? Big, eh? 크네요 (크-)?
Keuriseumaseuttae at Christmas time 크리스마스때
ki key 키
kkagdugi radish kimchi 깍두기
kkaji up to (and including), up until (a point), by 까지
kkakjaeng.i haggler, city slicker 깍쟁이
Kkakji maseyo (kkakk-, mal-) Don't shave (cut it short), please. 깎지 마세요 (깎-, 말-)
kkakkadallago hae (kkakk-, ha-) (You) ask for a discount 깎아달라고 해 (깎, 하-)

kkamansaek black 까만색
kke to, for someone (exalting the recipient) -께
kkeunnago (kkeutna-) after (it) ends 끝나고 (끝나-)
kkok for sure, definitely, without fail 꼭
kkwae quite 꽤
ko nose 코
kolla cola 콜라
kyeolle socks, shoes 켤레
Kyobomun.go Kyobo Book Center 교보문고

L

Lain Line (instant messaging application) 라인
laji large (size) 라지
lo choice marker after a noun ending in a vowel or ㄹ; to, towards, by way of -로

M

mada every, each -마다
ma.eul village 마을
maejin sold out 매진
maekju beer 맥주
maekju han byeong one bottle of beer 맥주한병
maenijeo manager, receptionist 매니저
maeun (maep-) spicy 매운 (맵-)
majayo (maj-) correct, right; (get) hit, hit the target 맞아 (맞-)
makgeolli unrefined rice liquor 막걸리
makigo (makhi-) is blocked up/congested and 막히고 (막히-)
makil geoyeyo (makhi-, i-) it will be blocked up, congested 막힐 거예요 (막히-, 이-)
mal language; talking 말
Mal no-eulkkayo? (noh) Shall we use casual speech? 말 놓을까요? (놓-)
malsseum words, stories (honorific) 말씀
Malsseum jom mutgesseumnida (mut-)? May I ask a question? (to a passer-by) 말씀 좀 묻겠습니다 (묻-)?
Malsseum mani deureosseumnida (deut-). I have heard a lot about you. (formal) 말씀 많이 들었습니다 (듣-)
mam (= **ma-eum**) mind, heart 맘 (= 마음)
mame deul (deul-) pleases you; is to your liking 맘에 들 (들-)

man only (noun marker); ten thousand 만
manayo (manh-) a lot, plenty 많아요 (많-)
maneul garlic 마늘
manhwa cartoon, comic strip, animation, graphic novel 만화
mani a lot, much, many 많이
mannagiro haesseoyo (manna-, ha-) decided to meet, are going to meet 만나기로 했어요 (만나-, 하-)
Mannaseo bangapseumnida. Nice to meet you/Pleased to meet you. (formal) 만나서 반갑습니다.
(mannaseo) ban-gawoyo (manna-, bangap-) Happy (to meet you). (informal polite) (만나서) 반가워요 (만나-, 반갑-)
mannayo (manna-) meets 만나요 (만나-)
mari animal 마리
maru traditionally wood-floored living room, space between/connecting rooms 마루
masinneun (iss-) delicious 맛있는 (있-)
masisseoyo (iss-) delicious 맛있어요 (있-)
mat taste 맛
matgiseyo (mat-) drop off, leave, entrust 맡기세요 (맡-)
Meksiko Mexico 멕시코
meogeoyo (meok-) eats 먹어요 (먹-)
Meokgo sipeundeyo (meok-, sip-) I want to/would like to eat… 먹고 싶은데요… (먹-, 싶-)
meongneun geon (meok-) act of eating; what one eats 먹는 건 (먹-)
meonjeo first, before others 먼저
meori head, hair 머리
meorigyeol hair (texture) 머리결
meositdeondeyo (meosiss-) it looked great (and I saw it personally) 멋있던데요 (멋있-)
midium medium (size) 미디엄+
Miguk U.S.; United States, America 미국
Miguk saram American (person) 미국 사람
mirae.e in the future 미래에
mit and, as well as, also 및
miting (= **hoe.ui**) meeting 미팅 (= 회의)
modeun all, every 모든
modu all together 모두
mogyok bathing, showering, to take a bath 목욕

Mokyoil Thursday 목요일
mom body 몸
momeneun joeunde (joh-) is good for your health, so… 몸에는 좋은데 (좋-)
more day after tomorrow, in two days 모레
mosilkkayo (mosi-) where to drive/take (you) (humble) 모실까요 (모시-)
mot can't 못
mu radish 무
Mullonijyo (mulloni-) It goes without saying; of course! 물론이죠 (물론이-)
mulnaengmyeon cold noodles in soup 물냉면
munhwa culture 문화
munjja text, texting 문자
munjjahaeyo (munjaha-) let's text, text (me) 문자해요 (문자하-)
munje problem 문제
mureoboseyo (mureobo-). Go ahead and ask. (informal, honorific) 물어보세요 (물어보-).
museun what kind of/what for 무슨
mutgi ttaemune (mut-) because (you can) get (something smudged) on it 묻기 때문에 (묻-)
mwo what 뭐
mwollo by what 뭘로
Myeochirieyo? What's the date? 며칠이에요?
myeodinnyong for use by how many people 몇인용
myeong counter for people 명
myeongham business card 명함
myeot how many 몇
Myeot si? What time? 몇시
Myeot wol what month 몇월

N

na or (after vowel-ending nouns) -나
nae my (informal casual) 내
naecheuk aisle 내측
naega I (informal casual form with the subject marker) 내가
naeil tomorrow 내일
naelgeyo (nae-) I will pay (informal) 낼게요 (내-)
naelkke (nae-) I'll pay 낼게 (내-)
naengjanggo refrigerator 냉장고
naeriseyo (naeri-) please get off (e.g., the subway) 내리세요 (내리-)

naeryeo deuryeoyo (naeri-, deuri-) drop you off, let you out (humble) 내려드려요 (내리-, 드리-)
naeryeo juseyo (naeri-, ju-) drop me off, let me out (honorific) 내려 주세요 (내리-, 주-)
naeryeogasipsio (naeryeoga-) Please go down(stairs) (formal) 내려가십시오 (내려가-)
naganeunde (naga-) going out/moving out so/but/and… 나가는데 (나가-)
naganneundeyo (naga-) went out; gone, sold out 나갔는데요 (나가-)
nagasimyeon (naga-) if you go out (honorific) 나가시면 (나가-)
nagasineun ge (naga-) act of going out, honorific 나가시는 게 (나가-)
nago (na-) come out and 나고 (나-)
nai age 나이
najung.e some time later; later 나중에
nal day 날
nalssi high school 날씨
namubang tree room, wood room 나무방
namul seasoned steamed vegetable 나물
naon (nao-) something that came out 나온 (나오-)
nara country 나라
naseoseo (naseo-) step up/out and 나서서 (나서-)
ne yes (humble form) 네
Nedeollandeu Netherlands 네덜란드
nega you (informal casual form with the subject marker) 네가
Neibeo Naver (a Korean search engine) 네이버
Neibeo baendeu Naver Band (mobile community application) 네이버밴드
neo you (informal casual, addressed to minors, childhood friends) 너
neo.eumyeon (neoh-) if put in 넣으면 (넣-)
neomu too, overly 너무
net; ne four (before a noun) 넷; 네
neujeojil geoyeyo (neujeoji-, i-) will be late, will get late 늦어질 거예요 (늦어지-, 이-)
neujeul kkeoya will be late 늦을 거야
neun topic marker after a noun that ends with a vowel -는

-neun ge act of doing (subject marker) -는게; **-neun geon** (topic marker) -는 건; **-neun geo** (what one does) -는 거

neyo Gee, … hmm! (suffix used with verb roots to express emotion) -네요

nolda gaseyo (nol-, ga-) have a good time/rest for a short while 놀다 가세요 (놀-, 가-)

nolgo (nol-) play and (then) 놀고 (놀-)

norae song, singing 노래

norae han gok one song 노래 한 곡

noraebang karaoke room, singing room 노래방

nuga/nugu who (as the subject)/non-subject 누가/누구

nuna older sister (said by males, to a male sibling) 누나

Nyujillaendeu New Zealand 뉴질랜드

O

o five 오

oenjjok left side 왼쪽

oi cucumber 오이

ojeon AM/before noon 오전

ojing.eo squid 오징어

ojing.eo bokkeum stir-fried squid 오징어 볶음

on geo gata (o-, gat-) seems to have come 온 거 같아 (오-, 같-)

Ondae? (o-) Do they say it is coming/it will come? 온대? (오-)

ondol heated stone floor 온돌

oneul today 오늘

oppa older brother (said by females) 오빠

orae(gan)man a long time (since) 오래 (간)만

Oraenmanieyo! (oraenmani-) It's been a long time! 오랜만이에요! (오랜만이-)

oreunjjok right-hand side 오른쪽

Oseyo! (o-) Please come! (honorific, polite) 오세요! (오-)

osyeoseo (o-) come and… (honorific) 오셔서 (오-)

osyeosseoyo (o-) came (honorific-polite) 오셨어요(오-)

osyeosseumnikka (o-) came (honorific-formal) 오셨습니까 (오-)

ot clothes 옷

otjang closet, cabinet, locker 옷장

Owol May 오월

P

pa scallion, green onion 파

paek pack, sealed package 팩

pal eight 팔

pama hair permanent treatment; a perm 파마

para (pal-) sell 팔아 (팔-)

Parwol August 팔월

pati party 파티

Peiseubuk, pebuk Facebook 페이스북, 페북

Peo juseyo (pu-, ju-) Scoop it out/serve it, please 퍼 주세요 (푸-, 주-)

Peurangseu France 프랑스

pigonhada (pigonha-) tired 피곤하다 (피곤하-)

Piryohaseyo? (piryoha-) do you need (honorific, polite) 필요하세요? (필요하-)

podo grape 포도

ppalgan (ppalgah-) red 빨간(빨갛-)

ppallayo (ppareu-) fast 빨라요 (빠르-)

ppalli quickly, hurriedly 빨리

ppuri root 뿌리

puk deeply, sufficiently 푹

pye kkichigesseumnida (kkichi-) I am imposing; causing inconvenience 폐 끼치겠습니다 (끼치-)

Pyeollihajiyo? (pyeonriha-) It's convenient, right? 편리하지요? (편리하-)

pyeondo one-way 편도

pyeong.il weekdays 평일

pyeonhaeyo (pyeonha-) convenient, comfortable 편해요 (편하-)

pyeonuijeom convenience store 편의점

pyo ticket 표

R

rago haeyo be called—after vowel-ending nouns (informal polite) -라고해요

rakeo locker 라커

rang together with; and (used after a noun that ends in a vowel) -랑

Reosia Russia 러시아

reul object marker after a noun that ends in a vowel -를

robi lobby 로비

(r)yuk six 육

S

sa four 사

sa julkkeyo (sa-, ju-) I'll buy for you, my treat 사 줄게요 (사-, 주-)

sae.u shrimp 새우

saek color 색

saenggakhaessneunde (saenggakha-) I thought 생각했는데 (생각하-)

saenggang ginger 생강

saenghwal X life, life as a..., life in ... (usually after a descriptive noun) 생활

saengmaekju draft beer 생맥주

saengseon fish 생선

saengseon gui grilled fish 생선 구이

sagwa apple 사과

sagwa han gae one apple 사과 한 개

saheul three days 사흘

saida Sprite 사이다

saijeu size 사이즈

sainyong for use by four people 4인용

Sajangnim company chief 사장님

sajin photo 사진

salgi (sal-) living, to live 살기 (살-)

salgo isseoyo (sal-, iss-) is living 살고있어요 (살-, 있-)

sam three 삼

samgeori three-way intersection 삼거리

samnimyok forest bath 삼림욕

samshibiril the 31st 삼십일일

samship bun thirty minutes 삼십분

Samwol March 삼월

sangja box 상자

saram/myeong person 사람/명

sarayo (sal-) lives 살아요 (살-)

Sawol April 사월

seilhaeseo (seilha-) it's on sale so... 세일해서 (세일하-)

seobiseu service (as an extra, complimentary service) 서비스

seolsa diarrhea 설사

seoltang sugar 설탕

seomyeong signature 서명

seonbae senior colleagues/co-workers/ schoolmates 선배

seonbul paying in advance 선불

Seonggyungwan Korea's top educational institution in the royal court during the Joseon Dynasty 성균관

seongham name (formal, official, honorific) 성함

seonsaengnim han bun one teacher 선생님 한 분

seonsu professional athlete, athletic team member 선수

seorap (meok-;, sip-) drawer 서랍 (먹-, 싶-)

seorapjang dresser 서랍장

set; se three (before a noun) 셋; 세

setakgi washing machine 세탁기

seteu set 세트

seukaendeul scandal 스캔들

seumol small (size) 스몰

seupa spa 스파

Seupein Spain 스페인

seutail style 스타일

Shibirwol November 십일월

Shibiwol December 십이월

Shiwol October 시월

ship ten 십

shibil eleven 십일

shibo fifty 십오

shiboil the 15th 십오일

si hour (on the clock; time of day) 시

Sicheong City Hall 시청

sigan duration of time 시간

sigeumnyo food and beverages 식음료

sijak beginning, to start 시작

sikdang restaurant 식당

Sikilkkayo? (siki-) Should I/we order? 시킬까요? (시키-)

siksa meal, to have a meal 식사

siku after a meal 식후

sikye sweet rice drink 식혜

Silla Shilla (Kingdom) 신라

sillyehamnida (sillyeha-) Excuse me (formal) 실례합니다 (실례하-)

simhaeseo (simha-) severe, so... 심해서 (심하-)

sinaebeoseu intra-city bus 시내버스

sinbunjeung identification card 신분증

Singgaporeu Singapore 싱가포르

sinjepum new product 신제품

sinse jigo isseoyo (ji-). I am being a burden, being indebted for the trouble. 신세 지고 있어요 (지-)

sinyongkadeu credit card 신용카드

sogeum salt 소금

sogogi beef 소고기

sojja small one, small size 소자

soju soju 소주

sonamu pine tree 소나무

song.i flower 송이

sonnim guest(s), customer(s), client(s) 손님

ssan (ssa-) cheap (used before a noun)
싼 (싸-)

ssan geo gatayo (ssa-, gat) seems cheap
싼 거 같아요 (싸-, 같-)

sseoleo (sseol-) chop 썰어 (썰-)

sseoleoseo (sseol-) having chopped
썰어서 (썰-)

-ssi Mr./Ms. (used after first or full name in
formal situations) -씨

ssik each (used like an adverb after a
number expression) -씩

ssiseul tenikka (ssis-) will wash so then
씻을테니까 (씻-)

subak watermelon 수박

Sugohaseyo (sugoha-) Thank you (to a
service provider) 수고하세요 (수고하-)

sobangseo fire station 소방서

sujeo spoon(s) and chopsticks 수저

sul alcohol; booze; liquor 술

sunapcheo service window 수납처

sundubu(jjigae) soft tofu stew, often spicy
순두부(찌개)

Sunsaengnim teacher, doctor
선생님

sup forest 숲

sutgarak spoon(s) 숟가락

Suyoil Wednesday 수요일

swigo simneyo (swi-, sip-) want to rest,
take a break. 쉬고 싶네요 (쉬-, 싶-)

swipge (swip-) easily 쉽게 (쉽-)

swiseyo (swi-) please rest (honorific)
쉬세요 (쉬-)

T

Taekkwondo Taekwondo 태권도

taeksi gisa taxi driver 택시 기사

tago (ta-) rides and 타고 (타-)

tangsuyuk breaded, glazed sweet-and-sour
pork 탕수육

teibeul table 테이블

tellebijeon han dae one TV
텔레비전 한 대

teniseu tennis 테니스

teniseujang tennis court 테니스장

teomineol terminal 터미널

Teuwiteo Twitter 트위터

ti kadeu T(ransit)-card 티카드

tim team 팀

timjang(nim) team captain 팀장(님)

tisyeocheu han jang, jong.i han jang
one t-shirt, one piece of paper 티셔츠 한 장,
종이 한 장

toegeun sigan quitting time (when people
get off work) 퇴근시간

toejang leaving, to walk out (of a stage)
퇴장

Toyoil Saturday 토요일

ttae at the time of, on the occasion when
때

ttaemune because of (something) 때문에

ttak exactly, abruptly 딱

ttalgi strawberry 딸기

ttaro separately 따로

tteollijiman(tteolli-) nervous 떨리지만
(떨리-)

**tteugeo.ul kkeot gatayo (tteugeop-,
gat-)** seems like it will be too hot 뜨거울
것 같아요 (뜨겁-, 같-)

tto what else. who else. and; again 또

ttwigo itjiyo (ttwi-, iss-) playing (*Lit.*,
running) 뛰고 있지요 (뛰-, 있-)

U

udeung premium, top-notch 우등

uiryoboheomjeung insurance card
의료보험증

uisa doctor 의사

un luck 운

undong sports; exercising 운동

undonghaeyo (undongha-) exercises
운동해요 (운동하-)

uri we, us 우리

uri jip my house (*Lit.*, "our house") 우리 집

uyu han jan one glass of milk 우유 한 잔

W

Wa! Wow! 와!

wae why 왜

wangbok round-trip 왕복

wanjeon completely, absolutely 완전

wasseoyo (o-) came (informal polite)
왔어요 (오-)

wayo (o-) come 와요 (오-)

weiteo waiter 웨이터

WoldeuKeop World Cup 월드컵

wollae originally, by nature 원래

Wollam, Beteunam Vietnam 월남,
베트남

wonrum one-room, studio 원룸

Woryoil Monday 월요일

X
X-hoseon Line #X X-호선

Y
-ya marker used with a child(hood friend)'s name ending in a vowel -야
yagan at night time 야간
yaho Yay! Hooray! 야호
yak medicine, drug 약
yakgan a little bit, kind of 약간
yakguk drug store, pharmacy 약국
yaksok promise, appointment 약속
yangbaechu cabbage 양배추
yangju hard liquor 양주
yangnyeom seasoning, seasoned (before nouns) 양념
yangnyeom chikin seasoned fried chicken 양념치킨
yangpa onion 양파
yennare in the olden days, long time ago 옛날에
(ye)jeone before, some time ago (예) 전에
yeoboseyo hello (on the phone) 여보세요
yeogi here 여기
yeohaeng travel, trip 여행
Yeojjwobolgeyo (yeojjwobo-) Let me ask (someone honored, older) 여쭤볼게요 (여쭤보-)
yeok train station 역
yeol fever 열
yeodeol eight 여덟
yeol ten 열

yeolahop nineteen 열아홉
yeoldul; yeoldu twelve (before a noun) 열둘;열두
yeolhana; yeolhan eleven (before a noun) 열하나;열한
yeolmyeon (yeol-) if open 열면 (열-)
yeolyeodeol eighteen 열여덟
yeommeori hair on the sides 옆머리
yeomsaek dye, dying 염색
yeon.gyeoldoe.eo (yeon.gyeoldoe-) connected 연결되어 (연결되-)
Yeong.guk United Kingdom 영국
yeonghwa movie 영화
yeongsujeung receipt 영수증
yeonpil han jaru one pencil 연필 한 자루
yeonseup practice 연습
yeop next to, beside 옆
yeoseot six 여섯
yeosimyeon (yeol-) if you open (honorific) 여시면 (열-)
Yeppeune (yeppeu-) Pretty, eh? 예쁘네 (예쁘-)
yesan budget 예산
yeyo be—after vowel-ending nouns (informal polite) 예요
yogeum fee, fare 요금
yojeum these days 요즘
yoksil bathroom (for taking a shower) 욕실
yori cooking 요리
yuhaeng trend, trendy 유행
Yuwol June 유월